SACRED BIOGRAPHY

Saints and Their Biographers
in the Middle Ages

Thomas J. Heffernan

New York   Oxford
OXFORD UNIVERSITY PRESS
1988

OXFORD UNIVERSITY PRESS

Oxford   New York   Toronto
Delhi   Bombay   Calcutta   Madras   Karachi
Petaling Jaya   Singapore   Hong Kong   Tokyo
Nairobi   Dar es Salaam   Cape Town
Melbourne   Auckland

and associated companies in

Berlin   Ibadan

Published by Oxford University Press, Inc.,
200 Madison Avenue, New York, New York 10016

Oxford is a registered trademark of Oxford University Press

Library of Congress Cataloging-in-Publication Data

Heffernan, Thomas J., 1944–
    Sacred biography : saints and their biographers in the Middle Ages
/ Thomas J. Heffernan.
        p.   cm.   Bibliography: p.   Includes index.
    ISBN 0-19-505225-0
    1. English prose literature—Middle English. 1100–1500—History
and criticism.   2. Religion and literature.   3. Christian saints in
literature.   4. Christian saints—Legends—History and criticism.
5. Christian hagiography.   6. Biography (as a literary form)
I. Title.
PR275.R4H44   1988   820′.9′382—dc19   87-30280   CIP

9 8 7 6 5 4 3 2 1

Printed in the United States of America
on acid-free paper

For Judy and Anne

Preface

The inspiration for this book began when I was a graduate student at Cambridge University. At that time my work on medieval manuscripts brought me in continual palpable contact with medieval artifacts. During the course of my studies, I was impressed by the sheer number of lives of the saints which survived in manuscript. Surely, I thought, such numbers were an indication of importance; I promised myself to look into this. Some years later, when I first began this book, I decided it was the compelling powers of saints' lives in the lives of medieval Christians which I wished to study. My interest was piqued in part by the knowledge that these very lives which so stimulated the intelligentsia from Augustine to Aquinas had fallen into desuetude. The cultural atrophy of these fabulous stories was indicative not only of a change in religious sensibilities but of a change in virtually every area of intellectual and affective endeavor. Miracles, mortification of the flesh, belief in demons, necromancy, magical healing, resurrection of the dead, and a host of other transcendent phenomena are rightly given short shrift by modern society. Yet these same characteristics which comprised the cultural traditions of the western world were the mainstay of equally intelligent people of the past. I was fascinated by the differences, by the intellectual and creedal rift which separated us from our ancestors, as well as deeply moved by the power the lives of the saints exercised for a millennium and a half.

Inevitably my perspectives have led me to concentrate on some aspects of this very rich tradition at the expense of others. Selection in such a broad study is necessarily individual. I have, I suppose, written what Augustine refers to in his *Confessions* as the conceits of my own heart. Since my primary interest in sacred biography is from a diachronic perpsective, I have perforce paid less attention to an exhaustive study of individual lives in their unique settings. Such intense local study, although important, was not my goal. Rather I wanted to follow the rise and fall of the tradition, to see it at its beginning and at its end, to follow the tradition from its expression in early Latin *vitae* to that of late Middle English. It was the seemingly timeless endurance of the paradigms expressed in the sacred lives which fascinated and still holds me in the grip of its power. Although we have replaced these ancient stories with our own constitutive fictions, the careful reader can learn much of the present's indebtedness to the past by a sympathetic reading of medieval saint's lives. It is my hope that my work arouses in the reader what Augustine refers to as a "pleasure for these fabulous narrations."

I am well aware that my interests have carried me far afield and given birth to a book which moves over much of the medieval landscape. Although I have tried to represent a fair sampling of the scholarship, I am well aware of the compressions and the oversimplifications which result from attempting to cover such a broad compass. Indeed, a study which cuts such a wide swath involves the use of a host of sources both primary and secondary. I have tried to make it as accurate as possible, but I remain fully aware that errors will remain, errors of simple fact, errors of commission, and more regrettably errors of omission. And although no single book can hope to present a comprehensive study of medieval sacred biography, I regret and take full responsibility for such lacunae.

I wish to thank a number of people and institutions which have supported me during the writing of this book. I have benefited from my students with whom I have discussed these sacred lives and with whom I first tried some of my ideas. My colleagues have been generous to a fault. I would like to thank Dr. James E. Shelton for his careful scrutiny of my citation of Latin and Greek. Professors John H. Fisher, David E. Linge, Robert Adams, Jerry Ball, David L. Dungan, James Fitzgerald, and Bruce Grelle have all read and contributed helpful suggestions to me. Daniel Pigg and Dr. Jerry Ball have helped considerably in the proof reading of my manuscript. As Andrew W. Mellon Fellow at the National Humanities Center, I was afforded the time, solicitude, and collegial interest to complete the writing of the typescript. Dr. Joseph B. Trahern, Jr., and the trustees of the John C. Hodges foundation of the Department of English at the University of Tennessee were generous in their assistance, as was the American Council of Learned Societies. I am grateful to the editors at Oxford University Press for their guidance during the preparation of this manuscript. Numerous libraries in both this country and Europe were unstinting in their generosity.

I would also like to thank those countless scholars whose works have so influenced me that I only vaguely recognize the depth of my intellectual indebtedness. I have tried in the notes to acknowledge this debt but I feel sure that I have not done justice to the learning I have received. I would also like to thank my parents without whose nurturing this book would have been impossible. My greatest support, apparent in my dedication, is to my wife who has shared her life with my fascination for these old stories.

Knoxville, Tenn.   T. J. H.
August 1988

Contents

Abbreviations

Sacred Biography

1 / From *Logos* to Canon: The Making of a Saint's Life

Sacred Life in Sacred Word

One of the most imaginative and prolific writers of the Middle Ages also happened to be one of the most influential early medieval sacred biographers. Gregory of Tours was born in Arverni (the present Clermont-Ferrand) in 538–39 and died in Tours on November 17 in 593–94. Gregory, named Gregorius Florentius at birth, was descended from a distinguished Gallo-Roman family closely related to the most illustrious houses of Gaul. His education, he tells us, was in church schools and principally confined to a study of Scripture. Given such a clerical education in this region of Gaul in the late sixth century, it is fair to conclude that his knowledge of the classics was limited.[1] Although he frequently lamented his lack of training in rhetoric and secular literature, he appears to have read voraciously and was continually busy at his writing.[2] Gregory tells us: *Decem libros historiarum, septem miraculorum, unum de vita patrum scripsi; in psalteri tractatu librum unum commentatus sum; de cursibus etiam ecclesiasticis unum librum condidi.*[3] This list is not complete; there are works undoubtedly from his pen which are not contained in it, such as his *Passio Sanctorum Martyrum Septem Dormientium apud Ephesum.* Such industry may suggest that his self-deprecatory remarks are not to be taken entirely at face value.

Gregory's most important contribution to the corpus of sacred biography is his *Liber Vitae Patrum,* composed about 591.[4] This is a

1. Max Bonnet, *Le Latin de Grégoire de Tours* (Paris, 1890), pp. 48–76. Bonnet's comments on Gregory's education remain the standard; see also Raymond Van Dam, *Leadership and Community in Late Antique Gaul* (Berkeley, 1985), pp. 202–9.

2. Edward James, *Gregory of Tours: Life of the Fathers* (Liverpool, 1985), pp. 10–11.

3. *Catholic Encyclopaedia,* Vol. VII, p. 20.

4. Gregorii Episcopi Turonensis Miracula et Minora Opera, "Liber Vitae Patrum,"

lively, albeit prolix, work of the lives of twenty Gallic saints, all but two of whom were connected to Gregory's family or with the two dioceses where he lived most of his life, Clermont and Tours. In the preface to this well-received work, he announced that his interest in writing it was

> to build up the church [*ecclesiam aedificare*] . . . [because] the life of the saints not only opens up their intentions but also excites the minds of listeners to emulate them [*verum etiam auditorum animos incitat ad profectum*].[5]

Gregory's intention is that his "Life of the Fathers" will prove exemplary. Such lives bestow benefit for both believer and unbeliever, and it is the latter who will contribute the most to the increase (*aedificare*) of the church in its missionary work. Gregory's point that readings from the lives of the saints can inspire individuals to take up the cross of salvation shares in the spirit of St. Augustine's reworking of the Pauline idea that the saints were the living *templum Dei*.[6] In his *De Mendacio*, Augustine, in an extension of Paul's remarks in 1 Corinthians 3:16–17, proposes that the saint's deed is a more useful depiction of Christian truth than the employment of complex language in Christian teaching.[7] Although Augustine may be making allowances for the illiterate, his argument also reflects his concern for the age-old dispute in rhetoric between *res* and *verba*. Gregory of Tours was unlikely to have known of this dispute in classical rhetoric, and yet his preface suggests that by the late sixth century the Augustinian position in the argument had become part of the common heritage of Christian thinking.

Scriptores rerum Merovingicarvm: MGH Vol. I, part II, ed. Br. Krusch (Hanover, 1885), p. 455.

5. Ibid., p. 622. Translations are mine unless indicated otherwise. For a valuable discussion of how Gregory's public received his teaching, see M. van Uytfanghe, "Hagiographie et son public à l'epoque Merovingienne," in *Studia Patristica* 16 (1985): 54–62.

6. *Biblia Sacra: Iuxta Vulgatam Versionem,* 2 vols., ed. R. Weber, (Stuttgart, 1983), Vol. II, p. 1772: "nescitis quia templum Dei estis et Spiritua Dei habitat in vobis." All quotations from the Latin Bible are from the Vulgate and will be from this edition.

7. St. Augustine, *De Mendacio, PL* 40, cols. 508, 513: "Ita pleraque in verbis intelligere non valentes, in factis sanctorum colligimus quemadmodum oporteat accipi, quod facile in aliam partem duceretur, nisi exemplo revocaretur."

For Gregory, and for the great majority of those who followed him in the composition of sacred biography, the truth or matter of a subject (*res*) was no longer to be exemplified primarily through ornamented language (*verba*) but through the depiction of specific action in the life of the saint. The change which upset the late-classical balance between matter and ornament was to favor matter over ornament in catechetical settings. The primary motive for this change was to make the learning of the classical handbooks (designed largely to teach eloquence) available to Christian teachers, to give them the rhetorical skills necessary to defend the truth of their Scriptures. In Jerome and Augustine, but also as late as Bede in *De Schematibus et Tropis Sacrae Scripturae Liber,* we see the Fathers adapting and rewriting texts of Cicero, Servius on Vergil, Donatus on Terence, the *Rhetorica Ad Herennium,* Horace's *Ars Poetica,* and other classical handbooks. Their intention was to take this classical tradition and turn it into a practical vehicle for their missionary program and for their scriptural exegesis. The very titles are indicative of this catechetical program, as in Fulgentius's allegorizing composition *The Exposition of the Content of Vergil according to Moral Philosophy* (ca. 550), perhaps the most influential commentary on Vergil for the Middle Ages.[8]

This legacy manifests itself most clearly in the propensity of medieval Christian sacred biography to emphasize dramatized action over complex argument. Gregory is one of the first sacred biographers in the Latin West to reflect this view unselfconsciously and hence stands at the beginning of the tradition.

There are two additional reasons for the primacy of the dramatic deed in medieval saints' lives: the paradigmatic actions of Christ in the New Testament and the illiteracy of the audiences for whom these texts were intended.

The lives of the saints were sacred stories designed to teach the faithful to imitate actions which the community had decided were paradigmatic. Christ's behavior in the Gospels was the single authenticating norm for all action. For actions (*res*) narrated in the lives of the saints to be binding for the community, they had to be an *imitatio Christi.* Thus, a particularly compelling instance of Christian charity in, the late-eleventh-century *Vita Aedwardi Regis* (composed 1068–75), which depicted Edward the Confessor healing the leprous woman, had authority for that community because it was a *speculum* in which they saw the curative hand of Christ. (The figure of Edward may have also

8. *Classical and Medieval Literary Criticism,* eds. A. Preminger, O. B. Hardison, Jr., and K. Kerrane (New York, 1974), pp. 284–85.

stood as a political allegory, with Christ reaching out in mercy to the beleaguered Saxon England after the recent debacle at Hastings.)[9]

Such actions, then, functioned as complex religious symbols and as such could synthesize a multilayered ethos with less ambiguity than argument (*verba*). The ability of such dramatic symbols to synthesize complex ideologies in narrative gave them a special place in a culture whose values were shaped by religious belief. In this narrative frame, action becomes ritual, and specific action becomes specific ritual. For sacred biographers, there existed a veritable thesaurus of established approved actions which they could employ in their texts. The repetition of actions taken from Scripture or from earlier saints' lives (often this practice extended to appropriating the exact language) ensured the authenticity of the subject's sanctity. Within this cultural setting, the saint's life, with its emphasis on right action, served as a catechetical tool much like the stained glass which surrounded and instructed the faithful in their participation at the liturgy. The sacred word no less than the sacred image, depicted vivid tableaux which communicated the Christian message unambiguously. Indeed, in the idiom of sacred biography, from Gregory to the *vitae* read in the second nocturns of the matins service, to learned Latin texts like the *Vita Aedwardi Regis* to the vernacular lives in the *South English Legendary,* to the lives written by John Capgrave at the close of the Middle Ages, paradigmatic action dominates the narrative structure. Thus, Gregory's central goal for his work is to present models of behavior so worthy of emulation that all will follow their example. Such a strongly mimetic orientation places the *Liber Vitae Patrum* firmly in a tradition of biographical writing as old as Isocrates' *Evagoras.*

Language and the Sacred

Gregory's next point in his preface is more difficult to construe. In a grammatical discussion of his preference for using the singular *vita* rather than the plural *vitae,* he concludes:

9. *The Life of King Edward the Confessor,* ed. F. Barlow (London, 1962), pp. 61–64: "A dish of water was brought; the King dipped in his hand; and with the tips of his fingers he anointed the face of the young woman and the places infected by the disease. He repeated this action several times, now and then making the sign of the cross. And believe in wonder one about to relate wonders. Those diseased parts that had been treated by the smearing softened and separated from the skin; . . . his healing hand had brought out all that noxious disease . . . when, all foulness washed away,

*Unde manifestum est, melius dici vitam patrum quam vitas, quia, cum
sit diversitas meritorum virtumque, una tamen omnes vita corporis alit
in mundo.*

Whence it is clear that it is preferable to speak of the life of the fathers
than lives, because, although there is a diversity of merit and virtue, in
the world one life nourishes all bodies.[10]

Gregory's conclusion is most important as it reveals his understanding
of the relationship between theological truth and language. Notice that
his argument moves beyond purely grammatical concerns into the
realm of theology. The precedents of Gellius, Pliny, and the grammar-
ians notwithstanding, the essential reason for his choice of the singular
when composing a book of more than one life is based on the developing Christian idea that the saints share collectively in the luminous
life of the incarnate Christ. In sum, sanctity is derived from the sacred,
which is radically singular.[11]

Like much of his thinking, Gregory's understanding of this interdependence of saint and savior is derivative. Indeed, it is this very lack
of originality in his remarks which makes him an ideal figure for our
discussion: Gregory's real importance is his ability to represent the
Weltanschauung of the age. In the present instance, although his remarks are not directly derived from Augustine, they owe much to Augustine's Neoplatonist teaching that human life was like a penumbra
reflecting the central brilliance of the divine. In Question 46 of his *De
Diversis Quaestionibus Octoginta Tribus*, Augustine stated:

---

the grace of God moulded her with beauty" (*cum dei gratia . . . eam uenusto decore
informat*). (Barlow's translation.)

10. Krusch, pp. 662–63: "Et quaeritur a quibusdam, utram vita sanctorum an vitas
dicere debeamus. A. Gellius quoque et conplures philosophorum vitas dicere volu-
erunt. Nam Plinius auctor in tertio artis grammaticae libro ait: 'Vitas antiqui cuiusc-
umque nostrum dixerunt; sed grammatici pluralem numerum non putaverunt habere
vitam.' Unde manifestum est, *melius dici vitam patrum quam vitas,* quia, cum sit
diversitas meritorum virtutumque, una tamen omnes vita corporis alit in mundo. Et
scripsi, fateor, in inferiore confessorum libro aliqua de quorundam vitam quae in corpore operati sunt breviora, idcirco quia, cum de Dei virtute ingentia censeantur, parva
tamen redduntur in scriptis; prolixiora quoque in hoc, quod vita sanctorum vocitare
voluimus, libro imperiti idiotaeque praesumimus propalare, orantes Dominum, ut dig-
netur dare verbum in ore nostro, qui ora mutorum ad usus praestinos saepius reser-
avit, et quod in sanctis praecipit scribi, reputet ea suis in laudibus declamari."

11. See Ephesians 5:8–14 and Romans 12:3–10.

*Sed anima rationalis inter eas res, quae sunt a Deo conditae, omnia
superat; . . . in tantum ab eo lumine illo intellegibili perfusa quodammodo et inlustrata cernit. . . .*

Now among the things which have been created by God, the rational soul
is the most excellent of all. . . . [It is] imbued in some way and illumined
by him with light, intelligible light.[12]

Gregory subordinates grammaticality, and with it language's ability
to represent reality, to the exigencies of religious truth. Language, it
appears, can be employed in discourse to depict contexts which violate
both the normative view of things (e.g., Gregory's use of the singular
rather than the plural) and its own syntactic structures so that it may
be a handmaiden to theology. Once again, the most influential teacher
for the Middle Ages on this subject is Augustine, who in Book IV of
De Doctrina Christiana, argues for the Ciceronian ideal that wisdom
and eloquence (*sapientia et eloquentia*) must be intimately yoked.[13]

For Augustine however, (and, it would appear, for Gregory), the
highest duty of the Christian writer was the clear expression of the
truth; the basis of Christian rhetoric under Augustine's guidance was
strongly antisophist. Indeed, the great feat that Augustine accomplished in *De Doctrina Christiana* was to reestablish the Ciceronian
ideal of *sapientia et eloquentia* against his sophist opponents. Truth
without the ornament necessary to persuasion cannot teach; persuasion without truth is empty. Augustine, paraphrasing Cicero in *De Or-
atore,* says:

*sapientiam sine eloquentia parum prodesse ciuitatibus, eloquentiam
uero sine sapientia nimium obesse plerumque, prodesse numquam.*

wisdom without eloquence is of small avail to a country, but that eloquence without wisdom is generally a great hindrance, and never a
help.[14]

12. Augustine, *De Diversis Quaestionibus Octoginta Tribus,* ed. Al. Mutzen-
becher, *CCSL* (Turnhout, 1975), p. 73; and D. L. Mosher, trans. and ed., *Saint Augustine: Eighty-Three Different Questions* (Washington, 1982), p. 81. In his *De Doctrina Christiana,* ed. J. Martin, *CCSL,* Vol. 32 Pt. 4, I (Turnhout, 1962), Augustine,
in an oblique reworking of a remark in the Epistle to James, refers to God as the
"Father of lights" (". . . *supernam quae 'a Patre luminum' descendit . . .*"). See Bk.
IV, V, VII.

13. Augustine, *De Doctrina Christiana,* Bk. IV, V, VII. See also the informative
discussion of this ideal by Peter Dronke in "Medieval Rhetoric," *The Medieval Poet
and His World* (Rome, 1984), pp. 7–38.

14. Augustine, *De Doctrina Christiana,* Bk. IV, V, VII.

Augustine's great work of biblical hermeneutics and exposition of Christian rhetoric had, as Baldwin pointed out more than half a century ago, a "significance . . . out of all proportion to its size."[15] Cassiodorus refers to the authority of *De Doctrina Christiana* in his work on the Psalms; Rabanus Maurus drew heavily on Book III in his *De Institutione Clericorum;* and in the thirteenth century, St. Bonaventure began his *Ars Concionandi* with a reference to Augustine's distinction between *inventio* and *elocutio.* Such an influential treatise must have affected the intellectual climate even of remote late-sixth-century Tours. Stancliffe has recently demonstrated that as early as Sulpicius Severus's completion of the *Vita Sancti Martini* (ca. 396) there was a considerable amount and variety of Christian writing in Gaul.[16] Thus, Gregory of Tours specific argument that language must be made to serve truth, even if such service required a suspension of the rules governing language, is part of a larger Augustinian tradition which by the late sixth century was already becoming normative in sacred biography.

The correlation between Gregory's subordination of grammaticality to religious truth and Augustine's arguments concerning the function of language in a catechetical situation has not been noted before, but it can readily be documented. In *De Doctrina Christiana,* Augustine considered the matter of the responsibility of the Christian teacher and his use of language, arguing that it was appropriate for the teacher to use less correct words (*utetur etiam uerbis minus integris*) if that was all there was available to him, provided that the content was taught and learned correctly.[17] Implicit in these remarks of Augustine and those of Gregory is the belief that language is capable of reflecting accurately not only the apparently random events of daily life but also the most abstract and metaphysical religious truths, even if language has to be bent (*ex novo*) into new significances. This argument belongs to a strongly antisophist tradition traceable to Aristotle's insistence that the *res* or the dialectic of an argument was more critical than *eloquentia.*[18] What is of fundamental importance for this view of narrative in sacred biography is the idea that language is syncretistic: it cannot only harmonize different ontological planes, heaven and earth, but, if

15. Quoted in T. Sullivan, *De Doctrina Christiana, Patristic Studies* XXIII (1930): 5, 41.

16. C. Stancliffe, *St. Martin and His Hagiographer* (Oxford, 1983), pp. 55–70.

17. Augustine, *De Doctrina Christiana,* Bk. IV, X, XXIV.

18. Sullivan, p. 57. See also R. Pfeiffer, *The Classical World* (Oxford, 1968), passim.

necessary, it can also contradict its own required structures to do so.[19]

More than a thousand years after Gregory's observation concerning the relationship between language and religious truth, Osbern Bokenham wrote in the preface to his *Legendys of Hooly Wummen* that all composition must contain four causes, and although Bokenham does not state this as unequivocally as does Gregory, the two are essentially in agreement about the primacy of meaning in the Christian rhetoric of saints' lives. Meaning for Bokenham is related to the clarity of exposition, which he considers a work's formal cause: "and the more clere/ That it may be, the formal cause/ Settyth in dew ordre clause be clause."[20] The Augustinian ideal that the work be a synthesis of wisdom and eloquence which should provoke emulation is also endorsed by Bokenham in the prefatory remarks to his translation of the *Vita S. Margaretae*: ". . . to excyte/ Mennys affeccyoun to haue delyte/ Thys blyssyd virgyne to loue & serue. . . ."[21]

The Two Worlds of Sanctity and Narrative

Gregory does not dismiss the ontology of events in an individual's life in his argument for the primacy of the collective life, but his language does suggest that his thinking on this matter was dualist. Gregory believed that the saint, unlike the rest of humankind, lived simultaneously in two worlds, the heavenly and the earthly. Although these two worlds intersect, they are fundamentally different. The heavenly has primacy and serves to guide the earthly. This belief was widespread and early on received the imprimatur of the papacy. In his "Moralia [In] Job," Gregory the Great also takes up this problem of how the saints participate in both the heavenly and earthly spheres:

> [The saints] innately possess within themselves a proper changeableness; yet while they always zealously desire to cling to the unchanging truth, by clinging to it they cause it to happen that they become unchang-

19. Although it is not an issue for this stage of the discussion, for the view that ontology is not a property of language—whose primary exponents are Wittgenstein, Austin, and Waismann—see J. Kaminsky, *Language and Ontology* (Carbondale, 1969), pp. 91–105.

20. Osbern Bokenham, *Legendys of Hooly Wummen*, ed. M. S. Sergeantson, *EETS* O. S. 206 (Oxford, 1938), p. 1.

21. Ibid., p. 3. See also Augustine, *De Doctrina Christiana*, Bk. IV, XII, XXVII.

ing. Whenever they hold to this with complete affection, they find that being led above themselves they overcome this, that changeable things were produced in themselves. Indeed for what else is change save only a certain type of death?[22]

Gregory views the saints as active agents in securing their sanctity; it is their desire to cling to the sacred which inheres in them and transforms their earthly lives.

If language and its story-making agent, narrative, are to represent the actual life of the saint as a historic event, they must be able to reflect the nature of the interaction and the meaning which erupts when these two ontological planes collide. Language will often have to depict contexts which defy all our understanding of probability and the natural world; as Augustine sanctioned and Gregory of Tours practiced, language will have to bend to the will of this more primary reality. Narrative in this genre is primarily a medium for symbolic representation, since the essential thing (*res*) being signified (the presence of the divine in the saint) exists outside a system where sign and signified can be empirically validated. It follows that our reading and interpretation of such narrative should take seriously its symbolizing structures.

Gregory of Tours presented his explanation of his choice of title with little rhetorical embellishment, and we can infer that he believed the meaning of his remarks to be obvious. Of course, it is anything but obvious to a modern reader. Such an understanding of the dimensions of the self (what Gregory would have expressed with the reflexive pronoun *seipsum*) and language's capacity to reflect such concerns is alien. Gregory's point here is of seminal importance in the genre of medieval saints' lives. It reflects an understanding of sanctity, and of language's responsibility in representing the essence of the holy, that is crucial to sacred biography and the mentality of these writers. In Gregory's view narrative can reflect both actual circumstances and metaphysical truth.

Although the problem of universals is not the subject of widespread debate until the eleventh century, the vocabulary of that debate does shed some light by way of analogy on what Gregory intended centuries earlier. From this theological perspective, the substance of the holy is contained fully in Christ; the saints partake wholly of this substance but contain this substance only as accident. Yet, because they all share

22. Gregory the Great, *Libri Moralium sive Expositio in Librum Job,* in *PL,* 75, col. 1004; for a discussion of Gregory's meaning in an Old English context, see R. E. Bjork, *The Old English Verse Saints' Lives* (Toronto, 1985), p. 20.

the same substance, they are fundamentally alike, despite their accidental differences.

Questions Posed by the Tradition

Gregory of Tours and Osbern Bokenham write as cultic biographers; yet, separated from them by so many centuries as we are, it is difficult to see how their remarks have anything to do with the genre of biography. Biography is, after all, a sister discipline to history, and it is historical narrative which claims to represent "reality." How is it possible to compose a biography which conflates the subject's life with the lives of others and still expect it to be a record of that subject's life? Whose life is recorded when such a work is finished? How can this marriage of disparate parts be construed as history? Did Gregory have a historiography fundamentally different from our own? What sort of reality are Gregory and Bokenham intent on illustrating?

Aside from questions about the historiography implicit in the text, there are questions which need to be asked concerning audience response. Is the biographer not bound to relate to his audience the facts of his subject's life as accurately as possible? And what might we infer concerning the literary expectations of such an audience? Would the audience be expected to know that the life they heard or read was a literary mosaic? If they did understand this method, what might their response have been? What is the relationship of the biographer to his subject and to his audience? Were there certain verbal cues in the work that signaled to the audience a conflated incident? If so, how exactly did these narrative signs work? Were such borrowings considered fiction?

Another important arena for inquiry concerns the question of authority and the tradition of the genre. For example, who decided what other lives to integrate into the subject's life and what aspects of these lives to use? Do only certain aspects of the life, such as the birth narrative, allow for such a method? Could the biographer licitly borrow bits and pieces from ages past and other cultures? Was it not only possible but even quite probable that something Gregory borrowed from, say, the *Vitae Patrum* for use in his life of the prominent Auvergne martyr St. Julian (*De Passione et Virtutibus Sancti Juliani Martyris*) might itself have been borrowed? What are the implications of such a method if practiced widely over a period of fifteen hundred years? Might such conflation of different lives require certain patterns of substitution? Was such a biography designed with a specific purpose in mind, besides that of a documentary record of a cult, such as for a liturgical ceremony? What aesthetic criteria guide us in our reading?[23]

A Rich Harvest

Although there was a dearth of autobiography in the Middle Ages, there was a considerable amount of biography.[24] Biographies of kings, courtiers, bishops, abbots, monks, nuns, hermits, and holy men and women from varied socioeconomic backgrounds abound.[25] Those which treat the lives of the saints seem to have been the most beloved. The *Bibliotheca Hagiographica Latina* alone lists more than eight thousand saints' lives, and in English there are hundreds of examples extant in verse and prose. These sacred tales survive in greater volume and variety than any other writing. If we consider that only a fraction of the lives that were written managed to survive the iconoclastic ravages of the reformers, we can get some idea of the extraordinary currency of the genre in its own time. Bale writes:

> They who got the religious houses at the dissolution of them took the libraries as part of the bargain and booty, reserving of those library books, some to scour their candlesticks, and some to rub their boots. Some they sold to the grocers and soapsellers, and some they sent over the seas to the bookbinders, not in small numbers, but in times whole shipfuls, to the wondering of foreign nations.[26]

23. Edgar de Bruyne's, *Études d'esthétique médiévale* (Brugge, 1946), is still the standard work.

24. On this question of autobiography, see G. Misch, *A History of Autobiography in Antiquity*, trans. E. W. Dickes, 2 vols. (London, 1950); B. Smalley, *Historians in the Middle Ages* (New York, 1974), pp. 67–78; W. C. Spengemann, *The Forms of Autobiography: Episodes in the History of a Literary Genre* (New Haven, 1980); C. Morris, *The Discovery of the Individual, 1050–1200* (London, 1972); P. Dronke, *Poetic Individuality in the Middle Ages* (Oxford, 1970) and *Women Writers of the Middle Ages* (Cambridge, 1984).

25. For a handy reference guide to this vast corpus in England, see A. Grandsen, *Historical Writing in England c. 550 to c. 1307* and *Historical Writing in England II c. 1307 to the Early Sixteenth Century* (Ithaca, 1974–82).

26. *Bibliotheca Hagiographica Latina Antiqua et Mediae Aetatis*, 2 vols. (Brussels, 1898–1901; 2nd ed., 1949) The 8,989 texts listed include variants of the same life. See also the *AS*, 2nd ed., ed. J. Carnandet, 69 vols. (Paris, 1863). Perhaps the most comprehensive single-volume bibliography to appear recently on the vast literature concerning Christian sanctity is S. Wilson, ed., *Saints and Their Cults: Studies*

Given such quantity of material, it is fair to assume that virtually everyone in the Middle Ages was exposed to the lives of the saints in one
form or another. Such variety makes categorizing these biographies quite difficult.
Sanctity was the prerogative of men, women, and children (such as
Chaucer's "litel clergeon") from all walks of life. There are saints who
were kings, bishops, members of the aristocracy, of the peasantry, and
of the bourgeoisie. As Weinstein and Bell have recently shown, there
was a radical democracy concerning the divine call to sanctity.[27] Although these lives were written under different circumstances at different times about individuals from vastly different social backgrounds,
the conservative ethos of the genre (inherent in its rhetoric and theology) tends to play down differences while extolling socially accepted
paradigms of sanctity. Such rhetorical and theological hegemony was
more easily maintained when the texts were exclusively in Latin. As
we might expect, the rhetorical traditions governing genre loosen
somewhat (from the thirteenth century) when the vernacular begins to
assume an increasing role in sacred biography. The majority of those
lives rendered in English in the thirteenth and fourteenth centuries are
rhetorically unpretentious, their *dispositio* substantiating Dante's com-
plaint in the opening lines of *De Vulgari Eloquentia*: ". . . no one before me has discussed the teaching of vernacular stylistic art in any
way."[28]
    Complementing the variety of their subject matter were the idiosyn-
crasies of the sacred biographers themselves. While we can say that
most were drawn from the ranks of the clergy, it is devilishly difficult
to characterize the particular training or preparation they received.
Some were learned, and some were dunces; some were ironists, while
some were pious; some were among the greatest figures in the Middle
Ages, and some were obscure individuals whom history has swal-
lowed; some were scrupulous in their research, while others did no

---

in *Religious Sociology, Folklore and History* (Cambridge, 1983), pp. 309–417. For a
discussion of the massive amount of destruction of this corpus during the sixteenth
century, see Thomas J. Heffernan, "The Rediscovery of the Bute Manuscript of the
Northern Homily Cycle," *Scriptorium: revue internationale des études relatives aux
manuscripts* 36 (1982): 118–29. See also May McKisack, "Leland and Bale," in *Medieval History in the Tudor Age* (Oxford, 1971), pp. 1–25.

27. D. Weinstein and R. M. Bell discuss the breadth of this vocation to sanctity in
Part 1 of *Saints and Society* (Chicago, 1982), especially "The Call to Holiness."

28. See Dronke, *Poetic Individuality*, p. 33.

research at all; some were contemporaries of their subjects, while others were separated from them by centuries; some worked from documentary evidence, and others, perhaps most of them, worked with oral legend (some of these biographers even constructed their narratives from wall paintings and from epigraphic materials); some were able to work in rich *scriptoria*, while some barely had the parchment to complete their task; some were duty bound by commands from superiors to write their lives, while others were moved by genuine zeal; some wrote lives which are deliberately polemic, while others tried to depict the actuality of the life as they received it.[29]

Given the diversity of their backgrounds and interests, what can we infer about these biographers and their subjects? I shall argue that we can establish the tradition which brings this diversity together. Indeed, one of the paradoxes of the genre is that out of such diversity the tradition has wrought what for some is such a stifling sameness. Although author and community may have differed on the interpretation of events, the biographies that emerged from this complex interaction followed well-established narrative models. These models were derived from Greco-Roman biography on the one hand and Hellenized-Jewish character sketches on the other. These two traditions present quite differing approaches to biography. They are harmonized, however, by the Christian biographer, most notably by the biographers of the saints; they typify, perhaps more than any other medieval genre, Augustine's penetrating remark concerning the difference between the Christian and the non-Christian orator and his use of rhetoric: "So that he may give forth that which he drinks in [divine inspiration], and pour out what he will be filled with (*ut ructet quod biberet, uel quod impleverit, fundat*)."[30] For Augustine, the Christian linguistic movement is circular; it begins and ends in God.

Why "Sacred Biography"?

I have chosen to call this volume *Sacred Biography* because this title communicates the matter of my subject more comprehensively than the term *hagiography*, whose traditional critical associations seem now largely outdated. To paraphrase Lucien Febvre, categories and their

29. For this variety of disposition, see the accounts of sacred biographers in Grandsen, *Historical Writing in England*, Vol. I, chaps. 4, 5, 7, 14, 16.

30. Augustine, *De Doctrina Christiana*, Bk. IV, XV, XXXII.

labels can become fossilized and falsify the psychological realities of a period.[31] This is true in the present instance where the perfectly suitable term *hagiography* is now virtually impossible to read except as an epithet signifying a pious fiction or an exercise in panegyric. To be sure, these are characteristics of hagiography, but they are not its exclusive concerns. In fact, labels, while pretending to describe a particular reality, can foster misreadings of these texts and obscure their originality.

Sacred biography, as understood here, refers to a narrative text of the *vita* of the saint written by a member of a community of belief. The text provides a documentary witness to the process of sanctification for the community and in so doing becomes itself a part of the sacred tradition it serves to document.[32] The appropriation of many of these texts into the liturgical celebration of the medieval church attests to the fact that many in the church believed the texts to be inherently sacred. Paulinus of Perigueux reports in a poem entitled "On the Sickness of His Grandson" (*De Uisitatione Nepotuli Sui*) (ca. 461?) that his grandson was healed by having a text containing the miracles of St. Martin placed on his body.[33]

This definition of sacred biography implies an interpretive circularity in the composition and reception of these texts. First, the text *extends* the idea that its subject is holy and worthy of veneration by the faithful, and, second, the text as the documentary source of the saint's life *receives* approbation from the community as a source of great wisdom. In its participation in the tradition, the text is canonized by the tradition and thereafter itself becomes part of the appropriating force of the tradition.

The three areas of my principal concern here will be the tradition of the medieval saint's life as biography, the conventions used in the de-

31. Roger Chartier, "Intellectual History or Sociocultural History? The French Trajectories," in *Modern European Intellectual History: Reappraisals and New Perspectives* (Ithaca, 1982), p. 16. Chartier's essay, which cites Febvre, is a sober analysis of the problems in modern French historiography, particularly as practiced by the followers of Foucault and other postmoderns.

32. F. E. Reynolds and D. Capps, *The Biographical Process: Studies in the History and Psychology of Religion* (The Hague, 1976), pp. 2–30.

33. Michael Petschenig, ed., "Paulinus of Périgueux," *CSEL* 16.1 (Vienna, 1888), pp. 1–190, especially pp. 160–64, "Carmina Minora." Gregory of Tours noted with approval this miraculous cure. The date of Paulinus's composition is vexed. The date of 461 was given to me in private communication by R. van Dam, who is currently working on this material.

velopment of the genre, and the characterization of the female saint as heroic victim. Of all the genres that survive from the Middle Ages, only the lives of the saints, arguably the richest in terms of extant records, are still treated by literary historians as documents for source studies (*Quellenkritik*) and little else. The genre has until recently fallen through the net of scholarly research, avoided by the historians because it lacks "documentary" evidential status and by the literary historians because saints' lives are rarely works of art. We live, moreover, in a pluralist age ruled by a post-Marxian secular materialism, in an age when fear of the avenging angel of the Lord has been replaced by fear of microorganisms. We have replaced the awe-full reverence for the Almighty with a minute examination of the specific. Microbes have replaced devils. Our literary language has followed this transference of belief. The leading theorists of the last twenty years, in both literary criticism and historiography, share two important methodological premises inherited from the logical-positivists: a skepticism of metaphysical inquiry and a disbelief in the ontological status of language. From this methodological vantage point, they argue that narrative is unable to reflect any reality other than its own. Their major premise which decisively veers from the mainstream of Western philosophical argument is that language—which they define as a rule-based system of mutually intelligible signs—cannot represent reality, for reality is itself a random series of unrelated discontinuities (i.e., is not rule-based). Language is a closed encoding system, and if it reveals anything about a "reality" outside itself, that "reality" is a fictive one. It is some considerable distance from this position to that wherein language is a vehicle for representing not only the "things" of the material world but also the numinous presence (e.g., the scriptural λόγος). Augustine, Gregory, Bokenham or—even the proverbial medieval man on the street—all would affirm the ability of language and narrative to represent not only this world but the divine as well.[34]

If we are interested in learning about the mentality of the Middle Ages, we can study no better text than the saint's life, for it quintessentially illustrates what Braudel has termed the *longue durée*.[35] Of any

34. J. Kaminsky, *Language and Ontology*, pp. 91–105. See also B. Herrnstein-Smith, *On the Margins of Discourse: The Relation of Literature to Language* (Chicago, 1978), pp. 19, 41–50, 154.

35. See also J. Le Goff, *Time, Work, and Culture in the Middle Ages* (Chicago, 1980) and *The Birth of Purgatory*, trans. Arthur Goldhammer (Chicago, 1984), pp. 3–4; Jean-Claude Schmitt, "Religion populaire et culture folklorique," in *Annales Economies, Sociétés, Civilisations* (1976): 941–53; the study by E. Delaruelle, *La piété*

medieval genres it has the longest continuous history, beginning with St. Luke's rendering of St. Stephen's martyrdom in Acts and having no *de facto* end; ironically, the reformers wrote saints' lives using models from their papist predecessors, and lives continue to be written and retold today.[36]

The Relationship Between Author and Audience

Texts have their beginnings not in the act of composition but in a complex series of anticipations. The primary anticipation in the composition of sacred biography is that which contains the interaction between the author and his audience. The reasons for this complex intersubjectivity will become clear, I hope, but for the moment let us say simply that "texts" written in and for a cultic function iterate a system of values with wide community acceptance. Such narratives are designed to promote social cohesion. If the normative values are not present or challenged by such a text, it is unlikely that the text will receive community approbation. Let us begin our analysis at the earliest stage in the composition of a saint's life, prior to the writing of the text, with the relationship of the sacred biographer to his audience.

populaire au moyen âge (Turin, 1975), and the important but comparatively unknown work of A. Ja. Gurevich, *Contadini e santi,* trans. from the Russian by L. Montagnani (Turin, 1986). Paul Zumthor comes quite close to a concise expression of the *longue durée* as this term applies to the Middle Ages: ". . . this essential fact remains: here is a period not impossible to delimit within the continuum of human time, using more or less constant criteria; it is a period long enough to exist in our laboratories on a more than microscopic scale, yet limited enough that its traits can be ascribed to more than mere probability," in *Speaking of the Middle Ages,* trans. Sarah White (Lincoln, 1986), p. 9.

36. H. J. Cadbury, *The Making of Luke-Acts* (London, 1961), p. 135; R. M. Grant, "Greek Literary and Historical Criticism," in *The Earliest Lives of Jesus* (London, 1961), pp. 38–49. For a recent and most complete bibliography on the *vitae* of Jesus, see W. S. Kissinger, *The Lives of Jesus* (New York, 1985); Baudouin de Gaiffier, "Hagiographie et historiographie," in *Recueil d'hagiographie* (Brussells, 1977), pp. 139–66. See also H. White, *Tudor Books of Saints and Martyrs* (Madison, 1963); *The Acts and Monuments of John Foxe,* 8 vols., ed. S. R. Cattley (Fulham, 1836); A. Monteverdi, "I testi della leggenda de. S. Eustachio," *Studi Medievali* 3 (1908–11): 489–98; Weinstein and Bell, *Saints and Society,* p. 26. There is some pronounced similarity with Islamic sacred texts; see Marshall G. S. Hogdson, *The Venture of Islam,* 2 vols. (Chicago, 1974), Vol. I, Book 2, Chap. IV, also pp. 254, 326–27.

The primary social function of sacred biography, understood in the broadest of terms, is to teach (*docere*) the truth of the faith through the principle of individual example. The catechetical imperative is the most fundamental of the shared anticipations between author and audience. Brown, Weinstein and Bell, and others have shown how the saint and the saint's life could be used to support a wide spectrum of social needs. Although none of the sacred biographers discussed here would deny the value of the Augustinian precept of *ut doceat, ut delectet, ut flectat,* the primary emphasis throughout the Middle Ages was *ut doceat.* The effect of this emphasis was to diminish the importance of the aesthetic dimensions of the text. Such diminished importance is crucial, for it underlies a central thesis of sacred biography: the art of the text is designedly not a reflection of individual ability, of virtuoso excellence but is part of a tradition and posits a different orientation between author, text, and audience from that which would exist if aesthetics were a chief concern. As a result of this secondary interest in a text's art, the major anticipation which unites author and audience is how the text reflects the received tradition, a tradition whose locus is in the community. Such tradition is neither monolithic nor frozen but changes as the community selects and reinterprets anew from within itself.[37]

The nature of this complex relationship between author and audience can reveal much about the final narrative. *Audience* refers to the community of belief, whether that community is many, a congregation, or one, such as a bishop who assigns the composition of the biography to one of his court. Although the term *author* has a certain usefulness about it, it is also somewhat misleading. *Author* as used here can range in meaning from someone who has little interpretive interaction with the text to someone who exercises considerable influence over the text. Authorship, however, is never identified as an act of virtuosic composition, an ideal which usually stands apart from the community and its traditions. The author as literary artist writes for the *cognoscenti,* for a limited number of individuals with some training and understanding of the tradition and how it can be challenged. Such an idea of authorship, however, is hostile to the necessary function of cultic biography. The author for sacred biography is the community, and consequently the experience presented by the narrative voice is collective. The principal reason for this is the dominant role given to the text's didactic

37. Ernst Kris, *Psychoanalytic Explorations in Art* (New York, 1964), pp. 64–84.

element. The author is not the expert; rather, the community is a collection of experts, and the narrative reflects this state of collective authority.[38]

The author must also construe a life which will illustrate the exemplary behavior of the subject—what we should call the ethical dimension—to a community which has definite expectations concerning the outcome of this biographical record. A most interesting aspect of this presentation of what the community has acknowledged as normative behavior is the transformation the text undergoes as a result of its acceptance. This ethical imperative illustrated for prescribing behavior by the deeds narrated in the life of a saint can itself become constitutive. Hence the dramatic moments, no matter how individual and heroic they might appear, are conventionalized and thus exist as paradigms for the community. For example, in Walter Daniel's *Vita Sancti Aelredi,* discussed in Chapter 3, the individual ascetic practices which Aelred learned and imitated from the lives of earlier saints became in his personal appropriation of them normative for the community of monks at Rievaulx. His behavior, once lauded as heroic and distinctively individual, was viewed after his canonization, as having become part of the tradition and as a model for public *imitatio.* Thus, the new sacred model reclaims past models and in turn is authenticated by them as these past lives are reintroduced in the present. By virtue of this constitutive or ethical imperative, the individual sacred biography continually renews for the faithful a tradition of great antiquity. As we shall see, Walter Daniel, Eddius Stephanus, and Reginald of Canterbury use these earlier texts to reclaim the past and in so doing validate the present. In this pattern of figural repetitions the singular character of sacred biography—what makes it different from, say, the way Dante uses Vergil—lies in the medieval understanding that the saint's life is the perfect *imitatio Christi.* Hence these repetitive mimetic patterns have as one of their primary objects the reconstitution of the divine in new historical dress.

The life of the text is bounded from its inception by a complex web of significances which in turn foster an intersubjectivity between author and audience. In this model, the audience for biography serves more deliberately as resource, censor, critic, and arbiter than we have come to expect since the eighteenth century. Such a complex interdependency makes it difficult to construe these texts as simply the arti-

---

38. J. Ferster, *Chaucer on Interpretation* (Cambridge, 1985), p. 46.

facts of the dialogue between a high and a low culture. Indeed, such a characterization obscures the real conceptual intimacy which author and audience appear to have shared. Given this model of intimate reciprocity, the claim for two distinctive cultures—a dominant clerical elite on the one hand and a subordinate illiterate peasantry on the other—most recently and persuasively argued by LeGoff and Schmitt, seems wide of the mark. Murray has written convincingly about the degree to which the Dominican Thomas of Cantimpre's (ca. 1201–70/80) *Bonum Universale de Apibus,* a rather typical collection of *exempla* used in preaching, incorporated comparatively recent anecdotes, the bulk of which were drawn from his own interaction with the laity. The very existence of Cantimpre's work (one might add to it the *exempla* collections of Etienne de Bourbon, Jacques de Vitry, Odo of Cheriton, etc.) plus the fierce rivalries for preferment which existed among the major mendicant orders, among the mendicants and the monks, between different groups of regulars, and between the regulars and the seculars, should make one chary about a monolithic view of "the clerical elite." Le Bras' view of the medieval clergy as a congeries of mutually competing interests is nearer the mark. Moreover, as Robertson has shown for fourteenth-century England, it is equally naive to view the peasantry as some homogeneous "mass" bound by similar economic, agrarian, religious, and cultural patterns occurring with cookie-cutter reproducibility throughout the land.

Let us now return to the nature of the relationship between the sacred biographer and his audience. One must resist the impulse to conclude that because of such intimacy between author and audience that the sacred biographer was a cipher simply reflecting the received opinion and that such compositions were mere cultural montages. The function of the text was not only to document the wondrous appearance of the divine in a man or woman but also to interpret for the community what was only partially understood, mysteriously hidden in the well-known public record, buried in the very ideal of sanctity itself. Such complex narrative structures possess what Clifford Geertz, borrowing a phrase from Gilbert Ryle, has called "thick description."

If, on the other hand, we inquire into the function of biographies since Boswell's *Life of Johnson,* we find that they present themselves rhetorically as the authoritative word on their subject's life. They exist not to confirm what the community may already understand but rather to increase that understanding, to bring a new, complete, and carefully documented understanding of the subject to the community.[39]

Types of Testimony: The Oral Tradition

Conversely, the raw materials for the saint's life were often stories which originated with the audience; stories which, although dependent on oral testimony, were considered admissible evidence. It is clear that before the late-eleventh-century consolidation of canonization by the Vatican (especially under the jurisdiction of Alexander III, 1159–81), virtually all the worship of saints began as local cults. Their legends, as we would expect, sprang from these local traditions. With some exceptions, after the machinery of canonization was in place, most stories, anecdotes, and legends which comprised the basic data of the sacred biographer were selected, adapted, and retold so as to conform to the dictates of the Vatican's administrative policy concerning canonization and to promote the cultus of the saint beyond its original locale. And yet, even in this climate of control, this new "authoritative" text could not conflict too greatly with the original community's stories lest it risk alienating itself from its cultic center.[40]

Such an interdependence does not allow for an easy distinction between author and audience, for these are terms which reflect modern notions of literary interaction. The medieval audience's primary role, as indicated above, is as resource and juror. Considerable skill was required to promote within a community a text that possessed what one might call a protective understanding of the subject of the biography. To complicate matters even further, the audience's understanding might at times be incompatible with the written text, since their understanding may have been dependent on the flexibility of a collective oral tradition. Moreover, different respondents, as we know from the work of the students of oral literature, although able to tell the same story, invariably would introduce differences, however subtle, in their retelling. Texts may fossilize such a fluid interpretive scheme.[41]

39. C. Geertz, *The Interpretation of Cultures* (New York, 1973), pp. 3–30.

40. W. Baldwin, *Alexander III and the Twelfth Century* (Westminster, Md., 1966). Alexander's pontificacy was from September 7, 1159, to August 30, 1181. See also André Vauchez, *La sainteté en occident aux derniers siècles du moyen âge: d'après les procès de canonisation et les documents hagiographiques, Bibliothèque des Ecole Françaises d'Athènes et de Rome, Pt. 241 (Rome, 1981).*

41. A. B. Lord, *The Singer of Tales* (London, 1960); see also J. M. Foley, *Oral-Formulaic Theory and Research: An Introduction and Annotated Bibliography* (New

   The oral tradition is important in a study of medieval sacred biography even if many of the texts appear primarily to be the products of the learned. For example, although Walter Daniel's knowledge of Aelred was based on a long-standing intimacy of many years, the traditions and historiography that informed the genre demand that he consider the oral record. In prefaces to works as distant as Pontius's *Life of St. Cyprian* (ca. 259) and the unquestioned place of oral supplement in the English *vitae* contained in the *South English Legendary* (ca. 1300), we see this emphasis on the importance of the *viva voce*. Walter Daniel was informed by this oral culture, and it is a culture that has a view of the past different from one built on an archival historicism. Its critical method did not depend so exclusively on an evidentiary system.

   The governing cultural stories within an oral society were reinterpreted in light of present experience. This manner of interpreting the past, which we may call reflexive, ensures that the past is never completely divorced from the present, never becomes a foreign artifact, but is always within the realm of the familiar. Indeed, since the past resides within the memory, the society is never alienated from its past. Critical access to and empathetic understanding of the past is not a problem. In the *Phaedrus,* Socrates tells of the rebuke given to the god Theuth, the inventor of writing, by Thamus, the king of Egypt:

> O most ingenious Theuth, the parent or inventor of an art is not always the best judge of the utility or inutility of his own inventions to the users of them. And in this instance, you who are the father of letters, from a paternal love of your own children have been led to attribute to them a quality which they cannot have; for this discovery of yours will create forgetfulness in learners' souls, because they will not use their memories; they will trust to the external written characters and not remember of themselves. The specific which you have discovered is an aid not to memory, but to reminiscence, and you give your disciples not truth, but only the semblance of truth; they will be hearers of many things and will have learned nothing.[42]

Socrates's anecdote underscores the idea that oral understanding is not one which considers the past a distant artifact with a fixed dimension in time. Rather, within the oral consciousness, an understanding of the

---

York, 1985). See Zumthor, *Speaking of the Middle Ages,* passim; M. Foucault, "The Being of Language," in *The Order of Things* (New York, 1970), pp. 42–44.

   42. Quotation from Plato in M. T. Clanchy, "Trusting Writing," in *From Memory to Written Record* (London, 1979), pp. 231, 233–257.

past is contingent upon present circumstance wherein the past is continually reconstructed by the present. The past and the present are in a dialogue within the individual consciousness. Such fluid accessibility between past and present is clearly part of the object of sacred biography; a major premise of that tradition is to document the continuing presence of past constitutive patterns of behavior as models for the present.

As indicated above, documentary evidence of the past produces an entirely different historicism from that of a system which makes use of oral evidence. Fifteen hundred years after Plato penned the *Phaedrus,* in the medieval England of the late thirteenth century, these two modes of recall and their respective evidentiary values entered their final struggle. The issue concerns a debate between Edward I and John, Earl de Warenne, concerning the legitimacy of de Warenne's ownership of his land. The king insisted that private rights had to be legally warranted; the crown by this time appears to have accepted the authenticity of charters and other documentary forms of testimony. De Warenne responds to this inquiry into the legitimacy of his ownership with an appeal to the nonliterate traditions of oral memory:

> The king disturbed some of the great men of the land through his judges wanting to know by what warrant [*quo warranto*] they held their lands, and if they did not have a good warrant, he immediately seized their lands. Among the rest, the Earl Warenne was called before the king's judges. Asked by what warrant he held, he produced in their midst an ancient and rusty sword and said: "Look at this my lords, this is my warrant! For my ancestors came with William the Bastard and conquered their lands with the sword, and by the sword I will defend them from anyone intending to seize them. The king did not conquer and subject the land by himself, but our forebears were sharers and partners with him."[43]

The rusty sword brought to England during the Norman invasion as evidence for ownership against the royal lawyers' demands for charters is a beleaguered attempt at maintaining the legitimacy of the nonliterate oral tradition.

The increasing complexity of institutions from the late twelfth century clearly elevated the importance of the documentary mode of re-

---

43. Ibid., pp. 20–21: "By then [the reign of Edward I] the province of myth and hearsay was the only appropriate place for a story which claimed priority for memory over written record in the king's court." See also M. Powicke, *The Thirteenth Century* (Oxford, 1970), p. 521.

cording traditions. As texts gradually replaced the oral stories, the oral stories in turn came to be viewed with increasing skepticism and as less than faithful repositories of the truth. As written narratives became a part of the Vatican's apparatus of canonization, they assumed an official status which the oral report never possessed. The oral witness became the product of the provincial, the rustic, and, as such, from the twelfth century lost its former importance within the tradition of the sacred tale.

Meaning in Rhetoric

How does the sacred biographer reconcile the tensions in the complex web which ties author, subject, and audience together to produce a text in a situation that was often overflowing with conflicting and fragmentary sources? Just as we saw Gregory of Tours subvert the grammaticality of language to contain his meaning, so too is language the consolidating, symbol-making force uniting these polarities.[44] The basic answer of how this task of consolidation is accomplished is to be found in the creative potential of the rhetorical structures sanctioned by the genre. The Augustinian ideal of the role of rhetoric acting to synthesize *sapientia et eloquentia,* although still the general goal, was to be modified in practice. Because of its role as the cultic history of Christian heroism and as the potential source for liturgical texts, sacred biography stresses the element of *sapientia* over that of *eloquentia.* Although meaning is designed to upset the delicate balance between these two elements, it is nonetheless still true that meaning must be served by language that is not consciously self-referential, not consciously seeking after artistic eloquence. To begin with, the sacred biographer must draw contradictions into the controlling rhetoric of his telling through the employ of particular linguistic devices, specifically through the use of metaphor, metonymy, synecdoche, and irony, in the selection of *topoi* and sources, and in variation of tone and point of view.[45] The display of such rhetorical language offers to the auditor or the reader a situation in which his comprehension of the text depends not

44. K. Burke, "Four Master Tropes," In *A Grammar of Motives* (New York, 1945), pp. 503–17.

45. H. White, *Metahistory: The Historical Imagination in Nineteenth-Century Europe* (Baltimore, 1973), pp. ix–42, and "The Historical Text as Literary Artifact," in *Tropics of Discourse: Essays in Cultural Criticism* (Baltimore, 1978).

only on the "documentary" nature of the text, the testamentary evidence presented as corroboration of the divine favor in the individual's life, but on the individual's ability to comprehend the linguistic formulae established in the text and sanctioned by the genre.

In sum, these rhetorical tropes are not mere linguistic adumbrations superimposed on the life of this or that saintly man or woman; rather they create the type of life being narrated, since our comprehension of the life comes exclusively through the filter of language.[46] Geoffrey of Vinsauf in the *Poetria nova* discusses the function of such rhetorical figures as metonymy, synecdoche, hyperbole, and catachresis and makes this very point that such figures exist to serve meaning:

> *Quae clausum reserent animum sunt verba reperta,/ Ut quaedam claves animi.*

> The expressions are found in order to unlock the sealed spirit: they are, as it were, the keys of the spirit.[47]

Let me offer an example of how a trope such as synecdoche is used by a medieval author and how that use, unless it is understood by the modern reader, can lead to a misinterpretation of the text.[48] The tradition of dividing history into six separate ages, begun by Augustine, was to remain the dominant view of Christian historiography for most of the Middle Ages. The hexameral literature which survives is copious.[49] For example, in his *Ecclesiastical History of the English People,* the Venerable Bede, following Augustine, proposed that history was divided into this hexameral scheme and that his own work was a record of the sixth age of mankind. Moreover, this sixth age was an age of

46. C. Taylor, "Interpretation and the Social Sciences of Man," in *Interpretative Social Science: A Reader* (Berkeley, 1979), p. 45: "The language is constitutive of the reality, is essential to its being the kind of reality it is."

47. Dronke, *"Medieval Rhetoric,"* p. 30. See also the editions and bibliography by J. J. Murphy: *Rhetoric in the Middle Ages: A History of Rhetorical Theory from Saint Augustine to the Renaissance* (Berkeley, 1981); *Three Medieval Rhetorical Arts,* (Berkeley, 1971); *Medieval Eloquence: Studies in the Theory and Practice of Medieval Rhetoric* (Berkeley, 1978); and *Medieval Rhetoric: A Select Bibliography* (Toronto, 1971).

48. I could use one of the other figures, but Bede's use of synecdoche nicely illustrates his method and my point.

49. A. J. Burrow, "Time," in *The Ages of Man: A Study in Medieval Writing and Thought* (Oxford, 1986), pp. 55–94; see also A. Ja. Gurevich, "Ideas of Space and Time in the Middle Ages," in *Categories of Medieval Culture* (London, 1985), pp. 26–39.

grace since it was ushered in by the redemptive glory of the Incarnation and would end in the consummation of the Last Judgment. The record of that age (viz. its history) was cotemporal with the age of the church, since the church was founded by Christ. Further, both that age and the church have as their mission the fulfillment of the Pauline ideal of bringing salvation to the entire world. Bede's Northumbrian church is part of a larger English church which is in turn part of the universal Roman church. It is through the use of synecdoche that Bede's Northumbrian or English church stands for the universal church. Thus, in writing about the English church, Bede is also writing about the soteriological mission of the entire church.[50]

It appears that Bede understood the political beginnings of Britain to be acts of Providence, that the arrival of the Romans, coterminous with the sixth age, and the growth of the English polity were caused by Divine Providence. For Bede, political and ecclesiastical history are inseparable. Thus, we can say that Bede's history of the church in England was also a history of the country of England, a history of the larger Roman church, and a history of the progress of the Pauline mission of the conversion of the world. Synecdoche allows Bede to compress all of human history into this grand design without diminishing the accuracy of his record of the English church.

It was through such rhetorical structures as these that the sacred biographer built his text and signaled to his audience the complex antique traditions to which the text was indebted.

Another approach (one which we will look at in more detail in Chapter 3) to this synthesizing of apparently disparate documentary testimonies involves an appeal to the presence of the omnipotence of God in the life of the saint. The saint is depicted as someone in whom the natural laws of causality are suspended because of divine favor.[51] Such an approach does not give the biographer excess license, nor is it an argument for the unbridled use of miracle stories. Rather, it simply acknowledges as a matter of theological principle—a theological principle that no one in the Middle Ages would have taken issue with—

50. C. Kendal, "Bede's *Historia Ecclesiastica*," in Murphy, *Medieval Eloquence*, pp. 145–46.

51. See John Capgrave's remarks in his prologue to *The Life of St. Katharine*, ed. C. Horstmann, EETS O.S. 100 (London, 1983), p. 3: ". . . next that lady a-bove [Virgin Mary] alle other in blys/ffolweth this mayde whiche we clepe kataryne./ Thus wene we, lord, becavse that thov and thyne/ have ʒove to hir *grace* so greet plente,/ That alle thy pryuileges whiche been in other fovnde/ Arn sette in hir as in souereyn of heygh de-gree/ffor in alle these rychely dooth she abounde."

that even the reality that seems most palpable to us, created flesh and blood, was, as Aquinas argues in his *Summa contra Gentiles,* continually being divinely reshaped in ways which violate the normative bounds of created nature, that is, the Eucharist.[52]

The Sacred Role Model: *Imitatio* and *Elocutio*

The most influential thinkers of the Middle Ages believed that the imperative to imitate the saints was sanctioned in Scripture. Augustine, for one, is very clear on this point in a number of places but perhaps nowhere more pertinent for this discussion than in *De Mendacio.* Arguing for this understanding in 1 Corinthians 9:13, he contrasts the power of their example with the power of language to teach:

> *Ita pleraque in verbis intelligere non valentes, in factis sanctorum colligimus quemadmodum oporteat accipi, quod facile in aliam partem duceretur, nisi exemplo revocaretur.*

> So in general, what in words we are not able to understand, in the deeds of the saints we gather how it is to be understood, which would easily be drawn to the other side, unless it were recalled by example.[53]

It was no small part of the sacred biographer's task to highlight those features of the saint's life which the pious laity were to emulate. Bede, for example, points out in the prologue to his *Ecclesiastical History* that

> if history relates good things of good men, the attentive reader is excited to imitate that which is good [*ad imitandum bonum*]; or if it mentions evil things of wicked persons, nevertheless the religious and pious hearer or reader [*religiosus ac pius auditor sive lector*], shunning that which is hurtful and perverse, is the more earnestly excited to perform these things [*ipse solertius ad exsequenda ea*] which he knows to be good and worthy of God.[54]

For Bede, history can relate both good and evil about men. The practice of historical writing is not undetached reporting, however. Objec-

52. Thomas Aquinas, *Contra Gentiles,* III, cii.

53. See *De Mendacio,* Bk. I, c. XV, XXX, *PL* 40, col. 508, and *Contra Faustum Manichaeum,* lib. Bks. XX, XXI, in *PL* 42, cols. 370–402.

54. Bede's *Ecclesiastical History of the English People,* eds. B. Colgrave and R. A. B. Mynors (Oxford, 1969), p. 2.

tivity in narrative played no more than a minor role in both medieval history and biography, if indeed the concept was understood at all.[55] We need to recall that within the medieval Christian's understanding of the world there was a time before the Fall. This prelapsarian world was a place where nature had existed without sin. Sin entered that world and broke that eternal harmony, but it did not efface all record of it.[56] Christian history reveals both the record of the time before the Fall, the Fall, and the promise of redemption. It was the record of the promise of redemption held out by God and made intelligible by history toward which mankind was to strive. The writer of history within such a teleological system had to make use of rhetoric since, as Bede acknowledged, his purpose was to stimulate the hearer or reader to action (*ipse solertius*).[57] Indeed, it seems clear that even if medieval biography had never been influenced by classical rhetoric, the medieval biographer's teleological scheme of redemption would eventually have led him to locate history within the purview of rhetoric, since the belief in redemption was contingent upon prescriptive formulae which regulated behavior. In short, the medieval historian's craft gave considerable attention to the art of persuasion.[58]

Bede's remarks indicate that it is the responsibility of the historian to present both virtue and vice in such a manner that the first is to be sought and the second to be avoided. But how does the historian or the sacred biographer manage this? In a word, through *style*. While not

55. For a discussion, see G. Evans, "St. Anselm and Sacred History," in R. H. C. Davis and J. M. Wallace-Hadrill, *The Writing of History in the Middle Ages* (Oxford, 1981), pp. 192–209; N. F. Cantor, "The Interpretation of Medieval History," in V. Murdoch and G. S. Couse, eds., *Essays on the Reconstruction of Medieval History* (Montreal, 1974), p. 14.

56. I. Sullens, ed., *Robert Mannyng of Brunne: "Handlyng Synne,"* (Binghamton, N.Y., 1983), p. 5: "We handyl synne euery day/ Yn wrde & dede al þat we may./ Lytyl or mochyl synne we do:/ þe fende & oure flesshe tysyn vs þarto./ Handlyng synne for oure mysbreyde./ For euery day and euery oure/ We synne, þat shal we bye ful soure."

57. Kendal, "Bede's *Historia Ecclesiastica*," pp. 146, 172.

58. S. Jaffe, "Gottfried von Strassburg and the Rhetoric of History," in Murphy, *Medieval Eloquence*, pp. 302–3 and passim. See also the helpful illustration of John of Salisbury's indebtedness to classical rhetoric and its influence on his historiography by R. Ray, "Rhetorical Scepticism and Verisimilar Narrative in John of Salisbury's *Historia Pontificalis*," in *Classical Rhetoric and Medieval Historiography*, ed. E. Breisach (Kalamazoo, 1985), p. 68: "In one place John seems to say that historical writing is a subdivision of grammar."

wanting to disparage the concern of the medieval historian or biographer for the reporting of actual events, it is important to point out that both history and biography were understood to be narrative genres—designed, as Bede tells us, *ad imitandum bonum.* That is, these narrative records were designed to inform and provoke approved behavior from their audiences by means of rhetorically sophisticated and avowedly mimetic reminiscences of the life of Christ. The effectiveness of the historical or biographical record depended heavily on the writer's persuasive skills, on what the medieval rhetorician would call the writer's *elocutio.*[59]

At the same time that the sacred biographer's narrative depicts the exemplary, those wise and judicious actions praised by all humanity, his biography must also strive to isolate the divine mystery present in the person. The subject must be made to appear fully human while that which is being written must confirm and celebrate his or her "otherness." Such a situation involved some degree of paradox, since it was a constant of medieval Christian apologetics that perfection in this life was impossible. Hence a narrative portrayal of the joining of the human and divine—the presence of God palpable in his creation but illustrated in language which did not explicitly claim for itself divine inspiration—was dangerously close to an acknowledgment that the mystery of the Incarnation had taken place more than once in a particular man or woman. The Incarnation was that most mysterious union of disparates to which most medieval thinkers believed perfection alone pertained. From the beginning of orthodox Christian apologetic writing, this idea of singular perfection is a constant. Clement of Alexandria, in his *Miscellanies,* stated the idea succinctly: "But I know of no one man perfect in all things at once while still human, though according to the mere letter of the law, except Him alone who for us clothed Himself with humanity."[60]

The sacred biographer sought to maintain a difficult balance between the narrative depiction of a not quite demigod (if the expression be permitted) and a moral everyman. If this characterization—a characterization which perforce finds its most complex expression in what we might call a biographical dualism—is weighted too far toward the supernatural, we lose the man, while if the exemplary is underemphasized, we end up without our saint.

59. On *elocutio,* see Kendal, "Bede's *Historia Ecclesiastica,*" pp. 148–52.

60. A. Freemantle, ed., *A Treasury of Early Christianity* (New York, 1953), p. 58.

Biographical Dualism

The division of the life of the saint into an ethical dimension on the one hand and an encomiastic celebration of the saint's intimacy with God on the other has a great antiquity. We find such biographical dualism in its infancy in the Athenian orator Isocrates' panegyric *Evagoras*—a text he claimed on somewhat dubious grounds to be the first encomium of a living person. His contemporary Xenophon borrowed from the *Evagoras* in his own panegyrical life of the Spartan king Agesilaus where, as Leo was the first to point out, the biography is divided for the first time into two distinctive sections: *praxeis,* in which the life is summed up in a chronological manner, and then *ethos,* which is a somewhat rigorous and interpretive discussion of character.[61] This interplay of *praxeis* and *ethos* became the dominant mode in Greek biographical writing. It was used extensively by Plutarch and was adopted in the Latin tradition to some extent by Suetonius, who in turn bequeathed it to medieval biographers such as Einhardt and Asser.[62] Contemporary with Suetonius were the Gospel writers, who, as Grant, Hengel, and Cox have argued, emphasized a particular aspect of hellenized Semitic biography: the miraculous. This narrative of miraculous anecdote, indicative of character, appears to have been in existence for some time prior to the formation of the Gospels and is known to have been widely used in the hellenized Semitic communities of ancient Palestine. Scholars have labeled this genre *aretalogy* since it is believed that it arose from the practice of reciting the wondrous deeds and miraculous acts (*aretai*) of the divinity. Indeed, in late-Hellenistic Greek, the word ἀρεταί is often used in contexts where its meaning is best construed as "miracle."[63] Hence, centuries before Gregory of Tours argued for the importance of presenting the deeds of

61. F. Leo, *Die Griechisch-Römische Biographie nach ihrer Litterarischen Form* (Leipzig, 1901), pp. 91–92: "Die Erfindung und Begründung dieses εἶδος gehort dem Isokrates. Der Euagoras (73 τὸν ἐπαινον τοῦτον) hat eine richtige Vorrede an Nikokles und eine zweite ans Publikum über die neue Gattung, die Isokrates mit dieser Schrift in die Litteratur einführt." See also P. Cox, *Biography in Late Antiquity* (Berkeley, 1983), pp. 12–13.

62. Cox, *Biography,* p. 13; see also C. G. Gianakaris, *Plutarch* (New York, 1979), pp. 39–40. For a somewhat different point of view from that of Leo, see A. Wardman, *Plutarch's Lives* (Berkeley, 1974), p. 2 and passim.

63. M. Hengel, *Judaism and Hellenism: Studies in Their Encounter in Palestine during the Early Hellenistic Period,* 2 vols. (Philadelphia, 1974), Vol. I, pp. 58–61.

the saints, we see the biographical tradition already fixing on this idea of the primacy of act (*res*) over argument (*verba*).

New Testament scholars, such as Hengel, have recently shown that the Gospels fit this classification, since they are the canonical transcriptions of no-longer-extant oral texts that depicted in an anecdotal narrative the wondrous deeds and sayings of Christ. It is this narrative aretalogy of the Gospels and models of Greco-Roman encomium and panegyric, such as Plutarch's *Life of Alexander,* Iamblichus's *Life of Pythagoras,* Porphyry's *Life of Plotinus,* or Suetonius's *Augustus,* which influenced the author of *Acts of the Apostles* and other early Christian writers. The classical and the early-Christian biographical traditions show the effect of a consolidating force by the time we reach such distinctive texts as the anonymous *Martyrdom of Saints Perpetua and Felicitas* (ca. 203), Eusebius's life of Origen in the *Ecclesiastical History,* (ca. 330), Athanasius's *Life of St. Anthony* (ca. 357), and Sulpicius Severus's *Life of St. Martin* (ca. 397), to name some of the more important early sacred biographies.

Fixing the Text in the Canon

Now let us consider the manner in which some of these early sacred biographies might have been composed. Let us assume that a hypothetical *vita* represents an early stage in the written transmission of the cultus. It is reasonable to assume that our hypothetical biographer has an understanding of the community's expectation concerning the figure whose life he is about to compose. Indeed, it appears often to have been the case that the audience's knowledge of the subject was as great as the biographer's own. Furthermore, there were usually entrenched legends, often contradictory, of the saint in the community. Of course, such a situation is a commonplace of this sort of composition, and contradictory elements can be found in the ultimate paradigm for all sacred biography, the Gospels. The persistence of textual contradictions suggests the lack of a dominant consolidating tradition. Nonetheless, the presence of contradictory motifs in the legend is especially difficult for the early biographers, since, if the biographical subject has recently died, the cult still exists in the memory primarily as oral record. At this early juncture the record acknowledging the sanctity of the subject depends chiefly on stories associated with the living man in different contexts. It does not yet depend on the claims of the miracles after the saint's death originating from the locus of the cult, the burial place.

The tomb, whether located in a church or a churchyard, was monitored by the clergy and hence gave to the clergy a legitimizing authority with respect to the variety and number of miraculous stories surrounding the relic.[64]

The movement from oral story to written text was a momentous step. It represented a broadening of the cult and as a consequence diminished the importance of the oral tales and the role of those who cherished such tales. It is difficult to underestimate the importance of the *viva voce* as a source for both the early biographer and the early historian. Indeed, the testimony of the living witness was of greater value, it would seem, than the documentary evidence. Eusebius mentions the interesting anecdote of St. John's putative disciple Papias, who sought the testimony of the apostles as it was remembered by those who had actually heard it. Papias shows deeper reverence for this oral record than for any written text as he says, "For I did not imagine that things out of books would help me as much as the utterances of a living and abiding voice."[65] Today, however, we are accustomed to an opposite point of view: it is to the bookish narrative that we surrender *a priori* our skepticism. But despite this preference for the eyewitness, the task of discerning the authentic witness, the true voice of tradition, was not easy. The sheer number of stories growing up around local cults could be enormous. And these numerous testimonies concerning the sanctity of living saints were, in turn, more difficult than written texts for the clerical hierarchy and the biographers to coalesce into a desired scheme.

Medieval sacred biographies are replete with the biographers' testimony to the variety of stories which surrounded their subjects during life. Sulpicius Severus wrote of St. Martin of Tours that in his life "he was already regarded by everyone as a saint." Walter Daniel tells us that even as a young abbot Aelred's "fame runs through the whole countryside. Bishops, earls, barons venerate the man and the place itself." St. Cuthbert's sanctity was so widespread that he was summoned from the solitude of the recluse's life on Inner Farne around 685 by King Egfrith and Archbishop Theodore to accept the bishopric of Hexham, a position he traded for that of Lindisfarne. Thomas of Celano says that after the miracle of the swallows St. Francis's popularity was so widespread that people from all over would come "to kiss the

64. S. Wilson, *Saints and Their Cults;* see the introduction and passim.

65. Eusebius, *The History of the Church from Christ to Constantine,* trans. and ed. G. A. Williamson (New York, 1966), p. 150; and R. Grant, *Eusebius as Church Historian* (Oxford, 1980), pp. 61–63.

hem of the saint's garment . . . [and indeed some became so frenzied
by Francis's nearness that] they laid hands on him, pulled his habit and
even cut pieces from it so as to keep them as relics."[66]
Indeed, these local traditions were vital and were not simply the
products of the lay side of the community. For example, long after the
process of canonization was under the control of the Vatican, we have
instances in which both lay and cleric came together to proclaim one
of their own as a saint. In the first *lectio* of the *Officium* for Richard
Rolle of Hampole, written probably in the 1360s, we learn that Richard
has been proclaimed a saint: *Sanctus dei heremita Ricardus in villa de
Thornton iuxta Pickering Eboracensis diocesis accepit sue propaga-
cionis originem.* Unfortunately for the good people and clergy of Yorkshire, the Vatican never canonized their man.[67]

The Text as Relic

Presented with a variety of such vital oral traditions, the early biographer must have found many of the events surrounding the saint's life
to be fluid, different in different locales, and (as suggested above) at
times contradictory. However, in spite of these contradictions, such
legends, even those clearly apocryphal, were readily incorporated into
the growing cultus and became articles of faith. At this early stage in
the growth of the cult, criticism, disagreement, and differing points of
emphasis are endemic; they are all undergoing continual interpretation;
this is a hermeneutic process which is facilitated by the lack of an established written text. If there are *vitae* beginning to emerge at this
early stage, then the presence of continued interpretation indicates that
none has, as yet, achieved a position of sufficient dominance to limit
the growth of new stories about the saint.

The "authorized" biography, to borrow a not completely appropriate

66. Stancliffe, *St. Martin;* Sulpicie Severe, "Vie de Saint Martin," ed. J. Fontaine,
in *Sources chrétiennes,* 3 vols. (Paris, 1967), Vol. I, p. 250. For Aelred, see M. Powicke, *The Life of Aelred of Rievaulx* (Oxford, 1950), p. 28. For Cuthbert, see B. Colgrave, *Two Lives of Saint Cuthbert.* For Francis, see Otto Karrer, ed., *St. Francis of
Assisi: The Legends and the Lauds* (London, 1947), pp. 41, 49.

67. R. W. Woley, ed., *The Officium and Miracula of Richard Rolle of Hampole*
(London, 1919), p. 23. Woley's edition is superior, being more complete than that
contained in G. G. Perry, *English Prose Treatises of Richard Rolle de Hampole,*
EETS O. S. 20 (London, 1886), pp. xv–xxxiii. Virtually all the historical background
we have on Rolle (d. 1349) is found in the nine *lectiones* for matins printed by Woley.

expression from modern parlance, besides its obvious interest in being viewed as the text of record, serves less well known but equally important ends: it acts to terminate unsanctioned oral tradition and coalesces the myth-making powers of the community around its paradigms. Within this varied biographical mélange, however, the sacred biographer's *primary* mission in writing the life is not to render a chronological record of the subject's life, Xenophon's *praxeis*, but rather to facilitate the growth of the cult.

For the Christian sacred biographer, this mission means stressing the encomiastic aspects, the *ethos*, of the subject's life. Such a task involves a considerable degree of interpretation, and it is an interpretive process which—if the life is to gain adherents for the cultic figure— must accomplish two vital objectives: it must complement and satisfy the specific community's traditional understanding of this holy person, and it must establish the text itself as a document worthy of reverence, as a relic. There is evidence for this belief throughout the tradition in both Latin and vernacular *vitae*. Gregory of Tours, in his life of Nicetius, Bishop of Lyons, reports how a deacon of Autun, suffering from blindness, placed a book containing accounts of the miracles of St. Nicetius over his eyes and was cured at once: "Immediately the pain and the shadows dissipated, and by the power [*ab virtute*] of this volume he recovered his sight." It was only after he was cured of his blindness that the deacon read the accounts of the miracles presented in the book. In the late-thirteenth-century account of the *Vita Sancti Kenelmi Regis* in the *South English Legendary*, we have a most explicit instance of a sacred narrative as cultic relic:

That writ was puyr on Englisch i-write: ase men it radden there;/And for-to tellen withoute ryme: theose wordes it were:/ "In klent covbache kenelm, kyngues sone, lijth onder ane thorne, is/ heued him bi-reued."/ this writ was wel nobleliche: i-wust and up i-do,/ And i-holde for gret relike: and ȝeot it is al-so;/The nobleste relike it is on thar-of: that is in the churche of rome.[68]

The potential cultic status of these texts marks, I believe, a major difference between Christian sacred biography, its Greco-Roman-Semitic ancestors, and the Renaissance biography which followed it. The text of the Christian saint's life is meant to serve two audiences, not only the present, temporal one but the divine as well, for the lives of the saints are meant to reflect honor and glory to God. The medieval sacred

68. James, *Gregory of Tours*, p. 77; C. Horstmann, *The Early South-English Legendary or Lives of the Saints*, EETS O. S. 87 (London, 1887), pp. 352–53.

biographer and the community interact and the fruit of this labor establishes what I call the text's iconicity.

The text should so appropriate the vitality and truth that tradition has bestowed on the *viva voce* that the populace will slowly begin to transfer their cherished beliefs from the oral renderings to the written composition. Such a process, however, can take considerable time. The text, as it slowly achieves recognition from an ever-widening circle of the pious, can be said to become increasingly "legitimized." This process is syncretistic as the text gradually incorporates and consolidates various traditions. At this stage in the emergence of a written text as the official text of choice—in order to ensure the text's continued dominance—the authority on which the text is based must be spiritualized. A concomitant of the process of legitimation, this spiritualizing of the text takes one of two methods.[69] First, we may find a steady disassociation of the text from the unique historical author. Such a process shrouds the document's origins in mystery and gives to the document an ahistorical, quasi-transcendental character; further, this process helps, paradoxically, to augment the document's status as an inspired text. Sacred biography is not sacred scripture, and no one in the Middle Ages would have equated the two. However, if they both partake of inspiration, then we ought to consider that Augustine's remarks that "these words were not written by human industry, but were poured forth by divine intelligence" were undoubtedly believed to apply to these texts as well as to Scripture.[70] The second method is simply to declare from the outset that the document is the product of a divinely inspired minister of God.

As our hypothetical saint's life moves from oral through multiple written versions, it moves toward being accepted as canonical undergoing the while a subtle but sure transformation from witness to tale, to text, to history, and finally to sacred history. The final version, if accepted by the community of believers, holds all these interpretive moments within itself. This complex process of transformation—from oral sayings through multiple written records, toward a recognition of either a single text or the broad outlines confirmed by a single tradition —is syncretistic. It is through this continual process of adding and excising that the text achieves iconicity, since the text has now not merely

---

69. R. E. Brown, "Hermeneutics," in *The Jerome Biblical Commentary*, eds. R. E. Brown, J. A. Fitzmyer and R. E. Murphy (Englewood Cliffs, 1968), pp. 605–23.

70. Augustine, *De Doctrina Christiana*, Bk. IV, VII, XXI.

joined a normative (viz. canon) list of documents but has at this stage become a document to be revered as a symbol (viz. icon) of the deity. The iconicity of the document is firmly established when the biographical record has become part of the community's worship and the text itself is revered as an essential part of the liturgy to accompany the worship of both saint and God.[71]

71. J. C. Turro and R. E. Brown, "Canonicity," in *The Jerome Biblical Commentary*, pp. 515–34.

2 / Sacred Biography as Historical Narrative: Testing the Tradition, Gibbon to Gadamer

> . . . an exhaustive and well-arranged statement of the facts of Shakespeare's career, achievement, and reputation that shall reduce conjecture to the smallest dimensions consistent with coherence, and shall give verifiable references to all the original sources of information.
>
> Sidney Lee, *A Life of William Shakespeare*

> *Mallem potius eorum auctoritati quam oculis credere meis.*
>
> I would rather believe their authority [the ancient authors] than to believe that of my own eyes.
>
> Boccaccio, *Genealogia deorum gentilium*

These quotations from Lee and Boccaccio highlight the gulf which separates the medieval from the modern sensibility on the issue of authority and judgment. For Boccaccio, and, no doubt, the majority of medieval men and women, the evidence of the senses was at best only a corroborating proof, and a secondary one at that, in the search to determine the truth. The "real" was always unapparent, hidden beneath some surface. Such a fideistic attitude is nowhere more pronounced than in the lives of the saints, where human flesh and blood have become the dwelling place for the God of Abraham, Isaac, Jacob, and Jesus. The saint is the medieval symbol for this interplay between the known and the unknown. Within this medieval system of belief, it followed that if a narrative pretended to describe the saint's life, it had to confront this intersection of the human and the divine. Such a narrative was thus concerned simultaneously with the historical—the story of the saint's life—and the metahistorical—the divine in-dwelling.

The rich texture of immediate experience and event in a subject's life was viewed dialectically against a canvas which only partially concealed the divine force. Nonetheless, such narratives were thought to be biographical studies since they were records purporting to describe the historical lives of individuals. This idea that such texts could pretend to be biographical, or even historical, was dealt a death blow with the growth of empirical biography at the end of the eighteenth century. However, modern understanding of medieval sacred biography remains overly committed to this post-Enlightenment position. Such an empirical view, although it gave us much of value, misunderstood and misrepresented the idea of history which sacred biography claimed for itself. Contemporary scholarship in sacred biography has been heir to both the insight and the blindness of those historians since Gibbon who have studied saints' lives. Yet if we are to develop a renewed understanding for this genre, an understanding more in tune with what medieval authors believed they were writing, a fundamental first step is to delineate the biases which we have inherited and which continue to shape our reading of these texts.

Empirical Biography

Let us begin with an examination of the opening quotation from Sidney Lee's preface to his one-volume *Life of Shakespeare,* quoted above. I could use any number of examples, but Lee was a popular biographer, and his work was well received. His biography, published in 1898, was in its fourth edition by 1899 and was revised as late as 1915. Such popularity is a litmus test of the intellectual appetites of the late-Victorian/ Edwardian age and a testimony to Lee's skill as biographer and his understanding of his audience.[1]

What were some characteristics of Lee's work that contributed to its wide appeal? We might expect to find in a work which enjoys continuous approval over a period of twenty years narrative strategies which contributed to its success. Is there a guiding principle discernible in the composition of his biography of Shakespeare? The answer to this question is that there is indeed such a principle in Lee's work, and it is, in a word, empiricism—an empiricism that pleased his late-Victorian audience. But what does it mean to refer to a biography as empiricist? Although labels often obscure more than they illumine, in this discussion the term does inform. Lee deliberately avoided a discussion of

1. Sidney Lee, *Life of William Shakespeare* (London, 1898), p. vi. See also I. B. Nadel, *Biography: Fiction, Fact and Form* (London, 1984), pp. 55, 217; and D. Aaron, ed., "Studies in Biography," in *Harvard Studies in English,* no. 8 (Cambridge, 1978).

any aesthetic questions in Shakespeare's work and how a consideration
of such an aesthetic dimension might have been an integral part of his
subject's life. Lee avoided such analysis because he believed aesthetics
was a topic to which the principle of verifiability could not be applied.
Lee tells us in his preface that he concentrated on "an exhaustive
and well-arranged statement of the facts of Shakespeare's career . . .
that shall reduce conjecture to the smallest dimensions consistent with
coherence, and shall give verifiable references to all the original
sources of information."[2] The crucial language in this passage, prose
which spoke, moreover, in a subliminal manner to his audience—subliminal because the arguments were and remain to some degree beyond
dispute, gospel—are the words "exhaustive," "facts," "conjecture,"
"verifiable," and "information." Lee's language exalts the role of biographer as archivist whose "exhaustive" research will reveal the dim
recesses surrounding Shakespeare's past. In short, it is such language
and the method of research that such language exemplifies which warrant the label "empiricist."

But how does the biographer with such a predisposition (even if that
predisposition is unconscious) proceed? And what is the effect of this
method on the reader? This method presents the biographer's work as
history and his role as that of historian, as antiquarian, who has recorded what the past holds locked firmly in place. The understanding
of history implicit in these remarks is the static vision of the past as a

2. Nadel, p. 4. The empiricist sentiment is very clearly stated by Boswell in his
discussion of his method: "I acquired a facility in recollecting, and was very assiduous in recording, his conversations. . . . I spared no pains in obtaining materials concerning him from every quarter." *The Life of Samuel Johnson* (London, 1791); I believe one can discern this positivist tradition even in such a twentieth-century master
of the form as Leon Edel in his remark, "The biographer may be imaginative as he
pleases—the more imaginative the better—in the way in which he brings together his
materials, but he must not imagine the materials. . . . He must respect the dead but
he must tell the truth . . . to discuss the quest for materials—that constant search for
significant detail, much of it irrecoverable." *Literary Biography* (Bloomington, 1959/
73). Although it appears that Edel has moved some distance from Boswell, he restricts
the use of imagination to the *dispositio*—what he refers to as bringing "together the
materials"—of the work while he attributes to the materials an apodictic hold on the
truth. Contrast both of these statements on method with Freud's remarks in his single
(rather, it must be acknowledged, disastrous) excursion into biography in *Leonardo
da Vinci and a Memory of His Childhood* (London, 1910), p. 69: "If a biographical
study is really intended to arrive at an understanding of its hero's mental life [but note
the original German is far more provocative: it reads *des Seelenlebens seines Helden*,
literally the spiritual life of its hero]. . . ." Freud is clearly skeptical of the value of
such complete encyclopedic biographies represented by Boswell and Edel.

vast frozen planet littered with time's unchanging debris. The scholar's task within such a historiographic frame is to learn two things: first, how to return to this frozen past and, second, how to recognize and then retrieve its artifacts for the present. But what was this scholarly method, and to what aspect of that past did Lee direct his labors? The method was the historical-critical one bequeathed to Lee by Gibbon but most influenced by Leopold von Ranke (1795–1886), whose *History of England in the Seventeenth Century* (1859–68) established the pattern for academic historiography from which the school of empirical biography grew.[3]

To what aspects of Shakespeare's life did Lee turn? To the "facts" of the bard's life. And why did Lee concentrate so exclusively on the facts of Shakespeare's life, and, more to the point, what precisely did he mean by the facts of Shakespeare's life? Because the Victorians saw no problem in identifying a fact, they did not discuss what they understood by "fact." The nature of historical fact for Lee was *something* that he could verify had happened. For example, surely we can agree that Shakespeare's role in the management of the Globe Theatre is a fact—one with personal, economic, theatrical, and social implications and one, Lee would argue, which we can fully grasp. But why must we limit "fact" to physical occurrences? For example, we might argue (to Lee's disapproval, I hasten to add) that Shakespeare's very considerable interest in language games, such as puns, was also a fact of the poet's life and had a decided impact on the popularity of his drama and hence on his wealth, which in turn affected his circle of peers, where he chose to live, how his children were raised, his consequent fame, and so on. Lee anticipated the first part of our question, that is, why the preoccupation with facts, for he went on to say that it was only through a concentration on the facts that he would be able to reduce conjecture to a minimum and, moreover, that these facts had the inestimable value of being verifiable. But concerning the second part of our query, the nature of fact—that is, the assumptions which underlie the positivist understanding of empirical reality—Lee, as a sensible Victorian, believed a fact to be self-evident, as apparent as heat on a summer's day. The very idea that one might question the importance of such events seems never to have occurred to him. Furthermore, he would have rejected my example of the investigation of the pun in the

3. Nadel, p. 217. White, *Metahistory*, pp. 163–90. See also the wonderfully concise account of the development of the historical method by A. Suelzer, "Modern Old Testament Criticism," in *The Jerome Biblical Commentary*, pp. 590–604.

tapestry of Shakespeare's life, since the choice of the pun, he would have contended, was too conjectural; that is, the causal bases that might exist among Shakespeare's language skills, his use of puns, the presumed audience appreciation, his popularity, and his increase in wealth were mere serendipity. And moreover, the importance of Shakespeare's use of puns to his success as a dramatist, to his popularity, and to his wealth, Lee would have argued, was not verifiable by any historically acknowledged method. Because such an argument lacked these essential constituents of Victorian biography, a biography which made use of such argumentation was thought to be lacking in what Arnold called "high seriousness."

Lee's argument boils down to an *ad hominem* appeal to his readers' intelligence and a respect for their antiquarian interest in the past. This argument is not made directly, but the reader is invited through a host of cues (e.g., tone, innuendo, and indirect statement) to undertake the same work that Lee has performed. The argument implicit in the remarks quoted above and directed to the reader—an argument no less pointed than the overt remarks—might be restated, "If you do not believe the *veracity* of this biography, you can, yourself, dear reader, check my fidelity to these facts by returning to the very documents I have used." Such an argument acknowledges an agreement between the reader and the author concerning the effectiveness of the historical method and the importance of facts. But Lee does not address, either explicitly or by innuendo, the second query that I raised above concerning the nature of the facts, since for Lee—and this is borne out from his biography—the facts were palpable *things* which happened, things which have chronologies and things for which records exist. In other words, the nature of fact was as commonsensical as the nose on one's face: it was physical; it could, to paraphrase Lee's contemporary, the great physicist Rutherford, be measured. Fact was observable event.

Another important concern of Lee was to present a life so well documented that conjecture would be virtually eliminated. Explicit in this position is an acknowledgment that the depiction of the individual in this biography and the actual life of the subject in its historical milieu agree. The biography must bridge the historical chasm and make the departed present to us. But how can such a claim, eschewing conjecture, be made for biography? And what are the bases for such a position? First, the claim is made precisely because the record, Lee believed, was now available for all to see, and the events that comprised Shakespeare's life could be verified by the historical method. The model underlying this approach to biography is analogous to the scientific one which verifies results by repetition.

In such a rigorously empirical system, interpretation is seen as a conscious distortion of the historical record and the imposition of the author's values at the expense of the historical record. I am not suggesting that interpretation may not, in certain situations, "in fact," cloud the historical record. Rather, what I am suggesting is that a method like Lee's does not acknowledge, and hence does not take into account, the inescapability of the act of interpretation—interpretation which is inherent *a priori* in the author's prejudgments, in the observation and selection of material, in the very act of composition, and in the choice, both deliberate and unwitting, of rhetorical paradigms which make up the author's style.[4]

The Primacy of Content

Biography is a genre exquisitely sensitive to the demands of verisimilitude, since the biographer's aim is to render, as ably as he or she can, the record of an individual life. And it is because of this aim, to present that life in all its facets, that biography is, at one level, historical writing. Part of its primary responsibility as a historical narrative is to represent reality. There is a special seductiveness in the writing of biography. The biographer is drawn to his subject, usually someone of note, out of a desire to learn more about this remarkable individual—perhaps, as Freud suggested, out of an unrealized identification with the subject or because through the writing of this biography the biographer may discover more about himself. This allure of the genre directs the biographer's imagination toward a primary concern with the *content* of the story. Content becomes all. The biographer searches every crevice for further evidence about his subject. The biographer's zeal is not only understandable but one we all share. The daily wonder

4. K. Popper, *The Poverty of Historicism* (New York, 1957), p. 3: "I mean by 'historicism' an approach to the social sciences which assumes that *historical prediction* is their principle aim, and which assumes that this aim is attainable by discovering the 'rhythms' or the 'patterns,' the 'laws,' or the 'trends,' that underlie the evolution of history"; and p. 150: "there can be no history without a point of view; like the natural sciences, history must be selective unless it is to be checked by a flood of poor and unrelated material. The attempt to follow causal chains into the remote past would not help in the least, for every concrete effect with which we might start has a great number of different partial causes; that is to say, initial conditions are very complex, and most of them have little interest for us."

with the beauty of creation, with our families, with our hopes and our fears, and with our finitude weighs heavily in the biographer's and his readers' imaginations. Indeed, the audience for biography reads biography to "find out what happened" and not to reflect on how what happened is presented. I am not suggesting that we ignore the value of what happened; rather, the language of biography is, for most readers, like a limpid pool with the subject shining intact deep in its depths. The language of the tale is overlooked in the search for the subject. Indeed, educated modern readers of biography seem far less acute concerning the presence and function of rhetoric in biography than were their medieval counterparts.

Such inattention to the narrative presents a serious obstacle for both biographer and reader. Nadel's comment is surely apt when he remarks that readers of biography "ignore what is written in favor of what is written about."[5] However, against this thesis which highlights the shaping function of language, one often hears such responses as: "Biography is concerned with actual people who lived in sharply etched historical moments as they went about the unique business of their lives in a past time. And it is the biographer's responsibility to communicate that life [i.e., focus on the primacy of events] as clearly as possible to his readers." To this point one readily agrees, with the proviso that the language of communication is not a neutral matrix for the historical narrative but an interpretive one. Language, as Gadamer argues, is quietly building toward its own teleology; hence the biographer's rhetorical strategies, the selection of metaphors, and even the syntax employed is shaping both the biographer's and the reader's comprehension of the subject. Thus, as the reader is led through the details of the subject's life, the language that vivifies those incidents is shaping what he sees, as well as shaping the lexicon which he will use to describe his understanding of what he believes he has seen. This latter point was not lost on medieval sacred biographers and is part and parcel of Walter Daniel's rhetorical strategy in the *Vita Aelredi*.

The biographical method, which I have been calling empirical (some have labeled it analytic or objectivist), is a stepchild of the closing decades of the eighteenth century and heir to the great strides in historiography made throughout the nineteenth century; it is a school of biographical writing which—to perhaps paint it in somewhat stark relief for the sake of clarity—believes it can reflect the actuality of a past as it actually happened, the Rankean *wie es eigentlich gewesen ist*. To

5. Nadel, *Biography*, p. 3.

do otherwise, the empirical biographer would argue, would be to betray the historical integrity of that life, its historical complexity, and to deny our experience of life as a comprehensible whole. Facts for these biographers are the verifiable truths of life. But surely the more basic issue, however, is not simply the opposition of "fact" and "interpretation" but the metaphysic which supports such heuristic procedures: the consideration given to evidence and judgment, how historical evidence is examined, and what it allows us to say confidently about the past.

It is one of the primary ironies of biographical writing that this exquisite feeling for life—an attitude that has given content the primary role in biographical writing—has caused the biographer to underestimate the unconscious biases inherent in selection, observation, and presentation; such an attitude has kept the biographer from an awareness of the judgments his choice of language is continually forcing on him. It is this zeal "to represent" the subject's life which has moved the biographer toward a depiction of the concrete, the unimpeachable, the facts. Without addressing here the manifold problems inherent in the idea of representation, it is well to acknowledge that at the very least representation requires the creation of a synthesis. And it is in the creation of the synthesis—the interpretive bridging between the verifiable, concrete events—that some severe methodological problems crop up, such as the degree to which causality can be attributed to a historic event on the basis of necessarily incomplete documentary evidence. Although other branches of historical writing have considered such questions as worthy of serious concern, the mainstream of the Anglo-American school of biographical writing continues to presume in the transparent causality of historical events and the ability of the biographer to chronicle them without distortion.

Froude, the biographer of Carlyle, wrote that "the facts must be delineated first. . . . We must have the real thing before we can have a sense of the thing."[6] I would like to propose, against Froude, that it is precisely our sense of the thing that sends us in search of the real thing. By "sense," I mean an apprehension of the thing, an incomplete knowledge, rather like the pleasure taken in the expectation of eating that comes from the smell of bread baking. The search for the thing begins with an intuition, with a partial understanding. It is through the application of scholarship that we can come to a more complete understanding. This intuition is a *Tiefsinnigkeit;* it reveals a deep identi-

6. Aaron, "Studies in Biography," p. vi.

fication with the subject. The philologist confronting the ancient text
or the biographer confronting the raw datum of his subject's life is
deeply aware within himself of a feeling that both he and the author
share. Everyone has had this experience. The depth of this intuition
can be seen in situations in which a subject is exposed to a completely
novel point of view. For example, many who have taught Sophocles's
Antigone for the first time have observed their students' shocked recognition that the ancient dramatic voice somehow offers an understanding for their *Angst*—indeed, as improbable as it may sound, appears to have lived their own situation, or one which they can identify.
This dynamic interaction can take place in a seventeen-year-old who
hasn't a hint about the "facts" of Sophocles's life and the complexities
of mid-fifth-century B.C.E. Greek culture. Although such a trans-
historical intuition is an inseparable part of the evaluative procedure,
and more likely to be "correct" given the breadth and depth of the
researcher's reading, it nonetheless arises out of the interpretive faculty and is not dictated by the weight of the evidence.

The search for comprehensiveness in biography, of course, entails
an enormous bibliographic labor. The researcher must have excellent
libraries and access to archives, private papers, letters, photographs,
tapes, audio and video, journals, diaries, and other minutiae which
might have some bearing on the subject's life. One continually reads
reviews which laud recent biographies as the "definitive" work on the
subject. All such aids support the public image of the biographer as the
unbiased "scientific" observer. Once the materials are assembled, they
can be scrutinized so that the biographer can bring to the reader a narrative portrait of his subject that he judges to be historically accurate.
This process presupposes that the biographer can reconstruct the historical moment in the present; that the "facts" so critical to the empirical "school" can be moved without distortion from one chronology to
another.

Lest it seem that I am belaboring a curiosity of nineteenth-century
biography and presenting a caricature, I hasten to add that this biographical method is still dominant despite the work by Kris, Erickson,
Turner, and others. For example, there is almost a century between
Froude's remarks on biography and the interviewer who asked Matthew J. Bruccoli what was new in his 1981 biography of F. Scott Fitzgerald, the third biography of Fitzgerald since 1954. Bruccoli replied:
"More facts." Indeed, one might ask how more facts would produce a
more comprehensive understanding of the subject. Bruccoli's response—which, I hasten to add, has the ring of genuine common

sense—brings up the problem of the relationship of a reasonable sample of statistical data and the idea of a representative depiction. The difficulty with this relationship between a statistical sample and its subsequent interpretation is that facts are not all equal, nor are they all measurable. If the new facts were taken from one period or series of incidents late in Fitzgerald's life, could one claim that such additional material, no matter how novel, would appreciably change the broad synthesis of the life which the biographer must present? Or indeed, even if the new material were to be distributed evenly throughout the subject's life, the biographer would still be faced with weighing the relative importance of this new material. Were some of the new facts more critical in determining the outcome of the particular circumstance he was chronicling, and, if so, why? Facts viewed from the perspective of value—and it would appear impossible to construe them otherwise in historical narratives of any kind—that is, viewed with an eye to how their worth shapes the outcome of the events being studied, are not subject to a neutral quantification. Experience demonstrates time and again that one single item might be the cause for a plethora of effects, while a whole series of facts might have little or no significance outside their immediate context.[7]

The Fallacy of Completeness

The empirical biographer presumes a special philosophical and ethical responsibility to his text. First, he is responsible for a rigorous fidelity in establishing the known boundaries of his subject's life within the historiographic frame he has established, a historiography which is unabashedly positivist.[8] The "known" boundaries of human history since the Enlightenment can be paralleled to those of a Newtonian universe, that is, a self-contained realm of immanent, causally related entities which are insulated against "outside" influences. In such an intellectual model, it is not so much that "transcendent" explanations of events are wrong (the sort made in medieval sacred biography) but rather that they are inappropriate, out of bounds. This attitude is concisely summed up in an anecdote about a conversation between Lamarck and Napoleon. Napoleon asked Lamarck about the place of God in his cosmology. Lamarck replied: "Sire, I have no need of that hy-

7. Nadel, *Biography,* pp. 210–11.

8. Ibid., pp. 38–39.

pothesis." For Lamarck, the idea of God was not "wrong" but simply irrelevant to his model of explaining natural history.

The assumption that people can be understood in their own terms, on the basis of publicly verifiable evidence, is also a basic given of "idealists" and "positivists" such as Collingwood, Dilthey, Ranke, and Momsen. The medieval view, however, when it considers the evidence of the self *seipsum*, the individual in history, invariably construes such data as an integral part of God's plan of salvation; hence it is inherently nonobjectivist. Such a view is profoundly at odds with those of both the positivists and the idealists. The principle of verification in medieval biography, of ascertaining what we can know about a self, is always "outside" the bounds of the known, for the self is itself a reflection of the creative act of God in Genesis: *Et creavit Deus hominem ad imaginem suam.* And hence the self is simultaneously both inside and outside the physical world. For medieval biographers, what exists embedded in the deepest recesses of the human psyche (what they would call the *anima*) is not the primal constituents of the individual— drives, inhibitions, fears—but the eternal *imago Dei.*[9] It follows from this medieval view of human psychology that their historical method will be mediated to a large extent by procedures which optimize value and meaning at the expense of event. The significance of the event, the act, in medieval sacred biography is largely subordinated to the mechanism which produced the action, a process which, since its *Sitz im Leben* is within the world, can be neither understood nor described apart from a heuristic method at whose center lies the unfathomable mystery of the transcendent deity.

Lee's biography of Shakespeare, for example, since it rests on a philosophical foundation opposed to a sociologic, structuralist, or psychoanalytic examination (or combination thereof) of events would *in principle* avoid any such speculation. Furthermore, the biographer who subscribed to an empiricist view would believe he was responsible for bridging the gap between the subject's actual existence and his narrative of that existence. Discounting for the moment the contemporary discussion concerning narrative's ability to represent reality, this empiricist view appears to contain an important contradiction, which, for lack of a more felicitous term, may be called the "fallacy of completeness." The model for biographical study which exists in the mind of the analytic biographer is tripartite: first, it contains an incomplete amount of information about the subject that is separable from the sub-

9. See Van Austin Harvey, *The Historian and the Believer* (New York, 1966).

ject (i.e., events, sayings, letters, witnesses); second, the subject exists here as object (i.e., as a sum of these events); and, third, the model assumes the correctness of the idea of the biographer as impartial witness standing outside both prior categories able to make a selection which will render an accurate depiction of the life of the subject. The imposition of order and arrangement—in short, structuring the raw historical data—of the items in the first category is seen as natural and evolutionary: the events "dictate" the frame for the judgment-making process. The interpretive, judgment-making aspect of the third category is "checked" by continual reference to the first; lastly, the emerging narrative is continually validated by reference to the biographer's understanding of how accurately the first category reflects the second. Although it is the avowed intention of such biographies to be factual, to exercise judgment within the bounds of all the evidence, in actual practice, as this model illustrates, there is much about this complex process that is syncretistic and arbitrary.[10]

Contending Views

There are serious flaws in the assumptions implicit in the above model. One might argue that, rather than being a rendering of a true portrait of a subject, it has, despite the scholarly care taken, unwittingly given birth to a facsimile of a subject. The view of the biographer as a witness able to make present these past events as they existed in their original historical context is naive at best. A number of serious problems arise from such an assumption. The first series of problems concerns what might be called problems of record. For example, the historical/biographical analysis is invariably based on a documentary record different in kind from the actual subject being studied, and that documentary record is necessarily incomplete. The archival materials, no matter how extensive or varied, can never hope to represent the infinitely varied world of experience of the historical subject. Another type of problem concerns the affective dimension of the researcher. Freud and others have shown the highly complex way in which we express iden-

10. Nadel, *Biography,* p. 151; W. Dilthey, *Pattern and Meaning in History,* ed. H. P. Rickman (New York, 1961); and White, *Metahistory,* pp. 6–7: "It is sometimes said that the aim of the historian is to explain the past by 'finding,' 'identifying,' or 'uncovering' the 'stories' that lie buried in chronicles; and that the difference between 'history' and 'fiction' resides in the fact that the historian 'finds' his stories, whereas the fiction writer 'invents' his. This conception of the historian's task, however, obscures the extent to which 'invention' also plays a part in the historian's operations."

tification with a subject through transference. The selection of a biographical subject may be so fraught with unconscious bias that the analysis is never able to locate the historical subject in a genuine past. The problem of identification and its role in understanding for historical inquiry has also been considered by Thomas Mann in *Joseph and His Brothers*. Ernst Kris, writing about Mann's discussion of this problem, has suggested that Mann "thought that the succession of generations may become indistinct, that proximity and remoteness of time tends to diminish by virtue of identification."[11] Those interested in contemporary German hermeneutic theory would probably agree with Mann and argue further that the objectivist model, described above, takes no account of prejudice. Indeed, in their view all judgment is conditioned by prejudgment which in turn is dictated by one's *Sitz im Leben*. If, as Gadamer says, the "task of hermeneutics . . . [is] the bridging of personal or historical distance between minds," then it must follow from this appropriation (Gadamer's word is *Aneignung*) that the bridge is built from the bricks and mortar of one's personal experience. Gadamer avoids the charge of radical solipsism by rooting all prejudgments in tradition. We are all in tradition; indeed, we contribute to and create tradition—the situation is unavoidable. Within this conceptual frame, rather than positing two distinctive entities, text and interpreter, the text and its interpreters exist within a historical continuum. The interpreter's task is not simply one of making the text's meaning available to contemporaries; rather, since the interpreter himself is part of the tradition of meaning which surrounds the text, he has the added task of recognizing his commentary within this tradition of critical commentary. Genuine understanding takes place when the other, something outside us, in this case a text or the raw materials of someone's life, seizes our attention. When we respond to this urgency of appeal, we are led to a proper awareness of our own prejudices and a consequent correction of them. The entire process entails what Gadamer calls a blending of horizons (*Horizontverschmelzung*). The interpreter, the biographer, actually arrives at this state of enlightened prejudice once his experience has been broadened by and included in the concerns of the text.[12]

11. Kris, p. 83.

12. Hans-Georg Gadamer, *Truth and Method,* 2nd ed. (New York, 1981), especially pp. 235–74, 460–91; for a very concise introduction to Gadamer's understanding of hermeneutics, see D. E. Linge, *Philosophical Hermeneutics* (Berkeley, 1977), introduction; and D. E. Linge, "Dilthey and Gadamer: Two Theories of Historiography," *Journal of the American Academy of Religion* XLI, no. 4 (1973): 536–53; see also Joel

A deconstructivist view would argue that the biographical model proposed above is a fiction because it, like its sister discipline history, purports to record the reality of life and refuses to recognize the impossibility of this task. Those of this post-Heisenbergian persuasion would contend that the events we encounter in life are random, not causally related, are representative of nothing outside of themselves, and cannot be represented in language. Life as Roland Barthes expressed it, is nothing but "scrambled messages."[13] In seeking to express in narrative a true representation of the world, of an individual's life, we attempt the impossible because we are using an ordered, rule-bound system with distinctive structural features, such as its "sign-making" faculty, to serve as a transparent reflection of a world which is rule-less and whose "significances" are only arbitrarily related to linguistic signs.

Narrative from this perspective—a view deeply indebted to a Saussurean conception of things—cannot present accurately the context for the historic past. As Hayden White recently argued, "The notion that sequences of real events possess the formal attributes of the stories we tell about imaginary events could only have its origins in wishes, daydreams, reveries."[14] White's argument is based on a metaphysic fundamentally at odds with that of either Lee or Bruccoli, but one which can be located in a historiographic tradition at least as early as Charles Beard's ground-breaking work of the 1930s. The credal system which proposes such a theory of narrative is secular and Lamarckian. Indeed, White's and Barthes's argument concerning the arbitrary nature of the relations between word and thing is such a part of the postmodernist canon that the major assumptions which underlie this position, the inherent randomness of events, frequently go unexamined. For example, in his discussion of time-consciousness, Husserl pointed out that all events, even the most passive, are anticipated. For Husserl all human experience exists within what Carr has called a "double aspect": events are not experienced as happening in the present, but rather, because of our anticipatory faculty, all events are experienced as following something and leading to something else. Thus, the world is not

---

C. Weinsheimer, *Gadamer's Hermeneutics: A Reading of Truth and Method* (New Haven, 1985) especially pp. 164–84 under "Prejudices as a condition of truth."

13. D. Carr, "Life and the Narrator's Art," in *Hermeneutics and Deconstruction,* ed. H. J. Silverman and D. Ihde, Vol. 10 in Selected Studies in Phenomenology and Existential Philosophy (New York, 1985), p. 109.

14. Ibid., p. 110.

experienced as a series of random happenings but as ordered sequences.[15] But to return to White's perspective and its implication for biography, the reader, because of the biographer's desire to "make" sense (I am tempted to substitute "impose") out of the past, knows the subject in a way the subject never knew or could have known himself or was known by his contemporaries. Indeed, the reader understands a subject who never lived in that way at all. In an extreme post-Saussurean model, it would not be difficult to see how one might construe a biography as a work of fiction for the historical context and the text are only intentionally related.

Those biographers of an objectivist persuasion, those who dispute, reject, or are unaware of their own acts of selection and interpretation, who ferret meaning out of minutiae, out of a reverence for the apparent facts of their subject's life, may, paradoxically, be unwilling—albeit they may be quite unaware of this attitude—to confront the most profound difficulty in biographical writing: that (to paraphrase philosopher Wilhelm Dilthey, the first to make this distinction) although they can explain (*erklären*) to their audience the life of their subject, they cannot genuinely claim that they can bring that same audience *to understand* (*verstehen*) that individual's life. Explanation is a mode of analysis derived from the hypothesis-making method of the natural sciences. Dilthey's concept of understanding (*verstehen*) refers to a deep realization of the modes of expression of those biographical subjects, their language, their gestures, and their actions; in sum, it represents a true *Geschichtswissenschaften.* Furthermore, Dilthey proposed that a genuine understanding of expression requires a familiarity with the social institutions, the laws, traditions, conventions, and the ordering of the cultural milieu since expression is embedded within these social patterns. Dilthey retained his belief that one could achieve a complete empathy with a past through such understanding. Indeed, Collingwood in *The Idea of History,* although not necessarily indebted to Dilthey in this instance, subscribed to the idea of empathy/sympathy as a vehicle for the reenactment of past experience. He praised the Romantics because the "intense sympathy" they brought to the Middle Ages made it possible for them to recognize the genuine achievements of that age which the historians of the Enlightenment missed.[16]

15. Ibid., p. 112.

16. H. P. Rickman, ed., *Wilhelm Dilthey: Pattern and Meaning in History, Thoughts on History and Society* (New York, 1961), pp. 38–50, 70: "It is the same with aesthetics. The work of a poet lies in front of me. It consists of letters, is put together by compositors and printed by machines. But literary history and criticism

New Testament scholar Rudolph Bultmann, considering the same problem, suggested that historical understanding depends on the ability to reconstruct the historical context in which an event or a text existed. But this reconstruction is a preliminary effort and produces only a superficial historical understanding. True historical understanding requires that the interpreter of the text enter into what Bultmann referred to as an *Existentialist* life relation with the subject matter. The problems, joys, and perennial human questions addressed in the text become our questions, ones we have already confronted. It is only by means of such profound identification that the past can be genuinely intelligible to the present. Bultmann's thesis is dependent on the crucial assumption that the interpreter in the present has access to the same reality with which those in the past wrestled. The importance of Bultmann's position, which he shared with Karl Barth, among others, was that it answered the naive assumptions of those historians of biography who believed that explaining the past (for example, those seeking to document the life of the historical Jesus) and understanding it are the same heuristic technique.[17]

In this brief survey, we have moved from a positivist view of biographical writing to a postmodernist one. Since these are important issues for a study which seeks to illustrate the different *mentalités* which govern medieval sacred biography from later biographical methods, it is well to iterate the main points of these arguments. Within the empirical frame of a Sidney Lee or a Matthew Bruccoli, we can identify at least three crucial methodological first principles: first, events are causally related; second, an extraordinary degree of fidelity exists between the surviving historical documents and the life in question; and, finally, present biases can be objectified and hence controlled. Thus, the historical events and their connective properties have the weight of facts; they can be reconstructed in a biographical narrative to support judgments without an outside appeal to a transcendent explanation. The most critical issue which separates the work of Lee or Bruccoli from such writers as Victor Turner, Eric Erickson, Hayden

---

are only concerned with what the pattern of words refers to, not—and this is decisive—with the processes in the poet's mind but with a structure created by these processes yet separable from them. . . . Thus the primary subject matter of literary history or criticism is wholly distinct from the mental processes of the poet or his readers. A mind-created structure is realized and enters the world of the senses; we can understand it only by penetrating behind that world."

17. R. E. Brown, "Hermeneutics," p. 614; see also Van Austen Harvey, *The Historian and the Believer,* p. 5.

White, Dominick LaCapra, Martin Jay, and other biographers and intellectual historians lies in their different assumptions concerning access to the historic past. To oversimplify, Lee believed that as we had
access to that past, we could reconstruct it in historical biography;
White in contrast seems to be following Beard's skepticism about historical knowledge or Foucault's belief that a radical *découpage* has
irrevocably severed our ties with the past. Texts, since they are made
of narratives which do not accurately signify "reality," have ontologies
divorced from particular historic contexts.[18]

Gadamer and, more recently, Jauss seem to offer a methodological
middle ground between these two polarities: the past and the present
are part of the tradition of knowledge.[19] We do have access to the past,
but such access is not in the persona of the objective historian reconstructing a distant time, for our own prejudgments, and indeed our very
way of knowing the past, have been shaped by that past which in turn
shapes our judgment. The text, which can be any historical document,
and critic exist in the same interpretive tradition. Moreover, it is an
interpretive tradition shaped by a history of past interactions with
these texts.

Gadamer's argument reinforces part of my thesis, namely, that much
of our current understanding of medieval hagiography has been unwittingly shaped by the Enlightenment response to sacred biography, the
parent of the dominant positivist tradition to which much biographical
scholarship is still heir. This tradition has not dictated this legacy, but
rather the present age has selected from the past certain characteristics
to emphasize. If we are to establish an understanding of the otherness
of medieval sacred biography, if we are to establish a genuine *Horizontverschmelzung,* we must first be aware of the prejudices which inform our reading of these texts. Such awareness has as its first goal the
discovery of our position within the tradition; it is a heuristic task
which seeks to distinguish "individual" prejudices from those that inform the "many" of tradition. Let us now turn briefly to that tradition.

18. LaCapra and Kaplan, *Modern Intellectual History;* see also LaCapra's recent
argument for the importance of rhetoric as an interpretive tool in historical writing:
"Rhetoric and History," in *History and Criticism* (Ithaca, 1985), pp. 16–44.

19. H. R. Jauss, *Toward an Aesthetic of Reception,* trans. T. Bahti, and *Aesthetic
Experience and Literary Hermeneutics,* trans. M. Shaw, Vols. 2 and 3 in the Theory
and History of Literature (Minneapolis, 1982). Jauss, formally trained in medieval
Romance philology, takes Gadamer's more conceptually based philosophical arguments and fashions from them a theory of hermeneutical literary criticism.

The Traditional View

Medieval biographical writing, especially that devoted to the saints, has long been the butt of the positivist school, which invariably used language redolent of incense and the chiaroscuro of flickering candles to describe it. "Hagiography," used as an adjective by these writers, became an epithet for the unreliable. The sacred biographies of the Middle Ages were, for a number of distinguished nineteenth- and twentieth-century scholars, leitmotifs for a benighted, mass-indulged credulity, as texts written in a time when the power of human reason seemed to exist as the prerogative of the very few. Some of these critics, found these texts to be pious frauds written by "monkish," "credulous," "primitive," "dishonest," downright "liars." It is important to discuss such critical remarks, however naive they may now appear, because some of these assumptions reflect and grow directly from the biases we have examined in our discussion of empirical biography.

Few historians could castigate with the gusto of Gibbon, and when it came to the lives of the saints, Gibbon's ironic voice cut savagely. He said that the lives of the saints showed "a total disregard of truth and probability."[20] In attempting to account for this utter disrespect for probity, Gibbon found an easy scapegoat in the religious biographers' pious zeal. He suggested that such a "total disregard of truth and probability in the representation of these primitive martyrdoms was occasioned by a very natural mistake. The ecclesiastical writers of the fourth and fifth centuries ascribed to the magistrates of Rome the same degree of implacable and unrelenting zeal which filled their own breasts against the heretics or the idolaters of their own times." Gibbon's accusation reveals his quite ahistorical assumption that the ancient Christian panegyrists distinguished, or should have, between causality and the miraculous in the same way as leading Enlightment intellectuals.

20. E. Gibbon, *The Decline and Fall of the Roman Empire* (New York, 1952), Vol. I, p. 467. B. Lyon, *The Origins of the Middle Ages* (New York, 1972), p. 27: "What is remarkable about Gibbon's interpretation is that so little of it was altered or questioned in the nineteenth century, that century of *Historismus* which fostered so many new trends and improvements in historical research arising from the 'scientific' methodology and from such European movements as romanticism, nationalism, and liberalism, but few new explanations for the end of the ancient world." See Peter Gay, *The Englightenment, An Interpretation: The Rise of Modern Paganism* (New York, 1966), pp. 210–11. See also Gay's perceptive remarks: "It was plain—at least to Gibbon—that in the centuries when Christianity had shaped men's minds, history, like philosophy, had obediently served as handmaiden to a glittering superstition," *Style in History* (New York, 1976), p. 31.

His skepticism of their motives stems from his belief that these writers could not have believed the nonsense they wrote because of its patent violation of the natural order, and hence what they wrote must be deceit. Gibbon's argument grows out of the great strides made in eighteenth-century science and the scientific method and England's humanist epistemology—even Pope's Catholicism did not deter the poet from his famous humanist dictum that the "proper study of mankind is man."

Three-quarters of a century later, Jacob Burckhardt surveyed the entire canvas of ancient historians and their writings and found Eusebius, Bishop of Caesarea, the one historian/biographer, among the many whom he considered, to be the "first thoroughly dishonest historian of Antiquity" and the "most disgusting of all eulogists."[21] Eusebius is often anecdotal, gossipy, impressionistic, repetitive, and somewhat lacking in analytical powers, but Burckhardt's splenetic charge, one which proved very influential, represents a deeply felt but unacknowledged bias. For Burckhardt, Eusebius as historian was a member of the same fraternity and thereby obliged to accept the same principles that he and his mid-nineteenth-century colleagues did. Accordingly, Burckhardt judged Eusebius exclusively from a point of view singularly unable to discern the enormous historical value of Eusebius's biographical work.

Eusebius's most recent biographer, D. S. Wallace-Hadrill, more accurately comprehends the genre of biography practiced by Eusebius in calling attention to the inability of the modern scholar to deal with all the facets of man who was at once historian, theologian, politician, bishop, chronicler, and rhetorician. Burckhardt's categories are, in fact, too limited. Although he was correct in his assessment that Eusebius was not a historian (given his understanding of that term), Burckhardt was utterly wrong in his judgment of what he was and the value of his work. For example, Eusebius's *De Vita Constantini*, which Burckhardt despised, is a complex work of panegyric, history, politics,

21. J. Burckhardt, *Die Zeit Constantin's des Grossen* (Basel, 1853), pp. 283, 260; compare with D. S. Wallace-Hadrill, *Eusebius of Caesarea* (London, 1960), p. 7; see also Cox, *Biography*, pp. 72–73, 136–41; and H. A. Drake, *In Praise of Constantine: A Historical Study and New Translation of Eusebius' Tricennial Orations* (Berkeley, 1976), pp. 3–11. Momigliano's terse remark captures something of what Eusebius may have considered his role as cultic historian: "Eusebius, like any other educated man, knew what proper history was. He knew that it was a rhetorical work with a maximum of invented speeches and a minimum of authentic documents." "Pagan Historiography in the Fourth Century A.D.," in *The Conflict between Paganism and Christianity in the Fourth Century*, ed. A. Momigliano (Oxford, 1963), p. 89.

and theology. It cannot be intelligently read, nor should it be, as a chronicle of Constantine's life. As Drake has pointed out, Eusebius considered himself the "interpreter" (ἑρμηνεύς) of the motives and the devout deeds of the first Christian emperor and not the mere chronicler of his deeds.[22]

Hippolyte Delehaye, while having made the greatest modern contribution to the study of hagiography, also attacked the genre for its lack of probity. Delehaye was concerned to authenticate a canon of texts that had some claim to historical legitimacy. Part of his interest in the texts of the early martyrs was directed toward establishing the actuality of the saints' existence, and his motivation was to provide a solid historical foundation for those saints whom the church worshipped. In part, then, his scorn for those texts which included apocryphal materials, or, as he put it, those "wretched plagiarisms," was a reflection of this rationale, perhaps an extension of his orthodoxy. Despite the unquestioned breadth of his erudition, Delehaye's historiography owes much to the belief of the nineteenth-century German school that credible history depends on modern ideas of causality.[23]

The Historical Solipsism

Gibbon, Burckhardt, and Delehaye were all chagrined at what they considered a lack of a concern for truth in the medieval saints' lives. If we were to ask what the components were which comprised these historians' imaginative grasp of the truth, we should find that historical truth for these three great scholars consisted of a synthesis of event, fact, impartiality, reliability, and verifiable evidence. These are five of the most important principles of the historical method. Their critical misjudgments, of course, are caused not by these categories but rather by the unexamined assumptions they held and the consequent misapplication of these principles of historical research.

While Gibbon, Burckhardt, and Delehaye were able to discern their rationale for truth, they apparently were not interested in considering—as a question possessed of serious intellectual merit—whether the truth in these medieval biographies was the same as or different from their own. Historical truth from their perspective had to conform to a probability grounded in common sense. Such a procedure of discovery

---

22. Drake, *In Praise of Constantine*, p. 9.

23. H. Delehaye, *The Legends of the Saints* (South Bend, 1961), pp. 78–81.

places a premium on events and tends to downplay other types of evidence, such as what the rhetoric of a text might reveal about the circumstances of its production.

Hyperbole is one of the stock rhetorical figures of medieval sacred biography. The ubiquity of hyperbole in a text—its tendency to promote typicality—was an element singled out as a barometer for judging the reliability with which a certain text might be used to draw historical inferences. Indeed, the degree to which the text employed those rhetorical strategies—and, ironically, the rhetoric which made the text representative of its age—was the degree to which the text's historical probity was questioned. For example, we know nothing about the historical figure of Ignatius of Antioch other than his journey to martyrdom from Antioch to Rome and that he wrote letters to Christian communities along the way. Remarks such as his desire "to be ground as God's wheat in the lions' jaws," from the *Epistle to the Romans* can easily be accounted for by appealing to a type of excessive Christian hyperbole and, as Gibbon would argue, the undoubted polemic intent of the community.[24] Such extreme remarks are a commonplace of the newly converted, and their typicality tends to diminish their value as evidence. However, such hyperbole can also serve as a window into a larger arena and help reconstruct in this instance both the man and the context. Ignatius's remark, redolent with the metaphor of sacramental theology, is an early figural statement of the Eucharistic celebration: Christ is God's wheat to the world. His other epistles testify—as do later commentators such as Origen and Eusebius—that he was gripped in a crucial debate with the early gnostic-Docetists who argued that Christ's presence in the world was apparent rather than real. Ignatius's hyperbole, his choice of metaphor, is thus his official episcopal affirmation of the real presence of Christ not only as a genuine historical figure but as a continuing presence in the breaking of the communion bread. Hence this remark of passionate hyperbole, of obvious religious polemic imbued with an almost breathless desire for martyrdom, points both to the flesh-and-blood Ignatius gripped in an intellectual debate and to the emerging ecclesial theology and political struggle with the Docetists during this formative period in the early church. Whether this remark was actually uttered by Ignatius or attributed to him by a disciple, although important as a historical circumstance, does not detract from what this piece of passionate polemic reveals about the intellectual cauldron of the early church.

24. K. Lake, *The Apostolic Fathers* (Cambridge, Mass., 1970), Vol. I, p. 230.

It would undoubtedly add to our knowledge of the context if we knew whether Ignatius himself uttered this striking remark, for it is the language of genius—language which seized the imagination, and gave voice to the religious imagination of many during this period. But one's zeal to know the identify of the author should not diminish what the remark reveals about the *Sitz im Leben* of the life of St. Ignatius, nor, because of the text's highly wrought rhetoric, should it cause one to treat the text as a less reliable historical document. The fact that the expression cannot be attributed to Ignatius with certainty makes him no less important as a historical figure. That his contemporaries believed he made such a statement is indicative of his heroic status in the community and reveals much about its apocalyptic expectations.[25]

The preoccupation with ascertaining whether Ignatius said what the *Epistle to the Romans* claims he said suggests an inattention to the contextual meaning of the remark, ignores what the community believed about this individual, misunderstands the method through which most of these documents achieved their canonical status, and—I would agree with the distinguished Old Testament scholar Gerhard von Rad— misrepresents the true historic value of these documents as reflective of a collective mentality, indeed the very sort that we saw Gregory of Tours discussing in his work on the *Vitae Patrum*.[26]

Von Rad, in discussing this very problem of the verifiability of event versus the historicity of biblical narrative, took the somewhat radical position that the attempt to determine the historical content of these biblical narratives was irrelevant.[27] To be sure, he argued, a historical

25. For a radical rejection of positivism in a hermeneutic applied to religious literature, see the discussion of M. Noth's and von Rad's historiography in Suelzer, "Modern Old Testament Criticism," p. 601. See also the remarks of Jaroslav Pelikan clearly indicating his understanding of a fundamental change wrought by the Gospels in the future development of historical writing, in *Jesus through the Centuries* (New Haven, 1985), p. 31; "For our present purposes *The Life of Antony* stands as a prime example of the new historiography and new biography inspired by the life of Jesus in the Gospels."

26. I do not for one instant intend to disparage the importance of establishing the authenticity of a text, or indeed the far more difficult procedure of determining if Ignatius was its author. I am intent on measuring the importance of this symbol-laden expression in its particular *Sitz im Leben*—that is, as a polysemeous linguistic construct which is not only an insight to the mentality of a particular community but also an expression which helped create that community's self-consciousness—as it shifts the focus of the historical question from problems of textual integrity to the heuristic value of the remark for the *Weltanschauung* in question.

27. Suelzer, "Modern Old Testament Criticism," p. 601.

kernel can be found in many of the biblical accounts, but the genuine historical concern is the ancient author's intention of illustrating God's special presence to the people of Israel.

Although historians can never have the epistemologic certainty inherent in the scientific method—for example, whether Ignatius of Antioch actually uttered this remark attributed to him—this very inability to place historical narrative in such a secure methodological frame, plus the obvious latitude of interpretation in humanistic study, although a difficulty for a student of the past, has ironically been the stimulus for greater empirical methods in historical writing. William Dray, in *Perspectives on History,* has argued persuasively against those historians who, attempting to secure this scientific certainty, couch their methodological utterances in language indebted to the physical sciences with its apodictic laws, its principle of causality and replicability. Much of the best recent philosophy of history views the study of history as the interpretation of past events with human character as the major element in the "drama." Since history is the continuum of unique human events, proponents of this school of historical narrative would argue, we cannot apply to its study theories which are founded on heuristic procedures based on the natural sciences.

The rationale which earlier twentieth-century historians had for employing both language and principles indebted to the sciences—in which laws are used to predict certain behavior—was to claim for the historical method an objectivity akin to the scientific. Today even the most statistically oriented social scientists would be chary about using models of the "hard" sciences in justifying their methodologies. Indeed, the physical sciences have of late moved away from the use of language conveying an apodictic certainty (e.g., "immutable laws") in favor of a language which discusses the "statistical probability" and the "randomness" of processes. To propose that biographers drop the behavioral archaisms implicit in their language does not imply a return to a historiography based on relativism or a return to the sort of historical method dominant before Kant's will-to-truth replaced the will-to-belief. What it does insist on is a more sensitive response to a wide spectrum of events which hitherto were judged by empiricist canons as being unimportant.

The critical legacy which the student of sacred biography inherited from the positivism of scholars as prominent as Gibbon, Burckhardt, and Delehaye and the practitioners of biography still survives in the works of some of today's most prominent scholars. LaCapra, Jay, Kaismann, Hughes, and others have recently argued that neopositivism is having a resurgence in historical writing. In his recent essay "Rhetoric and History," LaCapra quoted H. Stuart Hughes, who saw a regression in contemporary historiography to a "primitive positivism" and urged his colleagues away from this retreat from interpretation by reminding them of "the simple truth that what one may call progress in their endeavors comes not merely through the discovery of new materials but at least as much through a *new reading* of materials already available."

With Hughes's remarks in mind, let me survey a sampling of recent comment, taken from the work of medievalists in different disciplines but with a direct application to sacred biography. The point of this review is crucial: it is not my interest to create foils for an argument but rather to show how the persistence of historical *mis*reading since the Enlightenment has continued into the present, how it has shaped our approach to these texts and how as a consequence it has limited a deeper appreciation of the merits of sacred biography, perhaps the most "medieval" of all the narratives that survive.[28]

Sacred Biography as Pious Fiction

In his book on the Irish saints Declan and Mochuda, P. Power provided the following question and answer: "Did the scribe believe what he wrote when he recounted the multiple marvels of his holy patron's life? Doubtless he did—and why not! To the unsophisticated monastic and mediaeval mind, as to the mind of the primitive man, the marvelous and supernatural is almost as real and near as the commonplace and natural."[29] Surely, however, no one would suggest that Aquinas had an unsophisticated mind, and yet Thomas had great reverence for the saints and daily read their *legenda*. Augustine credits the *Vita Sancti Antonii* with his conversion. But Augustine's attitude should come as no surprise, for the tradition from Cyprian through Bonaventure shows that it was the intelligentsia, often as not, who took the lead in promoting the cult of the saints.

If we turn to the lives of English saints, we find a variant of Power's critique of excessive credulity being leveled by one of the most able

28. William Dray, *Laws and Explanation in History* (Oxford, 1957); LaCapra, "Rhetoric and History," p. 20.

29. P. Power, ed., "Lives of Saints Declan and Mochuda," in *Irish Texts Society* (London, 1914), Vol. XVI p. vii.

editors of Anglo-Latin hagiography, Bertram Colgrave, writing in his edition of the *Two Lives of St. Cuthbert* that "Science had not yet given man a conception of a universe ruled by unchanging laws. . . . The age of Bede was primitive in its outlook; it was naturally credulous, and the nature of evidence was but vaguely understood."[30] Power and Colgrave, unable to account for the miraculous in these texts other than as an indication of their authors' belief in the easy violation of the natural law (that is, to treat every event as requiring some causal explanation), viewed these texts, their authors, and the period as steeped in an age of blind faith.

Medieval historian W. J. Brandt, in his book *The Shape of Medieval History,* suggested that the narrative of the saint's life, which seemed to him "late classical in origin, is very difficult to characterize. It is neither a modern narrative, searching for meaning within experience, nor a value charged aristocratic narrative. It seems to me a narrative which exists for its own sake, [and] often manifests a peculiar sidewise movement, a kind of chronic indirection, which can be surrealistic in effect."[31] But Brandt's difficulty with the narrative never goes much beyond this early stage of bewilderment. His difficulty in understanding the genre stems from his obvious lack of study of antique narrative forms, such as the distinction between *praxeis* and *ethos,* and sacred biographies' employment of panegyric, the tension between *res* and *verba,* as these distinctions were used in biography.

In his excellent study of *Women Writers of the Middle Ages,* Peter Dronke remarks: "In the thirteenth century Jacobus de Voragine, even though he clearly had Perpetua's own text [*Passio Sanctarum Perpetuae et Felicitatis*] before him when he wrote the *Legenda aurea,* wanted to present her in coarsened hagiographic clichés."[32] This comparison is misleading. Notice that Dronke has compared the text of the original *Passio* with the "coarsened hagiographic clichés" of Jacobus's epitome. The comparison is between what may be a *sui generis* text (the original *Passio*) and the characteristics of a genre (Jacobus's epitome). Such a comparison fails to convince, since it compares two narratives which, although related, are fundamentally different: Jacobus was writing within the well-established tradition of producing a collection of epitomes for pious clerical reading while the author of the *Pas-*

30. B. Colgrave, *Two Lives of St. Cuthbert: A Life by an Anonymous Monk of Lindisfarne and Bede's Prose Life* (Cambridge, 1940).

31. W. J. Brandt, *The Shape of Medieval History* (New Haven, 1966), p. 68n.

32. P. Dronke, *Women Writers of the Middle Ages* (Cambridge, 1984), p. 282.

sio was composing a text to be used in evangelizing a most complex lay audience, those who faced persecution and those who persecuted them. Dronke's remarks, while more sophisticated than those positivist arguments of the empirical school, reveal a point of view which, for lack of a more precise term, we might call neoromantic. By this expression, I mean that implicit in Dronke's argument is the premium paid to the belief that the *Passio* is an authentic "historic" document dictated by Perpetua and that because it can make such a claim to authenticity —in language comparatively free from the idealizing tendencies of the genre—the scholar can confront the distinctive utterance of the individual Perpetua herself. If the original *Passio* is to be revered for its historic and authentic individualism, for the genius of its linguistic particularity, then the epitome of Jacobus—already part of a millenium-old tradition which has changed that singular historic feminine voice of the lady Vibia Perpetua into the idealized person of St. Perpetua— is to be sanctioned for having suffocated such individualism under the weight of a bloated rhetoric.

Few dispute that the account of Perpetua's imprisonment is a magnificent testimony to individuality—her language often spare and unadorned mixes in a perfectly natural way her plight with her domestic anxiety as a nursing mother—an individuality so imposing that it makes the argument for the text's autobiographical authenticity plausible.[33] However, the problem with comparing her narrative of her incarceration with that of Jacobus's rendering is, as I pointed out, a comparison of different things. It is impossible to read Perpetua's narrative and not be inspired by her conviction, by her maternal tenderness, to acknowledge the reality of her contradictory feelings between loyalty to family or to her newly adopted faith. In short, Perpetua emerges from the text as an individual woman of genuinely heroic dimensions. Conversely, although it would appear to make the best of sense to view the lives of the saints as the lives of the Christian heroes, as many scholars believe, the theology—a theology which developed only after the late fourth century—which animates the tradition of sacred biography is antagonistic to the concept of individual heroism. There are really no heroines or heroes in saints' lives; rather, there are men and women whom God has favored (with grace), and that favor has distinguished them in the eyes of their fellows.

Sacred biography, although it exalts the individual, does so only hav-

---

33. For an extended discussion of the *Passio Sanctarum Perpetuae et Felicitatis,* see Chapter 5.

ing made perfectly clear that the exaltation is a result of Providence. There are no genuinely autonomous acts of heroism in this genre; all actions, whether good or evil, are contingent acts. Such a situation presents a difficulty for the critic who, perhaps unintentionally guided by modern criteria, in the analysis of late-antique and medieval biography, places a premium on depictions which appear to be unique, independent, virtuoso—in short, the behavior of Perpetua. And thus, a comparison of the figure of Perpetua, as it is presented in the original *Passio* and in Jacobus's epitome, which does not take into account the different theological biases present in both texts and their accompanying rhetoric, is unlikely to elicit a useful conclusion.

Positivist's *Redux*

One final example of this legacy of misreading sacred biography by a prominent historian will conclude this discussion of the genre and its critics. In G. R. Elton's recent review of R. Marius's biography of St. Thomas More, Elton writes: "it takes some courage to venture beyond the hagiographical fiction and write about More as the man he really was."[34] Elton's remarks illustrate the traditional critique that hagiography must be a fiction because the actions and sayings attributed to More are clearly encomia, and they are thus inadmissible as historic evidence; and, as a fictional character, this hagiographic More can teach us nothing about the authentic character of Thomas More. Such is the belief in the intransigent polarity between historical fiction and fact and in the separability of such historical tradition from the historical record as it "really was."

If the tradition's use of epideictic language reveals how past audiences—both learned and lewd—became part of this tradition of Moreiana (as Gadamer's hermeneutics would understand them to) is of value for Elton, these narrative strategies are clearly of less value than

---

34. G. R. Elton, *New York Review of Books*, January 31, 1985. See also Georges Duby, *William Marshall: The Flower of Chivalry*, trans. R. Howard (New York, 1985), pp. 13, 28–31, 58. Although Duby does recognize the difference in genre represented by the saint's life ("According to the rules of that special literary genre constituted by saints' lives . . ."), he retains the traditional understanding which argues that the author's intention in presenting such evidence was to present these lives as intentionally factual accounts: "It allows us to rectify two fallacious kinds of evidence: first, that of hagiographic literature which paints every knight as a little Saint Alexis, a little Saint Maurice, steeped in docile devotion."

content and fact. Indeed, the genre's fictional More is in opposition to a historic More. There are two antipathetic poles in this argument: the fictional More and the historic one. The fictional More is the product of pious and perhaps designing individuals, who wove this cloak of sanctity about him for a variety of reasons, perhaps none of whom was interested in telling the "true" story. Hagiography has kept this aspect of More alive and dominant. Of course, there was another More, the historic man whom the autonomous, objective historian can discover. But such thesis/antithesis positions, although useful in certain instances, make for too easy a generalization. What I would propose is that the tradition that developed shortly after More's death, indeed during his life, may be didactic, may be fabrication, but it is nonetheless the reality which a large number of his peers choose to believe and write about, which he abetted—dare I suggest believed—in some instances and which is thus historic. It is historic for two reasons: first, because it is an emblem of the collective consciousness of a given community at a given time and, second, because later understandings of More have been shaped by it even as they reconstitute it. The hagiography surrounding More is both diachronic and synchronic. Elton's interest in establishing More as the man apart from the tradition—what Ranke called the effort to uncover the *wie es eigentlich gewesen ist*— seeks to isolate More, to free him from his context. Given this understanding of the tradition, the role of interpretation, and context, the task of the biographer is to place More's "actual" life within a matrix which sees More as an inseparable part of a multidimensioned tradition, pious or otherwise, with which he has come to be understood.

A related difficulty with Elton's remarks is their implicit acceptance of what I would like to call the organic fallacy, "More as the man he really was." This approach to biography purports to document a reality that, as we discussed above, never existed in such an atomistic state. More's life was a continuum of contingent events, of carefully planned maneuvers, of savage disappointments and unexpected turns. Since More's life can only be viewed by the historian as a narrative sequence of past events, it is well to keep in the forefront of our analysis that such an approach—one which derives its interpretation from the completed record of the life—may distort both the events being examined and any conclusions we might make about the life of More. The organic fallacy imposes an order on life that exists only in retrospect in the mind of the viewer gleaned from the extant documents. There is a paradox in this method, since the quality of historical interpretation is related to the amount of material which survives and the concomitant belief that more material can ensure the likelihood that greater coherency can be discerned among the often incongruous events of the individual's life. Such a method distorts the limits of what biography can do; it cannot claim in a substantial way that it can give us what actually *was*, since the past is accessible to the biographer only as a reconstituted present in which the original context is determined by the selectivity of the biographer.

Historical Truth in Sacred Biography

We have surveyed a tradition of historical criticism which I have been labeling empiricist. I have tried to define the general outlines of a critical position which has invariably found these medieval sacred biographies severely flawed as historical documents. The argument I would like to outline at this juncture, and which I present in greater detail in Chapter 3, concerns the following three points: what the sacred biographer understood as fact; how his understanding of the miraculous affected his understanding of verisimilitude; and in what way sacred biography can be considered historical writing.

The sacred biographers of the Middle Ages considered their work historical insofar as they developed categories which they reserved exclusively for this type of writing. History was a category of writing under the general aegis of grammar and had always been considered as part of the study of rhetoric. Cicero, commenting on the difference between the annalist and the historian, remarked that the annalist was a mere recorder whose guiding principle was "brevity without obscurity," while the historian was involved in a literary endeavor. His rhetorical skills were necessary since historical writing was either read or listened to.[35] Many medieval texts illustrate Cicero's remark, but I would like to cite one from the work of Agnellus of Ravenna (ca. 846) whom we will discuss in more detail below. Agnellus appears to have been a secular priest of some learning who was in the employ of the bishop of Ravenna. It seems that Agnellus read from his history of the church of Ravenna to an audience of clergy and laity. He must have

---

35. B. Smalley, *Historians in the Middle Ages* (London, 1974), pp. 15–25; see also D. Hay, *Annalists and Historians: Western Historiography from the Eighth to the Eighteenth Centuries* (London, 1977), pp. 1–11. See also the informative study by G. A. Press, *The Development of the Idea of History in Antiquity* (Montreal, 1982), pp. 46–50, for a summary discussion of the changing complexity of Cicero's understanding of *historia* as he grew older.

been an entertaining and animated person, for at what must be the end of each day's reading he concludes with a summary of what he believed the audience's response was: "You've been hanging on my words today" or "Yesterday you showed signs of boredom." Such remarks indicate the importance Agnellus assigned to the place of *elocutio* in *historia*.[36] It was a crucial part of the medieval historian's duty to ensure that his audience remained alert to what he was saying or what they were reading. Agnellus employed traditional rhetorical strategies to do this. The annalist's responsibility, on the other hand, was to make his entries short, pithy, and free from rhetorical embellishment.

This classical distinction between history and annal, a distinction with much left unsaid, was maintained in the Middle Ages. Indeed, even when a medieval author is explicitly discussing the characteristics of historical writing, his remarks can be maddeningly oblique. Isidore of Seville, whose *Encyclopaedia*'s influence was widespread, puts the matter in the broadest terms when he says that "grammar is the art of writing and history is a written narrative of a certain kind." Such lack of distinction between categories does not endear Isidore to a modern historian's search for exactitude.[37]

Hincmar of Reims

But what did the sacred biographer believe he was writing? The learned archbishop, Hincmar of Reims (ca. 805–82?) wrote the *Vita Remigii* late in his long life (ca. 877–78).[38] It is, as J. M. Wallace-Hadrill

36. O. Holder-Egger, ed. "Agnellus Liber Pontificalis Ecclesiae Ravennatis," *MGH: Scriptores Rerum Langobardicarum* (Hanover, 1878).

37. Press, *The Development of the Idea of History*, pp. 91–92; Hay, *Annalists and Historians*, pp. 38–86; and Smalley, *Historians in the Middle Ages*, p. 22.

38. B. Krusch, ed. "Vita Remigii Episcopi Remensis," *MGH: Scriptores Rerum Merovingicarium* III (Hanover, 1896), pp. 336–40; see also J. M. Wallace-Hadrill, "History in the Mind of Archbishop Hincmar," in *The Writing of History in the Middle Ages* eds. R. H. C. Davis and J. M. Wallace-Hadrill (Oxford, 1981), pp. 43–70: "In the massive *oeuvre* of Hincmar we find no history; not that is, history as conceived by Gregory of Tours, Paul the Deacon or Bede, who, for all their differences, had had in common the compulsion to look attentively at large tracts of the past and out of them to make a world, full of people. Hincmar, who knew both his Gregory and his Bede, was not like that. In his own way, however, he did imagine and use the past. Like Hugh of St. Victor 'his historical thoughts came to him not through writing history'; they came to him as allies in his long life's search for secure foundations."

says, the work of a lifetime and a most elaborate composition, far more elaborate than most works of sacred biography. In its broad outlines, it is a liturgical work; it praises not only the saint but also the province of the saint and the kingdom of France, for St. Remegius was the baptizer of Clovis. It contains popular instruction for the clergy as well as intellectual arguments of some consequence. And it has political overtones. But what did its author consider such a hybrid work to be? It is obvious from the text that Hincmar was well versed in the rhetorical tradition of the genre of sacred biography and that he used that tradition to good effect in this text. In the work, however, we find a most interesting remark: Hincmar refers to it as a history. For in the *Vita Remigii* he discusses the role of the true law of history as having as one of its primary functions the role of edification. There is little doubt that Hincmar's discussion of history was intended for anything other than to illustrate the truth of this remark in the *Vita Remigii*. In his own words: *vera est lex hystoriae simpliciter ea que fama vulgante colligitur ad instructionem posteritatis litteris commendare.*[39]

Thus, it is apparent that Hincmar did not see sacred biography and history as separate genres. Hincmar would have agreed with the proposition that sacred biography, since it was a narrative about the life of someone, was, whatever other elements it might contain, historical writing. Hincmar's remarks quoted above on the true law of history bear a moment's further scrutiny. In fact, these remarks are not original with him but have a long and distinguished antiquity. It is not my intention to derive the ultimate source for Hincmar. However, Bede, in virtually the same language, said as much in his *Ecclesiastical History*. And we find that Bede is, in turn, paraphrasing St. Jerome.[40] But, even more interesting, and pertinent for our discussion, is to ask why Hincmar cites a remark used by these two fathers. First, I believe that Hincmar, like all his peers, accepted, that the work of both St. Jerome and Bede was a careful combination of sacred biography and history. Thus, citing these two intellectual giants of Christianity in defense of his method is a powerful argument to authority and bound to limit the potential criticism of his *Vita Remigii*. Second, I believe that, Hincmar's use of St. Jerome allowed him to iterate an important point concerning what he believed was the crucial idea which comprised the historical method: the principle of *instructio*.

39. Hincmar, *Vita Remigii*, p. 253.

40. Wallace-Hadrill, "History in the Mind of Hincmar," p. 66.

Ethics and *Instructio*

I would like to place the context for examining Hincmar's remarks within the general category of ethics. Such a categorization may at first appear strange. However, the force of Hincmar's *instructionem* is not simply to edify or inform but to teach (*docere*). But to teach what? Hincmar's intention was to teach the proper mode of behavior in society, behavior which the saint offers as a model of supreme excellence, since the saint's behavior is grounded on the *imitatio Christi* or what Xenophon and Plutarch would call the *ethos*. Hincmar's remarks are similar in spirit to those of Bede discussed in Chapter 1: history should excite us to imitate the good (*ad imitandum bonum auditor sollicitus instigatur*). This good can only be understood as the truth of revelation as practiced by Christian living. I am suggesting that for the sacred biographer there are no historically neutral actions, no actions that simply have an ontology without an ethical dimension.

Medieval sacred biographers believed that every event which can occur in the world can occur because its potential for occurrence is sanctioned by God. There are no events which take place in creation that do not have a metaphysical dimension. The presence of the deity suffuses all creation. Such ideas, commonplaces of medieval theology, exist from the very beginning of Christian apologetics, as in St. Justin Martyr's *Dialogue with Trypho the Jew* (ca. 132–35). What is pertinent for our discussion is that within such a philosophical system in which an invisible umbilical cord, as it were, yokes the divine force and the created, there is an utter lack of intellectual and emotional polarization between the ideal and the real, between the unseen and the seen. They are points along an epistemological continuum—with the world of the unseen requiring the eye of faith and that of the seen requiring physical sight.[41]

41. The problem of causality and future contingency was a subject for considerable sophisticated discussion by some of the greatest thinkers of the High Middle Ages, such as St. Anselm in his *De Concordia Praescientiae et Praedestinationis et Gratiae Dei cum Libero Arbitrio*, Abelard in his *Logica Ingredientibus*, Peter Lombard in Book I of the *Sentences*, Robert Grosseteste in *De Libero Arbitrio*, St. Thomas in his *Summa Theologica*, John Duns Scotus in *Ordinatio*, Peter Aureoli in his *Commentarium in Primum Librum Sententiarum*, Ockham in *De Praedestinatione*. However, the most succinct remark I have found on God's omniscience and power serving as the immediate potential for the existence of the past, present, and future is that of Thomas Bradwardine in his *Summa de Causa Dei contra Pelagium et de Virtute Causarum ad Suos Mertonenses Libri Tres*, ed. H. Saville (London, 1618; reprinted Mi-

Perhaps this latter point is best illustrated through a story. In his *First Dialogue,* Sulpicius Severus has the holy traveler Postumianus, a very astute and credible witness, tell of his travels through the Middle East. Postumianus has just departed from a visit of six months with St. Jerome and has arrived at an unidentified monastery somewhere in Egypt not far from the banks of the Nile. Postumianus recounts the story of two young boys who were returning from bringing food from the monastery to one of the outlying hermitages. The boys came upon a huge, menacing snake which suddenly before their eyes became docile and allowed them to pick it up. They hid the snake inside their cloaks and on returning to the monastery displayed it "not without boastful pride." Their fellow monks extolled the faith and miraculous power of the boys. But their wise abbot reproved them lest in their weakness they should become haughty

> for having revealed the deed the Lord had done. What had happened did not come from their faith, but from [his] divine power. They should learn to serve God in humility rather than pride themselves on signs and wonders; it was better to be conscious of one's weakness than to draw vainglory from miracles.[42]

How does this excursus into the realm of medieval religious parable help us gain greater understanding of the method of the sacred biographer? It helps us to compare their understanding of events with the understanding of those historians cited above. For example, the great rationalist historians of the Enlightenment, such as Gibbon, Voltaire, and Montesquieu, did not recognize the tissue which connected reason and fantasy, nor did they recognize, as Hayden White points out, the process by which fantasy or the imagination contributed, as much as did reason, to the discovery of truth.[43] These historians saw reason allied with common sense and its capacity to judge sensory experience as opposed to the imagination with its propensity for wishing certain realities into existence. Medieval authors, especially sacred biographers, saw little that need be contradictory between the worlds of fact and fantasy; both fact and fantasy were signs to the acute observer of

---

nerva, 1964), p. 209: "Si Deus esse desineret, nihil esset praeteritum, nec futurum, verum nec falsum, possibile vel impossibile, necessarium vel contingens, nec etiam posset esse."

42. Sulpicius Severus, "Dialogi III," *PL* 20, 80, quoted in Freemantle, p. 512.

43. White, *Metahistory,* pp. 49–53.

the nature of things, different signs to be sure, but nonetheless signs revelatory of truth.

In the chapters which follow, I consider the implications of a historiography which accepts as a fundamental principle the idea of *instructio*. How are we to understand the nature of event and causality in these sacred tales? Does a historiography based on the idea of *instructio* ignore research, verifiability, and plausibility? What is the role of hermeneutics in such historical writing?

It seems that a vast gulf separates a historiography based on *instructio* and one based on the historical-critical method. In the chapters which follow, I hope to show a way to bridge these distant shores.

3 / Sanctity in the Cloister: Walter Daniel's *Vita Sancti Aelredi* and Rhetoric

Aelred, the saintly abbot of Rievaulx, died at approximately ten-thirty P.M. on the twelfth of January 1167, the day before the ides of January on the feast of St. Hilarius (d. 368), bishop of Poitiers, and within the solemnity of the feast of the Epiphany. His biographer, Walter Daniel, tells us that his death was not unexpected; that year's exceptionally bitter Northumbrian winter had sapped much of the elderly man's remaining vitality.[1] Aelred's fellow Cistercians knew that his death signaled a great passing. They believed the moment of his death was of major historical significance. Aelred was, after all, the acknowledged leader of the first generation of English Cistercians. He had met St. Bernard during his journey to the Roman Curia in 1142. Moreover, it was the great abbot of Clairvaux himself who had insisted that, although only the novice master at Rievaulx, Aelred must write what was to become his famous analysis of the Cistercian religious life, the *Speculum Caritatis*.[2] Lastly, Aelred's monastic brethren knew that his reputation for sanctity was well deserved. Not only did they weep, then, for the passing of a beloved monastic companion, but they wept for the loss of a great spiritual teacher, and, perhaps most importantly, they wept because they believed that they were present at the passing

---

1. F. M. Powicke, ed., *The Life of Aelred of Rievaulx by Walter Daniel* (London, 1950), p. 54: "Through the last year of his life a dry cough racked his breast and, added to all his other various infirmities, so weakened and wearied him that sometimes, when he came back from his cell after mass in the church, he could for an hour neither speak nor move but lay as though unconscious on his pallet . . . he endured this suffering for a whole year, until on Christmas eve, when bodily pain tormented him more than ever and his illness harassed his life here on earth, he began in his turn, in his strong and unconquerable soul, 'to depart and be with Christ.'" Translations from the *Vita Sancti Aelredi (VSA)* are from Powicke unless indicated otherwise.

2. A. Hoste and C. H. Talbot, eds., *Aelredi Rievallensis Opera Omnia: Opera Ascetica, CCCM* (Turnhout, 1971), see De *Speculo Caritatis*, pp. 3–161.

of an age. Aelred's death separated them from this representative of a heroic age, a more hallowed time; it separated them from the age of the historic beginnings of the Cistercians in Northumberland.

It is no exaggeration to suggest that the acute feeling of loss depicted in Walter Daniel's *Vita Sancti Aelredi* is analogous with the sense of nostalgia and irreparable isolation from the beloved past that the verses from the Old English *Wanderer* exemplify: "Homeless and hapless, since days of old,/ When the dark earth covered my dear lord's face."[3] For the monks, Aelred was that palpable, physical sign of a temporal lord, but a lord who exemplified, above all else, the sign of Christ's presence in their monastic home. He was, for his monastic brethren gathered at his deathbed on the night of the twelfth of January, within the solemnity of the Epiphany—the feast of the manifestation to the Gentiles—the biblical promise of salvation fulfilled, now suddenly taken from them. From that moment of his death, his brethren feared that they would be bereft of guidance as the gloom of the Yorkshire winter deepened.[4]

Vita Sancti Aelredi

Walter Daniel's biography of Aelred, despite the biographer's intimate knowledge of his subject, is a curious blend of panegyric and narrative realism. Walter writes with a passion for detail, and his use of idiom

3. When Gilbert, abbot of Swineshead, learned of Aelred's death, he was in the middle of his chapter sermon. It is reported that he broke off at once from his subject and made the following remarks concerning Aelred's sanctity: "What a honeycomb, how mighty and how rich a one, has passed in these days to the heavenly banquet. . . . It seems to me that in him, in his being taken from us, our garden has been stripped, and has given up a great sheaf of myrrh to God the husbandman. There is no such honeycomb left in our homes. His discourse was like the honeycomb, pouring out the honey of knowledge. His body was languishing with illness, but he himself languished more in spirit from love of heavenly things." See M. E. Laker, trans., *Aelred of Rievaulx: Spiritual Friendship,* Cistercian Fathers Series No. 5 (Washington, 1974), p. 14.

4. In the proem in the *Vita Sancti Aelredi* addressed to Abbot H. (he remains unidentified), Walter compares Aelred's passing, in good encomiastic tradition, to the disappearance of the daily sunrise: "To Abbot H, dearest of men, his servant W. Daniel, greeting. Our father is dead; he has vanished from our world like the morning sunshine, and many hearts long that this great light should flood with its brightness the memory of generations to come, and indeed of those still living for whom it shone in all its splendour."

and concrete imagery gives a very vivid portrait. His prose is richly evocative of the physical world. For example, in his response to anonymous critics who must have complained that Aelred took too much delight in his frequent bathing, Walter points out that Aelred had a severe case of kidney stones and that his consumption of wine and frequent baths were not the gratification of the sybarite but an attempt to lessen the excruciating pain: "The pain was severe and frequently his urine contained stone fragments as large as a bean" (*Quam passionen ita duram sustinuit ut sepissime in urina produceret fragmenta saxea ad grossitudinem fabe.*)[5] Such graphically descriptive prose, which seeks to vivify the narrative through its passion for the particular and the homely, is a powerful tool in the pen of the skilled biographer.

Aelred's Last Words

It is not, however, as biography alone that I am interested in Walter Daniel's *Vita Sancti Aelredi*. My interest is also in the manner in which Walter is able to combine the traditional idealizing *topoi* of medieval sacred biography, the use of the panegyric and the encomium, with his narrative skill for the particular. The biographer's attempt to bring the reader a deeper understanding of his subject cultivates a descriptive prose which conveys the peculiarities of his subject's life. The sacred biographer, proceeding from a different conceptual frame, is more interested in what his subject has in common with the sacred; thus, his prose eschews the particular for the ideal.

Walter Daniel's ability in combining these two distinctive methodologies is well illustrated in his depiction of Aelred's death and burial, scenes which in sacred biography are often stylized and deliberately intended to be idealized icons. Let us turn to Walter's testimony of

---

5. Ibid., p. 34: "the passage of [the kidney stone] was so unbearable that if in his suffering he had not tempered and softened the obstruction in the bath to ease its course he would have incurred sudden death. One day after no less than forty visits to the bath, he was so incredibly exhausted in the evening that he looked more dead than alive." Aelred seems to have been severely incapacitated for some considerable time during his abbacy. Indeed, he received the extraordinary permission to be excused from the harshness of the rule because of these multiple illnesses. It would appear from the record left by Walter Daniel that these illnesses were exacerbated by Aelred's especially severe ascetic practices. See Powicke, *The Life of Aelred*, pp. 39, 49–50. On this matter of Aelred's ascetic practices, see Aelred Squire, *Aelred of Rievaulx: A Study*, Cistercian Studies Series No. 50 (Kalamazoo, 1981), pp. 35–37, 127–29.

Aelred's final moments. Walter writes that just before Aelred's death, he bent his head toward Aelred and whispered softly to his friend and abbot: ". . . to look on the cross, let your eye be where your heart is" (*Domine, respice ad crucem et ibi sit oculus tuus ubi est etiam cor*). Aelred, on hearing these words, rallied for a moment, opened his eyes, and uttered his final words: *In manus tuas commendo spiritum meum*.[6] Most readers or listeners, medieval or modern, would find this scene deeply touching. In it, Walter brings together two quite different modes of expression: the individual and the ideal. Walter himself is a major character in the dialogue. The effect of this situation is that the biographer's persona becomes part of the narrative fabric, and thus, whenever this persona is itself dramatized within the narrative, we are reading text which is, for lack of a more felicitous term, autobiographical biography.[7]

6. Ibid., p. 61. The line, from Luke 23:46 (and found nowhere else in the Gospels), is actually Aelred's concluding remark. The entirety of his remarks appears to derive chiefly from Psalm 30. This last prayer of Aelred's is interesting for a number of reasons, but chiefly for the way it reflects the way his prayer is utterly bound up in the biblical texts. Notice that although the lines undoubtedly come from this psalm— traditionally understood to be a hymn of lament containing praise for God's expected deliverance of the distressed individual—Aelred's appropriation of them makes them entirely his own. Here is the entirety of Aelred response to Walter's request: "Tu es deus meus et dominus meus, tu refugium meum et salvator meus, tu gloria mea et spes mea in eternum. In manus tuas commendo spiritum meum." Although Psalm 30 seems to be the major source for Aelred's remarks, a number of these psalmic phrases have echoes in other scriptural passages as well. Such monastic prayer has a richly nuanced polysemous character about it, since the one allusion is continually pointing to yet another referent. For example, Psalm 30 contains echoes of a number of biblical texts, which Aelred surely intended his listeners to recognize: "Ego autem in te speravi Domine/ dixi Deus meus es tu" (Psalm 30:15; cf. Psalms 7:2, 15:1–2, 139:7); "esto mihi in Deum protectorem/ et in domum refugii ut salvum me facias" (Psalm 30:3). The line "tu gloria mea et spes mea in eternum" is a common conclusion to a doxology. Aelred's interior disposition was so shaped by his continual meditation on and praying of Scripture that his most heartfelt personal expression is deeply imbued with scriptural images; on this latter point, see Squire, *Aelred of Rievaulx*, pp. 14–21. For additional discussion of Aelred's spirituality, see D. Knowles, intro., *The Works of Aelred of Rievaulx: Treatises, The Pastoral Prayer*, Cistercian Fathers Series No. 2 (Spencer, Mass., 1971); and A. Hallier, *The Monastic Theology of Aelred of Rievaulx*, trans. C. Heaney, Cistercian Studies Series No. 2 (Spencer, Mass., 1969).

7. This is crucial, since one of the major attacks made on Walter's *Vita Sancti Aelredi* concerned its factual accuracy. The essential point here is that because Walter is both a character in the narrative and the narrator of his interaction with Aelred, his insistence on the truthfulness of the facts of the work is grounded in his belief that the issue of the text's factuality must be subordinated to the truth of his witness. Walter's biography of his friend reveals his own ability to interpret the events of

The single most crucial effect that this complex narrative can have on the reader's imagination concerns the degree to which the text can claim authenticity for itself. Through the use of his first-person narration and the dramatized persona, the biographer confronts his audience with his own personal testimony. Such witness creates a curious dialectic between reader and text; it is the text which forces the reader, in order to support his skepticism, to deny the reliability of the narrator. Such reader response concerning the integrity of the narrator, a response which we are used to making in works of fiction, is one not lightly leveled at works of biography.[8]

Walter's last words to his beloved Aelred are tender and solicitous. His attention to detail makes it easy to visualize him bending low over his abbot, who was the bulwark of the community, and whispering his last ministerial concern. His interest in directing Aelred's last moments to the cross is perfectly appropriate and what we would expect to be the real concerns of these two friends as they confronted death, the prelude to Aelred's glorified life in Christ.

And yet their interchange does not entirely have the ring of personal witness and the authentic moment about it. However personal that moment may have been for Walter and Aelred, the traditions of sacred biography were such that Walter needed to situate the moment within a typological frame. Although the narrative which leads up to the mo-

---

Aelred's life. However, those events, as Walter believed, transcended the world of phenomena, and part of his interpretive skills depends on his ability to penetrate to the truth of this other world. Therefore, the veracity of the final text cannot be guaranteed by objectivist criteria, but only by the witness of the author. Attacks on the text's factuality call into question Walter's own status as reliable witness. Indeed, to question the veracity of the text is to make central Walter's witness and the integrity of that witness to the events in question. Note the observation of J. Ayto and A. Barratt on the accuracy of Walter's biography: ". . . although it [the *VSA*] is not free from some of the usual exaggeration of the hagiographer, [it] is by and large a reliable work." See their *Aelred of Rievaulx's De Institutione Inclusarum,* EETS O. S. 287 (London, 1984), p. xi. See Also G. Gussdorf, "Conditions and Limits of Autobiography," in J. Olney, ed., *Autobiography: Essays Theoretical and Critical* (Princeton, 1980), especially pp. 42–45.

8. Gussdorf, "Conditions and Limits," p. 45. See the distinction Gussdorf makes between "objective biography, regulated only by the requirements of history", and autobiography, which "is a work of art and at the same time a work of enlightenment." Walter's persona intruding as agent in the text does tend to blur the distinction between strict biography and autobiography, since not only is he the agent for telling the story, but he is also a primary character who shapes events in the narrative. See also W. Ullmann, *The Individual and Society in the Middle Ages* (Baltimore, 1966), especially pp. 3–50.

ment of Aelred's final utterance and Walter's portrayal of himself speaking with the dying abbot does ask implicitly for the reader to accept the veracity of the moment as reported, Aelred's response to Walter disrupts the intimacy created by the narrative and supplies the needed typology. Aelred's answer breaks the narrative's spell and moves us from biography to sacred biography.[9]

Let us place this scene in a larger context and ask how the narrative conditions our reading of this passage. The reader's response to this brief deathbed interchange is complex. Initially, we are seduced by the persuasiveness of the text's argument, and we may imagine that we are present at this historic moment. However, once we recognize the source of Aelred's remarks, the biographer's attempt to convince us of the authenticity of the moment is open to serious doubt. Indeed, if we did not proceed further with our investigation into the method of the sacred biographer, we should at this point begin to doubt the intention of the biographer. Walter's narrative genius, his passion for detail—such small touches as his description of his need to bend over the frail Aelred, for example—transports us into the flickering candlelight of the monastic infirmary, which gives us the tangible feeling of being present as Aelred breathes his last. And yet we would be deceived if we believed that this attention to verisimilitude was among the chief goals of Walter's *Vita Sancti Aelredi*. On the contrary, it is the recognition of the moment's typological significance in the quotation from Luke—a recognition which for the modern reader serves paradoxically to destroy the narrative verisimilitude—that Walter was primarily intent on developing.[10]

Although Walter's *Vita Sancti Aelredi* is one of the great works of medieval English sacred biography, his dramatic narrative style has momentarily caused us to suspend our awareness of his mission as the appointed historian of a cultic hero, a hero whose sanctity needs to be documented from the resources of a well-wrought tradition. The narrative's persuasive power is such that the reader wants to believe in the literalness of the moment and in the uniqueness of the interchange between Aelred and Walter, to believe that the author actually intended

9. The quotation from Luke, because it had such wide recognition in Christian monastic tradition, joined for the listener two different historical moments, the deaths of Christ and of Aelred. It seems that at least some in the monastic community did question whether Aelred actually uttered these words or whether they were inserted by Walter to acknowledge the typological parallel between Christ and Aelred.

10. G. W. Lampe and K. J. Woollcombe, eds., *Essays on Typlogy* (Napierville, Ill., 1957).

to render the actual historic moment in those very words. However, in this very passage the text argues, albeit obliquely, against deepening our interest in the narrative's verisimilitude and for increasing our understanding in the text as cultic biography. For in this most precious of moments, the moment of Aelred's historic last words, destined themselves to become linguistic relics, Walter places in his mouth Christ's final utterance as recorded in Luke 23:46.

The use of a quotation at that precise moment is crucial, if and only if the modern reader has recognized the quotation, which, once recognized, acts to subsume the historical Aelred. The quotation places Aelred in a tradition, and the crucial point of such placement is to direct the audience's attention to Aelred's relationship to that tradition and not, for example, to underscore his unique historical attributes in his role as the abbot of Rievaulx.

Before we proceed further, I would like to raise some questions. How is the historical Aelred "subsumed"? What do I mean when I use language with such a metaphysical bias, and why is Aelred's individuality displaced only if the quotation is recognized? Does not such an argument concerning the importance of recognition place an enormous responsibility on the ability of the reader to catch every allusion no matter how slight? Such an argument, which proposes that the text is not fully realized—indeed, perhaps never fully realized—until the reader completes a certain series of connections, makes of the reader or the listener a major participant (perhaps too major) in the construction of the meaning of the text and as a corollary tends to diminish the ontology of the text.[11]

Walter's use of the quotation from Luke proposes on the most superficial of levels that Aelred's and Christ's deaths are related in a crucial manner; the quotation further proposes that their deaths are im-

---

11. Within the monastic milieu of the twelfth century, the ontology of texts was absolute. An argument which considered the question of the ontology of texts as worthy of serious speculation would perforce have to contend with the status of the Bible. No monastic writer would have questioned the Bible as the divine *logos*, which in turn guaranteed the ontology of language to represent reality and by extension that of books also to represent a reality. To suggest that a text has an ontology only when the text and the reader/listener interact confers on the reader/listener a creative force which the medieval world reserved to God alone. God alone could create *ex nihilo*; human creation was secondary, derivative. Jauss points out that even in that most sophisticated discussion of the role of human creation in the Middle Ages, that of Plato's *Timaeus* by the school of Chartres, the *opus hominis* is the most limited type of creation, one which merely reshapes matter. See H. Jauss, *Aesthetic Experience and Literary Hermeneutics* (Minneapolis, 1982), pp. 45–49.

portant for a more complete understanding of either death taken individually. The similitude which links their deaths and the thesis Walter is intent on deriving from our recognition of that similitude can be discerned only if the quotation is recognized. Although the scriptural quotation introduces another character, another man in his death throes, the effect is to lead the reader's attention away from the individual, away from Aelred, away even from Jesus. The quotation leads the reader to an apprehension of the general, to what is shared, to what is common, and not to what is private, unique, *sui generis*.

The event of Aelred's death is, of course, memorable in itself, but Walter would argue, and his monastic audience would agree, that Aelred's death has become more memorable because it is now able to arouse in us the memory of another death, the death of Christ, which is the paradigm for the manner in which all Christian martyrs are meant to surrender to God.[12] Walter's quotation of the well-known verse from Luke is easily recognized. However, the biographers of the saints often make use of many such allusions, obscure allusions often not based on Scripture but on other saints' lives. Many modern readers do not recognize these allusions and are unable to make the connections necessary to complete their understanding of the meaning of the saint's biography. Such partial reading only plays on the text's surface and distances the modern reader from a genuine understanding of the genre of medieval sacred biography.

The Scriptural Skeins

My remarks above do not preclude the possibility that Aelred actually uttered the verse from Luke. Such an utterance from someone who had spent his entire life in corporate spiritual prayer and *lectio divina*

---

12. G. W. H. Lampe, "Martyrdom and Inspiration," in *Suffering and Martyrdom in the New Testament,* ed. W. Horbury and B. McNeil (Cambridge, 1981), p. 118: "For Christians, however, the conviction that the martyr was the ideal disciple held an even more central place in belief and practice, for it was rooted in the event that stood at the heart of the Gospel, the death of Jesus." The Greek word μαρτύς before the period of the New Testament simply meant witness and was frequently used to refer to witnesses in courtroom situations. The notion of suffering joined to that of witness and expressed in the word μαρτύς is a uniquely Christian concept. See Origen's "Ad Martyrium," in *PG,* Vol. 11, cols. 563–636. An excellent discussion of martyrdom and its influence in the early church is H. Le Clercq's in *Dictionnaire d'archéologie chrétienne et de liturgie* (Paris, 1932), cols. 2359–2619; see also H. Delehaye, μάρτυς Note sur un terme hagiographique," Académie des Inscriptions et

was entirely possible. The monastic records from the period are replete with examples of monks, far less able than Aelred, celebrated for their verbatim recall of Scripture. For example, the *Gesta Abbatum Monasterii Sancti Albani* credits John, abbot of St. Albans (1195–1214), with the remarkable feat of repeating the entire psalter backwards verse by verse.[13] My concern with the verse is not with its verifiability as an authentically historic utterance, a perfectly appropriate area of examination, but rather I am interested in what light this particular verse can shed on the interpretive frame of the entire *Vita Sancti Aelredi*. For example, our understanding of the importance of these words in this particular context is not dependent on whether Aelred actually said them or whether Walter spuriously attributed them to him. Walter's report is our only historical record of that moment, and it appears to have been a report that, aside from some skepticism from the clerical hierarchy, was widely accepted. I believe the more basic questions are why was this particular passage selected from the Gospels (regardless of whether that decision was made by Aelred or Walter); what does the scriptural verse contribute to the portrayal of Aelred; and, lastly, why does Walter give the quotation such prominence? To answer these questions, we need to turn briefly to the Lucan narrative.

Walter's Use of Luke

Walter's decision to quote from the Gospel of Luke is interesting from a number of points of view. To begin, it was Luke who wrote the first Christian sacred biography, the story of the protomartyr St. Stephen

---

Belles-Lettres: Comptes rendus des seánces de l'année 1919, pp. 128–34; and G. Kittel, *Theological Dictionary of the New Testament* (Stuttgart, 1967), Vol. 4, pp. 474–514.

13. H. Riley, ed., *Gesta Abbatum Monasterii Sancti Albani* (London, 1867), Vol. 1, p. 232: "Sciendumque, quod numquam in Ecclesia Beati Albani aliquis tam inoffense, tam secure, omnes Psalmos medullitus scivit, aut scitos crebius iteravit, vel tenacius ipso illos in memoria thesaurizavit. Hoc enim, quasi in confusionem nesciorum, fecisse ipsum profecto meminimus, quod, quasi ad experimentum et exercitium, primo Psalterii ultimum versum psallendo pronunciabat, deinde penultimum, popostea antepenultimum; et sic, ordine retrogrado, totum Psalterium, sine offendiculo aut defectu—quod etsi verum, sit tamen incredibile—transcurrebat; cum nec de hoc Psalmo multum usitato, scilicet—'Miserere mei Deus,' hoc se facere quilibet diffidat."

(Acts 5:59).[14] Stephen's discourse is the longest single speech in Acts, and the language placed in Stephen's mouth is significant for its bold typologies. Further, Luke alone among the Synoptic Gospel authors was likely to have known, as Grant convincingly argues, the traditions of Greek rhetoric, Greco-Roman biography, and Greek historical writing. St. Jerome acknowledged the eloquence of Luke's Greek, remarking [*superat*] *omnes evangelistas Graeci sermonis eruditissimus* and further that it sounded to him rather more like a bare history, *nudam sonare videntur historiam*.[15] Kennedy, in his recent work on rhetoric in the New Testament, goes so far as to suggest that

> [the] Book of Acts resembles a classical historical monograph. . . Luke's choice of this form suggests that he expects an audience with some education, who would appreciate it, and that he thinks of himself in the role of a Greek historian—not a scientific collector of facts, but an interpreter and dramatizer of the direction and meaning of events.[16]

It was Luke's knowledge of these traditions which, I believe, contributed to his decision to place the words "*In manus tuas commendo spiritum meum*" in the mouth of the dying Christ. Luke's is the only one of the Synoptic Gospels which attributes this final utterance to Christ. Not only is Luke's use here unique in the Synoptic portrayals, but these words of Luke's—which he substituted for the more agonized, despairing, and (perhaps somewhat vulgar to his hellenized sensibility) Aramaic *Eli, Eli, lema sabachthani*—are themselves borrowed.

The Lucan image of a suffering Christ gasping out *In manus tuas commendo spiritum meum* makes use of a direct quotation of the sixth verse of Psalm 30. The monastic audience certainly recognized the relationship between the psalm and the Gospel. The verse from the psalm was frequently interpreted by monastic exegetes as an expression of thanksgiving sung by someone freed from the imminence of affliction, and its use in the Lucan narrative has a thematic appropriateness (see the commentaries of Jerome, Prosper of Aquitaine, Cassiodorus, Re-

14. H. J. Cadbury, *The Making of Luke-Acts* (London, 1958), pp. 184–93, 221–23, 299–316.

15. Ibid., p. 239; see also R. M. Grant, *The Earliest Lives of Jesus* (London, 1961), p. 14 ff.

16. G. A. Kennedy, *New Testament Interpretation through Rhetorical Criticism* (Chapel Hill, 1984), p. 114.

migius of Antissidorensis, Theodore of Mopsvesteni, and the *Glossa Ordinaria*.)[17] The verse in Luke, as we might expect of any scriptural text which purported to be the actual words of Christ, was also glossed frequently. It, too, was commonly interpreted by early Christian and medieval biblical commentators as a prayer of thanksgiving for an escape or deliverance from distress. In his commentary on this verse in the psalm and in Luke, Bede makes a most interesting observation extending the interpretation beyond that of the idea of thanksgiving for deliverance. Bede's remarks suggest that the verse as it is used in Luke represents Christ's triumphant announcement to his heavenly father that the salvation brought to the world through his incarnation is complete. Read from this perspective, the verse, as it occurs in Luke's account of the Crucifixion, is an affirmation of the essential oneness of the Father and the Christ and hence supports a view which attempts to demonstrate these final moments as an exemplification of the Trinity.[18]

17. It is worth pointing out that the more sophisticated of the biblical exegetes approached the interpretation of Scripture with extreme caution. The psalms were thought to be especially difficult texts. Jerome warns of the difficulty in understanding the meaning of the psalms in his commentary on verse 14 ("Repleti sumus mane misericordia tua") of Psalm 89, where he states: "Mysteria sunt quae dicuntur in psalmis, et figuris plena sunt omnia." See his *Tractus in Librum Psalmorum, CCSL,* vol. 78, part II (Turnhout, 1958), p. 419. Augustine: D. E. Dekkers and J. Fraipont, ed., *Enarrationes in Psalmos,* in Vol. 38 (Turnhout, 1956), pp. 186–90. On God's protective mercy, see Prosper of Aquitaine, *Liber Sententiarum, CCSL,* ed. P. Callens, Vol. 30, part II (Turnhout, 1972); Cassiodorus, *Magni Aurelii Cassiodori: Expositio psalmorum,* ed. M. Adriaen *CCSL,* Vol. 97, part II (Turnhout, 1958), pp. 260–74, especially *Conclusio psalmi,* p. 274. The *Glossa Ordinaria* collects what had become the standard commentary on this psalm; see *PL* 113, cols. 884–85. The *Glossa* cites Augustine and Cassiodorus. See also Theodore of Mopsuestia, *Expositionis in Psalmos,* ed. Lucas De Coninck, in *CCSL,* Vol. 88a (Turnhout, 1977), pp. 135–38; Remigius of Antissiodorensis, *Enarrationium in Psalmos, PL* 131, cols. 289–300, especially cols. 292–93. Pseudo Jerome, *Breviarium in Psalmos, PL* 26, cols. 961–62, draws an explicit comparison between the verse in the psalm and the verse in Luke.

18. Bede quoted in D. Hurst, ed., *In Lucam Evangelium Expositio, CCSL,* Vol. 120, part II (Turnhout, 1960), p. 407: "Patrem invocando, filium Dei se esse declarat spiritum vero commendando non defectum suae virtutis sed confidentiam eiusdem cum patre potestatis insinuat. Amat enim dare gloriam patri ut nos aedificet gloriam dare Creatori. Commendat itaque Patri spiritum iuxta hoc quod delectato corde et exultantibus spe resurgendi labiis in alio psalmo loquitur: Quoniam non derelinques animam meam in inferno nec dabis sanctum tuum videre corruptionem"; see also J. A. Giles, *Venerabilis Bedae: Commentaria in Scripturas Sacras* (London, 1844), Vol. 5, p. 369. The *Glossa Ordinaria* indicates that Luke's expression was deeply imbued with the spirit of triumph: "Patrem invocans, se filium Dei declarat. Spiritum com-

The Very Words

The noun *spiritum* in this verse from Luke was the subject of some commentary, and a discussion of its interpretations can help us understand something of the philosophical basis of medieval sacred biography, as well as offer specific insight into Walter Daniel's purpose in featuring the verse (see the pertinent commentaries of Jerome, Fulgentius of Ruspe, Theodulphus of Orleans, and St. Anselm of Canterbury). Let us begin with a brief introduction to the word as it was commonly glossed. The majority of the commentators who examined the passage suggested that Luke's use of *spiritum* refers reflexively to the individual who utters the verse and the spirit as an independent entity. *Spiritum* is the eternal spirit freely bestowed by the Creator, the animating life principle which the Father shares coequally with his Son. The line was frequently given this Trinitarian interpretation.

There was another understanding of *spiritum* shared by prominent medieval exegetes which I would like to consider. *Spiritum* was also understood as a reference not primarily to the spirit as the life principle which adhered in the individual body but more particularly as the literal spirit of God, the very creative breath of life which gave birth to the universe. In making this observation, patristic commentators argued that the psalmist's use of the word *spiritum* in the verse *In manus tuas commendo spiritum meum* was intended to be a deliberately obscure reference to the fecund spirit of the Lord depicted in Genesis 2:7: . . . *et inspiravit in faciem eius spiraculum vitae.*[19] And it was this con-

---

mendans, non defectum virtutis, sed confidentiam ejusdem cum parte potestatis insinuat. Amat enim dare gloriam Patri, in quo nos informat, ut gloriam demus Creatori." See *PL* 114, cols. 348–49. For Richard of St. Victor, Christ's surrender of the spirit is the single crucial acknowledgment that the spirit is to receive divine peace. See his *Adnotationes Mysticae in Psalmos, PL* 196, cols. 273–76.

19. Fulgentius of Ruspe, *Contra Fabianum Fragmenta,* ed. J. Fraipont, in *CCSL,* vol. 91a (Turnhout, 1968), pp. 763–866; Theodulphus of Orleans, *De Spiritu Sancto,* in *PL* 105, cols. 239–276. Although his commentary is more indebted to John's Gospel, Theodulphus's work is a florilegium of citations from past commentators; indeed, his commentary gives the prevailing orthodox position concerning the relationship of the persons within the Trinity. Once again, although Theodulphus does not explicitly cite this verse in Luke, he sees Luke's theology as deeply Trinitarian; see cols. 268, 274. Given the litmuslike quality of Theodulphus's work, we can assume that his opinions would have been shared by the mass of the clergy. Theodulphus concludes his work with a fragment of a verse he attributes to Prudentius which also sums up his theology on the Trinity: "O Trinitatis hujus/Vis una, lumen unum/ Deus ex Deo per-

tinuous creative spirit or breath of life (*spiraculum vitae,* from the Hebrew חַיִּים נִשְׁמַת) emanating from God which in turn distinguished mankind from every other form of earthly life. Jerome's translation of the Septuagint account of Genesis 2:7 καὶ ἐνεφύσησεν εἰς τὸ πρόσωπον αὐτοῦ as *et inspiravit in faciem eius spiraculum vitae* suggests that πνοὴν/ζωῆς *spiraculum vitae* is a reference to God the animator, the creator who creates *ex nihilo.* The *spiraculum vitae* from the Genesis verse and the Lucan *In manus tuas commendo spiritum meum* are to be connected because of their shared theological concern; they are part of the continuing affirmation of the power of the *spiritus Dei* to reanimate creation.[20] The sixth verse from Psalm 30 provides the means for connecting the verse from Genesis to that in Luke. Walter Daniel, when he attributed Christ's cry to Aelred, believed that the same *spiritus Dei* which the author of Genesis identified as resident in mankind was actually present at the very moment of release as Aelred expired.

Having suggested something of the complexity of this skein of scriptural and textual interdependencies, we are bound to ask how such an inquiry can further our understanding of the methods of the sacred biographer, in particular those of Walter Daniel. The author of Genesis, the psalmist, Luke, Walter Daniel, and all medieval practitioners of *lectio divina* understood this expression, "breath of life" (*spiraculum vitae*), as an acknowledgment of the single fact of Providence which held the world in moment-to-moment existence.

The Old Testament author understood the "thingness" of the world,

---

ennis/Deus ex utroque missus." See also Anselm of Canterbury, *PL* 158, cols. 259–84; quoted in Ambrose, M. Adriaen, ed., *Sancti Ambrosii: Expositio Evangelii, CCSL,* Vol. 14, part 4 (Turnhout, 1957), p. 185. Ambrose's interpretation of the Lucan verse is deeply Trinitarian. Christ's old body is replaced, he argues, with a new body which is the church: "Corpus eius traditiones sunt scripturam, corpus eius ecclesia est"; see also pp. 381, 391.

20. Avitus, Bishop of Vienna, *Carmen de Initio Mundi, Liber Primus, PL* 59, cols. 323–30, but especially the bottom of col. 326. Cassiodorus, in his *Expositio Psalmorum* in *CCSL,* Vol. 98, part II (Turnhout, 1958), p. 1300, makes explicit the relationship between Luke 23:46 and Genesis 2:7 in his discussion of verse 4 of Psalm 145. Jerome, *Liber Genesis, PL* 28, col. 147. This continual reanimation of the universe is an aspect of the Augustinian idea of the *seminales rationes;* see also Bede's remarks in *In Genesim,* ed. C. H. Jones, *CCSL,* Vol. 118, part II (Turnhout, 1967), p. 44. Bede, having just quoted the verse from Genesis 2:7, writes: "cum ei substantiam animae ac spiritus in qua viveret creavit. Nam ita recte intelligitur spirasse Deum *in faciem* hominis spiraculum quo viveret creasse sicut supra intellectum est, Vocavit Deus lucem diem, pro eo positum quod vocari ab hominibus fecit."

the physical properties of creation, as substances which are the products of a continuous event, a continuous creation, suspended intact in time and space by God's spirit.[21] All material creation, although it has the appearance of having been created at a particular time and place, is being continually held together by God's continual providential interaction in the world. For the sake of this broad comparison, the *kosmos* of the Greeks was static; nature was impersonal and objective, with regular and predictable behavior governed by "laws." The Hebraic understanding of the universe was as a personalized one, a universe whose opulent diversity was not subject to prediction and whose totality was bound in a mysterious harmony by the divine will. In the main, this understanding of creation was dominant in medieval Christianity (at least until the thirteenth century and the resurgence of Aristotelianism)—especially in the mentality of monastic contemplatives—and such an understanding is continually affirmed in their radical insistence on humanity's utter and complete dependence on God.[22] In his *On Consideration,* Bernard of Clairvaux makes this brilliantly clear:

> Yes, God is eternity, just as he is charity; He is length without tension, breadth without extension. In one way no less than the other, he surpasses the narrow limits of space and time, but by the freedom of his nature, not by the vastness of his substance. Thus he who made everything to measure is himself beyond all measure; and yet, even so, he remains the measure of this same immensity.[23]

If we now examine Aelred's death cry, *In manus tuas commendo spiritum meum,* in light of the above discussion, Walter's intention that this verse stand as a universal affirmation of the vital principle, the *spiritus Dei,* shared by all mankind is more easily apprehended. Since Aelred's utterance not only recalls the death of Christ, the praise of the psalmist, and the cosmology of the author of Genesis, Walter Daniel and other sacred biographers would argue that the very repetition of such linguistic formulae or *logoi,* because they serve to reveal the

21. M. Chenu, *Nature, Man and Society in the Twelfth Century* (Chicago, 1968), pp. 134–35: "The universe is a system of symbols more than it is a chain of effects. But the potentialities of this system tend readily toward imbalance; symbolic value tends to empty *things* of their earthly reality, their ontological reality, their conceptual reality . . . [while on the contrary for] Aristotle, ideas are *within* things."

22. J. Le Clercq, *Bernard of Clairvaux and the Cistercian Spirit* (Kalamazoo, 1976).

23. Ibid., p. 154.

essential unity connecting all these texts, effectively collapses historical chronology. Through the discernment of such recurrent themes
(made apparent by lexical and theological parallels), these *logoi* return
both the speaker and the audience mysteriously and simultaneously,
from Aelred's utterance to Luke's account of Stephen's stoning and to
the moment of Christ's Crucifixion. Aelred's utterance is an expression
of the hope of the psalmist and a reaffirmation of the belief in the fecund spirit of the God of Genesis erupting anew in creation. This last
point, which underscores the idea that creation is a continuum constantly unfolding before our eyes, an unfolding which we can only ob-
serve in its surface effects, is very important for our understanding of
the method of the sacred biographer. For if *spiritum meum* is related
to *spiraculum vitae/*"breath of life," then the force which guided
Aelred on his saintly pilgrimage is the Lord actually resident in his
body. Such a concept is not in the least foreign to the medieval mind,
nor does its acknowledgment suggest a theology which was possessed
of a pantheism of immanence. One can cite a number of orthodox medieval biblical commentaries which point to a striking, one might almost say inextricable, union between the soul and the body. For instance, Alain de Lille, in his commentary on Genesis 2:7, explains that
the author of Genesis used the expression *spiraculum Dei* to indicate
the essential unity of the human spirit and the flesh.[24]

Such a method of composition was absolutely essential for the sacred biographer. The task that faced Walter Daniel, for example, in
illustrating the character (what Xenophon first chose to call ἔθος) of
Aelred was one which all sacred biographers faced, namely to depict
in narrative that utterly baffling mystery of the divine and human union
which Alain saw as an essential truth of human creation. To put it
baldly, the saints whose lives were chronicled exhibited behavior
which they believed was contingent on the shifting interstices between
the human and the divine presence. Such an understanding presents a
unique ideology of personality. If one of the tasks of the biographer is
to illustrate character, then the idea of person (which is, after all, a
larger category than character and would encompass character) that
we must imagine confronted the sacred biographer was one grounded
not in a psychology, judgments of which are derived from observations
of behavior but rather in a psychology that was utterly theological: all
human beings, but to a greater degree the saints, were, as discussed

24. Alanus de Insulis, *Sermo I: De Spiritu Sancto, PL* 210, cols. 221–23, beginning:
"Spiritus Domini replevit orbem terrarum, et hoc quod continet omnia, scientiam
habet vocis."

above, literally *templa Dei*. We might say that for the sacred biographer, human behavior could often be *prima facie* evidence for the divine. Thus, when Walter Daniel attempts to illustrate Aelred's character, to present an analysis of Aelred's motives for a particular action, Walter is forced because of his belief in the theological dimensions of human personality to confront the presence of God. His narrative responsibility is broadened to chronicle the life of an individual in whom the human and the divine are not easily distinguished. Such a theological basis for human personality is the *raison d'être* for the type of narrative strategies adopted in the genre of sacred biography.[25]

The Psychology of Sanctity and Time

Such an understanding of personality contains other important assumptions accepted implicitly by the sacred biographer, assumptions which will illustrate the sophistication of the method of the medieval sacred biographer. If we consider the manner in which writers such as Walter Daniel, Eddius Stephanus, and John Capgrave understood personality, it follows that we should then be better equipped to understand the way they represented it. The depictions of deeds in most sacred biographies do not function to sharpen the relief with which we see the subject but rather serve as guides to behavior which exist within the popular imagination as cultural paradigms. Hence, all behavior in sacred biography should ideally represent exemplary types.

These "types" of behavior have received the approbation of the society, and they make up patterns which derive their authority from paradigmatic models. Of course, such a conceptual basis for the depiction of human personality may seem curious; it appears to dismiss *a priori* the belief in a *sui generis* individual, a criterion which is an unquestioned assumption of the modern biographer. However, as one studies this most interesting of medieval genres, one finds that the idealization of character which resulted from this method was paradoxically not intended by these biographers to diminish the importance of human personality. On the contrary, such a method, they would argue, allowed them to present human individuality in its complete fullness, to augment it, by placing the concept of the individual within the larger frame of a collective personality.

25. Cox, *Biography in Late Antiquity*, p. xi. Cox uses the happy expression "inscape" to describe biography's efforts at describing the character of its subject.

The Theology of Daily Life

Herbert of Bosham, a contemporary of Walter Daniel, besides being the most celebrated Hebraist of his day, wrote a most creditable biography of St. Thomas Becket (ca. 1186). In his work, Herbert tells us that his "purpose is not only to record the works of the archbishop, but the causes of these works, not only the facts, but the mind of the doer."[26] If we examine Bosham's remarks in light of the entire biography, it appears that his understanding of the expression "the mind of the doer" (*animum facientis*), although it includes examples of behavior and the rationale for such behavior, has a very decided theological foundation. Bosham accepted the fundamental premise that the basis, the very core, of human personality was the incorporeal spirit. Being incorporeal, it was not subject to the same laws governing the rest of creation. And as it was related to the divine spirit, Herbert concludes that his presentation of Becket's acts in a narrative of that man's life must tend more to "theological edification than to historical exposition."[27]

The "inscape" of the saint, which is frequently depicted through narratives of exaggerated physical events, makes use of traditional patterns of composition and well-established *topoi*. Because these patterns, as indicated above, are idealized and determined by culturally accepted paradigms, the narrative structures in which they are realized must themselves have been sanctioned by a specified set of traditions. Tradition, the fidelity to an established narrative rhetoric, plays such a vital role in these narratives because these lives illustrate the timeless reality of the sacred. It is a commonplace of the history of orthodoxies that both liturgically and in their sacred writings, they develop traditions which themselves become fixed and a necessary corollary of their worship. All Christian sacred biography, then, has as an absolutely necessary philosophical first condition the recording of the crucial

26. Grandsen, *Historical Writing in England, c. 550 to c. 1307*, p. 296. For the original text of Herbert's life of Becket, see *Memorials for the History of Thomas Becket*, ed. J. C. Robertson and J. B. Sheppard, (London, 1875–85), Vol. 3, p. 248: "Verum quivis notans nos sic saltem non judicet, sed advertat prius nos non solum pontificis opera, sed et causas operum, quod et supra jam nos dixisse meminimus, explicare: quasi non solum facta, sed et animum facientis, quem ab ipso sic accepi factore."

27. Robertson and Sheppard, *Memorials*, p. 247: "et potius theologicae aedificationi quam gestorum viri historicae explanationi insistere, et ita nimis theologum, historicum vero parum, sapere."

nexus linking the divine and the human. The medieval sacred biographer, because of this belief, did accept (as we shall see in more detail below) as a theologically sound position the fundamental sameness of people *sub specie aeternitatis,* whether they were Palestinian Jews living under the joint rule of Caesar and Herod Antipas, or Northumbrian Saxons under Henry II and Pope Alexander III.

Such an understanding of the basis of human personality which dramatically extends the similitude of the concept of "individual," must also construct an understanding of the nature of time and of event to support such an ideology of personality.[28] Time is seen from this biographical perspective in a cosmic context which emphasizes not the distinctiveness, the separability of human chronology, but rather its continuity; human chronology possesses a deliberate movement which is both teleological and divinely maintained. For the Christian and for the Jew, as opposed to the Greek and the Roman, time is linear with an end, not cyclical and repetitive. The world is ever moving toward its fulfillment in the *Parousia.* Besides the obvious point of all time progressing toward the final judgment where the good will be separated from the wicked and the just from the unjust, the Creator, medieval Christians believed, would explain the relationship of God to his creatures and the purpose for creation at the last judgment. Once this divine purpose was accomplished, the human race would have achieved its apogee and would from that instant live in harmony under the tutelage of Christ. These ideas are ancient in Christianity and can be found in the Gospels, in the Acts of the Apostles, in the Nicene and Athanasian creeds, and in the commentaries of Tertullian, St. Clement of Alexandria, St. Ambrose, St. Augustine, and St. John Chrysostom.

This philosophy of time, with its radical belief in the role of Providence, is heavily indebted to and evolved from the Hebraic conception of the universe found, for example, in the introductory chapters of Genesis and even in those largely historical books of Joshua, Judges, Samuel, and Kings. For example, the dying King David tells his newly anointed son Solomon, "If your descendants take care to walk faithfully in my [the Lord's] sight with all their soul, you shall never lack a successor on the throne of Israel" (1 Kings 2:4). Although we do have in the Old Testament different expressions of history—one need only compare such different treatments as the largely mythopoetic patriar-

---

28. For recent discussions of the medieval understanding of time, see Burrow, "Time," in *The Ages of Man,* pp. 55–94; and Gurevich, in *Categories of Medieval Culture,* pp. 26–39.

chal narratives in Genesis and the largely genealogically based material
in the first book of Chronicles—it is largely true that the ancient Jew
understood history, the chronicle of human time, to be the revelation
of God's Law as it is manifest in creation.

Time began with the creation of the world, but history did not begin
until the sixth day, when God said, "Let us make man in our image,
after our likeness." History is not realized until the Hebrew God in-
trudes himself into physical creation through the simulacrum of man.
Indeed, for the Jew, the true beginning of time can be dated from the
covenant God made with Abraham in which he promised to stand by
him and his descendants forever; once again, the emphasis is on God
placing himself into human creation (see Genesis 17:7–8).[29] This covenant was not unilateral; humanity had a responsibility to God to maintain his laws as given to Moses on Sinai. And thus, human history,
because of these theological foundations, has from its covenantal inception a dialectical structure.

Although the Decalogue, as the summation of the Law, was the
guide for the ancient Jew, orthodox Judaism recognized from the earliest time that God's revelation was continuous. Given this need to
manifest further interaction between God and his people, Judaism accepted the idea that throughout the ages, special men and women
would be the vessels for these revelations. The testimony of these individuals was a valid form of revelation, and through their prophecy
one could discern God's will. Indeed, it is pertinent to note that the
Jews paid homage to these singular individuals by building shrines and
encouraging pilgrimages to these shrines. The early Christian church
often appropriated these shrines for their worship of the martyrs.[30]

29. "I will fulfill my covenant between myself and you and your descendants after
you, generation after generation, an everlasting covenant, to be your God, yours and
your descendants' after you. As an everlasting possession I will give you and your
descendants after you the land in which you now are aliens, all the land of Canaan,
and I will be God to your descendants."

30. E. R. Dodds, *Pagan and Christian in an Age of Anxiety* (London, 1965), pp.
30–32. Dodds gives a balanced and informative discussion of pagan and Jewish ascetic movements in late antiquity, remarking, "There is some rather slight evidence
for the existence of 'pagan hermits' before the Christian ermetic movement, but it
would be rash to conclude that their example influenced the Desert Fathers; we can
only say that the same psychological impulses may have been at work in both. If there
was a model, it was probably Jewish [Elijah, John the Baptist, the Therapeutae] rather
than pagan." See also St. Jerome's remarks in his *Adversus Jovinianum, PL* 23, col.
298: "Nam et Pythagoraei hujuscemodi frequentiam declinantes, in solitudine et desertis locis habitare consueverunt." W. Manson, "Martyrs and Martyrdom," *Bulletin*

Because God was in himself utterly incomprehensible to the religious Jew, a knowledge of God's presence in creation could be inferred from the signs of his presence reflected in creation. The interpretation of these signs was exceedingly difficult. The key to unlocking these secrets lay in the Torah. Scholars were urged to study the Torah and natural creation, the latter as if it, too, were a text with the signs of the Creator's presence. Philo wrote that for such study to be fruitful one had to look beyond the literal sense of words or the concrete fact of creation because all acts of interpretation, if they were truly motivated by philosophical zeal, had to acknowledge the presence of the divine in the world and thus must take with the utmost seriousness, as a statement of literal truth, the act of creation wherein humans were made "after our [God's] likeness" (*demut*) (Genesis 26:27) and the eternal which is present in that creation.[31]

The profound anthropomorphisms of this verse in Genesis were accepted as an article of faith by most medieval philosophers. A theological belief which proposes that the physical world is a speculum which can, if viewed properly, reveal God's omnipresence necessarily requires of language a narrative which allows for the creation of additional dimensions sufficient to exemplify this hidden reality.

Allegory or the allegorical method was, for Philo and the Alexandrian school, a method of composition which reveals as no other the interplay between the temporal and the eternal. Moreover, being a composition that allowed greater freedom of expression when exploring types, it was an approach to composition which was used early on as a way to illustrate the interior, moral life of its subjects. Philo's allegorical approach was to have considerable impact on patristic ex-

---

of the John Rylands Library 39 (1957): 468–84, suggests that the idea of a martyr as one requiring a blood sacrifice was joined with the Old Testament understanding of the role of the prophet; see also M. R. James, *The Lost Apocrypha of the Old Testament* (London, 1920), pp. 68–70.

31. Philo's religious philosophy is deeply indebted to Platonism. Indeed, his second series of writings on the Pentateuch, his *Legum Allegoriarum*, is a highly figurative reading of the first seventeen chapters of Genesis. Philo's understanding of the Pentateuch was entirely mediated by Greek; there is no evidence that he was even able to read Hebrew. His Hebrew etymologies, which he used in his allegorized interpretations, are derived from onomastica in which the Hebrew name appeared with its Greek translation. Aside from his exegetical work on the Scripture, Philo also wrote sacred biography. His *De Vita Moisis*—deeply indebted to Greek rhetorical methods—is perhaps his best-known work in this genre. See E. R. Goodenough, *By Light, Light: The Mystic Gospel of Hellenistic Judaism* (New Haven, 1935).

egesis, especially on Origen and those who followed his decidedly spiritualized interpretation of Scripture.[32] Allegory also played an important and continuing role in the sacred biography. One need only consider the *Passio Sanctarum Perpetuae et Felicitatis,* perhaps the greatest of the early saints' lives, and virtually any of the Middle English lives in important collections such as the *South English Legendary,* the work of Capgrave, or Mirk's *Festial,* to name but a few.[33]

The Waning of the World

It is commonplace but important nonetheless to iterate how very different from our own are the assumptions concerning time that we find in medieval sacred biography. Time for Walter Daniel or John Capgrave is an example of the Lord's creative power. Time, having begun

32. Philo's religious thinking, informed as it is by Platonism, is strongly dualist and given to an extreme view of transcendence. For Philo, God is beyond even such abstract concepts as the good and the beautiful. Further, because Philo's dualism made a rigid distinction between matter and the spirit, the will must choose between matter ("the world") and the spirit ("God"). Philo's dualism leads him to incorporate an element of Stoic ethics into his thinking: if the will chooses to follow the spirit, then reason must be employed to govern the passions. Stoicism is thus joined to his Platonism. See H. A. Wolfson, *Philo: Foundations of Religious Philosophy in Judaism, Christianity, and Islam,* 2 vols. (Cambridge, Mass., 1947).

33. Preminger, Hardison, and Kerrane, eds., *Classical and Medieval Literary Criticism,* pp. 264, 277–78, 283, 286. An important and often overlooked reason which helps to account for Alexandrian allegorism becoming the dominant way of interpreting texts in the Middle Ages can be traced to the Council of Constantinople II (553). The Council condemned the teaching of that great proponent of the Antiochene school of exegesis, characterized by a greater tendency to emphasize the literal sense of the text, Theodore of Mopsuestia. Theodore's work was thought to contain the roots of Nestorianism. His exegetical "literalism" made it difficult for him to countenance a system which used the typological method as a means of bridging the Old and New Testaments. Hence, the psalms for Theodore are to be understood as being irrevocably rooted in their idiosyncratic historical circumstances. They do not exhibit shadowy prophecies of Christ. Theodore's method is diametrically opposed to that of Philo and Origen. For an interesting discussion of the differences between these two "schools" and the distinction between Philo's method and Theodore's, see J. M. Wallace-Hadrill, *Christian Antioch: A Study of Early Christian Thought in the East* (Cambridge, 1982), pp. 33–38: "These passages [excerpted from Theodore and others] of comment on the minor prophets point out the contrast between Alexandrian use of the text as a jumping-off ground for spiritual exhortation and Antiochene insistence upon the historical foundation of interpretation even if the interpretation goes on to refer to Christ" (p. 35).

with the creation of the universe, will itself cease to exist at the final judgment. Moreover, because time is a part of creation, it can be shaped and separated from other aspects of that creation by divine power. The understanding of time which we confront in these sacred biographies is an important aspect of their *Weltanshauung* and must be addressed in any study of medieval sanctity, because Christian sanctity concerns the achievement of a state of blessedness in this world. The saints were constantly urging men and women to forsake temporal pleasures; *contemptus mundi* was a doctrine which had a wide appeal from Paul's Epistles through Innocent III's efforts at reform.

How did these different attitudes concerning time affect the overall portraits of sanctity that are presented in Christian sacred biography? The first point that our sacred biographers accepted was a belief in the chronologically fixed age of the world. The earth had a temporal beginning approximately six millennia earlier, St. Jerome claimed. The popularity of the Hexameral literature points to the widespread nature of this belief. The Incarnation was God's way of interrupting what many believed was the growing evil of the world. Christ was born into a world which was already thought to be fully mature (indeed, some would have said senescent). The old and new Adams were separated by more than five thousand years. Human creation seems to have grown increasingly corrupt and liable to sin as the world grew older. Aside from what else it may teach us about the medieval mind, this Hexameral tradition exemplifies a deep suspicion of the appropriateness of human pleasure in created things. This senescent world which Christ came to save was a world besotted with sin. What is not generally remarked on is that in the popular imagination, there was a sense that the gates of heaven, if not closed to the just, were virtually impregnable. Indeed, even the most learned, when expressing themselves outside the confines of their scholarly commentary, reveal this dark side of the plan of salvation. Examine John Damascene's graphic verses on this state of affairs in his poem "The Last Kiss":

> Sin in this world let us flee,/ That in heaven our place may be./ . . . Draw nigh, ye sons of Adam;/viewing A likeness of yourselves in clay:/ Its beauty gone;/its grace disfigured; Dissolving in the tomb's decay;/The prey of worms and of corruption,/In silent darkness mouldering on.[34]

What is important for our study of the biographical method employed by writers such as Walter Daniel or Eddius Stephanus is that

34. Freemantle, *A Treasury of Early Christianity*, p. 612.

the belief in a child savior sent to renew an old world extends to all the covenant God made with Abraham. God reveals himself in his creation through men and women who, like Jesus in their humanity, carry within themselves the promise of redemption for all humanity. The ideology of sainthood is really quite a radical one in a monotheistic religion, holding as a possibility the chance for an individual to be a place of habitation for the timeless, eternal God. It was for medieval civilization the most graphic locus of the eternal in the present.

Augustine on Time

The most influential thinker on the philosophy of time for medieval Christians was St. Augustine. Augustine's authority was acknowledged as early as Pope Celestine I's letter to the bishops of Gaul in 431. In his *De Genesi ad Litteram,* Augustine argued that God created the universe out of nothing, *ex nihilo,* in six days and that this original creation held all future possibility. His position here is twofold: to refute the Platonists who argued that God created the world by emanation, and to harmonize the Genesis account of creation over six days with the verse in Ecclesiasticus (18:1) which states "that God created all things at once" (*Qui vivit in aeternum creavit omnia simul*).[35] For Augustine, everything created and which exists in the present is a product of the first divine creation.[36] Augustine believed that those things whose occurrence has become a commonplace to us—the sun, the stars, the rainfall, the round of seasons—are the continuance of that first creation. Their predictability has hidden their true "miraculous" nature. Because we have lost our understanding of the exact nature of these daily miracles and, as a consequence, our awe of their majesty, Augustine believed that God had created other miracles, miracles which *seemed* to contradict nature but were designed to arrest the attention of mankind. These miracles only appear to contradict nature, for they too were created at the first creation. They are known as the *seminum semina* or *seminales rationes* expressions Portalie says Augustine undoubtedly borrowed from the Neoplatonists.[37] These *sem-*

35. *Biblia Sacra,* p. 1050.

36. E. Portalie, "Creation and Creatures," in *A Guide to the Thought of Saint Augustine,* trans. R. J. Bastian (Chicago, 1960), pp. 136–42; see also Augustine, *De Genesi ad Litteram, PL* 34, col. 231, beginning: "Nam in ipsa ratione operationem contemplatus est in Spiritu Sancto . . . quam istis oculis cerneretur."

37. Portalie, "Creation and Creatures," p. 138: "These seedlike principles (*ra-*

inales rationes, "hidden causes," erupt periodically throughout human history to remind men that the "natural world" is permeated by the divine, which itself is immutable and unchanging. Augustine's *seminales rationes* can be understood as latent potentialities (he refers to them as *elementis latent* in *De Trinitate*), as germinal principles, which were created at the original creation and are continually being actualized in time.

These miraculous events were most often made manifest to men and women through the lives of the saints. The saints were a unique conduit for this continuing act of creation. Even those biographies replete with phantasmagoric miracles were not written to show the triumph of metaphysical sleights of hand over the hard facts of daily reality, but rather the depiction of these miraculous events was meant to illustrate a theological view of material creation. In *De Civitate Dei,* Augustine makes this point: "For how can an event be contrary to nature when it happens by the will of God, since the will of the great creator assuredly is the nature of every created thing? A portent therefore does not occur contrary to nature but contrary to what is known of nature."[38] And in *De Trinitate,* Augustine suggests that the ability of holy men and women to perform miracles is made possible by the ministry of angels.[39] We shall see the importance of Augustine's remarks when Walter Daniel defends himself from those members of the clergy who disputed the credibility of some of the more remarkable feats he presented in his portrait of Aelred.

Augustine's pronouncements on time had great influence throughout

---

tiones seminales), a term undoubtedly borrowed from the Neoplatonists and to become quite famous later in the Scholastic era, are nothing else than the energy latent in the germs which are destined to develop not just during the six days of creation but during all the centuries of the history of the world." Augustine, in W. J. Mountain, ed., *De Trinitate, CCSL,* vol. 50, part XVI (Turnhout, 1968), p. 140, beginning: "Omnium quippe rerum quae corporaliter visibiliterque nascuntur occulta quaedam semina in istis corporeis mundi huius elementis latent . . . uel laudem bonorum."

38. Augustine, in B. Dombart and A. Kalb, eds., *De Civitate Dei, CCSL,* Vol. 48, part XIV (Turnhout, 1955), p. 773, beginning "Sicut ergo non fuit impossibile Deo, quas voluit instituere, sic ei non est inpossibile, in quidquid voluerit, quas instituit, mutare naturas . . . huic operi iudicavi"; see also Benedicta Ward, *Miracles and the Medieval Mind* (Philadelphia, 1982), p. 222.

39. Augustine, *De Trinitate,* Vol. 50, Book III, chap. XI, pp. 151–52: "Hinc ostendit illa omnia non solum *per angelos* facta sed etiam propter nos facta, id est populum dei cui promittitur haereditas *uitae aeternae.* . . . Deinde quia tunc *per angelos* nunc autem per filium *sermo factus est* . . . propterea volui ex hac epistula manifestius testimonium dare ubi non dictum est: *per* angelum, sed: *per angelos.*"

the Middle Ages. With the exception of the school of Chartres in the twelfth century and the influence of Aristotle, especially works such as *De Interpretatione* (chapter 9) and Boethius's two commentaries on it (important for the late thirteenth and fourteenth centuries), there were few thinkers who could avoid having to consider the Augustinian theories of time.[40] This is true even of thinkers such as St. Bernard of Clairvaux, whose own deep experience of the world coupled with his *elocutio* may blur his indebtedness to Augustine. Augustine's most celebrated commentary on time and creation was in the eleventh book of the *Confessions*. Here he clearly states his idea that God is anterior to time and is the creator of time: *omnia tempora tu fecisti et ante omnia tempora tu es, nec aliquo tempore non erat tempus.*[41] God is prior to all creation, prior to duration, and prior to all linguistic constructs such as past, present, and future. Augustine would argue that God is the ultimate simplicity of whom we can only speak in metaphor.[42] Hence all phenomena, no matter how they may *appear* to violate this spatial or temporal frame, nonetheless do have their own ontology and are part of the divine plan.

But how do these philosophical speculations of Augustine play a part in the method of the sacred biographer and in particular our Northum-

40. Chenu, *Nature, Man and Society* pp. 60–63: ". . . we must be no less aware of the enduring influence of Augustine's Platonism as the common ingredient of all these syncretistic forms." Portalie, in *Guide to the Thought of St. Augustine,* (pp. 84–85) quotes Harnack: "It would seem that the sorry existence of the Roman empire in the West had been prolonged until then only to permit Augustine's influence to be exercised on universal history." Eucken, restricting his comments to Augustine's influence on Christianity, commented: "Augustine made his own all the influences of the past as well as the movement of his own age. He gathered them together in himself only to achieve something that was both greater and newer. Although his cultural roots were in the Latin tradition, he underwent strong Greek and Oriental influences. From primitive Christianity and Neoplatonism he worked out a new synthesis in which the Christian element, with his own originality, is predominant. The result of this synthesis could be debated, but it was to dominate the entire history of Christianity."

41. Augustine, in L. Verheijen, ed., *Confessionum Libri XIII, CCSL,* Vol. 27 (Turnhout, 1981), p. 202. The whole of Book 11 had a marked influence on medieval theories of time; see also W. Watts, ed., *St. Augustine's Confessions* (New York, 1925), p. 236.

42. Augustine, *De Mendacio, PL* 40, col. 492. In discussing the use of figurative language in the Old Testament, Augustine argues that the truth behind the figure is, as it were, guaranteed by God. Augustine says this truth is anchored in the "truth of the Holy Spirit."

brian Cistercian, Walter Daniel? Augustine's ideas on time are crucial precisely because they completely dominate the way medieval man understood the importance of event, *qua* event, and the writing of history. Because biography was thought to be a close relative of historical writing, philosophical constructs that were the underpinnings of historical writing were transferred to the genre of biography.

Sacred history or sacred biography in the Middle Ages assumes as part of its responsibility the recording of those instances when God manifests the divine in the world. Medieval man believed that the theophany was most appropriately manifested through an incarnation in God's elect, his saints. I would argue that one of the principal activities of sacred biography is to chronicle the appearance of the inbreaking of the divine in the world, or what Augustine referred to as the *seminales rationes* interrupting the continual flux of the world. Secular history, on the other hand, has as its responsibility to chronicle and interpret activities, points of view, and institutions all of which have little metaphysical orientation. Thus, these two types of historical writing, although they are sometimes fused in a single work, as in Bede's *Ecclesiastical History of the English People,* are fundamentally different in their evaluation of the importance of human events and what these events signify.[43] Medieval sacred biographers saw sacred history as the single narrative which reveals the timeless and the unchanging—the condition toward which they believed the universe was inevitable progressing. Sacred history exists outside human agency; it is an evolving panorama which we are invited to view, but it is one, as Peter Damian asserts in his *Dominus Vobiscum,* from which nothing can be added or subtracted.[44]

---

43. Although Bede would have found the distinction between secular and sacred otiose, his work is a grand synthesis of historical reporting and *Heilsgeschichte.* One need only compare his carefully detailed accounts of the various opponents in the dispute between the Roman and Celtic practices for calculating the date of Easter (e.g., Wilfrid, Ceolfrid, and Colman) against such impressionistic narrative accounts as the miraculous preservation of Queen Eheldrida's body and the miracles her burial linens engendered. See J. A. Giles, *Venerabilis Bedae Opera quae Supersunt Omnia* (London, 1843), Vol. 3, pp. 237–97, 89; see also Grandsen, *Historical Writing,* pp. 13–28.

44. Peter Damian, *Dominus Vobiscum, PL* 145, col. 234; see also G. Evans, "St. Anselm and Sacred History," in *The Writing of History in the Middle Ages,* ed. Davis and Wallace-Hadrill, *Christian Antioch,* p. 192.

The Timeless and Personality

One of the central points of sacred biography, although it is seldom discussed, was the singular revelation that the immutable God exists personally in his creation, in his saints. There was some degree of philosophical speculation devoted to this aspect of God's attributes, that is, his immutable presence. As Chenu has pointed out, and most notably during the twelfth century—the time when Walter Daniel was a monk at Rievaulx—the *opuscula sacra* of Boethius were being read with renewed interest. It is interesting to note that in his *De Trinitate*, Boethius takes special care to examine the quality of God's immutability.[45] Boethius proposes that the subject of theological inquiry should be directed at that which is *sine motu, abstractum atque separabile*, without movement, distant and bodiless. Boethius is reworking one of the standard arguments for Neoplatonic ideas. God's immutability was a subject of serious concern with some, such as Arnobius, who argued in his *De Trinitate* that God was the antipathy of change.[46] Change for Arnobius is the sine qua non of creation; therefore, where we have elements which can change in substance, we cannot have God. Change is a result of humanity's fall from the splendors of Paradise, a result of sin. Thierry of Chartres, whose commentaries on Boethius's *opuscula sacra* were most influential, concluded that there was no mutability in God, *nulla in deo quidem mutabilitas*. The concern with God's immutability is invariably dependent on theories of the nature of time, and time becomes a consideration in these arguments.[47] Anselm of Havelberg makes the point in his *Dialogus* that God is beyond time and the vagaries of the events of this world:

> But this variety [he is discussing human events] is not caused by the changeableness in the unchanging God, who is always the same and whose years do not fail, but by the weakness of the human race and the changes brought about by time from generation to generation.[48]

45. Chenu, *Nature, Man and Society*, pp. 64–78.

46. Arnobius, *De Trinitate*, ed. H. F. Stewart and E. K. Rand (London, 1973), p. 8.

47. N. M. Haring, ed., *Commentaries on Boethius by Thierry of Chartres and His School* (Toronto, 1971), pp. 75, 138, 162, 164, 547: "Quoniam ergo actus sine possibilitate est necessitas ideoque immutabilitas, necesse est deum utpote inmutabilem inmateriari non posse. Esse namque in materia idem est quod mutari vel variari. Quod quia de deo impossibile est nec deus quidem inmateriari potest. Nulla in deo quidem mutabilitas, pluralitas nulla. Quare et deus est unitas."

48. Anselm of Havelberg, *Dialogus*, ed. G. Salet, in *Sources chrétiennes* (Paris,

From such a theological orientation, we can appreciate something of the reverence in which medieval culture held the works of sacred biographers; it was these works par excellence which attempted the difficult task of rendering a narrative record of the operation of this immutable God in his continually changing creation. Also from this theological perspective, we are in a better position to comprehend Denys Hay's observation that by the time Augustine had completed his *De Civitate Dei,* his thinking on historiography had become so radically eschatological that he had abandoned his concern for those events which postdated the Ascension; Augustine's eschatology had considerable influence in later works of history.[49]

The Hallowed Body: Burial Eulogy and Borrowed Lives

Although it is no longer a credo of literary historians, it remains eminently plausible to affirm that literary forms reflect the *Sitz im Leben* in which they were produced, even if the mirror they hold up to that age is out of step, critical, or reformist. The conventions of sacred biography, however, because of the genre's theological conservativeness and adherence to traditional forms, embodies philosophical positions on time, personality, and the miraculous which often antedate individual examples of the genre by centuries. Moreover, these three particular categories play a fundamental role in shaping sacred biography's conceptual frame. Part of the reason for this predisposition to traditional forms is that medieval saints' lives sought to depict their subjects' exalted election by illustrating how these three normative categories of experience were dislocated by the power of Providence. For this reason, these categories tend to be more in the foreground in Christian biography than in related genre, such as the romance.

The locus for illustrating Providence's vast power as it turns the world upside down and reverses all our normative expectations of creation is the very person of the saint. Time, ego, and the commonplace experience of life are bent, refracted, wondrously changed, and refuse to obey the logic which has governed the universe hitherto. New cat-

---

1966), Vol. 118, p. 116: "Facta est autem haec varietas non propter invariabilis Dei, qui semper idem est, et cujus anni non deficient, mutabilitatem, sed propter humani generis variabilem infirmitatem, et temporalem mutationem de generatione in generationem." See also Evans, "St. Anselm and Sacred History," p. 193.

49. Denys Hay, *Annalists and Historians* (London, 1977), pp. 19–20.

egories of understanding are proposed by the saint's life; time must be understood paradoxically from outside time; the ego must cease to be viewed as a habitation for the experience of the self alone but is now enlarged to incorporate other personalities; and, finally, one's understanding of the logic which governs the behavior of the world has to be broadened to include experiences which appear utterly to contradict this logic. The dead can rise, evil men become good, and water can flow uphill. The Christian saint embodies all of these (what we might call) meta-understandings of experience. There is no more interesting way to illustrate how these experiences shape medieval sacred biography than through a discussion of the manner in which sources were employed.

Sources and Their Meaning

Let us return to the verse from Luke 23:46. This verse was understood throughout the medieval period as an utterance redolent with optimism. A number of commentators (see Augustine, Gregory the Great, and Bede) discussed it from at least two complementary perspectives: as the cry of someone who has lived a saintly life and as a recognition and sign to others that the creative presence of God was palpable. Moreover, the verse suggested that this creative power of God was now in complete control of nature. Luke's verse, to restate this last point in the Augustinian language discussed above, was believed to be an acknowledgment of the presence of the *seminales rationes* again breaking forth into creation.[50]

Walter Daniel was aware that Luke's Gospel was possessed of manifold levels of meaning. Walter, like most of his monastic brethren, read the sacred word from the perspective of the celebrated fourfold method of exegesis, a method so familiar that it was celebrated in rhymed distichs: *Littera gesta docet, quid credas allegorica,/moralis quid agas, quo tendas anagogia.*[51] I believe that part of the reason for the central place of this verse from Luke, figuring as it does as Aelred's last words, suggests Walter's intention that, like this scriptural quotation, his *Vita Sancti Aelredi* was also to be read on a series of interpretive planes.

50. Augustine, *PL* 38, col. 657, 1115–25; Gregory the Great, *PL* 76, col. 1181; Bede, *PL* 94, col. 427.

51. H. de Lubac, *Exégèse médiéval: les quatre sens de l'écriture* (Paris, 1959–64), Vol. I, p. 23.

The literal meaning of the Lucan verse is an illustration of Christ's recognition of two things: the end of his human life and the incorruptibility of his spirit. Viewed from the perspective of *sensus allegoricas,* Christ's remark is a sign (*allegorica*) of the fecund, atemporal, creative power of God. The tropological sense of this cry from the heart is an affirmation of divine approval of Christ's filial obedience. Lastly, the astute monastic reader faithfully performing his *lectio divina* knew that the verse was an adjuration to the faithful that they were meant to strive (*tendas anagogica*) to achieve the same spiritual enlightenment in their death that Christ had achieved in his. Walter intended that those who recognized the quotation from the Gospel of Luke apply all four of these senses to Aelred.

Hallowed Bodies—Precious Relics

Walter tells us that when Aelred's monastic brethren began the ritual washing of his corpse,

> *Cum autem corpus eius ad lauandum/ delatum fuisset et nudatum coram nobis, uidimus quodamodo futuram gloriam reuelatam in patre, cuius caro uitro purior, niue candidior, quasi quinquennis pueri membra induerat, que ne parue quidem macule neuus fuscabat, set erant omnia plena dulcedenis decoris et delectacionis . . . lucebat pater defunctus ut carbunculus, ut redolebat, apparebat in candore carnis ut puerulus purus et inmaculatus.*

When his body was laid before us to be washed, we saw how the glory to come had been revealed in the father. His flesh was clearer than glass, whiter than snow, as though his members were those of a boy five years old, without a trace of stain, but altogether sweet, and composed and pleasant . . . the dead father shown like a carbuncle, was fragrant as incense, pure and immaculate in the radiance of his flesh as a child.[52]

These are the words of the panegyrist replete with the requisite degree of hyperbole; one might add that these are also the words of a comrade who passionately believed his dead friend the best of men and believed that what he wrote was not sophistry.

Although there have been some notable critics of the use of hyperbole—Aristotle, in his *Rhetoric* 3.11 (1413a)[53] considered it a juvenile

---

52. Powicke, *The Life of Aelred,* p. 62.

53. Aristotle, *The "Art" of Rhetoric,* trans. J. H. Freese (Cambridge, 1975), p. 416:

form—the literary tradition in the West has, in the main, acknowledged
the effectiveness of hyperbole in encomia and especially in those narratives in which, as the *ad Herennium* allows, there is a need to mag-
nify or minimize something: *Superlatio est oratio superans veritatem
alicuius augendi minuendive causa.*[54] At least part of the rationale underlying the importance of the use of this trope is the simple recognition on the part of rhetoricians that there are times when plain language
(language free from conscious figurative intention, e.g., the use of metaphor or simile) fails to satisfy our imaginative recall of certain events.
Hyperbole has always been a trope whose use acknowledges the limitations of language, especially in instances when language is employed
in rendering a satisfying and adequate reflection of intense personal
experience.

When we examine Walter's eulogy of Aelred, however, we find to
our surprise certain characteristics which differ markedly from the normative tradition associated with the funeral panegyric. The manner in
which Walter's encomium differs from the basic constraints of the tradition is a key to unlocking the assumptions built into his methodology
and in turn illustrates quite clearly sacred biography's use of sources.

The most profound methodological difference which separates Walter's work from that of typical biographical encomia can be found in
his description of Aelred's body. Although his description of the dead
Aelred has a stylized beauty about it, its most striking characteristic is
that it is entirely a pastiche of quotations from Scripture and from the
lives of other saints, but especially from Sulpicius Severus's *Vita
Sancti Martini.*[55] Before we look more closely at Walter's remarks, I

"Attic orators are especially fond of hyperbole. Wherefore it is unbecoming for elderly people to make use of them." The context for this discussion is one which in
which Aristotle considers the broader question of style and the use of figures which
represent things in a state of change.

54. [pseudo-Cicero], *Ad Herennium,* trans. H. Caplan (Cambridge, 1981), p. 339.

55. Powicke, *The Life of Aelred,* p. 62, n. 4: "Testatique nobis sunt qui affuerunt
iam exanimi corpore glorificati hominis uidisse se gloriam. Vultus luce clarior reni-
tebat, cum membra caetera ne tenuis quidem macula fuscaret. In aliis etiam et in illo
tantum artubus non pudendis septennis quodammodo pueri gratia uidebatur. Quis iustum unquam cilicio tectum, quis cineribus crederet inuolutum? Ita uitro purior, lacte
candidior, iam in quadam futurae resurrectionis gloria et natura demutatae carnis ostensus est." It is worth noting that there is clearly some difference in the manuscript
tradition of the *Vita Sancti Martini;* the above passage printed by Powicke is different
from that used by Fontaine in his *Vie de Saint Martin,* in *Sources chrétiennes* 133,
134, 135 (Paris, 1967–69), Vol. 1, p. 342: "Cum hac ergo uoce spiritum caelo reddidit.

want to underscore that this weight of borrowing did not occur because Walter was not intimate with his subject and used ancillary texts as aids in creating a document because he lacked firsthand knowledge. Walter and Aelred lived together at Rievaulx for at least seventeen years, and, as Powicke suggests, it appears very likely that Walter was Aelred's personal physician during that time.[56] The human tie that bound these two men was strong, and we can assume from the practice of the early Cistercian life that Walter knew his subject intimately.

Why, then, did Walter, a writer of some ability and Aelred's companion for many years, borrow passages from other biographies to augment some of the most poignant moments in the life of his beloved friend? It is well to point out that these were not obscure passages which he hoped would not be recognized and thus be thought part of a genuine Aelredian tradition, but, on the contrary, these were well-known texts within the monastic community. Did such borrowing point to the adoption of a particular persona for this important work? Did his understanding of his role as narrator play an important part in the final shaping of this text? If Walter deliberately steps outside the traditional ideal of funeral panegyric, does he do so intentionally and with sanction from another tradition? It is fortunate that we can supply the answers to these questions. Walter addressed many of these issues in his *Letter to Maurice,* a penetrating and at times pugnacious defense of his method.

The *Epistola ad Mauricium*

Walter's biography of Aelred was vehemently attacked by some influential but (unfortunately for historians of sacred biography) anonymous prelates who, it appears, shared with Dickens's Mr. Boffin a cer-

---

Testatique nobis sunt qui ibidem fuerunt uidisse se uultum eius tamquam uultum angeli; membra autem eius candida tamquam nix uidebantur, ita ut dicerent: 'Quis iustum umquam cilicio tectum, quis in cineribus crederet inuolutum?' Iam enim sic uidebatur, quasi in futurae resurrectionis gloria et natura demutatae carnis ostensus esset." Fontaine, in his discussion of this passage (see Vol. III, pp. 1332–36), does not discuss this variant reading.

56. Powicke, *The Life of Aelred,* p. xxvii: "Lamentor non pro se rei eventum, sed pocius pro me casum eventus. Et licet mihi sim in officio medicus, non tamen sine acerbo dolore curo. Sed nunc cura certa huius artis constat, que pendet e medicina remota a corpore." Powicke notes that the "passage" is suggestive rather than conclusive."

tain skepticism concerning the accuracy of the details presented in such biography: "What to believe in the course of his reading [Plutarch's *Lives*] was Mr. Boffin's chief literary difficulty indeed; for some time he was divided in his mind between half, all, or none; at length, when he decided as a moderate man, to compound with half, the question still remained, which half? And that stumbling block he never got over."[57] We have no surviving evidence about the nature of the attack made against the *Vita Sancti Aelredi,* whether it was made orally or in writing, whether it was made only to the abbot of Rievaulx or to a local bishop, or, indeed, whether Walter was summoned before some sort of examining body; nor do we know how widespread was the sentiment expressed by his accusers. What we can infer from the *Letter to Maurice* was that the attack was substantial enough for Walter to need to defend himself before his abbot.

Walter's reply to his critics, his *Letter to Maurice (Epistola ad Mauricium),* with which he prefaced his *Vita Sancti Aelredi,* is not only a defense of his *Vita* but also a defense of his method and thus a window into the workings of the genre. His *apologia,* which is a rebuttal of those critics who impugned his credibility, argues passionately that his biography is consonant with the ancient traditions of the genre and that he has taken no liberties not fully represented both in the Bible and in the thousands of sacred biographies which have preceded his. If we accept Walter at his word, then, we have a good example of someone who avoids innovation, and we can see the genre of the saint's life unalloyed, because the perfect text to study for the continuity of a tradition is one which avoids any attempt at virtuosity. Fortunately, in his *Letter to Maurice,* Walter highlights the use of sources, the role of rhetoric, and the employment of tropes in the composition of the saint's life, especially when the biographer must describe physical events which appear to violate the natural order.

We shall examine his *Letter to Maurice* in more detail below, but one crucial preliminary point concerning Walter's use of sources is the utter lack of discussion of the correctness of appropriating motifs from the biographies of other saints for subsequent use in his life of Aelred. Walter borrows readily from Sulpicius when constructing his depiction of Aelred's body. His silence on this matter surely piques our interest; we are conditioned to expect biographical details to be uniquely illustrative of the subject at hand. What are we to make of this practice and Walter's silence concerning it? Of course, we do face the difficulty of

---

57. C. Dickens, *Our Mutual Friend* (London, 1952), p. 86.

constructing an argument from silence, because Walter really does not directly address this important issue. I do believe, however, that his very silence allows us to draw the following conclusion: Walter's critics did recognize his use of such borrowings, such as Sulpicius's *Vita Sancti Martini,* and they accepted such usage as normative in the biographical process. This conclusion offers an explanation for why Walter does not defend himself from any charges concerning these appropriations from other *vitae.* Walter does not appear to have been challenged concerning his use of sources.

The *Letter to Maurice* is typically detailed and impassioned. It seems inconceivable, given the general tone of his argument, that if he had been attacked for what seems unscrupulous use of other sources, he would not have made some response. Given the nature of the response in the *Letter to Maurice,* I believe that the main thrust of his critics' disagreement was with the improbability of some of the miracles he attributed to Aelred, and not with his use of details and entire passages—no matter how this latter point confounds the modern sensibility—from the biographies of other saints in completing his portrait of Aelred, because it is these matters of the miraculous which he inveighs against most mightily. Walter's response to his critics is harsh, being no less than to accuse them of ignorance of their Christian interpretive tradition. Such an attack, although never stated explicitly, also impugns their understanding of *lectio divina* and the rhetoric that surrounds that tradition.

Walter's Use of Rhetoric

From the few references to Walter in contemporary documents, he appears to have been at times an irascible, pugnacious individual. The abused and arrogant tone of the *Letter to Maurice* seems to confirm this. Examine his skillful opening proemium to Maurice:

> Far be it from thy son [referring to himself] who knows that without truth there is no salvation, that he should knowingly allow himself to branded a liar [referring to the charges of his critics]. . . . Let them take heed that ignoble minds always breed unworthy affections and dismiss as false things sealed with the seal of truth.[58]

58. Powicke, *The Life of Aelred,* pp. 66, 69: "Set absit a filio tuo ut scienter cauterio falsitatis uri uelit uel ualeat, qui nouit quod sine ueritate salus nulla consistat

These lines present a narrator who assumes the pose of the humble, beleaguered servant, the submissive contemplative, "thy son" (*a filio tuo*), who labors to uphold the sanctity of truth against those with ignoble minds (*animos*). Although Walter's language is sometimes overwrought and histrionic, the *Letter to Maurice* shows his considerable skill in the ability to polarize, to develop an argument, and in his knowledgeable understanding of the tradition of sacred biography.

Walter's passion for rebuttal has somewhat obscured the exact nature of his critics' charges and makes one a bit chary in reconstructing them. However, as mentioned above, because we do not have either an accurate oral tradition concerning the critique leveled against his biography or the documents which contained the critique of his *Vita Sancti Aelredi*, we can only reconstruct his critics' positions through an interrogation of Walter's defense. The principal challenge seems to have been directed at the veracity of the miracles attributed by Walter to Aelred:

> *ni fallor, illos prelatos qui uobis legentibus ipsa miracula credere noluerunt.*

> If I am not mistaken, those prelates who, when you [Maurice] read these miracles to them, were unwilling to believe them.[59]

Walter, however, felt that their attack was even more basic than one leveled at his credibility as an accurate biographer of Aelred. He viewed it as an attack which impugned the accuracy of the entire life: *suspicionis impellere uoragine et infidelitate maculare* ("to cast it into the pit of suspicion and defile it [the life] as being unfaithful"). In this way, these anonymous prelates raised the issue of Aelred's sanctity; to doubt the presence of the miraculous in Aelred's life implied, for Walter, a suspicion of his sanctity.[60]

But let us turn directly to Walter's rebuttal. His basic strategy was to mount an *ad hominem* attack against the two anonymous prelates. His anger at their skepticism of his report of Aelred's life is directed, as I said above, primarily toward demonstrating their ignorance of the rhetorical traditions which have governed sacred biography from the very beginning. Although his defense does not deny the literal truth of

---

... dum tamen aduertant semper ignobiles animos degeneres parturire affectus, resque ueritate signatas non aliter approbare quam falsas."

59. Ibid., p. 66.

60. Ibid.

the miraculous events he has reported, he attempts to broaden the scope of the argument from one primarily concerned with the truth of depicting the literal happenstance of an event, *qua* event, as an isolated phenomenon, to an argument more heuristic in kind, in which an event cannot be fully understood apart from an observer and his report of that observation. As a result of his broader approach in portraying how accurately language conveys the truth of individual events—his aim is essentially to broaden the argument into a discussion of Christian epistemology—he attempts to show the importance of rhetoric (especially the use of the trope of hyperbole) as a linguistic tool essential to conveying to the reader the complete circumstances which governed the way the events were experienced.

Walter's intention as manifest in his discussion does not countenance or propose a radical solipcism or historical relativism. Walter accepted the position that physical events have their unique ontology and that the imagination cannot logically claim for itself the power to change an action into a different action and still retain a claim to be telling the truth. Rather, he is attempting to lay out an argument which will illustrate the crucial role of metaphoric language as indispensable vehicle for conveying to an audience, in language designed to revivify the original experience, the imaginative response of those who witnessed events which appear to have violated the natural order. He is intent on conveying his experience of the phenomenon which, for him in that moment under those exact circumstances, is inseparable from the phenomenon, even if at all other times his experience and the phenomenon are different. The vehicle which must communicate this deeply felt nonnormative experience is figurative language.[61]

Walter begins his explanation of the value of rhetoric with a discussion of the function of hyperbole (*superlatio*) and its place in narratives which depict emotionally charged situations, and we can assume that he believed this figure to be of fundamental importance. I would like to use his discussion as a means of demonstrating his method. He begins by turning to his narrative of the night on which Aelred died. Walter argues that it is only through *superlatio* that he has been able to

61. Augustine, in *De Doctrina Christiana,* III, 29, 40, comments: "And what illiterate man is there that does not use such expressions [figures of speech], although he knows nothing at all about either the nature or the names of these figures of speech? And yet the knowledge of these is necessary for clearing up the difficulties of scripture; because when the words taken literally give an absurd meaning, we ought forthwith to inquire whether they may not be used in this or that figurative sense which we are unacquainted with; and in this way many obscure passages have had light thrown upon them."

bring some semblance of what he and his fellow monks felt (*sic sensimus omnes*) during that time. He tells us that the events immediately leading up to and including Aelred's death were the cause for extreme feeling within the community:

> The brethren, hearing these things, for he was speaking in chapter [Aelred], hearing, I say, these things, began to sigh and weep [*audientes fratres suspirabant et lacrimabantur*]. . . . But the following night brought the father great pain, and us most pain of all [*nobis autem maximum*] for his was only of the body while ours was the pain of a sorrowful mind [*animi merentis*] exceeding sad because of him.[62]

We can recapture some sense of this heightened emotional pitch if we call to mind the immediate setting for Walter's life of Aelred: an isolated, cohesive community faced with the imminent loss of their abbot, their spiritual father, heaven-appointed shepherd, and source of their physical and economic well-being. Within such a community, the imminence of Aelred's death had sharpened all their senses, which were painfully acute, heightened as perhaps never before; the intimate monastic brethren were drawn even closer together in the expectation of the great but painful event. Indeed, even nature was drawn into an expectant collusion, for the heavens might signal the time of the great portent. Walter compares Aelred's presence to that of the sun:

> *Quoniam quidem pater noster obiit et quasi lux matutina euanuit e terra nostra et multorum animo insidet ut radius tanti luminis refundatur ad memoriam et illuminacionem futurorum.*

> Our father is dead; he has vanished from our world as the morning sunlight, and many spirits yearn that such a great light should flood with its brightness the memory of the future.[63]

It surely was the topic of every furtive whisper and nod in the hours immediately preceding Aelred's death. One can imagine the hand signs used by these silent Cistercian brethren concerning the state of Aelred as they passed one another that January morning.

Now, amid this throbbing communal expectancy imagine Walter Daniel, monastic *infirmus,* physical minister to the dying Aelred. His awesome responsibility is to record for the community, for the order, for posterity, and *ad majorem gloriam Dei* the passing of Aelred, a passing of which every detail was being woven into the hearts and

62. Powicke, *The Life of Aelred,* p. 57.

63. Ibid., p. 1.

minds of his monastic brethren; of which every event, no matter how small or trivial, was being viewed in light of this greater event. Is it any wonder that Walter argued that the only way an accurate account of such a moment could be conveyed was in a narrative which used hyperbole as the principal rhetorical device? He argued passionately that those individuals (clearly referring to his critics) who would insist on a more factual account asked for the impossible; this moment existed only in and was inseparable from the imaginative recall of those who were present:

> Is it supposed that the dead body of Aelred did not shine when it was washed? It was a light to all of us who stood by. And how? Much more than if a carbuncle had been there. That its fragrance exceeded the smell of incense seemed so to us; all of us were sensible of it.[64]

Walter's thesis is not as extreme as it may sound. In a brief analogy from recent history, Americans asked about the assassination of President John Kennedy commonly recall the event by references to what they were doing when they heard news of it. One hears events of that day recalled through a dramatic kind of spatial dislocation: "I was just returning from a delivery I had made and turned on the radio when I heard the shocking news. I'll never forget that. . . ." Such a material or circumstantial recall is an attempt to weave oneself into the fabric of the historic moment and to fix the larger event into a personal narrative. This type of historical recreation changes the orientation of the event from one in which the witness is a spectator to one in which the witness is a participant. The telling is no less accurate, but the focus of the narrative has shifted from the event to the observer. To paraphrase Karl Popper, observation is always selective no matter how faithful we intend our report to be. The real consequence of what is being conveyed in this historical retelling is that the narrator creates a story through the use of the plot and other narrative devices ("I was returning from a delivery") in which the main action (the death of a

64. Ibid., p. 77: "Quid enim? Alredi corpus num mihi non luxit cum lauaretur defunctum? Vere lux nobis omnibus qui affuimus. Et quomodo? Plus multo quam si carbunculus affuisset. Quod eciam super odorem thuris redolebat, sic nobis uisum est, sic sensimus omnes." Although the Latin *carbunculus* is a diminutive usually referring to a small piece of coal, in later Latin it identified a semiprecious reddish stone. There is a reference to *carbunculus* in the famous description of the bejeweled breastpiece worn by Aaron as a sign of his consecration to the priesthood in Exodus 28:18: "in secundo carbunculus sapphyrus et iaspis." Given the importance of the figure of Aaron for the priesthood, it is entirely possible that Walter's use of *carbunculus* was deliberate.

leader) is seen only through secondary plot devices which record the actions, events, and feelings of subsidiary witnesses. Oral records of the assassination of the president, which juxtapose the events in Dallas with where someone was, what he was doing, and at which precise time, all testify to this emplotment of personal history in the frame of the larger issue.[65]

Walter Daniel's *Letter to Maurice* is in part a defense of this sort of narrative (e.g., the narrative description of the death of Aelred), although in this instance the crucial part of the narrative is inseparable from the witness's recall of that event despite the fact that such recall may stretch the credulity of other witnesses, who may have emplotted the event in a different manner. There is a striking contrast between, on the one hand, the skepticism of his critics who asked for facts somehow separable from the experience of those present and, on the other hand, Walter's ideas on the inseparability of the exact quality of the experience from the narratives of those who were there. Walter's pugnaciousness was never more to the fore than regarding this critical difference. Losing his temper, he refers to his attackers as dullards (*O! Hebetes*).[66] This passage, in which Walter defends his use of hyperbole, is so crucial that we should have it before us in its entirety:

> Hyperbole [*superlatio*] indeed, is a form of speech which extends the truth [*superans ueritatem*] with the object of making something greater or less. By this and other colors mother wisdom employs her skill on the picture of eloquence. The heathen writer who said "Speech sweeter than honey poured from his mouth" is an example of this. And again in our books "Swifter than eagles, stronger than lions." Or again in the Life of Saint Martin "purer than glass, whiter than milk." Oh, you dullards. These are not extraordinary expressions [*note iste non sunt notabiles*], but, on the contrary, are plainly commendable. They emphasize great matters, and annoy foolish critics. For what are the facts [*quid enim*]? Is it supposed that the dead body of Aelred did not shine when it was washed? It was a light to all of us who stood by. And how? Much more than if a carbuncle had been there [*Plus multo quam si carbunculus affuisset*]. That its fragrance exceeded the smell of incense seemed so to us; all of us were sensible of it [*Quod eciam super odorem thuris redolebat, sic nobis uisum est, sic sensimus omnes*]. And no wonder; for never before in life was that fair and seemly man habited in flesh so bright as when he lay in death. I say without a grain of falsehood [*dico sine*

65. H. White, "The Historical Text as Literary Artifact," in *Tropics of Discourse, Essays in Cultural Criticism*, pp. 84, 91–92, and "Introduction" to *Metahistory: The Historical Imagination in 19th Century Europe*.

66. Powicke, *The Life of Aelred*, p. 77.

scrupulo mendacii] that I never saw such bright flesh on any man, dead
or alive. You must pardon me, therefore, if I magnified the incomparable,
as it deserved, by using a permissible hyperbole [*licta superlacione*]. If
you do not, the experts in rhetoric [*alioquin auctores eloquencie*] will
publicly trounce your stupidity.[67]

Walter's remarks, although they acknowledge that *superlatio,* as a
figure, does range beyond the sheer empirical or literal fact of a truth,
support his interest in a level of interpretation beyond the rigidly
empirical while not denying the literal or claiming the prerogative of
the allegorist. It is for this reason that I have chosen to translate *superans* as "extends," because it is in this sense of broadening without
falsifying the event or even subjecting it to the standard exegetical
method that Walter intends us to understand the phrase *superans
ueritatem.*

His stance on the use of hyperbole has considerable antiquity, and
the authorities he cites in his defense are among the most distinguished. The three from whom he quotes in the above passage are the
pseudo-Cicero's *Rhetorica ad Herennium,* 2 Samuel 1:23, and Sulpicius Severus' *Vita Sancti Martini,* respectively.[68] Indeed, his very definition of hyperbole, quoted above from his *Epistola ad Mauricium,*
although he does not acknowledge its source, is taken verbatim from
the definition of the category *superlatio* in the *ad Herennium.* Even

67. Ibid., p. 77: "Etenim superlacio est oracio superans ueritatem alicuius augendi
minuendiue causa. Hoc colore mater sapiencia in pictura eloquencie cum ceteris ar-
tificiose operatur. Hinc est illud ethnici dicentis: cuius ore sermo melle dulcior pro-
fluebat. Et in literis nostris: 'aquilis uelociores leonibus forciores.' Illudque in uita
beati Martini: uitro purior lacte candidior. O hebetes! note iste non sunt notabiles,
immo plane commendabiles, res magnas commendantes et stultos reprehensores ir-
ritantes. Quid eniim? Aelredi corpus num mihi non luxit cum lauaretur defunctum?
Vere lux nobis omnibus qui affuimus. At quomodo? Plus multo quam si carbunculus
affuisset. Quod eciam super ordorem thuris redolebat, sic nobis uisum est, sic sensimus omnes. Nec mirum. Nunquam enim antea in uita sua carnem sic candidam gessit
pulcher ille et decorus quomodo quando iacebat defunctus. Dico sine scrupulo mendacii, nuncquam ego tam candidam carnem uidi alterius cuiuslibet uiui uel defuncti.
Ignoscite ergo michi quod rem incomparabilem licita superlacione merito magnificaui.
Alioquin auctores eloquencie stoliditatem uestram publica redargucione dampna-
bunt."

68. *Ad Herennium,* IV, xxxiii, 44: "Superlatio est oratio superans veritatem alicuius augendi minuendive causa." Walter's allusion to 2 Samuel 1:23 is also of interest. The context for the verse in 2 Samuel is one of lamentation at the loss of a loved
one. David has just learned the news of Saul's and Jonathan's deaths and sings a dirge
which contains these verses: "Saul et Ionathan amabiles et decori in vita sua/ in morte
quoque non sunt divisi/ aquilis velociores leonibus fortiores." In the *Vita Sancti Martini,* "Ita uitro purior, lacte candidior."

this minor aspect of his argument has a calculated effect. Walter certainly hoped that the learned among his readers would recognize such unacknowledged citations, credit him with perspicacity and care in handling the traditions, and thus think less of his critics, who, it would seem, failed to recognize them. Had his critics recognized the unidentified quotations, Walter's argument implies, it would have suggested that they understood the nature of the tradition and hence would not have criticized his handling of it.

Having established the importance of using *superlatio* (an importance sanctioned by the ancients and by the Bible, as his quotations point out) as a device to augment or extend an understanding of the truth of an event, Walter next makes an application of his use of *superlatio* in his biography of Aelred. His argument is decidedly self-referential. If we push his argument to what appears to be its logical conclusion, it seems that Walter is arguing that the authentic "truth" of a situation is inextricably linked to a personal experience of it. If an individual is then to render an account of that truth, he can only do so through the theory of emplotment discussed above and the use of such figures as *superlatio*.

We might say that the corollary of that situation exists for the reader who is, in turn, only able to recreate that experience, once again, through figurative language which works to extend the truth (*superans ueritatem*) through a stimulation of his imagination. This interpretation, however, depends rather heavily on Walter's use of the distinctions made about *superlatio* in the *ad Herennium* only. To complete Walter's understanding, we must consider his other authorities, especially his allusive remark that "mother wisdom employs her skill on the picture of eloquence." Walter's use of the expression *mater sapientia* as a reference to wisdom as the guardian and font of human eloquence was a commonplace in medieval thinking on the source of eloquence. The expression derives ultimately from the deuterocanonical *Liber Sapientiae*, one of the most popular texts in the monastic *lectio divina*.

The Book of Wisdom personifies Wisdom as the mother of all (7:12), as capable of understanding all turns of phrases and subtlety of argument (*scit versutias sermonum, et dissolutiones argumentorum*, 8:8), as God's creative word (9:1), as immanent with the Holy Spirit (9:17), and as the source for Solomon's astonishing eloquence: *tacentem me sustinebunt,/Et loquentem me respicient,/Et sermocinante me plura, manus ori suo imponent* (8:12). Walter's allusion to *mater sapientia* gives to his conception of rhetoric, but in particular to his employment of *superlatio* to extend the truth (*superans ueritatem*), a necessary theological basis. Walter believed that figurative language, such as hyperbole, was necessary to communicate what his imagination had confronted and what simple, declarative language was unable to convey—in particular those instances when human reason confronted the majesty of divine Providence.[69]

Moreover, and this should be stressed, Walter believed that metaphoric language, in its ability to construct new orders of meaning, worked in an analogous way to the unseen creative power of God. Hence, those who sought to use *superlatio* in their writing were striving toward the highest, most spiritually enlightened of ideals (*quo tendas anagogia*). Indeed, such employment of these rhetorical tropes was a recognition that it was only through the use of such inspired eloquence —and here, once again, we come back to the principle of the deity's creative spirit, *et inspiravit*—that one could not only reanimate the circumstances being depicted (the imaginative response of those present at the time) but also make palpable the creative power of the divine word to one's audience.

Walter's theory of narrative eloquence is derived from his theological belief that the Lord created the universe through language and has bequeathed his *logos* to humanity for our salvation. For Walter, it is only by means of such eloquence that the true meaning of human experience can be conveyed, no matter how difficult it may be for some to see the similitude between the expression and the experience.[70]

The Importance of Recognition

Walter Daniel's account of certain events in Aelred's life was taken, sometimes verbatim, from other sacred biographies. This is undoubtedly a curious practice. However, this use of source materials would be of little interest if the practice were simply indicative of the biographer's need to supplement his text from what he had at hand. This is surely an inadequate explanation for the complex series of associations we can discern in the saintly lives, such as Eddius Stephanus's use of

69. *Liber Sapentiae* 7:12: "et ignorabam quoniam horum omnium mater est"; 9:1–2: "Deus parentum meorum et Domine misericordiae tuae qui fecisti omnia verbo tuo, et sapientia tua constituisti hominem"; 9:17: "sensum autem tuum quis sciet, nisi tu dederis sapientiam, et miseris spiritum sanctum tuum de altissimis."

70. Augustine, *De Doctrina Christiana,* III, 6, 7.

Victorius of Aquitaine's *Easter Calendar.* Moreover, as we shall see below, such textual embedding appears to be virtually *sui generis* to the *vitae sanctorum* and as such is enormously important for a complete appreciation of the genre. Such embedded narratives seem to play a crucial role in the dialectic with which the medieval Christian conceived the ideological foundations of sanctity. Of course, the entire edifice of this system of embedded structures would be utterly meaningless if the audience was ignorant of its presence. Let us now look at how this ideal of recognition was intended to function and the framework for the meanings it was designed to generate.[71]

Because Walter does not rebut his critics concerning his borrowings in his *Letter to Maurice,* I think we can fairly assume that Walter's audience, even those who were hostile to his *Vita Sancti Aelredi,* accepted such borrowings as part of the *amplificatio* of the text, indeed as part of the well-established convention governing this genre. I would go further and propose that the use of such embedding was itself a sign of narrative sophistication to a literate audience. Indeed, the more artfully embedded and complex the series of associations provoked by the embedding, the more they contributed to the sacred biographer's reputation. I believe this to be a reasonable hypothesis in light of Walter's painstaking defense of his *elocutio* in the *Letter to Maurice,* with precious little effort devoted to defending himself from a charge of having used his sources unwisely or without sufficient subtlety.

This substitution of motifs from other sacred biographies, this *amplificatio,* was viewed as an act of filial *pietas* and not one of literary theft. There is little evidence to suggest that the sacred biographer was consciously deceiving his readers into believing that an embedded selection was in fact from the writer's own hand. The literary thief wants to deceive, wants his readers to believe the work is his alone. Walter's intention, on the other hand, as in the tradition of such borrowing in sacred biography, seeks to establish a new polysemous understanding of the saintly hero or heroine through a complex skein of associations which can only create the desired objective, if the reader recognizes them. The intentions of the literary thief and of the sacred biographer with respect to their use of sources could not be more opposite.[72]

71. The embedded structures, although borrowed, become a structural part of the text. They function differently from an allusion by not simply calling to mind another text, but rather making the borrowed *topos* an inseparable part of the meaning of the new narrative.

72. The method I will discuss bears some resemblance to the classical employment of *cento* in verse. Briefly, the *cento* was the unacknowledged borrowing of words or, less frequently, entire lines from earlier poets—Homer and Vergil were the favorite

The new understanding of character sought by the sacred biographer is corporate and indebted to the doctrine of *communio sanctorum*. We have seen how sacred biography makes deliberate use of borrowings to stimulate the reader's associative faculty. Such audience recognition was widely employed. This associative faculty, or recognition is quite similar to the classical notion of ἀναγνώρισις a technique used prominently in both the classical drama and the epic. Aristotle discussed its effectiveness as a literary convention designed to deepen one's understanding. It was also employed in classical biography by Nepos and Plutarch. Although little scholarly study has focused on the evolution of *anagnorisis,* it seems reasonable to see it moving from the great tragedians (from whom Aristotle takes his examples) to the comedy, especially the New Comedy. The plots of the plays of Terence and Plautus, for example, depend to a considerable degree on *anagnorisis*. This theme of discovery is also marked in Hellenistic romance; one need only note such classics as Achilles Tatius's *The Love of Leucippe and Clitophon* (ca. early second century A.D.) and Heliodorus of Esema's *Aethiopica* (ca. third century A.D.). Indeed, this principle of recognition is also the major plot device in the popular *Pseudo Clementine Recognitions* which survive in more than one hundred manuscripts.[73]

---

texts through the fifth century A.D.—for use in one's own poetic composition. The *cento* never seems to have been employed in prose. Classical practitioners of the *cento* included Aristophanes, Lucian, and Ausonius, who gave to his work the title *Cento nuptialis.* Scholars find less evidence for the existence of the *cento* in the Middle Ages, with the exception of the tenth-century *Ecbasis Captivi* and some *centones* composed by Anicia Faltonia Proba, Pomponius, Luxorius, and possibly Sedulius. R. Yeager, to whom I am indebted for a copy of his paper on Gower and the *cento* (forthcoming), makes a convincing case for Gower's use of the *cento* in the *Vox Clamantis.* For additional work on the *cento,* see O. Delepierre, *Revue analytique des ouvrages écrits en centons, depuis les temps anciens, jusqu'au XIXième siècle* (London, 1868), pp. 107–36, 141–47; M. Manitius, *Geschichte der Lateinischen Literatur des Mittelalters,* (Beck, 1911–31), Vol. 1, p. 618; F. J. E. Raby, *A History of the Secular Latin Poetry in the Middle Ages* (Oxford, 1957), Vol. 1, pp. 44–45. Raby makes the very interesting remark that "reminiscences of Vergil, Ovid, Horace, Juvenal, Claudian, and Sallust, to say nothing of Prudentius, are to be found in the prose and poetry of Columban," in *A History of Christian-Latin Poetry from the Beginnings to the Close of the Middle Ages* (Oxford, 1953), pp. 138–39. There is clearly a need for more work in this area, as the one thing the medieval monastic community could supply par excellence, and something which the *cento* required, was the existence of a very literate audience deeply learned in an established canon of texts; the common practice of monastic readings would have supplied this common ground of literary experience.

73. Aristotle, *Poetics,* ed. J. H. Freese (Cambridge, 1975), 1452a, 36. Aristotle's discussion of *anagnorisis* is drawn exclusively from the drama: "A discovery is, as the very word implies, a change from ignorance to knowledge, and thus to either love

Its importance in sacred biography, although first noticed by Charles Jones more than forty years ago, has drawn little attention, despite the fact that it deepens our understanding of how the genre's narrative conventions work and must therefore change the way we read saints' lives.[74]

The application of *anagnorisis* in Christian sacred biography developed early. It was employed, although this has not been pointed out before, at the very birth of the genre in the very first saint's life. Luke's depiction of the death of St. Stephen in Acts (7:54–60) is the first deliberate use of the technique in sacred biography. If we think it unlikely for one of the evangelists to be making use of this technique from Greek drama, we need only remind ourselves of Luke's background. New Testament scholars are in agreement concerning Luke's sure understanding of Greek rhetorical traditions. Heinrici pointed out that Acts "is the only book in the New Testament that permits of classification in the contemporary Greek literature," and Blass noted that many classical idioms are found in Acts, though they are unusual in most of the New Testament.[75]

Luke was also indebted to the other Synoptics for his depiction of Stephen in the conventional biblical role of the persecuted prophet. Aside from acknowledging these influences, the important issue before us is how Luke, the author of the first Christian saint's life, employed *anagnorisis* to deepen his portrait of the beleaguered Stephen. Luke uses this convention borrowed from the drama most effectively in Stephen's speeches. Intending *anagnorisis* to point to the spiritual likeness which unites Stephen and Christ, Luke attributes to Stephen both the sentiments and some of the actual expressions given to Christ in the Gospels. Stephen and Christ both forgive their executioners; both were accused of threatening to destroy the Temple; in the entire corpus of early Christian literature, the epithet "Son of Man" (as a reference

---

or hate, in the personages marked for good or evil fortune." On the subject of the influence of *anagnorisis* from Greek romance to Christian authors, see H. Dörrie, "Die Griechischen Romane und das Christentum," *Phil* 93 (1938): 274. Dörrie makes the interesting proposal that the romance of Leucippe and Clitophon is the basis for the martyrology of Leucippe and Clitophon in the *AS* for November 5, and it is the account in the martyrology which explains the survival and wide propagation of the pagan romance. See also B. E. Perry, *The Ancient Romances* (Berkeley, 1967), pp. 346–47.

74. C. Jones, *Saints' Lives and Chronicles in Early England* (Ithaca, 1947), p. 61.

75. H. J. Cadbury, *The Making of Luke-Acts*, pp. 133, 224, 228.

to Christ) is used only by Stephen and by Christ; and, lastly and most importantly for this discussion, Luke places Christ's final words in Stephen's mouth.

Luke wants the reader to recognize the similarity between Stephen and Christ. He also intends something more. In his depiction of the stoning of Stephen, Luke places in Stephen's mouth an abridged verbal parallel of Christ's final words, *Domine Iesu, suscipe spiritum meum.* The depiction of Stephen that we have from Luke up to this moment in Acts is broadly modeled on that of Christ in Matthew and Mark, the innocent, beleaguered prophet preaching God's word to a community that refuses to take his message to heart. Stephen's iteration of remarks borrowed from Christ represents an effort to move the reader or listener from the simple recognition of the obvious correspondences which exist between the two martyrs to the deeper recognition that Stephen, in the act of patterning his witness (in both utterance and deed) on Christ, has mysteriously become one with Christ.

Luke's use of *anagnorisis* was to illustrate the power of Providence to shape the disposition of the human heart. The Christian theological substrate of the Greek literary device is the identification of divine Providence as the active ingredient causing these similitudes. Indeed, it is this theological dimension which distinguishes the technique from simple typology which sees Stephen as a type of Christ. For the Christian sacred biographer, at the moment of his death, Stephen is not merely a type of Christ but an actual part of Christ, not so much a later historical representative of Christ, but Christ *redux*. We shall consider this religious extension of human personality in more detail in our discussion of the *Passio Sanctarum Perpetuae et Felicitatis* in Chapter 5.

Before returning to Walter Daniel and his use of *anagnorisis,* let us sum up by acknowledging that Luke's was a great bequest to the legion of medieval sacred biographers who employed the Greek dramatic technique of *anagnorisis.* Luke's portrayal of Stephen's death legitimized the use of Christ's death as a paradigm in saintly tales and thus exerted a seminal influence on later Christian sacred biography.

But now let us move the historical pendulum forward eleven centuries to Walter Daniel's use of borrowed motifs and ask whether he employs this same *anagnorisis* within a theological frame and, if so, how? My point of departure will be the scene of the washing and anointing of Aelred's body before burial:

Cum autem corpus eius ad lauandum/ delatum fuisset et nudatum coram nobis, uidimus quodamodo futuram gloriam reuelatam in patre, cuius

*caro uitro purior, niue candidior, quasi quinquennis pueri membra in-
duerat, que ne parue quidem macule neuus fuscabat, set erant omnia
plena dulcedenis decoris et delectacionis.*

When his body was laid naked before us to be washed, we saw how the
glory to come had been revealed in the father. His flesh was clearer than
glass, whiter than snow, as though his members were those of a boy five
years old, without a trace of stain, but altogether sweet, and composed
and pleasant.[76]

We recognize at once the element of encomium in Walter's depiction
of Aelred. Indeed, as Fontaine has pointed out, this description of a
body for burial, in particular the celebration of the miraculous white-
ness of the dead limbs, has broad literary parallels in antiquity.[77] Walter
did not turn to the classics for his depiction of his beloved Aelred,
however. He did indeed borrow directly some of the above language
(and perhaps the idea for the actual setting) as he himself explicitly
tells us. Walter acknowledges in his *Letter to Maurice,* with some
pique directed at his critics' ignorance, a similar expression in Sulpicius Severus's *Vita Sancti Martini,* from which he quotes: *Illudque in
uita beati Martini: uitro purior lacte candidior.*[78] His reference is
couched in a tone of exasperated disbelief that his critics did not immediately recognize this expression, used in one of the very greatest
of saints' lives and found throughout the Old and New Testaments and
in classical literature. Further, the fact that his critics did not recognize
this explicit correspondence made it perfectly clear to Walter that they
could not have followed the entire skein of causal relationships that the
phrase *niue candidior* was meant to summon up. In light of Walter's
expressed concern, it would be sheer folly to construe his remarks as
a blustering apology for an unacknowledged citation from Sulpicius.

Walter's acknowledgment of the similarity of this passage to that in
Sulpicius is merely a small branch taken from a large tree of possible
correspondences. Restricting myself to an examination of the number
and nature of the associations produced by this single expression from
Walter's *Aelred, cuius caro uitro purior, niue candidior* (the very one
which he himself drew a parallel with in Sulpicius, *membra autem eius
candida tamquam nix uidebantur*), I have identified no less than thirty
correspondences that would have been recognized by a typical member

76. Powicke, *The Life of Aelred,* p. 62.

77. Fontaine, Vol. 3, p. 1334.

78. Powicke, *The Life of Aelred,* p. 77.

of Walter's audience, recognitions which he clearly intended and expected to take place. It is not my purpose to discuss how these associations interact and create new meaning; that task would itself fill a small book. Rather, I shall limit myself to illustrating how I believe they were meant to function.

These embedded borrowings are typically signaled through verbal parallels, with excerpts of similar or identical language, as in the present example. Further, the contexts of the different texts which are being associated by the parallel language should have some thematic complementarity. Once these two primary associative factors of language and context which link the two texts are recognized by the audience, the author's rationale for embedding the text can begin to unfold. In short, the dynamic aspects of the principle of *anagnorisis* take hold. For example, Walter's verbal echo of Sulpicius in his *superlatio niue candidior* justifies the use of his hyperbole through an *argumentum ad auctoritas* and compares the abbot of Rievaulx with one of the greatest saints of Christendom. We might say that by extending the association to Martin, Walter has created a typological correspondence; Aelred is a second Martin. But this method of embedded borrowings extends the idea of typology, as indicated above, into the realms of theology and *Heilsgeschichte,* because the intention is not simply to work within a theory of types, to hold up one figure as the allegorical embodiment of an earlier one, but rather to illustrate the dogma of *communio sanctorum* as it operates in this world, in human lives fettered by historical circumstance. Those two sacred lives, as Augustine would say, give evidence of the deity's first creative act (*seminales rationes*), and the recognition of the similitude uniting them bridges time's chasm and connects the utterly pristine instant of creation, the beginning of time, to this senescent present.

Walter's acknowledgment of a parallel in Sulpicius was not meant to limit the associative power of the comparison to that text alone. Indeed, the discussion of *superlatio* in the *ad Herennium* shows the application of this figure in "comparisons formed from superiority" with the following example of Agamemnon from Book 10 of the *Iliad:* "His body was as white as snow, his faced burned like fire."[79] Walter's knowledge of the *ad Herennium,* as was shown earlier, was quite intimate. Surely he would not have missed this reference to the tragic leader of the Greeks. There were, for Walter, bolder associative correspondences intended by his use of the *superlatio niue candidior,*

---

79. *Ad Herennium,* p. 340.

which he intended but does not reveal. After acknowledging his initial indebtedness to Sulpicius, Walter ceases to give any additional correspondences. What are his reasons for this silence? His reasons are methodological, ánd he recognizes that the associative mechanism which results from *anagnorisis* is audience-determined. The learned member of his audience will follow the association of the snow-white skin through a far greater series of correspondences than his less literate brethren.

With respect to Walter's particular choice from Sulpicius, the comparisons branch out in a ever-widening matrix of associations. The most important set of associations after that of Sulpicius is that with Christ in the Synoptic Gospels. Matthew's and Mark's depictions of the transfiguration of Christ offer the most primary parallel. Matthew illustrated the intensity with which Christ felt the Lord's presence by surrounding the figure of Christ with light: "and he was transfigured before us. His face was as bright as the sun and his robes were as white as the snow" (*et transfiguratus est ante eos. Et resplenduit facies eius sicut sol: vestimenta autem eius facta sunt alba sicut nix*). (Matthew 17:2) In Mark, we have the similar *Et vestimenta eius facta sunt splendentia, et candida nimis velut nix* (Mark 9:2). Both associations have considerable importance in furthering Walter's thematic intention in his depiction of Aelred. Walter intended that Aelred's demise be seen in a broad eschatological context. Aelred's death, like those of Sulpicius and Christ, was a signal to those who could see that their mortality was fleeting. Walter's use of the phrase *sicut nix* in reference to Aelred's corpse gives rise to correspondences which force this eschatological interpretation; this is the immediate context for the transfiguration of Christ, the two most important of the verbal parallels. If we were to stop our examination of the associative pattern (Aelred/Martin/Christ) with these two related passages from Matthew and Mark, it would appear that Walter is presenting a depiction of a type of the transfiguration of Aelred no less than the evangelists were doing for that of Christ. But the associations ripple out into a pattern that is broader than the eschatological alone.

The next set of correspondences branches out from strict verbal parallels to those which, although they employ similar language, make use of different plots and different syntactic structures. For example, Walter's comparison of Aelred's flesh with snow finds a verbal echo in Matthew's apocalyptic description of the appearance of the angel to the three Marys at the tomb. The angel's robe is like snow: *et vestimentum eius sicut nix* (Matthew 28:3). Bright, snowlike clothing is a frequent apocalyptic image of otherworldly glory. In Daniel 7:9, we see it in the figure of the ancient of days who has robes as bright as snow: *Vestimentum eius candidum quasi nix.* It is worth noting in this context that we find in this narrative in Daniel (see 7:13) the reference to the savior to come, the *Filius hominis,* Christ's most characteristic way of referring to himself and an epithet, as I have indicated above, used only by Jesus and Stephen in the whole of early Christian literature: *aspiciebam ergo in visione noctis/ et ecce cum nubibus caeli quasi filius/ hominis veniebat.* As association follows association, we surely must ask what is the cumulative hermeunetic generated by these correspondences. For example, the reference to the passages from Matthew and Daniel cited above associate the person of Aelred with the resurrection of Christ and the promised advent of a savior for Israel. If we simply consider the most obvious interpretations, we must conclude that Aelred, just deceased, is here identified with the risen Christ and is being portrayed as the promised redeemer who brings salvation to those who follow in his footsteps; he is the new *Filius hominis,* Son of Man. While this interpretation seems to reconcile the broad contexts of all three narratives, without undue disregard to the autonomy of the texts, it is one that a devout Cistercian would not or could not venture to proclaim with less circumlocution, because it moves perilously close to deifying Aelred, moving outside the bounds of *latria* into the area of *dulia.* Hence, the use of the embedded text has the flexibility of pointing to the theological association without dictating to the individual the meaning produced by the recognition.

Thus far, we have examined six primary texts considerably conflating what was a brief passage describing Aelred's corpse, which Walter admitted he took largely from Sulpicius Severus's *Vita Sancti Martini.* These six passages are primary because they exhibit close verbal parallels, and have an obvious directness about them; they operate at the first level of association, boldly directing, through the linguistic echos they stimulate, the audience's frame of reference. There are, however, at least thirty more passages in the Old and New Testaments alone which, although they do not use the same language, show a thematic similarity with the scene in the *Vita Sancti Aelredi.* Because these texts do not share similar language, their correspondence with the passage in Walter is less programmatic and much more dependent on the acumen of the audience. These passages display similarity of plot, of event, or even of an organizing idea which develops the themes we have accrued from the associations already made, such as the eschatological. It is not my purpose to develop each one as it permutates additional meanings in the passage from Walter's *Aelred,* as I think I have accounted for his method, but I would like simply to present them prefaced by the interpretive categories to which they belong: *Apocalyptic*—Old Testament angels (Genesis 16:10, 22:11; Exodus 3:2; Judges 6:12, 13:3; 2 Samuel 24:16); the just dressed in white garments (Enoch 46:1, 71:10; Daniel 7:9; Matthew 28:3; Mark 16:5; John 20:12; Luke 24:4; Acts 1:10). *Eschatological*—the glory of the saints (Revelation 3:4, 5, 18, 4:4, 6:11, 7:9–12). *Theophanic*—brightly resplendent faces indicative of a divine presence (Exodus 34:29–35, 24:15–18, 40:34–38; Isaiah 42:1; Matthew 3:17). *Transfiguration*—change of appearance of the just in the promised world (2 Baruch 51:3–10; Daniel 12:3; cf. 1 Corinthians 15:40–44; 2 Corinthians 3:18).

The hermeneutic process to which this number of associations can give birth varies from individual to individual and depends entirely on the degree of intimacy the audience has with the tradition. It is entirely credible that the single scene depicting the shining corpse of Aelred was recognized and followed through all of these associative layers, augmenting meaning at each new step, by Cistercians, even those in Aelred's own house, steeped in the daily practice of *lectio divina.*

4 / A Theology of Behavior: *Communio Sanctorum* and The Use of Sources

> Whosoever does the will of my heavenly Father is brother and sister and mother to me.
>
> Matthew *12:50*

> *Ibi namque tanta in membris est confederatio, ut totum sit proprium quod est commune, et commune quod est proprium . . .*
>
> Reginald of Canterbury, *Vita Sancti Malichi*

The narrative conventions of the medieval saint's life are indebted to religious ideals which laud antifraternal, solitary, and ascetic practices. Such ideals shaped the way medieval sacred biography illustrated both the public and the private character of sanctity. By the mid-fourth century, these austere ideals had formed a congeries of complex beliefs rooted in the church's theological and philosophical teaching and can be seen complete in Athanasius's *Vita Sancti Antonii*. These ideologies make up the conceptual skeleton which girds the narrative, and as such they inform the crucial antinomian dialectic, exemplified throughout the breadth of medieval sacred biography, of the conflict between the *civitas Dei* and the *civitas hominis*.

These socioreligious principles retained their force in the saint's life even when a narrative was contaminated by a large number of motifs from competing traditions with differing emphases, such as influence of Greek romance in the earliest Latin *Vita Sancti Eustachii.*[1] As late as the eleventh century, when the vernacular cultures began to mark their independence in their national literatures—notably in the growing

---

1. *AS, De Sanctis Eustachio, uxore ejus et filiis,* September 6 (Antwerp, 1757), pp. 123–37; see also A. Monteverdi, "I Testi Della Legenda di S. Eustachio," *Studi Medievali* 3 (1908–11):489–98. For the romance influence, see H. Dörrie, *Die Griechischen Romane,* p. 274; and B. E. Perry, *The Ancient Romances,* (Berkeley, 1967), pp. 346–47.

popularity of the romance and the romance's influence on the vernacular *vitae* written in France, Germany, and England from the thirteenth century—the biographical paradigm which continued to exercise the most profound influence on the sacred biographer remained the figure of Christ and the theology of human behavior which the legion of medieval Gospel commentators had wrought from Scripture.[2]

To understand the importance of the sacred biographer's use of these theological traditions and the complex manner in which the traditions shape the structure of the saint's life, we need to examine the more important of them, notably those which influenced the very ideology of the cult of the saints. This chapter illustrates the role played by the doctrine of *communio sanctorum* in the use of sources. This doctrine was to prove of considerable importance in providing the intellectual and spiritual rationale for the cult of the saints and in helping to shape the conventions which governed the genre.[3]

The first stage in the interpretive process in biographical writing— the development of a *Tiefsinningkeit*—depends on the nature, kind, and quantity of sources. Few today would contest the simple truth that the art of biography, no matter how elegantly conceived and written, could make little claim to authenticity without reliable sources. Freud's interesting but flawed study of Leonardo da Vinci is a perfectly good example of extreme selectivity in the use of sources.[4] The biographer's employment of sources reveals the historiography which governs the work and allows the reader to judge the interpretive skill with which the biographer has completed his task. These observations are somewhat less true for medieval sacred biography. The change in the sensibility of the medieval and modern biographers and their audiences is nowhere more striking than in their respective use and understanding of the value of sources.

2. For the clergy's anger at the romance's imitation of the saint's life, see P. Meyer, "La Vie de st. Grégoire le Grand," *Romania* 12 (1883): 147; and M. D. Legge, *Anglo-Norman Literature* (Oxford, 1963), p. 285.

3. On the doctrine of *communio sanctorum*, see J. P. Kirsh, *The Doctrine of the Communion of Saints in the Ancient Church* (Saint Louis, 1910); and S. Benko, *The Meaning of Sanctorum Communio* (Napierville, Ill., 1964).

4. S. Freud, *Eine Kindheistserinnergung des Leonardo da Vinci* (Leipzig, 1910). Freud's interpretation of Leonardo's sexuality is overly dependent on his interpretation of Leonardo's childhood dream and the figure of the hawk *del nibio*, a term which could have had a number of other meanings in the sixteenth century and one which Freud rather reductively limits to a symbol of the male genitalia.

The Scriptural Call to Sanctity

The Gospels are biographical documents which purport to tell of the life of Jesus. Although Matthew, like his modern counterpart, seeks to reveal his subject to his audience, his main intent is to reveal how the individual deeds in Christ's life point to a unique relationship with God, and secondly how these events, although emblems of Christ's messianic charisma, nonetheless exist as new paradigms for human action. The quotation from Matthew which opened this chapter has engaged the best exegetes and called forth quite different interpretations from the earliest periods of Gospel commentary. As a number of modern scholars have pointed out, Matthew presents this particular instance of Jesus's call to discipleship in an uncharacteristically spare style. The absence of figurative language or other indicators that the verse is to be understood metaphorically makes the interpretation even more tangential; its literalness seems even more prominent. The major thesis concerns the proper disposition of the human heart and the creation of a new model of kinship, a model which, I believe, is a kernel for the idea of Christian sanctity. Matthew proposes the novel thesis that even as blood relatives share a common inheritance, so too will members of this family of belief; this new inheritance will derive not from blood (as in the tribalism of Judaism) but from the spirit, not from the independence of the will but from the subjection of the individual will to that of God, with Jesus as the supreme model of that dependence of the human on the divine will. The verse read in this light was a radical call to spiritual discipleship and became one of the major supports in the intellectual foundations of the development of Christian sanctity.

Without entering into the history of the exegesis which surrounded this verse, it is reasonably clear that at least one interpretive constant which the medieval church sanctioned in its teaching of this verse was that of Christ's personal establishment of a class of individuals to be regarded as the models of Christian behavior, the saints. The exegetes who regarded the passage in this light, as in the pertinent commentaries of Augustine, Gregory the Great, and Haymo of Halberstadt, wrote that Christ proposed a new social unit to replace that of the family—a novel, radically different idea of kinship nourished not by blood or tradition, as in Judaism, but by faith.[5]

This verse from Matthew, plus Paul's remarks in Colossians 1:18,

5. Augustine, *De Genesi ad Litteram, PL* 34, cols. 25, 26, and *PL* 38, cols. 445, 467; Gregory the Great, *PL* 76, col. 1086; Haymo, *PL* 118, col. 208.

Ephesians 4:15–16, and Hebrews 12:22–24, not only provided the Fathers a scriptural basis for the later ideology of sanctity but also shaped the ideal of sanctity that was to develop.[6] For example, the verses from Matthew and Paul helped establish an understanding of sanctity as a charismatic personal witness, a witness which could exist outside a strictly hierarchical episcopal system. As early as the formation of the Gospels, we see Christian ideals of holiness joined to the separate issues of personal witness and the suffering prophet. The author of the First Letter of Peter (1 Peter 4:14) salutes the laity who suffer for their charismatic witness: "If Christ's name is flung in your teeth as an insult, count yourselves happy, because then that glorious spirit is resting upon you."[7] Such scriptural authority allowed for the incorporation within the institution of the established church of the idea of the holy man not wholly constrained by the framework which was to govern the great majority of the faithful. In his essay on "The Rise and Function of the Holy Man in Late Antiquity," Peter Brown, although he did not seek to establish a scriptural basis for such charisma, illustrated the complex series of relationships which existed between the holy man and society—relationships at once intimate and necessarily estranged—in the late Roman society of the eastern Mediterranean.[8] In such a scriptural call to witness and deeply held asocial interpretations of these scriptural verses, such as Origen's extension of the Pauline idea of witness μάρτυς to "one who dies for the faith,"[9] lay the foundation for the type of charismatic behavior later exemplified in such

6. Colossians 1:18: "et ipse est caput corporis ecclesiae/qui est principium primogenitus ex/mortuis/ut sit in omnibus ipse primatum tenens." Ephesians 4:15–16: "qui est caput Christus/et quo totum corpus compactum et/conexum/per omnem iuncturam subministrationis/secundum operationem in mensuram/uniuscuiusque membri/ augmentum corporis facit in aedificationem sui in caritate." Hebrews 12:22–24: "sed accessistis ad Sion montem et/civitatem Dei viventis Hierusalem/caelestem/et multorum milium angelorum frequentiae/et ecclesiam primitivorum qui conscripti sunt in caelis/et iudicem omnium Deum/et spiritus iustorum perfectorum/et testamenti novi mediatorem Iesum/et sanguinis sparsionem melius loquentem quam Abel."

7. 1 Peter 4:14: "si exprobramini in nomine Christi/beati/quoniam gloriae dei Spiritus in vobis requiescit." See also Hebrews 11:32–40; 1 Corinthians 4:9; and Acts 1:8, 5:41.

8. P. Brown, "The Rise and Function of the Holy Man in Late Antiquity," *JRS* 61 (1971): 91–92; see, however, his "The Saint as Exemplar in Late Antiquity," *Representations* 1 (1983): 1–25, which extends his discussion.

9. Origen, *Exhortation to Martyrdom*, trans. J. O'Meara (London, 1954), and *Exhortatio ad Martyrium*, *PG* 11, cols. 563–638. Origen's language in discussing the role of the martyr is typically impassioned; he refers to martyrs as a type of [Pauline] spiritual athlete.

important late-fourth-century lives as the *Vita Sancti Antonii* and the *Vita Sancti Martini*.[10]

Moreover, this same early spirit of charismatic sanctity provides a helpful rationale for the apparent disdain that medieval Christian saints are depicted as showing toward the established societal patterns. Saints are not respecters of social class; they do not follow the norms concerning sexually determined roles (e.g., women are often depicted as rebelling against male authority); and, finally, this early charismatic understanding of sanctity can provide the saint with a vehicle for the achievement of celebrated public status regardless of birthright within a rigidly hierarchical and often hostile social and ecclesiastical system.[11]

As we shall see below, even the depictions of the later medieval Christian saint were not bound by the normative social strictures which regulated the lives of king and peasant, prelate and parish priest, wife and mother, despite the very changed social milieu. The implications of such a charismatic understanding of sanctity that grants to the saints this gift of rapturous witness—a witness despite the constraining efforts of Jerome, Augustine, and other clerical leaders in the fourth and fifth centuries—which in turn frees them from the accepted commonplace traditions that bind society into cohesive units, are far-reaching. In endowing the saint with the aura of otherness, such an ideology requires that this theologically endowed separateness be manifest, that the gifts of the spirit proclaim themselves. Palladius tells of the female ascetic in the Egyptian desert who

10. Athanasius, *Vita Sancti Antonii*, *PG* 26; and Evagrius, *Vita Beati Antonii Interprete Evagrio Presbytero Antiocheno*, *PL* 73. There are some influences from the lives of prominent pagan holy men in Athanasius's *Life of Saint Antony*, the *Life of Pythagoras* (presumably because of Pythagoras's founding of a religious community with some predilection for quasi-ascetic practices recorded in the *acusmata*) being the most prominent example; see W. Burkert, *Lore and Science in Ancient Pythagoreanism* (Cambridge, Mass., 1972), pp. 166–92; see also E. R. Dodds, *Pagan and Christian in an Age of Anxiety*, p. 31. But see M. A. Williams, "The *Life of Antony* and the Domestication of Charismatic Wisdom," *Journal of the American Academy of Religion* 47 (1982): 31, who argues a fairly singular position that Antony's "charismatic dimensions" were subdued, "harnessed" by Athanasius.

11. Violet MacDermot, *The Cult of the Seer in the Ancient Middle East* (Berkeley, 1971), pp. 32, 294: MacDermot catalogues hundreds of instances in which the asceticism has at its base a deep antifraternal, antisocial bias: "For they dwelt in a desert place and their dwellings were remote and also they were separated, one from another, so that a man may not be known to his fellow and he may not be seen quickly nor his voice heard, but they live in great silence and each one of them is secluded in his cell."

left the city and shut herself in a certain tomb until the end of her life.
She received her food and her necessities through a window and no man
and no woman saw her face and neither did she see the face of any man
for twelve years.[12]

The *South English Legendary* life of St. Dunstan notes that his
sanctity—employing a common *topos*—was foretold while he was yet
in his mother's womb:

ȝwat was þat ore louerd crist: fram heouene þat liȝt sende
And þat folk þat þare stode aboute: heore taperes þarof tende,
Bote þat of þulke holi child: þat was in hire wombe here
Al enguelond scholde beo iliȝt: bet þane hit euer er ware?

The miracle stories in the narratives of the saint's life, aside from their
importance as agents in the drama of the tale, serve to authenticate the
genuineness of an individual's sanctity. Moreover, the miracle, standing as it does outside the normative round of experience, paradoxically
becomes the *topos* which is the most accurate location of the dwelling
place of the holy in this world, that is the saint.

Early Christian ideas concerning sanctity were often apocalyptic,
anti-establishment, and severely ascetic. The Roman authorities, who
were normally tolerant of religious pluralism insofar as it did not jeopardize the empire's political stability, considered those whom the
Christians believed to be saints as the ring leaders of a novel, barbarous
Oriental religious fifth column. During the period of the historical persecutions, many Christian leaders preached an ideology of sanctity
which urged a militant belligerency on the part of the faithful as the
norm for Christian membership. Such dire apocalypticism overflows
from such texts as the *Martyrdom of Polycarp*[13] or from the Roman
judicial accounts of the trials of Christians or from such inflamed teach-
ings as Tertullian's *De Fuga in Persecutione*.[14] Here Tertullian argued

12. Ibid., p. 297.

13. Herbert Musurillo, *The Acts of the Christian Martyrs* (Oxford, 1972), p. 11:
"But the other [the prosecuting governor] insisted once again, saying: 'Swear by the
emperor's Genius!' He [Polycarp] answered: 'If you delude yourself into thinking that
I will swear by the emperor's Genius, as you say, and if you pretend not to know who
I am, listen and I will tell you plainly: I am a Christian. And if you would like to learn
the doctrine of Christianity set aside a day and listen."

14. Tertullian, in J. J. Thierry, ed., *De Fuga in Persecutione, CCSL*, Vol. 2, part
II (Turnhout, 1954), pp. 1146–47: "Porro quis fugiet persecutionem, nisi qui timebit?
Quis timebit, nisi qui non amabit? Spiritus uero si consulas, quid magis sermone illo
Spiritus probat? Namque omnes paene ad martyrium exhorta[n]tur, non ad fugam, ut

that the Christian has a duty not to flee persecution, even if that persecution is likely to result in death, because God's providence had planned for the persecution! Personal sacrifice, even of one's life, was an obligation of the faithful if the state infringed on the free exercise of his religious belief; to act otherwise was to thwart Providence.

The secular authorities, no matter how benign or judicious their rule in other matters, were to be hindered in implementing civic policy if and when that policy conflicted with Christian teaching. Such a position which believed the Christian community and the state to be necessarily in opposition, was held by many prominent Christians. It seems to have been sanctioned even in the most dire of times. Even if the very existence of the state were threatened by invaders from outside, Christians had a moral duty to refuse service in the armed forces. In his *De Corona,* Tertullian concluded that no Christian could be a soldier without seriously compromising his faith.[15] Such anti-establishment views did not survive for very long once the period of persecutions was over. There was little need for such combative rhetoric once the Christian church had itself become the official religion of the state under Constantine.

The Communion of Saints

What survived the polemics, the persecutions, and the memory of the mutilated corpses of the saintly martyrs of the first two and a half centuries of the church was an old idea given new life, an idea of enormous power which grew slowly at first and provided for the vocation of sanctity without the same fervid hostility to authority, and most crucially without the necessary sacrifice of one's life. This new thinking on the role of the charismatic leader made one fundamental change: it recast the earlier understanding of sanctity from that of the isolated

---

et illius commemoremur . . . sed in martyriis uti glorificetur qui est passus pro uobis"; see also Frend, *Martyrdom and Persecution* pp. 254–84.

15. Tertullian, *De Corona,* ed. A. Kroyman, in *CCSL,* Vol. 2, part II (Turnhout, 1954), p. 1039. Tertullian urges believers to become soldiers of Christ; he is not intending this remark to be taken as metaphor: "O militem gloriosum in deo! Suffragia exinde, et res apud acta, et reus ad praefectorem." See also H. Musurillo, *The Acts of the Pagan Martyrs* (Oxford, 1954), pp. 236–46. It is interesting to note how Tertullian's language influenced the later Middle Ages; see Peter Damian's understanding of the saints as God's special athletes in *Sermo XIII, PL* 144, col. 568.

figure of the heroic charismatic individual diametrically opposed to the existing order, the Christ or an Origen, to a view which presented sanctity in more communal terms, more as a product of corporate responsibility. The glory and encomiastic celebration reserved for the *unus sanctus* was now to be extended to one based on a vision of *fraternitas sanctorum*. Viewed from an administrative vantage point, this changed understanding of sanctity may be related to the increased desire for centralization and consolidation taking place in the church at roughly this time. The Council of Nicaea meeting in the late spring of 325, particularly Canon 6, effectively moved to strengthen its Metropolitans and thus enhanced the powers of traditional bureaucratic centers.

Although the important doctrine of *communio sanctorum* was formally introduced in the first quarter of the fourth century, perhaps as part of a response to the growing power and separatism of the Donatists,[16] and was not referred to by name until it appeared in the pseudo-Augustine letters attributed to Caesarius of Arles, it was to continue to shape Christian thinking on sanctity long after that heretical group was forgotten.[17] It is well to note that worship of the saints amongst the people had been going on for some considerable time. Roman catacombs bear third-century inscriptions which read *vivas inter sanctos* and *refrigera cum spiritu sancto*. But let us return to the theology of *communio sanctorum*. The doctrine asserts that communion of saints is a mystical union of the faithful on earth, the suffering in purgatory, and the saints in heaven into one spiritual body with Christ as its head. Although Kirsch and others have suggested that we can see the doctrine implicit in the works of the Alexandrian school, notably in Clement of Alexander's *Stromateis* and in Origen's *Exhortatio ad Martyrium,* the doctrine is fully expressed only in the works of the later Latin Fathers.[18] Both St. Ambrose in his *De Poenitentia* and St. Augustine in his *Enchiridion* discuss it.[19] Although Augustine never referred to

16. F. L. Cross, *The Oxford Dictionary of the Christian Church* (Oxford, 1974), p. 419.

17. The power of the Donatists declined steadily after Augustine's vigorous attack during the Conference of Carthage in 411.

18. Kirsch claims that we can see the doctrine of *communio sanctorum* in Clement of Alexandria, *Stromateis, PG* 8, cols. 1289–96. Clement, arguing from the position of Basil's *Exegeticorum,* develops the idea that one can be called a martyr if one intensely desires to be one; this idea places a premium on the intensity of one's spiritual life; see also Origen, *Exhortatio ad Martyrium, PG* 11, cols. 563 ff.

19. The doctrine is really only given its first full expression in Ambrose, *De Poenitentia, PL* 16, cols. 510–13. Ambrose derives his argument from what he believed to

the doctrine by name, he presented one of its earliest and clearest elaborations, arguing that there was a logical necessity in the *Civitas Dei* for the idea of a communion of saints, one in which a *unitas caritatis* embraces the saints in heaven, the angels, and the believers on earth.[20] The Augustinian position became the basis for the dogma as it was later formalized in the syncretistic writings of Peter Lombard and in the theology of Aquinas.[21]

The crucial point for our study is to ask whether this doctrine influenced the genre and, if so, how. The genre was unequivocally affected by the doctrine, but in some quite specific areas, chiefly in the way the sacred biographer viewed the idea of human personality and in the way sources were employed. As we might expect in a religious climate where the teaching descended to the faithful through the ministry of the clergy, there were two dominant traditions governing a given teaching at any one time: the learned and the popular. Of course, there likely were innumerable subtle derivations from these two positions, but in the main, given the distance between the hierarchy and the laity in matters theological, such a theological dialectic seems to have existed. The nuanced understanding of the theology of *communio sanctorum* as it was carefully shaped under the scrutiny of an Augustine, a Gregory the Great, or an Aquinas only slowly entered the mainstream to become part of the religious mentality of the uneducated laity and its ministers. In the hands of teachers, priests, and monks more pious than thoughtful, we find that—rather than a sophisticated theological dis-

---

be Paul's remarks (in 1 Corinthians 5:7) on the universality of the Eucharist as it unites the church of the faithful. Augustine, in E. Evans, ed., *Enchiridion, CCSL*, Vol. 46, part XIII (Turnhout, 1969), pp. 79–80. In Augustine's *Ennaratio in Psalmum XXXVI, PL* 36, cols. 385–86, he discusses this ideas that the *unitas caritatis* creates an effective union by embracing the saints with the angels in heaven: "ut ipse totius caput civitatis Jerusalem, omnibus connumeratis fidelibus ab initio usque in finem, adjunctis etiam legionibus et exercitibus Angelorum, ut fiat illa una civitas sub uno rege, et una quadam provincia sub uno imperatore, felix in perpetua pace et salute, laudans Deum sine fine, beata sine fine."

20. Augustine, *De Civitate Dei, CCSL* ed. Bernard Dombart and Alphonse Kalb, Vol. 47, 48 (Turnhout, 1955).

21. J. Pelikan, *The Christian Tradition: A History of the Development of the Doctrine*, Vol. 3, *The Growth of Medieval Theology 600–1300* (Chicago, 1978), pp. 174–84. Aquinas's Aristotelianism, in its insistence on the integrity of the particular, would have caused him to view with some skepticism these idealizing ideologies; see J. Collins, "The Thomistic Philosophy of the Angels," *Catholic University of America Philosophical Studies* (Washington, 1947), Vol. 89, pp. 175–76; and M. M. Schen, "The Categories of Being in Aristotle and St. Thomas," *Catholic University of America Philosophical Studies* (Washington, 1944), Vol. 88, p. 76.

cussion of the commonality of belief uniting heaven and earth—the doctrine of the communion of saints is now presented in a populist frame, stripped largely of its theological baggage, whose central theological point argues that righteous individual Christians are identical *sub specie aeternitatis*. One can imagine the generations of congregations repeating the ancient formula from the Apostles' Creed, *Credo in . . . sanctorum communionem,* while surrounded by glass and sculptural images of the saints. Surely, from what we know of literacy levels throughout the Middle Ages, it is fair to presume that these congregations little understood the sophisticated theological speculation that supported the doctrine of *communio sanctorum* which made possible the glass and sculptural representations surrounding their worship. In sum, a popular theology which proposed the diminishment of the individual replaced, for the bulk of the populace, a learned discussion concerning the manner in which *caritas* unified the mystical body of the church. The effect on sacred biography of this populist idea of sanctity, although seldom discussed in a study of literary structures, reveals the method governing the use of sources in these biographies.

Reginald and the *Communio Sanctorum*

In his *Life of Saint Malchus,* Reginald of Canterbury framed his discussion concerning the use of sources and textual conflation in the composition of saints' lives within the larger conceptual frame of the doctrine of the *communio sanctorum*.[22] Reginald, born in France sometime between 1030 and 1050, emigrated to England and by 1092 had entered the famous Benedictine monastery of St. Augustine's Canterbury, perhaps the most influential of English Benedictine houses. We know precious little about Reginald's personal life. He appears, however, to have been a gifted poet—indeed, he was elected to the post of abbey poet—and brought to Canterbury the compositional traditions of quantitative verse and a penchant for an epic-didactic style practiced so gracefully in his homeland by such contemporaries as Marbod, bishop of Rennes (d. 1123); Balderic, abbot of Bourgueil (d. 1130); Hildebert of Lavardin, bishop of Tours (d. 1133); and Lambert of St. Bertin, abbot of St. Omer (d. 1125).[23] Reginald exchanged verses with

22. Levi Lind, "The Vita Sancti Malchi of Reginald of Canterbury," *Illinois University Studies in Language and Literature* 27 (1942): 5–245.

23. Ibid., pp. 9–11.

Lambert, some of which are extant. Unfortunately, we lose track of Reginald after 1109. Some have read into this documentary silence an indication of his death, while others have suggested that he lived as late as 1136.[24] What is interesting about these scant details of his life is that Reginald was a distinguished Benedictine poet writing as the official poet of the most prestigious monastic house in twelfth-century England during the apogee of Latin verse compositions from the pens of monks. Given such circumstances, it is not unreasonable to assume that Reginald had achieved a modicum of fame in monasteries outside Canterbury. Perhaps that fame as versifier of the *Vita Sancti Malchi*, and that very text, reached his younger Cistercian brother to the north, Walter Daniel.

Reginald's major work, the *Vita Sancti Malchi*, although it may have been begun in France, was completed in England. According to L. R. Lind, his modern editor, it was Reginald's most important work and took more than a quarter-century to complete, from 1082 to 1107. Reginald's work celebrates Malchus, the celibate Syrian hermit saint of Chalcis, in 3344 rhymed hexameter lines. Although Reginald acknowledges St. Jerome's life of Malchus as his direct source, Lind has demonstrated Reginald's indebtedness to Vergil, Ovid, Martianus Capella, Persius, Terence, the Bible, and his contemporary Hildebert of Le Mans.[25] Such reading indicates Reginald's scholarly disposition; certain of these classical authors, such as Martianus Capella and Persius, were not common fare in twelfth-century Benedictine houses. This long poem (Lind has called it epic in proportions) was intended for his monastic brethren at Christ Church: *Intendit igitur auctor in hoc suo libellulo/se et alios quosque praesertim sui homines ordinis, monachus monachos.*[26]

But it is not the work itself that I want to discuss; rather, it is Reginald's *exordium*, the *De Intentione in Sequentem Librum.*[27] The *exordium* had by Reginald's time become almost an integral part of the *dispositio* of sacred biography. Like his monastic counterparts Walter Daniel and Eddius Stephanus, monk of Ripon (d. 722?), Reginald presented his readers with a carefully argued account of his method. In his *De Intentione*, Reginald argues issues pertinent to this discussion, namely his use of sources, the credibility of the incidents he attributes

24. Ibid., pp. 11–13, especially notes 13 and 17.

25. Ibid., p. 11, note 13.

26. Ibid., pp. 19–21.

27. Ibid., p. 39.

to Malchus, and his own integrity as biographer. Reginald takes up his argument with the familiar trope of *captatio benevolentiae,* depicting himself as a humble servant having been asked to complete a work which far exceeded his ability. He refers to this, his life's most ambitious work, as *in hoc suo libello.* His hopes for his little book are great; he seeks nothing less than to have created a narrative which will give to the reader genuine insight into Malchus's life.

What could Reginald have intended the reader to experience? He tells us that he did not intend his narrative to render a depiction of refracted reality, the literary work as *speculum naturae,* a type so dear to medieval audiences. He claims that the *Vita Sancti Malchi* presents the reader with the chance of a "face-to-face contemplation" of the deeds of his hero, Malchus: *Cuius vitam et actus auctor iste propterea describit quoniam ibi/lector non quasi in speculo sed tamquam facie ad faciem intueri poterit.*[28] Reginald's remarks underline his conviction that he has told his tale in an attempt to depict Malchus's life with exactitude. They further suggest his attention to the appropriate use of language and remind one of Walter Daniel's intention to convey the immediacy of feeling he and his fellow monks experienced *sic sensimus omnes* the night Aelred died. Both Reginald and Walter insist that the nature of their experiences was so intense that the requisite presentation of those searing experiences requires a text which employs language explicitly designed to move the reader's affective apprehension of the moment. Such an argument is not terribly distant from Bultmann's insistence that genuine understanding for the past is based on an existential experience.

Reginald's interest in his narrative's persuasive ability has a basis beyond both the sheer aesthetic delight it must have afforded him and the presentation of the facts of Malchus's life. Reginald expected that through a dramatic recreation of the life of the holy Malchus, one in which he employed both classical and Christian rhetoric, his biography would lead his readers to avoid vice and live a virtuous life, as the pseudo-Horace said, *incitare ut vitia respuant, virtutes appetant, patientiam scilicet pudicitiam et cetera.*[29]

Having expressed his hopes for his composition, Reginald then turned to a discussion of his method. Like that of Walter Daniel, his discussion has the tone of *apologia* about it. The issue he confronts again turns on the nature of the miraculous deeds he has ascribed to his holy hero and his own credibility as biographer in light of his re-

28. Ibid., pp. 38–40.

29. Ibid., p. 39, 231.

porting of these deeds. Reginald opens his argument justifying his use of varied sources independent of Malchus by stating the general principle of the doctrine of *communio sanctorum* as he understood it. He begins, curiously, with an example of a city and the many relationships it contains, discussing both the corporate identity and the individual identity of members living within the polity. He concludes, through analogy with the polity, that the saintly individual and the saintly community are indivisible; they exist both individually and interdependently. Although the individual saint lives within the larger world of the community of saints, this pluralist corporate world exists also as a unity within the individual saint:

> *Ibi namque tanta in membris est confederatio, ut totum sit proprium quod est commune, et commune quod est proprium, sic et in corpore aecclesiae fidei quae per dilectionem operatur tanta vis est ut quecunque sunt bona fidelium singulorum, sint et omnium, et quae sunt omnium, sint et singulorum.*[30]

Reginald's language is unusually precise for an *exordium* in a work of sacred biography, and it underlines the importance of the doctrine for the genre. Reginald argues that his discussion of *communio sanctorum* has an actual application in the figure of the holy Malchus himself. His remarks, although a slightly disingenuous *argumentum ad hominem,* are paraphrased as follows: it would be impious for anyone to believe that the saintly Malchus was anything other than just and holy and beloved of the Lord (*Malchus igitur quem nefas est credere*). Indeed, Malchus was so exemplary a man that he was filled with the spirit of the just (i.e., the saints: *Spiritu omnium iustorum plenus fuit*).[31] Reginald's argument thus far is the very spirit of orthodoxy and a commonplace of medieval pious writing. It is Reginald's wish that his readers acknowledge the presence of this sentiment in his remarks prior to his introduction of the more controversial heart of the argument. He resumes: Since you believe that it would be a sin (*nefas*) to believe that Malchus was anything other than just, holy, and beloved of the Lord and filled with the spirits of our saintly ancestors (at this point, the argument takes an abrupt *ad hominem* turn but one which he shrewdly justifies by an appeal to dogma), then I do not lie, however great the deeds I attribute to Malchus himself (*quantaslibet ergo vir-*

---

30. Ibid., p. 40.

31. Ibid., pp. 40–41: "Malchus igitur quem nefas est credere non fuisse iustum, sanctum, domino dilectum, spiritu omnium iustorum plenus fuit. . ."

tutes Malcho personaliter ascripserimus non a vero deviavimus).[32] Before we examine Reginald's argument, I would note that my translation of *virtutes* as "deeds" reflects its application in medieval Latin religious tracts as a synonym for deeds that are often of a miraculous nature, and, as I discuss below, this medieval understanding of *virtutes* is derived from the use of the word in Greco-Roman biography.[33]

Reginald's justification for his method comes on the reader suddenly; and it is a quite staggering position, claiming for itself considerable authorial prerogative in the phrase *quantaslibet ergo virtutes* ("whatsoever, or howsoever wondrous or great the deed").[34] Although separated by almost seven centuries, it is the same argument Gregory of Tours used in his treatise on the *Vitae Patrum*, that is, the appeal to the substantial similarity of the behavior of Christian saints. Gregory wrote that one life nourishes all lives: *una tamen omnes vita corporis alit in mundo*.[35] Reginald and Gregory alike believed that in a theological system which presumed the indivisibility of divine truth, one whose most profound truths sanctioned the possibility of transcendence through an enactment of the life of Christ, those mortals who achieved this sanctity came into full possession of this divine truth and became in turn possessed by it, one with it. The logical extension of this argument for both Gregory and Reginald was the incorporation of human ego into the divine personality. The argument was not received as warmly by the philosophical intelligentsia of the church. Aquinas, for one, explicitly rejected this notion of the loss of unique human characteristics.[36] And, although this ideology of sanctity posed the greatest of barriers to the growth of a critical religious historiography, it was nonetheless held by sacred biographers against those critics who might accuse them of the improper use of sources or attack their work because of a lack of any rational historical method. Let us now turn to a less theologically circumspect but not untypical presentation of this doctrine in another English Benedictine setting.

32. Ibid., p. 41.

33. On this issue of *virtutes*, see B. Colgrave, ed., *Two Lives of Saint Cuthbert: A Life by an Anonymous Monk of Lindisfarne and Bede's Prose Life* (Cambridge, 1940), p. 62: *De Prefatione Scribendi*. Bede occasionally uses *virtus* in this manner; see P. F. Jones, *A Concordance to the "Historica Ecclesiastica" of Bede* (Cambridge, Mass., 1929), p. 574.

34. Lind, *The Vita Sancti Malchi*, p. 41.

35. See Chapter 1, above; and Gregory of Tours, in Krusch, *MGH* 1, pp. 662–63.

36. Thomas Aquinas, p. 131, n.21.

Eddius Stephanus and the Case of St. Wilfrid

A less sophisticated and rather dramatic application of this idea of *communio sanctorum* to justify quite extraordinary borrowings can be seen in the *Vita Sancti Wilfridi* by Eddius Stephanus.[37] Unlike Reginald's life of St. Malchus, which celebrated one of the acknowledged heroes of the faith, a Syrian hermit from the early Christian era, Eddius's biography was of his contemporary, indeed a friend. We know little about Eddius Stephanus. It is believed that he was a newly professed quire monk with some musical ability when he was first noticed by Wilfrid at the Benedictine house in Canterbury.[38] In 669, on Wilfrid's movement to reascend the see of York (he was first chosen by Alcfrith in 663/64 but was ousted by Chad, who was nominated by King Oswy in 666), he brought Eddius north with him and had him installed in the Benedictine house at Ripon.[39]

Ripon was a monastery dear to Wilfrid; he had once been its abbot, had introduced Benedictine monasticism to its brethren, and had himself been the primary reason why Ripon adopted the Roman method for calculating Easter. Eddius appears to have lived uninterruptedly at Ripon; he is present in 709 on Wilfrid's retirement there shortly before the old bishop's death. Eddius lived within the shadow of Wilfrid for a period of forty years, and in light of such proximity we might presume some intimacy between the two men, certainly in the late 660s and early 670s. Corroboration of this long friendship exists in the circumstances which dictated Eddius's undertaking to write Wilfrid's biography.

Eddius was asked to write the life by Acca, a disciple of Wilfrid, who later became bishop and his successor to the see of Hexham. It is unlikely that Acca would have asked someone to write Wilfrid's life

37. W. Levinson, ed., *Vita Wilfridi I*, in *MGH: Scriptorum Rerum Merovingicarum, Passiones Vitaeque Sanctorum Aevi Merovingici* 6 (1913): 163–263. Levinson's introduction remains excellent. For a brief introduction to the figure of St. Wilfrid of York, see E. S. Duckett, *Anglo-Saxon Saints and Scholars* (New York, 1947), pp. 101–214. For more on Wilfrid's activities as a reform-minded evangelical minister, see Bede's remarks in Books IV and V of his *Ecclesiastical History of the English Nation*, ed. J. A. Giles, Vol. 3, especially pp. 236–56.

38. Bede, *Ecclesiastical History*, p. 11: "primusque, excepto Jacobo, de quo supra diximus, cantandi magister Northumbrorum ecclesiis Eddi cognomento Stephanus fuit, invitatus de Cantia a reverendissimo viro Wilfrido, qui primus inter episcopos, qui de Anglorum gente essent, Catholicum vivendi morem ecclesiis Anglorum tradere didicit."

39. Levinson, *Vita Wilfridi I*, pp. 180–82.

who was either hostile toward or ignorant of the man and his many
deeds. One would therefore presume a high degree of accuracy
throughout the biography. But such a presumption would be incorrect,
for one of the more fascinating facts to emerge from Eddius's biography of Wilfrid, a fact made all the more curious when we consider
Eddius's half-century of acquaintance with Wilfrid, is that not only
does his life of Wilfrid contains many extraordinary elements, but it
makes use of a variety of source materials, some of which have nothing
at all to do with the dynamic Wilfrid of York, as Eddius well knew.[40]

Eddius prefaced his *Vita Sancti Wilfridi* with a dedicatory epistle to
his patron, Acca, bishop of Hexham. His epistle, like those of Walter
Daniel and Reginald of Canterbury, tells us much of his method and
has, as I hope to show, much in common with these two works. Eddius
opens by adopting the traditional personal of the humble narrator, employing the rhetorical pose of *captatio benevolentiae*. He presents himself as a man who has been asked by his superior to assume a lofty
task far beyond his meager rhetorical skills: *Est enim et hoc opus arduum et meae intellengentiae et eloquentiae facultas exigua*.[41] The use
of the *captatio* persona, *facultas exigua*, although a stock motif in the
classical exordium, was to become part of the tradition of medieval
sacred biography in the West through the influence of Sulpicius's dedicatory letter to his friend Desiderius with which he prefaced his *Vita
Sancti Martini*.[42]

Aside from Eddius's awareness and use of the tradition of the *captatio* persona in his exordium, there remains another far more striking
example of this sacred biographer's use of sources. Eddius's opening
gambit, his language and employment of the traditional *captatio*, is itself borrowed. This is quite an extraordinary instance of the appropriation of another's work; there is little imagination required to proclaim
one's limitations in one line of prose. Indeed, carefully copying the
remark would seem more time-consuming than merely making up some
ingratiating and self-deprecatory untruth. Nonetheless, the line is
taken verbatim from Victorius of Aquitaine's mid-fifth-century Easter

40. Ibid., p. 193: "Praeceptorum vestrorum magnitudine, O venerabiles domini
Acca episcopus et Tatberchtus Abbas [abbot of Ripon], et totius familiae ambitu su-
peratus, utinam ut tam effectu parere valeam quam voto."

41. Ibid., p. 193.

42. Fontaine, ed., *Vita Sancti Martini*, vol. 1, pp. 248–50: "Seuerus Desiderio fratri carissimo."

calendar, a work of computation which fixes the date for Easter, written at the request of Hilarius, bishop of Rome.[43] Victorius's treatise is a learned and rather specialized text for the sacred biographer to be searching in for such rhetorical crumbs. It would have been far easier to copy such a remark from a prefatory epistle in any one of the number of *libri vitae sanctorum* in the monastic library. Why did Eddius quote verbatim from this somewhat obscure text? Given the availability of such sentiments in other *vitae sanctorum*, I believe he intended considerably more than the borrowing at first suggests.[44]

Although to impute motives to individuals who are long dead and who have not expressed themselves specifically on a subject is fraught with methodological pitfalls, I feel confident that we can accurately interpret Eddius's motives and moreover that we can group them under two major categories. First, the borrowing from the Easter calendar allows him to display his learning and to acknowledge one of Wilfrid's major triumphs at the Synod of Whitby in 663/64. Wilfrid championed the primacy of the Roman practice over that of the Celtic for deciding Easter at Whitby. Wilfrid and those involved in that intense struggle would have known and possibly used Victorius's work on the calendar, because it too reflected the Roman view. Thus, Eddius's citation accomplishes some complex associations with a marvel of economy: it rings a responsive chord in those to whom the debate was so crucial; it reminds them of Eddius's awareness of their struggle and his reading of the learned tomes they used in their winning arguments; and it is an encomium which celebrates their triumphant struggle with Wilfrid for the church. Such praise, albeit oblique, was bound to curry favor and guarantee an audience from Wilfrid's supporters. Second, the encomium would also have served as a mild rebuke—rather like being reminded of a long-forgotten unpleasantry—to those responsible, at the Synod of Austerfield in 703, for Wilfrid's loss of the see of York. Seen in this light, what might appear at first glance as a simple case of what a modern reading would call a plagiarism is on examination a

43. T. Mommsen, ed., *Victorii Aquitani: Cvrsus Paschalis Annorum DXXXII ad Hilarum Archidiaconum Ecclesiae Romanae*, in *MGH: Auctorum Antiquissimorum, Chronica Minora Saec. IV, V, VI, VII* (Berlin, 1892), pp. 667–735.

44. Ibid., p. 677: "Domino vere sancto et in Christo venerabili fratri Hilaro archidiacono Victorius. Utiniam praeceptis tuis, archidiacone venerabilis Hilare, tam effectu valeam parere quam voto. Est enim et opus hoc arduum et meae intellegentiae facultas exigua."

narrative tool of considerable subtlety and extraordinary economy. It is clear that such recognition—similar to that observed in the case of Walter Daniel—depended on an audience intimately acquainted with such materials, which seems to have been true in this extraliturgical case.

Eddius's Appeal to Confidence

Like his Benedictine brother Reginald of Canterbury, Eddius in his epistle to Acca appealed to his readers for their faith in the truth of his narrative: *Obsecro itaque eos lecturi sunt ut fidem dictis adhibeant.*[45] Rhetorical convention as antique as the *Rhetorica ad Herennium* sanctioned such an address to the reader's confidence. Eddius goes even further, however, and concludes this appeal with a truly grand gesture as to his text's authenticity. He says that he would rather remain silent than to report those things he knows to be false, *alioquin tacere quam falsa dicere maluissem.*[46] A reader not sensitive to the traditions of sacred biography would have little reason to doubt such sincere and, for biography, such reasonable behavior on the part of the author. However, such a gesture is also part of the tradition. If we were to take the remark at face value, we would not only misunderstand the intention of the statement, but, if we were able to defy time and query Eddius face to face, would surely find him bemused and not a little piqued by our obtuseness. Once again, Eddius's very appeal is itself a borrowing. It is taken in its entirety from the anonymous *Vita Sancti Cuthberti* (composed ca. 699–705).[47] Before we suspect Eddius of some special predilection for laziness or some pathological addiction to lying, involving a wanton disregard of his readers' trust and a disrespect for the life of St. Cuthbert, I want to point out that once again Eddius was simply following the exemplary models of his ancestors; he is following an *argumentum ex auctorite.* This very passage which he has taken

45. Levinson, *Vita Wilfridi I*, p. 193.

46. Ibid., p. 193: "Neque enim me quicquam audaci temeritate, nisi quod conpertum et probatum a fidelibus sit, scripsisse arbitrentur; alioquin tacere quam falsa dicere maluissem."

47. Colgrave, *Two Lives of St. Cuthbert,* p. 62: "Obsecro itaque eos qui lecturi sunt ut fidem dictis adhibeant, neque me quicquam nisi quod compertum et probatum sit, scripsisse arbitrentur, alioquin tacere quam falsa dicere maluissem."

from *Vita Sancti Cuthberti* was itself lifted by that unknown author from Sulpicius's *Vita Sancti Martini*.[48]

In fact, of the first three hundred fifty words of the prologue to the *Vita Sancti Cuthberti,* only six cannot be accounted for from other compositions.[49] Another important example of this rather unfamiliar practice of what we might call textual embedding, an example which could not have escaped Eddius, also exists in the prologue to the Cuthbert. The anonymous author gives thanks to Bishop Eadfrith for having offered him the chance to complete so worthy a task. He says that he believes the composition of the life of the holy Cuthbert will be of great value to him: *Magna namque cum laetitia suscepi uestre caritatis imperium. Etenim ingens mihi lucrum est atque utilitas hoc ipsum quod recordor sancti Cuthberti.*[50] Once again, these very simple sentiments are borrowed; they have been taken verbatim from one of the most widely read saints' lives, Evagrius of Antioch's translation (ca. 373) of Athanasius's *Vita Sancti Antonii* (ca. 356–62).

The line from Evagrius's Antony reads, *Magna cum laetitia suscepi vestrae charitatis imperium. Etenim mihi ingens . . . quod recordor Antonii.*[51] The sheer audacity of this borrowing—the simple substitution of the seventh-century English saint's name for his fourth-century Middle Eastern counterpart—surely confirms that indeed such embedding has a very sophisticated purpose: it is by conscious design different from a system designed to display learning through a plethora of obstruse allusions (although this is often part of the product of this practice, as I show below). Such practice is also conceptually unlike the sort of systematic use of unacknowledged citations one commonly finds in such exegetical aids as a *catena* or *glossa*. The primary purpose of such textual embedding is theological; that is, it argues the case

48. Fontaine, *Vita Sancti Martini,* Vol. 1, p. 253: "Obsecro autem eos qui lecturi sunt, ut fidem dictis adhibeant."

49. See Levinson, *Vita Wilfridi I,* p. 193; and Colgrave, *Two Lives of St. Cuthbert,* p. 310.

50. Colgrave, *Two Lives of St. Cuthbert,* p. 62.

51. Evagrius of Antioch, *Vita Sancti Antonii Abbatis, PL* 73, cols. 126–27: "magna cum laetitia suscepi vestrae charitatis imperium. Etenim mihi ingens lucrum est atque utilitas hoc ipsum quod recordor Antonii et vos cum admiratione audientes." That these manuscript traditions were subject to some change is evidenced by this quotation in the recent edition by C. Mohrmann, ed., "Vita di Antonio," in *Scrittori Greci e Latini* (Verona, 1974), pp. 4–5: "Magnum [lucrum] enim mihi est ex hoc, et si tantum memoriam faciam Antonii."

for the doctrine of *communio sanctorum* (the essential oneness of the
individual in Christ and his saints) in biography.

Agnellus of Ravenna, *Virtus*, and Talking Pictures

The embedding method employed to accomplish this spiritualizing of
the *acta sanctorum* provides for a bold associative frame of correspondences between a variety of otherwise unrelated texts and argues that
any understanding of individual sanctity must be achieved through this
collective association. I would now like to demonstrate a classic instance of this technique of embedding as it is used by a master, Agnellus of Ravenna, in his *Liber Pontificalis Ravennatensis*. Although not
strictly a *liber sanctorum*—though some of the bishops were revered
as saints—Agenellus's great collection of biographical sketches of the
bishops of Ravenna nonetheless uses this technique most skillfully.

The saint's life shares some features with ancient travel literature
and the romance. Christian sacred biography not only constructs plots
which develop narratives of spiritual *peregrinatio* but also employs elements more commonly thought of as picaresque: long, arduous jour-
neys with accompanying perils, saccharine scenes of separation and
return (inspired by the pseudo-Clementine *Recognitions*), depictions
of maidens being threatened sexually by pirates or other brigands, and
a veritable bestiary of miraculous beasts.[52] Virtually all saints' lives
exhibit some of these characteristics, while some, such as the *Vita
Sancti Eustachii* to name just one, contain them all. Undoubtedly both
Monteverdi and Dörrie are correct in their judgment that Achilles Tatius's *The Love of Leucippe and Clitophon* (ca. second century A.D.)
and Heliodorus of Emesa's *Aethiopica* (ca. third century A.D.) exercised an influence in the formative composition of the Eustace tale.[53]

A comparison of the saint's life with its counterpart from the world
of romance is illustrative because it also reveals the singular difference
which distinguishes between these genres. Although one could present
a convincing case that the essential structure of the plot of the sacred
biography, like its counterpart in Hellenistic romance, relies on the

52. Graham Anderson, *Ancient Fiction: The Novel in the Graeco-Roman World*
(Totowa, N.J., 1984).

53. Angelo Monteverdi, "I testi della leggenda di S. Eustachio," *Studi Medievali*
3 (1908–11): 489–98; H. Dörrie, "Die Griechischen Romane und das Christentum,"
Phil 93 (1938): 274; see also B. E. Perry, *The Ancient Romances*, pp. 346–47.

dramatic tension inherent in scenes of separation and return, on the struggle between good and evil, on continual shifts in setting and time, and on an episodic narrative line,[54] there is one crucial thematic difference between the genre: their mutually distinctive understandings of the nature of heroic virtue.

The differences between the heroism of the saint and that of the romance hero is analogous to the difference between dependent and autonomous actions: the saint is moved whereas the romance hero moves. The sacred biographer locates the locus for the heroism, the correct behavior of the saint, in the gift of Providence. The romance hero is depicted as self-directed, the motivation for correct behavior coming from personal choice.

Both genres isolate the actions of the hero as they defy one life-threatening adventure after another in the pursuit of opportunities to exhibit and realize greater virtue. In the saint's life, the emphasis on deeds performed according to a religiously sanctioned plan, on appropriate public behavior as both a sign and a measure of saintly heroism, on the virtuous act as a mimetic paradigm, is derived from two closely related but distinctive traditions: The Greco-Roman and the Semitic. A convincing case could be made that the cult of the saints evolved from certain practices taken by the early Jewish-Christian community from the hellenized Judaism which, as Meeks points out, they would have encountered in the more populous trading cities of the eastern Mediterranean, exactly the sort of places where Pauline Christianity was evangelized with greatest success.[55]

These early Christians, like most religious groups which preceded them, borrowed much of their cultic practice and their ideology. Indeed, although not often the subject of scholarly investigation, even the Greeks and Jews had their "saints" and their cults of saint worship; the early church could hardly avoid being influenced by such practices. In some instances, ancient testimony concerning the evolution of these traditions survives. In his *Adversus Jovinianum,* Jerome makes benign reference to the Pythagoreans who turn away from the world to live solitary lives in the desert.[56] Lucius states unambiguously that the fifth-

---

54. Anderson, *Ancient Fiction,* pp. 30–31.

55. W. A. Meeks, *The First Urban Christians: The Social World of The Apostle Paul* (New Haven, 1983), chap. 1.

56. Jerome, *Adversus Jovinianum, PL* 23, col. 298: "Nam et Pythagoraei hujuscemodi frequentiam declinantes, in solitudine et desertis locis habitare consueverunt."

century cult of the Christian saints Cosmas and Damian, worshiped at
Cyrrhus in Syria, was a sequel to the worship of the Greek god Ascle-
pius, who was worshiped at the same shrine in antiquity and for the
same reason, the hope of healing. In Judaism, we have the important
heroic "saintly" figures of Elijah, the Therapeutae, the figures of Eleazar and the Maccabeean Mother and her seven sons in 2 Maccabees,
plus the popular apocryphal works, the *Martyrdom of Isaiah* and the
Lives of the Prophets. These latter two works take deliberate pains to
point out that the prophets died as *martyrs* for their religion, and they
present unambiguously the virtuous ideal toward which members of
the community were meant to strive. Medieval Christianity saw the
close connection between these pre-Christian saints and their Christian
descendants and, as Grabar points out, often used these Semitic figures
as subjects for their art.[57]

The Christian ideal of virtue—inherited from antiquity and revivified
in the intellectual cauldron of early Christian dialectic—was to become
a powerful conceptual tool in fashioning one of Christian sacred biography's unique characteristics, its use of historical sources. In the
hands of a master, the historical records which support the sacred biography are sometimes drawn from the most unlikely of sources and
utterly transformed.

Let us now examine Agnellus of Ravenna's extraordinary argument
for the justification of the sources he employed in his *Liber Pontificalis
Ravennatis.*[58] To begin, Agnellus derived his narrative accounts from
the evidence of the pictures in an unidentified church. He did not use
these depictions as guides in a work which purports to be a metaphor-
ical narrative of his subject's deeds but in an avowedly biographical
study which relies on the depiction as direct sources for events recounted in the biographies.

The justification of this questionable historiography is based on Agnellus's thesis concerning the function of Christian virtue in his subjects. In the ensuing discussion of *virtue,* in order to show the shift
between classical/Semitic heroic ideals on the one hand and those typ-
ified in medieval Christian sacred biography, I am using this term in its
broadest sense to describe a complex bundling of attitudes which include but are not limited to such categories as charity, piety, humility,

57. A. Grabar, *"Martyrium,"* *Recherches sur le culte des reliques et l'art chrétien
antique* (Paris, 1946), Vol. 2, pp. 20–21; for more on these Semitic antecedents of
Christian sanctity, see J. Downing, "Jesus and Martyrdom," *JTS* 14 (1963): 279–93.

58. O. Holder-Egger, ed., *Agnellus Liber Pontificalis Ecclesiae Ravennatis, MGH:
Scriptores Rerum Langobardicarum,* XVIII, 32 (Hanover, 1887).

and so on. Agnellus appeals to his readers' belief in the virtuous lives of his subjects as a guarantee of the authenticity of these lives. If the subject was a virtuous Christian, then any representation of him could not fail to capture the essential truth of that character. That character, in turn, was the single crucial aspect which validated the narrative's ethical historiography. Human behavior was inseparable from an ethical and theological matrix; indeed, for Agnellus, behavior outside this matrix was inconceivable. Within this frame, on the other hand—because of the human-divine hypostasis—all human behavior ceases to be bounded by the temporal spatial limits which are part of our normative experience of the world.

It is a curious method, to say the least, and one whose rationale can be understood if we first understand the tradition Agnellus is steeped in. His appeal to his audience's belief is based on the conviction that his subject's virtue was a guarantee of the heuristic worth of his narrative. His method, although radically novel in this application, is derived from a tradition which is an inextricable part of ancient biography. The classical idea of virtue was incorporated into the emerging Christian idea of sanctity, and it is this hybrid ideal of virtue which is the key to understanding Agnellus's rationale. The pomp and circumstance of the ancient world was ever present in Agnellus's beloved Ravenna. Ravenna was the urban benefactor of a wealth of Romano-Byzantine architecture, sculpture, and decorative civic embellishments of many kinds. Indeed, in Agnellus's mid-ninth-century city, a good deal of ancient Rome's grandeur must have still stood comparatively unscathed. Surely the equally rich legacy of ancient historical and biographical writing was as alive to this antiquarian-minded cleric as the stone monuments which enfolded him in their civic embrace.

Classical antiquity saw virtue as its own reward, the attainable *summum bonum* toward which all citizens should strive. In Latin texts, we often see the word *virtus* used to illustrate an internal, spiritual change which results from right action. Quintillian, in his *Institutes*, sees *uirtus* as a moral good, the absence of vice: *uirtus est fuga uitiorum*. In the *Bacchides*, Plautus uses the word to suggest excellence of character: *Mnesilochum . . . uiso ecquid eum ad uirtutem aut ad frugem opera sua compulerit*. Cicero sometimes restricts the attainment of virtue to the consequences of good actions, *virtus in usu sui tota posita est. . . .* Such a position was not limited to the great sages, such as Cicero, nor was it a phenomenon limited to the late republic. Biographers as early as Xenophon in both the *Memorabilia* and the *Agesilaus* and Isocrates in his *Encomium on Evagoras* (ca. 365 B.C.E.) believed that one of their chief responsibilities, if not the most important one, was the depiction of the deeds of virtuous men for the moral well-being of their audiences. In short, virtue is viewed by the preponderance of classical authors as an ethical consequence of the correct act.

The Peripatetic school, under the guidance of Aristotle, and the zealous interest in ethics that characterized this philosophical school forced a closer examination of motives, behavior, and human personality. Perhaps the leading biographer of the early Peripatetics, Aristoxenus, was, according to Jerome, one of the predecessors of Suetonius and *omnium longe doctissimus.* Aristoxenus's *Bioi Andron,* which included such lives as those of Pythagoras, Socrates, and Plato, established once and for all the Peripatetic school of biography, which, as Jenkinson suggests, proposed that "a man revealed his character through his actions."[59] Plutarch, heir to this tradition, whose importance to Christian biography is of the first order, makes this point quite clearly in the following remark in his *Life of Pericles:* "we must apply our understanding to objects which, when contemplated by the mind, give it delight and inspire it to aim at its own proper good. These objects consist of *virtuous deeds,* when a man has learnt about them he is filled with an eager desire *to imitate them.*"[60] For Plutarch, the achievement of virtue is efficacious both socially and morally: the serious study of proper actions in others, as depicted by the biographer, gives delight to the mind and emboldens the will to repeat those actions. Thus, the lives of the virtuous are pregnant reminders about moral responsibility both civic and private. Plutarch believed that the core of his biographical studies was the exemplification of correct living. Seneca proposed much the same thing in the concise remark *proponamus laudanda, inuenietur imitator* (let us set out to praise worthy things, an imitator will be found).[61]

However important the classical biographers believed the celebration of exemplary deeds was to their biographical form, they did not feel constrained to view these virtuous deeds as necessary constituents of actual historical events. Although this may appear contradictory, I am not proposing that they considered the depiction of these noble actions without historical value. Their understanding is somewhat more involved than a simple either-or equation would allow. Let me

59. D. R. Stuart, *Epochs of Greek and Roman Biography* (New York, 1967), pp. 131–54; E. Jenkinson, "Nepos—An Introduction to Latin Biography," in T. A. Dorey, ed., *Latin Biography* (London, 1967), p. 4.

60. B. Perrin, ed., *Plutarch's Lives* (London, 1916), Vol. 3, pp. 2–3.

61. A. J. Gossage, "Plutarch," in T. Dorey, *Latin Biography,* p. 45.

give an example of the complex attitudes that existed in antiquity concerning the nature of biographical writing, its relationship to its cousin historical writing, and the importance of the concept of the virtuous deed to this genre. Although St. Jerome attributes to Suetonius the remark that the founder of Roman biography was M. Terentius Varro, not a single scrap of Varro's putative biographical work survives. The earliest Latin biographer whose work is extant is Cornelius Nepos (ca. 99 ?–24 B.C.E.). Nepos, aside from being the earliest Roman biographer, was, according to Catullus, responsible for a three-volume outline history of the world written in the annalist fashion, his *Chronica*. As both biographer and annalist, Nepos is an excellent subject for our discussion.[62]

What did Nepos understand the scope of biography to include, and within that frame, what importance did he assign to the depiction of virtue as a didactic model to stimulate audience response? We must begin by saying that Nepos's style in *De Viris Illustribus* places him in the Peripatetic school, acknowledging at the outset his interest in the ethical dimension of the human story. But, like a number of his contemporaries, Nepos felt a certain ambivalence about the nature of the biographical art. In his opening remarks to his life of the Theban Pelopidas, Nepos expressed concern about the kind of narrative he employed. Nepos writes, because Pelopidas is better known to the historian, that he is "uncertain as to how to expound his deeds" (*cuius de virtutibus dubito quem ad modum exponam*).[63] Why does Nepos show such timidity, such doubt? What difference can it make that Pelopidas is better known to the historian? And what exactly does this last remark mean? Briefly, Nepos's doubt is grounded on the sharp shoals that he believed separated history and biography; he says that if he does explain these deeds of Pelopidas, he may appear to be writing history rather than recounting the life: *quod vereor, si res explicare incipiam, ne non vitam enarrare, sed historiam videar scribere.*[64]

Nepos's distinction is a curious one but not uncommon in the discussions concerning history and biography in antiquity. For Nepos, this distinction is based on the deeply held belief that the state and the public good transcended private interest, indeed, even acts indicative of private morality. Deeds done in the public interest have greater merit

---

62. E. O. Winstedt, (Oxford, 1904); the Loeb edition ed. and trans. by J. C. Rolfe, and the Oxford Classical Text, ed. by E. O. Winstedt, 1904.

63. Jenkinson, "Nepos," p. 5.

64. Ibid.

than those done by individuals for individuals. One feels in reading Nepos that the very motivations for these actions, the social versus the individual, are thought to be inherently antagonistic. Furthermore, because the tradition of the Peripatetic school, which he followed in the main, required that the subject be one whose life would serve as a sign of virtue to the reader, the subject invariably had to be a famous individual who was socially prominent. The biographer, in order to maintain the tradition of the genre, was required to use encomium and exemplary anecdote to excite his readers with a desire to imitate the virtue of the subject of his biography. On the other hand, the writing of history for Nepos and other intellectuals of his day was a serious affair (that is, with a more deliberately social venue) which, as Aristotle said, has to aim primarily at depicting truth with accuracy. Aristotle's distinction is based largely on his distinction of the roles of poetry and history: poetry aims at pleasure, history at truth through accuracy.

A second reason for Nepos's hesitancy concerns the issue of rhetoric broadly defined: each of the literary genres was identified by virtue of the type of language, style, decorum, and subject matter traditionally ascribed to it. Thus, for Nepos, a discussion of Pelopidas ought to be *a priori* a historical one, free from the obligatory employment of the tradition of encomium. As McQueen succinctly says in his study of the problem of history versus biography in the work of Quintus Curtius Rufus, "history describes in detail what its personages *do,* biography is more concerned in revealing what sort of person they *are.*"[65] However, as we read Nepos, we see that things are not so easily categorized; something else is eating away at his confidence, and there is more to his ambivalence than an intellectual apprehension that he may be mixing those things that belong to history with biography or with epic.

Biography was believed to be the youngest of the traditional genres. It may have been brash, ambitious, and exhilarating for both author and audience, but biography was still believed to be a bit awkward, gangling, and somewhat déclassé. Furthermore, and this seems to be a very telling aspect of Nepos's hesitancy, he seemed to believe that anyone with any intellectual stature knew it to be a less learned genre than historical writing. Nepos wrote to his friend Atticus, Cicero's close friend and correspondent, and explained that he was without any illusions that a great number of people (and here, of course, he is re-

65. E. I. McQueen, *Quintus Curtius Rufus,* in T. Dorey, *Latin Biography,* p. 18.

ferring to the *cognoscenti*) would judge the genre (biography, *genus scripturae*) unimportant and of little merit: *non dubito fore plerosque, Attice, qui hoc genus scripturae leve et non satis dignum summorum virorum personis iudicent.*[66] By the time of Suetonius (ca. A.D. 70–130), who grew up in an age of transition, classical Latin literature was near its end. His older contemporary, and for Suetonius the most brilliant of historians, Tacitus, had completed his work shortly before. If we can say conditionally that *historia* for Nepos was the record of the worthy deeds of great men whose deeds affected the state, by the time we reach Suetonius, we find a loosening of the standard to which this word formerly was restricted. He writes toward the end of a long catalogue of the debaucheries of Tiberius that Tiberius was especially fond of mythology or of fabulous history: "his special aim was a knowledge of mythology (*notitiam historiae fabularis*) which he carried to a silly and laughable extent." Suetonius also appeared to accept the writing of history by ordinary men as nothing out of the ordinary, and he seemed aware of a difference between this understanding and that of his older colleague Nepos when he remarks that L. Voltacilius Plotus "set forth the exploits (*res gestas*) of Pompey, as well as those of the son, in several books. In the opinion of Cornelius Nepos, he was "the first of all freed men to write history (*scribere historiam*), which had been written only by men of the highest position before that time."[67]

Although Suetonius does not follow the Plutarchian scheme of a developed chronology with anecdotes purporting to give the development of human personality, he is nonetheless much concerned to illustrate character through examination of behavior; the virtuous deed or indeed its opposite remained an important part of what he was intent on illustrating. His *Lives of the Twelve Caesars,* besides giving important historical details, is really more in the tradition of the informed memoir, presenting a political vignette, followed by a section on the emperor's depravity, either sexual or otherwise, followed by a description toward the end of the work of the emperor's physiognomy, and so on. Townsend makes the interesting observation that this disjunctive narrative (the use of the technique of *partitio* or *divisio*) forces on the reader the additional task of imposing an intellectual order on the nar-

66. Jenkinson, "Nepos," pp. 5–6.

67. J. C. Rolfe, ed. and trans, *Suetonius,* 2 vols. (Cambridge, 1913), p. 392; see also G. B. Townsend, "Suetonius and His Influence," in *Latin Biography,* pp. 79–111; W. Steidle, *Sueton und die Antike Biographie* (Munich, 1951).

rative.[68] Although Suetonius's influence (his influence on Einhardt's *Vita Karoli* has been well remarked) has not been marked in medieval sacred biography, it is well to note that this disjunctive or episodic narrative quality, this use of *divisio,* is present in many Christian saints' lives.

By the time of the late first century, the line between history (*historia*) and tale (*fabula*), which Nepos saw so keenly, was less clearly drawn. Indeed, authors such as Aulus Gellius believed that history could be written by an ordinary man about ordinary men. The proscriptions which determined the style and the content of the traditional genre had loosened. Gellius believed the genre of historical writing to be all-encompassing, even able to record events which he claimed comprised an entertaining history (*iocunda historia*). Although Book 8 of *Noctes Atticae* is not extant, many of the titles of its chapters survive. For example, Gellius entitled chapter 16 "A pleasant and remarkable history" (*historia . . . iocunda et miranda*).[69] It was this more expansive—indeed, one might say democratic and dynamic—tradition regarding classical antiquity's understanding of historical writing that influenced the early Christian sacred biographers.

The Christian Response

The Christian sacred biographer, and even his counterpart, the secular biographer (e.g., Einhardt's *Vita Karoli* and William of Poitiers's *Gesta Guillelmi Ducis*), inherited classical biography's emphasis on the importance of illustrating the virtuous deed as a paradigm for appropriate social behavior.[70] Such a methodological premise has its roots in a philosophy in which ethics and not metaphysics is dominant, and, it must be acknowledged, in a creedal system which seeks to control public behavior by means of such texts. Moreover, such a first premise must lead to a narrative which is *epideictic,* because the goal of the text is not authentication, but persuasion. Further, the narrative, being biographical, however broadly that term is conceived, must perforce be construed as a type of historical writing, as part of the genre of history.

---

68. Townsend, "Suetonius," pp. 84–88.

69. G. A. Press, *The Development of the Idea of History in Antiquity* (Montreal, 1982), p. 65.

70. See Townsend's remarks on Einhardt in "Suetonius," and T. A. Dorrey, "William of Poitiers: *Gesta Guillelmi Ducis,*" in *Latin Biography,* pp. 98–107, 139–55.

Of course, the biographical writing we are concerned with, biography as paradigm, only fitfully inhabits the world of historical writing; its avowed primary goal is not the presentation and interpretation of the record of the *vita* but rather the celebration of modes of behavior which exist as cultural symbols and not as autonomous *sui generis* acts. The historical record which we confront in such biography is history as *emblem*.

Medieval Christian biographers, both sacred and secular, do exhibit some of the ambivalence of a Nepos in their understanding of the differences between *historia* and *vita,* a distinction which, as we have seen, became increasingly blurred by the time Gellius wrote *Attic Nights.* As late as the late seventh century, we see, for example, in the work of Bede both distinctions in his *historiae,* the *History of the Abbots* or his *Ecclesiastical History of the English People* on the one hand, and in *fabulae* (to borrow Suetonius's expression) his translation of the encomiastic *Beati Felicis Vita* and his *Vita Sancti Cuthberti,* on the other.[71]

Although Christian biographers wrote out of a conviction that biography was an *epideictic* narrative containing an encomiastic celebration of heroic virtue, they reshaped the dominant classical philosophical understanding which supported such rhetorical narratives. Indeed, their most fundamental change was in their reinterpretation of the very motivation for human action: in short, sacred biography, although heir to the value system which governed the classical idea of *virtus,* succeeded in utterly changing this ideal of *virtus* and the philosophical environment which nourished it. It was by means of this critical interpretive decision to change the ethical system which had supported the classical notion of *virtus* that Christian sacred biography distinguished itself from the governing classical idea of biography as encomium.

The Christian sacred biographer was only seldom imbued with a predisposition to philosophical speculation, with the result that philosoph-

71. Bede's preface to his *Vita Sancti Cuthberti* goes to some length to assure Bishop Eadfrid of the great care and scrupulousness (*sine certissima exquisitione*) with which he has written this work. Depsite this exhaustive concern for the truth of the life, the text opens with an anecdote (Bede even cites his source, one Trumwine) about the three-year-old boy who, urged by the Holy Spirit, pleads with the eight-year-old Cuthbert to refrain from childish sports and concern himself with the things of the Lord. Bede guarantees the accuracy of this anecdote by appealing to the precedent of the Holy Spirit in the tale of Baalam and the ass. Here the veracity of the contemporary historical event is proven through an appeal to one of the more fabulous incidents from Scripture.

ical categories, as categories, exist as wholly integral parts of the narratives of the *vitae sanctorum*. Thus, when we come to inquire about the understanding of a very complex issue such as the concept of virtue, we find that in the corpus of sacred biography, one sees the subject not in terms of the philosophical controversy which may have surrounded it at any one time—a subject of intense discussion throughout the Middle Ages, from Augustine's observation in the *Enchiridion* that all of moral theology is merely a category of the virtue of *caritas* to Thomas Aquinas's and Albert the Great's differences on the *liberum arbitrium*—but rather these philosophical arguments were dramatized concretely by nonphilosophers in the biographies of the saints. The abiding view of virtue in the traditional genre of the *vitae sanctorum* was to place it within a broader theological matrix as a power to act within certain sanctioned categories, typically spelled out in considerable detail, for the achievement of a good born from grace (*libertas gratiae*). Such power is properly bestowed on certain individuals by God for the specific purpose of performing particular deeds which, although rooted in the specific of human behavior, transcend the everyday, the commonplace, by reason of those individuals' being practitioners of the divine law. Divine law not only provides to the medieval Christian all the rudiments of the natural law, but it also prescribes all the possible acts of all the virtues. Finally, *virtus* is the enabling power to action for the achievement of the end of all Christian life, the hope of heavenly salvation.

This complex ideal of *virtus* is not, despite its apparently volitional status, only a product of the will or the intellect, the *liberum arbitrium;* it is not something that one can strive for and be certain of achieving. In a mysterious way, the virtuous action remains at least partially outside human volition alone. Virtue can be sought, and, indeed, one's propensity to the practice of virtue is shaped through living within the parameters outlined by the language of Christian teaching on the divine law. Within the Christian economy of salvation and the accompanying ideal of virtue, there is never the guarantee that what is sought will be achieved, despite the status of the penitent. What does this theological and philosophical speculation on virtue give birth to in the less philosophically acute genre of sacred biography? Virtue is born out of struggle, whether that psychomachia is with conscience, a *bellum intestinum,* or with a demonic spirit. The depiction of the saints practicing virtues is almost always established within a dialectic which shows the difficulty of following the Christian virtues; for example, the young maiden Catherine struggles to protect her virginity against the rapaciousness of the pagan governor. Such struggles do not exist to exemplify the heroism of the individual, but, on the contrary, and this is often overlooked, they exist to promote an understanding that it is the gift of grace in those whom God has favored which is critical to the outcome of the struggle. Given this understanding, the single-minded pursuit of virtue depicted in medieval *vitae sanctorum* gives rise to a glorification of a type of transcendent solitude, because the primary objective of the saintly hero or heroine is not the perfection of character for the sake of self or *communitas* but rather for the achievement of a singular union with Christ. Innumerable examples of this characterization exist throughout the corpus of Christian sacred biography, from the anecdotes in the *Apophthegmata Patrum,* to Walter Daniel's depiction of Aelred's heroic ascetic suffering in the *Vita Aelredi,* to Osbern Bokenham's *Lyf of Seynt Elyzabeth.*

Let us now briefly review pre-Christian (chiefly those of classical antiquity and Judaism) ideals of virtue. Meeks is undoubtedly correct in his remark that personal morality varied considerably from group to group in the late Hellenistic period.[72] In those cosmopolitan urban centers where the early church established itself, differing systems of values were commonplace, and not only did these early Christians come into contact with different attitudes concerning virtue, but, as Paul's Epistles suggest, they amalgamated them to their nascent Christianity.

Although such generalization is fraught with problems, even within such a cultural crucible as the early Christian period we can for the sake of our discussion discern certain fairly normative positions concerning virtue. At the outset, it is well to acknowledge the absence of a hierarchical religion with a concomitant systematic theology and designated priestly class in classical antiquity. Within the Greco-Roman world, there were three general categories of behavior (these categories themselves are not virtues, but their practice produces virtue) whose successful pursuit by an individual *might result* in such moral fruits as piety, prudence, humility, wisdom, and so on. First, there is *virtus* as a type of a natural good, ἀρετή, the pursuit of which—as Aristotle points out in the *Nicomachean Ethics* (1102a, 6) and the *Politics* (1295a, 37)—can lead to a state of happiness. ᾿Αρετή is that quality which all individuals possess and which, if pursued, will give them their fullest potential. The second dominant understanding of *virtus* is contained in the Stoic figue of the wise man, the Senecan *Sapiens,* an individual of unassailable character but one who is at one remove from

72. Meeks, *The First Urban Christians,* pp. 127–31, 164–92.

the society around him. In the Stoic ideal, the *virtus* is a quality of mind and affect which makes the *Sapiens* impervious to the vagaries of daily life. For the sake of this discussion, I would include Epicureanism and Cynicism as types of extreme Stoicism. The Stoic stress is on self-possession and the capacity for self-regulation. Those factors which are outside this regulatory mechanism (politics, etc.) can be the source of disorder and should be avoided. Ideals similar to such Stoic positions find themselves in the theology of the Christian ascetic movements of the fourth and fifth centuries. In Augustine's Sermons 107 and 115 and in certain of Jerome's epistles, both return to an earlier ideal of the martyr as an ascetic witness who confesses (hence the growth of the ideal life as *Confessor*) the truth without the demand of blood sacrifice.

The final classical understanding of *virtus* is one which became and remained the dominant ideal of the Roman aristocracy and extended to many levels of society in late antiquity. This is the ideal of *virtus* inseparable from communal welfare. Such an ideal can be seen in Sallust's examination of the differing temperaments of Caesar and Cato in his *Bellum Catilinae*. Although Sallust is given to a dialectic, almost binary presentation of their respective characters, the *virtus* he celebrates is nonetheless one which, although rooted in an individual's unique *bonae artes*, is social, with a very keen interest in the welfare of *communitas*, heroic because it is sought not in solitude for the sake of solitude but with the good of the other in view. This *virtus* celebrates the inherent choice of the correct social action; it is a quality or disposition to behave (which may or may not have come from the gods) which does not depend on the gods for its efficaciousness.

The difficulty of describing in summary Jewish ideals of virtue in the period just preceding and during the early-Christian era is equally vexing. As in the Greco-Roman world, there were undoubtedly competing understandings of virtue in the Jewish communities and particularly in their dominant parties, the Pharisees and the Sadducees. Although certain texts are putatively assigned to the Pharisees, such as the *Psalms of Solomon* and *4 Esdras*, these writings are in no manner representative of the traditions as a whole. Further, the accounts of the Pharisees and the Sadducees and the growth of the rabbinic authority which comes from intermediaries are not the most reliable. For example, Josephus's design was to present both Pharisaism and Sadduceism in the best light to his Greek readers, and so he played up their similarities to Greek philosophical thought and in so doing misrepresented their original teaching. The New Testament, although certainly an important source for Pharisaism, presents the most unfavorable side of the movement as a foil for its message. It nonetheless seems to be the current scholarly consensus that for that part of the population which tried to follow the Torah, virtue was a quality arrived at through the faithful practice of the Law, whether explicitly stated in the Scripture, a part of the oral teaching, or *targum,* which served as an interpretation of the Scripture. Virtue in mainstream Judaism at this period was quantifiable behavior. The Law presented a program and a detailed prescription for living the good life. Virtue is not an interiorized state of being or a gift from God, but rather, it is character achieved through prescribed behavior. Although there were undoubtedly variations on this ideal and the movements of heterodox groups, it is interesting to note that in the opening of *Ecclesiasticus* (ca. 180 B.C.E.), the author, in accounting for the great legacy of the Jews, identifies the Law as primary.

The point of this review has been to illustrate that the distinctions between classical/Semitic and Christian ideas concerning *virtus* were pronounced. We are witnesses to a major shift in sensibility. Where the typical ancient biography celebrated the life of a socially prominent individual for his performance of the socially correct deed, Christian biography attributed the performance of such actions to the beneficent mercy of the Creator for *ad maiorem gloriam Dei. Virtus* is no longer lauded as a social ideal with the power to perfect human character, to contribute to the commonweal, to uphold the law, but it is now seen as a gift endowing one with the potential for certain action redolent with the numinous power. Virtue is a product of the grace of God working on human will. The pursuit of virtue is a deliberately solitary endeavor. Such emphasis on the transcendent, solitary nature of Christian virtue inevitably led to the judgment that those who were deemed especially virtuous were endowed with greater than human characteristics. *Virtus* was to become in Christian sacred biography a synonym for *miraculum.*

The *locus classicus* which ties *virtus* and *miraculum* together into a complex semantic web for the rest of the Middle Ages is the passage in Mark 5:25–34 concerning the hemorrhaging woman who approached Jesus as he stood unaware of her in a large crowd. The woman believed that if she just touched Christ's garment, she would be cured of her affliction. As soon as she had done so, Jesus was aware of it. The Gospel reports the following exchange: "And Jesus, immediately aware that *power* had gone out of himself, turned to the crowd and asked, 'Who touched my garments?" (*Et statim Iesus in semetipso cognoscens virtutem quae exierat de illo, conversus ad turbam, aiebat: Quis tetigit vestimenta mea?*).[73] Here the connection between *virtus* (power) and miracle (in this case, the cure) is made quite explicit. The woman's belief in the power of Christ to manifest the healing power of God was a sign of her faith, and her belief was rewarded with the miracle of her cure. The conjunction of *virtus* and *miraculum* is also evident in Jonas of Bobbio's *Vita Sancti Columbani,* in which we are given an account of an action *virtutes,* which can only be construed as the examination of miracles in the church of St. Peter: *vir quidam nomine Jocundua ad regem venit, qui regi indicavit se in solitudine ruribus Apenninis basilicam B. Petri apostolorum principis scire, in qua virtutes expertus sit fieri.*[74]

Medieval sacred biography makes the case repeatedly that power or *virtus* is given to the believer according to his merit, that is, to the extent to which he makes proper use of these gifts. For the Christian, this meant an emphasis on *virtus* as grace and the fundamental direction of these actions for *ad maiorem gloriam Dei.* The ancient Greek and Roman, on the other hand, saw *virtus* as a means of perfecting human character.

It would appear that the Christian and antique understandings of *virtus* are opposed at the most basic level. Classical man hopes through the cultivation of *virtus* to contribute to his own well-being and that of his society; the Christian, conversely, strives toward the good so as to manifest to this postlapsarian world God's special favor in him. The Christian psychology of the self—to place the matter in the broadest of terms—viewed from this perspective of the understanding of *virtus,* is self-deprecating and solitary, whereas its classical counterpart is self-aggrandizing and social. Although both classical and Christian biographies are *epideictic* narrative forms which share a number of rhetorical forms, classical biography celebrates the virtuous man who works as an *individual* in and for his *society.* His Christian counterpart, the sacred hero, is dependent on a radically different ideal of *virtus,* an ideal which diminished the importance of the individual and as a consequence placed in sharp antagonism the *civitas Dei* and the *civitas hominis.*

---

73. Weber, p. 1582. This anecdote proved to be extremely influential and became the basis for the development of the legend of Veronica and her veil; see M. R. James, "Acts of Pilate," in *The Apocryphal New Testament* (Oxford, 1924), p. 102; Ewa Kuryluk, "Mirrors and Menstruation," in *Formations* 1 (1984): 69–73.

74. B. Krusch, *Vita Sancti Columbani, MGH: Scriptores Rerum Germanicarum* Vol. 35, p. 221.

But how does this discussion of *virtus* assist us in our examination of Agnellus of Ravenna and his use of pictorial representation as sources in his *Liber Pontificalis Ecclesiae Ravennatis?* It will help immensely, because sacred biography illustrates this Christian concept of *virtus* in its most extreme form. For example, in opposition, say, to the Peripatetic school of biography, in which the investigation of motives in order to illustrate personality is of primary interest, we see in Christian saints' lives the representation of personality as a type of transparent membrane through which the author is intent to show the continual passage of God's grace. The concept of the autonomy of the individual action which we accept so unconsciously is an anomaly in this genre; individuality, and all its attendant qualities, is purposefully diminished, expunged, so as to give greater latitude to the idea of corporate personality. The theological substrate of sacred biography creates a portrayal of the self as semiautonomous: the self is capable of sustained action because of the favor of divine will. Such a system of belief—which in the main rejected the idea of person as a unique conｓ　ｔ uct, as a self-sufficient center of autonomous, integrated drives and needs utterly distinctive in the universe of human psyches—finds nothing contradictory in the extraordinary use of sources as seen above. Indeed, the features of biographical writing which since the eighteenth century give distinctiveness to the subject are in sacred biography accidental and unnecessary for revealing the true substance of the narrative, the subject's *virtus*.

If it is arguable that language is Adamic, arising out of an obsession to identify particulars, then it follows that a genre which is interested in the universal at the expense of the particular will seek to limit its lexical breadth; its language will be deliberately conventional and stylized and will abound in well-recognized formulae. Within such a narrative matrix, the sort of intertextual borrowings discussed above are seen as entirely appropriate; this is exactly the rhetorical situation we find in the medieval *vitae sanctorum*.

Agnellus and His Pictures

Having outlined some of the preparatory arguments, let us return to our discussion of Agnellus and his pictures. As indicated earlier, one of the most novel explanations justifying the types of sources available to the sacred biographer is that made by Abbot Agnellus of Ravenna. Agnellus, working at the behest of the bishop, lived in Ravenna during the first half of the ninth century (806?–46?). We know little about his actual background other than what he tells us—he is passionately anti-Greek, knew Vergil well enough to echo him, is materialistic, and supports rigid social strata[75]—and this is not always accurate; for example, his claim that he was a descendant of an aristocratic family, Brown says, is not only self-aggrandizing, but spurious.[76] Agnellus is important for his *Book of the Bishops of Ravenna,* a work commissioned by the occupant of the episcopal throne, Georgius, and indebted for its format to the earlier Roman *Liber Pontificalis;* it is arguably the most important mid-ninth-century history for Ravenna.[77]

What sort of work is Agnellus's *Liber Pontificalis?*[78] It is important to note at the outset that although it is a work which proceeds chronologically, providing information on the bishops of Ravenna—in this regard, it is somewhat prosopographical—Agnellus did not entitle it *Historia* or *Vita* but *Liber.* His somewhat ambiguous title may suggest the model of the Roman *Liber* noted above, but both of these may in turn be indebted to the survival of the old tension observed by Nepos and Suetonius between history and biography. The scope of the work is ambitious, as it contains the lives of all the bishops of Ravenna from the first, Apollinarius, whom Agnellus identifies as a disciple of St. Peter (a mark of his civic patriotism and an attempt to objectify Ravenna's sense of its own ecclesiastical antiquity), to the occupant of the see at that time, Agnellus's Bishop Georgius. In sum, there are forty-five biographies spanning the eight centuries of the history of the episcopacy in Ravenna. The *Liber* was written to be read aloud to younger clergy to stimulate their pride in their city's ancient ecclesial heritage.[79]

The biographies vary considerably with respect to both length and narrative design; some are merely a few lines, whereas others run to many pages. Although we do not find the application of a consistent methodological format in the presentation of the lives, Agnellus is usu-

75. O. Holder-Egger, *Agnellus Liber Pontificalis Ecclesiae Ravennatis;* T. S. Brown, *Gentlemen and Officers: Imperial Administration and Aristocratic Power in Byzantine Italy A.D. 554–800* (London, 1984), pp. 101, 126, 146.

76. Brown, *Gentlemen and Officers,* p. 80.

77. Ibid., p. 188.

78. G. Fasoli, "Rileggendo il 'Liber Pontificalis' di Agnello Ravennate," in *Settimane di Studio del Centro Italiano de Studi sull'Alto Medioevo* 17 (1970): 457–95; G. Cortesi, "Andrea Agnello e il 'Liber Pontificalis Ecclesiae Ravennatis,'" in *Corsi di Cultura sull'Arte Ravennate e Bizantina* 28 (1981): 31–76.

79. Brown, *Gentlemen and Officers,* p. 188.

ally consistent in his introductions to the individual lives, introducing
his subject either through a brief commentary on his virtuous life or
through a certification of the subject's sterling character derived from
an etymology, often spurious, of the bishop's name (the latter technique is of great antiquity and was well established by that time in
sacred biography). An example of the first technique appears in his life
of Bishop Liberius VIII. He begins with a brief encomium, mentioning
the virtues which he believed established Liberius's sanctity. He writes
that Liberius was a "great man, [because he was] filled with charity, a
font of healing water, distinguished in his faith and rich in intellect
(*magnus homo, caritate plenus, irriguus fons, fide praecipuus, mente
benignus*)."[80] The bishop's greatness is secured on the ready foundation of the cardinal virtues of faith, hope, and charity. An example of
Agnellus's second technique, the illustration of the sanctity of the individual through an interpretation of the individual's name, occurs
when he writes that "Eleuchadius II's name in Latin should be understood to mean unblemished (*cui nomen Latine candidus intelligitur*)."[81]
In this instance, besides the fact that the etymology is incorrect, Agnellus is using *candidus* in the figurative adjectival sense and not in the
more common nominal usage of a candidate for some office; I try to
account for this by translating it as "unblemished."

After introducing a life through one of these two strategies, Agnellus
moves directly to narrating the deeds of the bishop. These deeds are
the body of his narrative, and they consist essentially of encomia which
celebrate the episcopal holiness and substantiate the bishop's sanctity
through the presentation of appropriate miracles. Many of the lives end
with an identification of the burial place of the bishop—a necessary
ingredient to substantiate the historicity of his subject as well as to
propagate the bishop's fame as a Christian leader—and mention of the
length of the episcopal reign.

The prologue to Agnellus's *Liber Pontificalis* is a curious document
both for what it argues and for what it leaves unsaid. His major preoccupation in the prologue is to defend the use of the oral record in his
composition. He begins with an invocation followed by the traditional
captatio benevolentiae and moves immediately to his main argument.
The prologue is highly rhetorical and employs a number of traditional
strategies useful in argument, namely *aponmemonysis, procatalepsis,*
and *proecthesis.* For example, he carefully uses *procatalepsis* in antic-

80. Holder-Egger, "Agnellus," p. 283.

81. Ibid., p. 281.

ipation of possible objections to his reliance on the use of the oral record; he uses *proecthesis* in the defense of his method and *apomnemonysis* through the careful citation of approved authorities, chiefly the Old and New Testaments.

Agnellus shrewdly bases his argument concerning the efficacy of the use of the oral witness on the claims that his method is similar to the one used in the Gospel of St. Mark (his choice of Mark is related to that saint's importance in ninth-century Italy). He argues that we think no less of St. Mark's Gospel because Mark was not a disciple of Jesus. The reason for the credibility of Mark's account is that we reverence the source of this Gospel, namely St. Peter's oral witness of these events to Mark.[82] Agnellus's *argumentum ex auctoritate* is not restricted to individuals of Peter's unimpeachable rank; he also cites Gregory the Great's comments on the value of the oral witness.

But why does Agnellus broach such an elaborate defense of the pertinence of the oral witness in his prologue? He gives no explicit reason for his remarks and does not suggest that they pertain to the text of his *Liber Pontificalis*. Surely this entire prologue is an anticipation on Agnellus's part of his readers' possible objections to the sources he used in his lives. His prologue presents an oddly lopsided argument, pursuing this issue of the value of the oral witness quite single-mindedly while ignoring the really more basic issue of method. (I say more basic because I feel Agnellus himself believed the question of method to be of fundamental importance in a work of biography.)

When Agnellus does address this important question of his method much later on in the *Liber*—almost as if the answers had been inchoate until that very moment—the result is a kind of *argumentum in medias res*. In his life of St. Exuperantius, Agnellus suddenly breaks his narrative of the bishop's life—wherein he also discusses the problem of the paucity of his sources—and launches into a discussion of his method.[83] It is presumably a discussion to which he attached some considerable importance; in it, he identifies himself for the first time by name as the author of this work. Moreover, his commentary reveals for us yet another aspect of the considerable creativity of the sacred biographer and his use of source materials.

The discussion picks up the earlier theme of the prologue regarding the importance and value of the oral witness, especially oral testimony from senior members of the community, witnesses who, because of

82. Ibid., p. 279.

83. Ibid., p. 297.

their age, possess a probity and wisdom which protect both them and us from being deceived: *Et ubi inveni, quid illi certius facerunt, vestris aspectibus allata sunt, et quod per seniores et longaevos audivi, vestris oculis non defraudavi.* Such remarks are designed to convince the listener of the zeal of the author in his pursuit of sources for his narrative. At this point, Agnellus makes an abrupt and startling departure from his discussion of the value of the oral witness to make a most curious proposal. He discusses a method for the composition of sacred biography when an author—and here he most certainly has his own situation in mind—has *no* record of the past events of an individual's life. Even the most benign reader can feel his natural sympathies being tested by such a bold remark.

What kind of biography other than the most brazen fiction can he create with such a method? Yet Agnellus never believed that what he was writing was not true. If he were attempting a genuine deception, he surely would not argue in his text the merits of a system of biographical composition which has no past textual sources. But what was he about? In order to peer a bit more deeply into the rationale which governs this remark, let us have the entirety of this interesting passage before us:

> *Et ubi inveni, quid illi certius fecerunt, vestris aspectibus allata sunt, et quod seniores et longaevos audivi, vestris oculis non defraudavi; et ubi [h]istoriam non inveni aut qualiter eorum vita fuisset, nec per annosos et vetustos homines, neque per haedificationem, neque per quamlibet auctoritatem, ne intervallum sanctorum pontificum fieret, secundum ordinem, quomodo unus post alium hanc sedem optinuerunt, vestris orationibus me Deo adiuvante, illorum vitam composui, et credo non mentitum esse, quia et horatores fuerunt castique et elemosinarii et Deo animas hominum adquisitores. De vero illorum effigie si forte cogitatio fuerit inter vos, quomodo scire potui: sciatis, me pictura docuit, quia semper fiebant imagines suis temporibus ad illorum similitudinem. Et si altercatio ex picturis fuerit, quod adfirmare eorum effigies debuissem: Ambrosius Mediolanensis sanctus antistes in Passione beatorum martirum Gervasii et Protasii de beati Pauli apostoli effigie cecinit dicens: "Cuius vultum me pictura docuerat."*[84]

And when I discovered what those men certainly did, those things were brought before your gaze, and that which I heard from the elders and aged men I did not deny to your eyes. And when I did not find an account or how their life had been, neither through the years and through

---

84. Ibid., p. 297. (Emphasis added.)

old men, nor through inscriptions, nor through any authority at all, lest
there be a gap in the [list of] holy bishops, in order, how one after another
obtained this see, with God aiding me by your prayers, *I contrived [put
together] their lives, and I believe that it was not false,* because they
were encouragers and chaste and charitable and acquirers of the souls of
men for God. But concerning their appearance, if by chance there will
be a discussion among you, as to how I was able to know: you must
understand that portraiture taught me, because always images were
made in their times after their likeness. And if an argument shall arise
from the portraits to the effect that I should have confirmed their ap-
pearances: the holy bishop Ambrose of Milan in the Passion of the
Blessed Martyrs Gerrase and Protase with regard to the appearance of
blessed Paul the Apostle stated in these words, "A portrait had taught
me his face."

Agnellus tells us that where he has not found an account (*ubi
[h]istoriam non inveni*) or has been unable to determine what type of
life the bishops in question led (*eorum vita fuisset*), either from the
very old or through epigraphy (*neque per haedificationem*), and as he
was not inclined to leave gaps in his narrative (*ne intervallum*), he has
with the help of God and with the assistance of our prayers *contrived*
(*composui*) a life of those men. Agnellus's use of *historiam* and *composui* is, I believe, quite particular to his overall intention. Both words
have a richly ambiguous linguistic history. Although in classical Latin
historia usually referred to the record of past facts, it could also signify
a narrative, tale, or, less frequently, simply a theme. Agnellus appears
to restrict its meaning to a record of past facts, which record, however,
if it did exist, is no longer extant and available to him. In the entire
Liber Pontificalis Ravennatis, he makes very infrequent use of the
word *historia.* If we now turn to his use of the perfect form of the verb
componere, composui, it is well to note that, although this is a word of
broad application (to place things together, to compare, to position
something, to organize, to fabricate, to write, to compose a history, to
make up, to concoct, to calm down, to subdue), in both classical and
medieval Latin, the verb *componere,* when used in contexts which
concern texts mainly, indicates a type of composition in which disparate existing elements are brought together to form a whole. My translation of *composui* as "contrived" points to the very *absence* of existing elements and attempts to bridge Agnellus's prior acknowledgment
on this very nonexistence of sources in his work, *ubi* [h]*istoriam non
inveni.* Such an interpretation of the word can be seen in Livy, Cicero,

Tacitus, and Ambrose.[85] In sum, Agnellus is declaring the incredible *modus operandi* for some of these biographies of *componere ex nihilo*.

Although every historian has felt the pain and perhaps even the temptation to fill the gap (*intervallum*) which Agnellus complains about, none would argue that such lacuna is license for such behavior. This is precisely the behavior Delehaye excoriates, calling such saints' lives "mere hagiographic antholog[ies]." Confronted with such a methodology and after our initial shock and, perhaps, dismissal of the author's credibility as biographer (not as an important chronicler of Ravenna), our curiosity prompts us to ask if there is a rationale at work here that might present this problem in a different light, by going beyond Delehaye's judgment that such behavior represents the "[moral and intellectual] destitution of . . . editors."[86] And, indeed, Agnellus has once again anticipated this objection or one like it and provided us with a response. In the very next clause following his acknowledgment that he has contrived this life, he unambiguously states that the method is not meant to be a deception (*et credo non mentitum esse*). The skeptical reader may be piqued by such a claim, since Agnellus's *ad hominem* argument (*et credo*) may reveal more about his intention than the truth of his biography. Agnellus's remarks, however, remind us at once of the similar remarks of Walter Daniel, Eddius Stephanus, and Reginald of Canterbury and are something of a rhetorical *topos* even in the mid-ninth century. But does Agnellus believe that such a method can give birth to a text that is not a biographical *fabula*, not a figment of his imagination? What paradoxical truth does Agnellus believe keeps his *Liber Pontificalis* from being a deception (*mentitum esse*) when he has acknowledged that at least certain biographical aspects of it are contrived (*illorum vitam composui*)?

To begin, nowhere in the entire work does Agnellus claim to echo Bede's quotation of Jerome that the lives in his *Liber Pontificalis* are *vera lex historiae*. The absence of such a remark must prompt us to inquire into what genre Agnellus believed he was working in and what he understood its traditions to be. I believe his argument assumes two things: first, that his listeners were aware that this was a work of bio-history and, second, that these listeners were conversant with the tension between the matter appropriate to biography and that to history, tensions we saw expressed in Nepos's letter to Atticus a full millen-

85. *Oxford Classical Dictionary.*

86. H. Delehaye, *The Legends of the Saints*, pp. 78–81.

nium earlier. This distinction was observed in Christian sacred biographies from the very beginning. Agnellus understood the genre of the saint's life to be one which depicts in nonchronological fashion the exemplary actions of virtuous men. Indeed, although many of his bishops were not saints, the model presented by the saint's life was ubiquitous, and well before this time it had influenced related genre and was certainly appropriate for a composition which, for whatever other political, social, and familial narratives it contained, nonetheless was a record of the deeds of some of the most revered leaders of the Christian church in Ravenna.

But let us now turn to examine the belief system on which Agnellus founded his argument for the text's authenticity. Agnellus argues that his lives of the bishops are preeminently Christian lives; these men were preachers who were also chaste and charitable procurers of the souls of men for God (*quia et horatores fuerunt castique et elemosinarii et Deo animarum hominum adquisitores*). The logic of this argument is circular: it moves from the historically public acknowledgment of the bishops' Christian virtue to the position that this God-given virtue, which shaped their every action, is a guarantee to the faithful that they did good deeds. However, it is not the singular, temporally bounded act performed on a given day embroiled in its peculiar historical circumstance—what we might call an accidental act—which is essential to understanding and securing their sanctity. Rather, it is the Deity's presence in the *animae* of the bishops and the gift of virtue that that presence ensures. Such a method clearly diminishes the importance lent to the particulars of historical chronology as they might serve to legitimize sanctity. It would be a misjudgment to construe this method as contemptuous of the value of the historical chronicle. Rather, it views such historical data as unnecessary criteria in identifying the verities which constitute Christian sanctity. For Agnellus— and I am not being insouciant—one good deed is *in substance* the same as any other.

Virtue, being derived from divine grace, is indivisible; it is the motivating constitutent of all action. Actions done by virtuous individuals, then, give expression to this transcendent, freely given gift of God. Given such religious mentality, an exacting narrative account of an individual's specific virtuous deeds, although of great importance as a paradigm of correct living and as a model to be imitated, is not thought to be a success or a failure to the degree to which the author has accurately presented the actual events which transpired in that life. Agnellus's historiography is inseparable from his metaphysics; it is not a historiography that is rooted in an empirical epistemology but rather one which is dependent on religious, ethical, and moral values.

For Agnellus of Ravenna, the exacting recovery of the particular circumstance of the formal deed, an investigation of the causal relationships which bound events and ideologies, the weighing of the claims of conflicting evidence—although he and most educated medieval authors would acknowledge them as important tools for recovering the past and ones which he uses in certain instances—is not as crucial to his work's *raison d'être* as a narrative which carefully seeks out deeds which exemplify the quality of the ethical expression of the bishop's life. Agnellus, no less than the sacred biographer, when the intention is to laud, fills the life with deeds, narrative emblems, deliberately intended to point to the universal truth such deeds symbolize.

Pictures into Print

Bearing this in mind, we can now briefly consider the raw data from which Agnellus fashioned some of his lives. Toward the end of his discussion of method, Agnellus reveals that he was inspired to write the lives of certain bishops after having viewed pictures of them:

> *De vero illorum effigie si forte cogitatio fuerit inter vos, quomodo scire potui: sciatis, me pictura docuit, quia semper fiebant imagines suis temporibus ad illorum similitudinem.*[87]

We do not doubt that a picture was indeed his teacher (*me pictura docuit*), for in a number of the biographies the opening description of the bishop has a pronounced visual feel to it, in the almost lineal way his presentation segments the subject's features. The opening descriptions of certain of the bishops' lives render vividly the pictorial ancestry of the narrative. The language presents vivid physical images undoubtedly inspired by the mosaic with the accompanying interpretation. For example, Bishop Gratioso (784–88) is said to be slight of stature but gentle, somewhat bald, disposed to obesity, with large eyes, but in all a handsome appearance and possessed of sweet eloquence: *Iste humilis et mansuetus, pulcher aspectu, modice recalvatus, extenso in quantitate gutture, oculos grandes, decora forma et dulcia eloquia.*[88]

87. Holder-Egger, "Agnellus," p. 297.

88. Ibid., p. 383.

Agnellus's method, although somewhat novel, had a historical precedent in the discussion of biographical composition at least as old as
the funerary depictions in Prudentius's *Peristephanon*. Prudentius presented an elaborate description of the martyrdom of St. Hippolytus
based entirely on funeral art.[89] Representational art would have been
readily available to Agnellus; ninth-century Ravenna was well endowed with churches, twenty monasteries, and chapels. With a little
effort, we might imagine Agnellus with, as he tells us, no written or
oral history for a particular life, standing in the half-light of a beautiful
old church (perhaps the mosaics of certain of the bishops of Ravenna
which decorate the interior of the Church of St. Apollinare in Classe,
ca. 549, served as models), looking up at the likeness of his subject,
peering intently at the image in an effort to transcend the years separating him from his subject in order to fashion (*composui*) a biography
of the individual whose personal qualities, whose God-given *virtutes,*
he believed (*et credo non mentitum*) were embedded and accessible in
the tiny squares of brilliantly colored glass which shimmered in the
shadows before his eyes.

Agnellus's understanding of the utility of figural representation is
complex, and it is difficult to know exactly what he believed. Some of
his remarks suggest that he believed the figural representation was invested with a certain personal immanence. Two reasons suggest this:
his final clause in his remarks on his use of the mosaics, *quia semper
. . . similitudinem,* and the understanding of the icon in Byzantium and
in some areas of the West at the time. First, the final clause implies a
belief that the earlier artists who created the pictures of the bishops
were able to give an authentic representation of these bishops, in which
one could read spiritual as well as physical characteristics. Given this
understanding of the past artists' ability, it appears that Agnellus believed the pictorial text could serve as an anchor for his interpretation
and the resultant veracity of his narrative.

Agnellus's ability to "read" the meaning in the likeness presented in
the pictorial "text" may have been prompted, as suggested above, by
a belief in the power inherent in the representations. This raises the
issue of what he believed icons capable of. Iconolatry grew ever more
important from the late sixth century and was increasingly associated
with an effort to reinforce in the populace awe for the emperor, as
Cameron, Grierson, Brown, and others have suggested. For example,

89. H. J. Thomson, ed., *Peristephanon Liber* (Cambridge, Mass., 1961), Vol. 2,
book xi. See also H. L. Kessler, "Pictorial Narrative and Church Mission in Sixth-
Century Gaul," *Studies in the History of Art* 16 (1985): 75–91.

the Patriarch Sergius's placing the icon of the Virgin Mary atop the walls of Constantinople during the Avar siege (626) was not novel and designed to promote such behavior, but rather he was repeating an action which bishops in beleaguered provincial towns had been performing for some time.[90] The idealized, depersonalized, spiritualized image in painting, mosaic, and coins was the norm by the middle of the sixth century in Italy. However, by the eighth and ninth century in Italy, the difficulty of carefully determining attitudes on icons in a particular city is enormous; the Iconoclast controversy of the eighth century very likely produced a broad spectrum of positions on the subject. Brown suggests that in mid-eighth-century Ravenna—although Leo III's efforts at enforcing the doctrine of iconoclasm through his exarch Paul in Italy met with much resistance—an element of the population was strongly supportive of the imperial policy of iconoclasm.[91]

Indeed, the case of Ravenna for this period (715–840s) seems especially complex. However, Agnellus is writing shortly after the so-called Second Iconoclast Controversy (814–42), which ended with the restoration of the belief in the power of the icon—and in some circles the belief in the real presence of the subject in the representation—under the Patriarch Methodius in 843 (whose exile in Rome for some twenty years confirms a sympathetic Greek community in this city).[92] Further, it is likely that the work of well-known proicon polemicists, such as those of the theologian John of Damascus and works such as the *De Imaginibus Oratio III,* were known in the clerical milieu in which Agnellus traveled and would have been more accessible after 843.[93] John was a powerful proponent of those who believed that the sacred image, whether it be sculptural or pictorial, was more than a representation. He argued that the representation could become for the viewer the very

90. A. Cameron, "Images of Authority: Elites and Icons in Late-Sixth-Century Byzantium," *Past and Present* 84 (1979): 3–35; P. Grierson, "Symbolism in Early Medieval Charters and Coins 601–630," in *Simboli e Simbologia nell'Alto Medioevo, Settimane di Studio del Centro Italiano di Studi sull'Alto Medioevo* 23 (Spoleto, 1976), p. 619; Brown, *Gentlemen and Officers,* p. 157.

91. Cameron, "Images of Authority," p. 20; Grierson, "Symbolism," p. 619; and Brown, *Gentlemen and Officers,* p. 169.

92. Brown, *Gentlemen and Officers,* p. 160.

93. J. Nelson, "Symbols in Context: Rulers' Inauguration Rituals in Byzantium and the West in the Early Middle Ages," *Studies in Church History* 13 (1976): 97–119. Surely it must have been the case that the political and religious motives attached to the consecration of the emperor were part of Methodius's rationale. Michael II, repeating the practice of his predecessor Justinian II, had his image placed on one side

figure it was meant to signify while at the same time making no pretenses at realism. Deichmann's remarks concerning the iconist's disinterest in depicting the actual likeness of the living man (*Das Bild des lebenden Menschen*) ring true.[94] There was undoubtedly a wide spectrum of belief concerning the power of the icon, ranging from the sophisticated Platonism of John of Damascus to a simple piety which felt that the subject was literally present (and yet the representation was not portraiture in any sense) in the depiction. Even if one cannot determine precisely Agnellus's inclinations, which existed between these two extremes, living as he did in a city deeply indebted to Byzantine culture (it was the capital of the Exarchate from 541 until 751) and working at the bequest of the Metropolitan of Ravenna which had never supported the official policy of iconoclasm, we should not be far off base in suggesting that Agnellus's remarks reflect a belief in the ability of the inspired artists to render the true image in their compositions, the *veri eikon* which made manifest to his sight the saintly character of the long-deceased bishop.

John Capgrave and the Tradition's End

In the LV. ʒere of his regne [1271], this Kyng [Henry] deied, in the fest of seint Edmund, Archbishop—his age was LX. and VI.—and was byried at Westminster; whech werk he reisid, and biggid oute of the ground.

In this ʒere, in the XX. day of August [1384], in the feast of seynt Oswyn, the Kyng being at New Castelle upon Tynne, a wright hew on a tre, whech schuld long to a schip; and at every strok he smet ran oute blood, as it had be of a beste. He bethought him of the festful day, and left his

---

of coins issued during his reign and that of Christ on the other; John of Damascus, *De Imaginibus Oratio III,* in *PG* 94.

94. F. W. Deichmann, *Frühchristliche Bauten und Mosaiken von Ravenna* (Baden-Baden, 1958), p. 21. Deichmann's remarks are so penetrating that they are worth quoting: "Das Bild des lebenden Menschen, das Portrat, ist in der Sakralen Kunst nur wenigen, erlesenen Personlichkeiten vorbehalten. . . . Diese Gestalten prasentieren sich, frontal feierlich verharrend, in Voranschreiten. Sie erscheinen entruckt, mit den weiten, geradeaus gerichteten Augen im ruhig-entspannten Antlitz. Sie blicken nicht einen Beschauer an, sondern greifen über ihn gleichsam hinaus in den Raum, als seien auch sie, wie die anderen Bilder, uber Zeit und Gegenwart hinaus greifend auf das Geistige bezogen und mit höheren Bereichen verbunden." See also E. Dinkler, *Das Apsismosaik von S. Apollinare in Classe* (Cologne, 1964), which reproduces pictures of some of the bishops referred to by Agnellus.

werk. His felaw stood beside, having no reverens to this myracle, took the ax and smet, and anon blod ran owte. He fel for fere, and cryed mercy. And al the town merveylid, and gaf worchip to God. The tre was bore to Tynmouth, in token of this myracle.

The above quotations are taken from the first vernacular history of England, *The Chronicle of England,* completed in the spring of 1461 by John Capgrave. The quotations are concise, follow the accepted style of the monastic annal, contain little explicit editorial comment, and yet could not be more different. The death of Henry is the account of an event for which we have corroborating evidence, whereas the report of the bleeding timbers is the stuff of legend. Capgrave, however, did not make such a distinction. He presents both remarks in the same matter-of-fact tone, and he does not distinguish between their historical merit. Of course, the first entry's historical importance is attested to by the faculty of reason and common sense. Henry's death meets the test of probability; such an event, even if we had no knowledge of the particular monarch, could have happened as described. The second quotation's justification in a work of chronicle history is more problematic; it must be based on a historiography different from that governing the report of Henry's death. The incident of the bleeding timbers depends for its validation on a religious historiography and not on one which depends on a principle of verifiability. Furthermore, this incident of the bleeding timbers, in order to have some legitimacy in the *Chronicle*—no matter how fantastic it appears—also had to satisfy the demands of probability. This was a probability that was not empirically based, but rather implicit in the religious faith of a mid-fifteenth-century populace. In short, this fantastic episode had to satisfy the expectations of a system of belief which fully accepted the dislocation of causality as normative. If we return to our earlier discussion of the Augustinian concept of the miraculous, we can locate the episode of the bleeding timbers in the Augustinian idea of the inbreaking of the divine, the *seminales rationes,* in time. The historical context for the first quotation is political; that for the second is metaphysical. The first event is an anecdote in history as deed; the second is a sign in history as emblem. Emblematic history for John Capgrave, no less than for Walter Daniel, Eddius Stephanus, Reginald of Canterbury, and Agnellus of Ravenna, is an open system which seems to mirror the reflections of men through time but in so doing to make part of the patrimony, through testimony, those events from outside of time, whose imprint, although nowhere immediately visible, is nonetheless evident to the careful observer.

John Capgrave, last of the five sacred biographers to be discussed here, is the only one who left a record of his work in the English language. In his saints' lives, we come to the historical period which ushered in the end of the unselfconscious practice of the tradition of sacred biography in medieval England. Capgrave lived his entire life during a period of considerable upheaval in every sphere. His world knew the incessant warfare of the Hundred Years' War (1338–1453) and the civil dislocation which resulted from the War of the Roses (1455–85). His traditional piety is contemporary with the public disenchantment of a number of reform movements (e.g., that of the Lollards and Hussites), the weakening of papal authority, the growth of dispensations (in violation of canon law) for pluralists and absentee clergy with the responsibility for *cura animarum,* and the increased interference of the crown in episcopal appointments which interference spelled the *de facto* collapse of one of the central points of Gregorian reform and ultimately turned the English episcopacy into positions of social and political importance, devoid of a full-time commitment to a pastoral ideal. Later this situation reached an apogee in a figure such as Cardinal Wolsey, who, as Dickinson points out, did not visit the Archdiocese of York until after he had fallen out of favor. And yet Capgrave illustrates that it was still possible for those of his generation (in England) to live wholly nurtured by medieval ideologies despite the great creedal rift begun at the end of the fourteenth century. The images of disrepute were all about. The reputation of the mendicant orders and the religious life, especially that of the regulars, including Capgrave's own Augustinians, was somewhat tarnished by midcentury. The idea that the contemplative life represented the highest of ideals, an attitude which in England helped the massive building program of the Cistercians in the mid-twelfth century and so obvious a given in Walter Daniel's view of the world, was dead. By 1519, Bishop Oldham, founder of Corpus Christi College, exclaimed somewhat prophetically: "Shall we build houses and provide livelihoods for a company of bussing monks whose end and fall we may live to see? No, no, it is meet to provide for the increase of learning and for such as by learning shall do good to church and commonwealth."[95] The educational reforms of the Fourth Lateran Council with respect to the state of the clergy are virtually impossible to summarize for the country as a whole, some regions having received more attention than others. Purvey castigates the parish clergy's ignorance, while a writer such as Mirk is busy turn-

95. J. C. Dickinson, *The Later Middle Ages* (New York, 1979), p. 294.

ing out treatises, his *Manuale Sacerdotis* and *Festial,* which point to a
genuine concern for *cura animarum.* Alexander Carpenter, writing in
his *Destrutio Viciorum* (ca. 1450), lauded the frequency with which
priests were performing their preaching duties. For every paean of
praise, one could cite a damning satire of equal strength. It was clearly
the worst of times and the best of times. Capgrave lived through it all
and, on some level aware of it all, tried to nurture ancient cherished
ideals which fell about his feet one after another. The *vitae sanctorum*
was a genre which allowed Capgrave full rein. In particular, here was
a genre wherein he might use his vast learning *ad maiorem gloriam Dei*
and follow in the footsteps of those revered intellectual ancestors Augustine, Jerome, Benedict, de Voragine, and Tynemouth.

Although he was one of the more important sacred biographers to
write in English, Capgrave's compositions have been somewhat
eclipsed through comparison with the works of contemporaries who
were more forward-looking, more a product of their age, and who did
not exhibit Capgrave's ready nostalgia for a past long gone: "And
thouȝ it be so that these dayes be not used with myracles as the former
dayes were, in whech wer doo many myracles . . ."[96] Capgrave's sacred biographies illustrate his indebtedness to Walter Daniel, to Eddius
Stephanus, to Reginald of Canterbury, and especially to the role played
by virtue in the ideology of Christian sanctity which we saw Agnellus
of Ravenna use so shrewdly. Capgrave's presence in the great tradition
of hagiographical writing can be nicely illustrated in his use of rhetorical *topoi* traditional to the genre, his understanding of *manneris* or
virtue, and the role virtue played in securing audience belief in the
sacred biographies he composed. Capgrave's "anachronisms" make
him all the more valuable as the representative of a last burst of bloom
from a withered stock. Capgrave was definitely not alone in his zeal to
recover the glory of a past age. Pius II (1405–64), arguably the best
pope from this period and one of the leading lights of humanism, unceasingly and to no avail preached a Crusade against the Turks from

96. F. C. Hingeston, ed., *The Chronicle of England by John Capgrave* (London,
1858), pp. 162, 240. Note Capgrave's remarks about the veracity of his biographies in
his prologue to his life of St. Norbert: "In this story riht thus I wil procede/Of this
same Seynt to telle the lyf real." In C. L. Smetana, ed., *The Life of Saint Norbert by
John Capgrave, O.E.S.A. (1393–1464)* (Toronto, 1977), p. 22. Smetana remarks in the
introduction that "neither Capgrave nor his source [for the life of Norbert] was interested in delineating a profile of Norbert; God's favor was evident." I do not believe
the distinction for Capgrave between the "real" and the "apparent" was so easily
made.

1460 through 1463, only to die in Ancona, his ideal of pan-Christian hegemony utterly unrealized.

Capgrave tells us in the prologue to his *Life of St. Katherine* that he was born in Lynn, Norfolk, on the twenty-first of April in 1393.[97] He entered the Augustinian order about 1410, studied at the *studium generale* in London, appears to have been ordained a priest about 1417, and progressed to the *magisterium* at Cambridge about 1425. We know nothing of his whereabouts or the type of work in which he was engaged until October 1437, the date which appears in the manuscript colophons of his commentary on Genesis and Exodus. In light of the considerable scholarship which flowed from his pen after 1437, it is reasonable to assume that these unaccounted-for twelve years were spent in study. Between 1437 and his completion of *De Fidei Symbolis* in 1462, which most scholars believe to have been his final work, Bale, Leland, and Pits credit him with having written around forty-three compositions, ranging from commentaries on books of the Old Testament, to treatises on the Pauline Epistles, to sacred biography, to royal panegyric and chronicle history and a guidebook to the eternal city of Rome, *Ye Solace of Pilgrimes*.[98]

Capgrave, for all his great output, did not confine his work to the monastic scriptorium. He appears to have been prior of the Augustinian house at Lynn, having served as the host during Henry VI's visit to that house in 1446.[99] Furthermore, he was twice elected prior provincial of the English province of Augustinians in 1453 and again in 1455, a time of considerable stress for the church. He himself tells us, in the dedicatory epistle prefixed to his commentary on the Acts of the Apostles, that he made one major and arduous journey in his life, and that was to Rome.[100] He died on the twelfth of August in 1464 in his

---

97. In the *Life of St. Katherine*, he remarks that "If ye wil wete what that I am,/ Myn cuntre in Northfolk, of the toune of Lynne:/Oute of the world, to my profite, I cam/Onto the brotherhode wiche I am inne." See also J. J. Munro, ed., *John Capgrave's Lives of Saint Augustine and Saint Gilbert of Sempringham and a Sermon*, EETS O. S. 140 (London, 1910), p. 74; *The Chronicle of England*, pp. 259, 353. The entry reads: "In this ȝere [1393], in the XXI. day of Aprile, was that Frere bore whech mad these Annotaciones."

98. F. C. Hingeston, *The Book of the Illustrious Henries* (London, 1858), Appendix I, pp. 221–34, and Hingeston's catalogue in *The Chronicle of England*, pp. ix–xx. The best catalogue of his works is in Smetana, *The Life of Saint Norbert*, pp. 10–13.

99. Hingeston, *Illustrious Henries*, pp. 158–59.

100. Ibid., p. 228. Capgrave dedicated his "Acts of the Apostles" to William Gray, archbishop of Northampton and bishop of Lincoln (1454), who comforted Capgrave

seventieth year in his native Lynn and was buried, Bale tells us, in the priory choir: *et ibidem inter Augustinianos sepultus fuit sub Edvuardo Quarto.*[101]

Although his personal life strongly indicates that he dwelled mostly in the comparative isolation of the Priory in Lynn, there is a comment in a manuscript in the general archives of the order in Rome which refers to Capgrave as *doctissimus omnium Anglorum ordinis nostri.* This praise certainly appears to attest to some degree of fame outside England. Capgrave's reputation has seesawed from praise for his genius to attacks on his uncritical reverence for the traditions of the past. Bale, in a eulogistic moment, celebrated what he believed to be Capgrave's unique strengths, calling him somewhat grandly *Philosophus enim ac Theologus illa aetate praecipuus.*[102] Bale's encomium may reveal more about the limited milieu for genuine philosophical and theological speculation in mid-fifteenth-century England. Capgrave's real talents lie not so much in the originality of his thought but rather in his antiquarianism. Furnivall's comments, although utterly capricious, should at least be acknowledged, being an extreme example of Capgrave's opponents: "Capgrave, being an Englishman, was of course by race and nature a flunkey, and had an inordinate reverence for kings and rank. This vice or quality is ingrained in the nation."[103] Capgrave's real love was the study of old texts, whether scriptural, classical, apocryphal, or the lives of the saints. His major works reflect this; they are chiefly exegetical compilations and translations.

Capgrave is quite candid about the nature of his interests and the extent of his abilities. The prologues to his works often hint at something of this interest and his method. In his *Life of St. Gilbert of Sempringham,* he says, "This is the preamble or elles the prologue of Seynt Gilbertis lif, wheche lyf I haue take on hand to translate out of Latyn rith as i fynde be-fore me, saue sum addicionis wil I put therto wheche men of that ordre haue told me, and eke othir thingis that schul falle to my mynde in the writyng wheche be pertinent to the mater."[104] In his

---

when he fell ill in Rome (*atque Romae infirmum*); see also *The Chronicle of England,* p. xii.

101. *The Chronicle of England,* p. 327.

102. Ibid., p. 324.

103. See C. Horstmann, ed., *Capgrave's Life of St. Katherine* (with a foreword by F. J. Furnivall), EETS O.S. 100 (London, 1893), p. xv.

104. Munro, *John Capgrave's Lives,* p. 62.

Liber de Illustribus Henricis, he tells us (and I paraphrase the Latin) that in order to promote the sovereign's desire to follow the example of the best men, he has decided to publish a book in which he has collected (from writers who preceded him) the praises of those men who bore the name of Henry.[105] And in the dedication of his *Chronicle of England* to King Edward IV, he says he desired "specialy to gader eld exposiciones upon Scripture into o collection; [so that] thei which schal com aftir schal not haue so mech laboure in sekyng of her process."[106] In the prologue to his *Life of St. Augustine,* he writes: "A noble creatur, a gentill woman, desired of me with ful grete instauns to write on-to hir, that is to sey, to translate hir treuly oute of Latyn, the lif of Seynt Augustyn, grete doctour of the cherce."[107] Capgrave's *oeuvre,* although it can be anecdotal, witty, and ideological, is most accurately understood as one of compilation.

Although Capgrave wrote a considerable amount of work that we might label chronicle history, he is important to us principally for his work in sacred biography. He wrote four saints' lives: the *Life of St. Norbert,* the founder of the Premonstratensians, in English verse; the *Life of St. Katherine,* in English prose; the *Life of St. Gilbert of Sempringham,* the founder of the Gilbertines, in English prose; and the *Life of St. Augustine,* the patron of his order, in English prose. He has been credited with having composed the *Nova Legenda Anglie,* but it seems more likely that, in recopying this text, he only rearranged some of the *vitae,* the work itself being the product of John Tynemouth. All four of these lives are translations; there were well-established Latin versions of them all available to him. It is curious and quite inexplicable that, given his interest in the vernacular, he left the *Nova Legenda Anglie,* a work he knew and the greatest single corpus of English saints' lives extant in his lifetime, untranslated.

Because I am intent on showing the persistence of the ancient tradition of sacred biography, and demonstrating how the genre fixed its rhetorical conventions and extended them to the vernacular, I would like to begin with an examination of lines from the prologue of Capgrave's *Life of St. Katherine.*

Smetana suggests that the *Life of St. Katherine* was completed in

105. F. C. Hingeston, *Johannes Capgrave, Liber de Illustribus Henricis* (London, 1858), p. 2, beginning "Nomini ergo vestro . . . ubi laudes eorum qui nomen vestrum sortiuntur ex veterum libris collegi . . . ."

106. *The Chronicle of England,* p. 1.

107. Munro, *John Capgrave's Lives,* p. 1.

1445. Capgrave tells us that his translation is from Arrek's Latin translation of St. Athanasius's original Greek. We know nothing of Arrek other than what Capgrave tells us, and there is no reliable tradition associating the learned Athanasius with Katherine's *Acta*. Capgrave believed that Arrek was from the west of England ("Be his maner of speche and be his style"), was the rector of St. Pancras in London, and died in Lynn of the plague in 1349.[108] Capgrave's translation is in seven-line verse stanzas, usually rhyming *a b a b b a c*, and, depending on the manuscript version one uses, it is just under two thousand lines in length.

St. Katherine of Alexandria was one of the most popular saints of the later Middle Ages. Delehaye has dated the beginning of her cult in the West from the eleventh century. The situation in England was typical of the enthusiasm the cult inspired: she was depicted in manuscripts, ivories, paintings, and embroidery. In England, some sixty-two churches were dedicated to her, and at least one hundred seventy bells bear her name. The earliest record of a miracle play was performed in her honor in Dunstable around 1110. Wilson has discussed the depictions of Katherine's life in mural paintings, of which thirty-six examples are extant, with those in the chapel of the Holy Sepulchre in Winchester Cathedral the earliest (ca. 1225). Events from her life were depicted in stained glass throughout the country in churches great and small, such as in York Minster, in Clavering (Essex), in Combs (Suffolk,), and in Balliol College, Oxford. She was celebrated in Latin *vitae,* in the *sanctorale,* and, from the end of the first quarter of the thirteenth century, texts of her life begin to appear in English. This catalogue could be continued, but the point is that the cult of St. Katherine was quite widespread and had an active following from different socioeconomic groups throughout the land.

The *Acta* which narrate this young maiden's protests against the cruel persecutions of the emperor Maxentius have no historical basis. Her cult was late in developing and seems to date from the ninth century at the monastery located on Mount Sinai, where angels were said to have transported her body. In the West, interest in the cult began with the period of the Crusades, presumably because her story, already extant in the East, was brought back by the returning troops. Although her biography pays homage to her intellectual merits—she is depicted as successfully defeating the polemic of fifty pagan philosophers—the popularity of the cult of St. Katherine throughout medieval Europe, I

108. *The Chronicle of England,* p. 352.

believe, owes much to the central motif depicted in her biography (possibly a contamination from the romance): the beautiful young virgin who has repudiated the offer of marriage from the sexually threatening emperor to become a martyred *sponsa Christi*.[109] For her refusal to marry the emperor and renounce Christ, she was sentenced to death. Her punishment was to be strapped to a wheel and tortured. When this proved unsuccessful, she was beheaded. As an unmistakable sign of her sanctity, her decapitated corpse brought forth nourishing milk, not blood:

> Oon was, in token of vyrginal clennesse
> In stede of blood mylke ran[e] at hir nekke,
> Whiche of hir purite that tyme bar witnesse.
>   (11.1898–1901)

Let us turn to some crucial lines from the prologue to Capgrave's *Life of St. Katherine*. I have selected this single stanza from the prologue because it exhibits in microcosm his familiarity with the rhetorical tradition of sacred biography, his understanding of the importance of *virtus* as an ideological justification for Christian sanctity, and a considerable revelation of his method:

> Aftyr hyme nexte I take vp-on me
> To translate this story & set it mor pleyn
> Trostyng on other men that her charyte
> Schall help me in this caas to wryght & to seyn
> Godd send me part of that heuynly reyne
> that apollo bar a-bowte, & eke sent poule;
> It maketh vertu to growe in mannes soule.
>   (11.232–38)

The first two lines acknowledge this as a translation, indicate Capgrave indebtedness to his immediate predecessor, the Latin text of Arrek, and thus point, albeit silently, to the ancient textual tradition stemming from the original composition by St. Athanasius. In this manner, Capgrave not only establishes his indebtedness (a type of the *topos* of humility) but legitimizes his text by referencing its millennium-old tradition. Although he has made his disclaimer that this is a work of translation, the second half of line 2 is really a statement of authorial prerogative. He has set himself the charge of making Arrek's text "more pleyn." Because Arrek's text is not extant, we cannot know with cer-

109. C. L. Smetana, ed., introduction. See Horstmann, ed., *Life of St. Katherine*, pp. 81, 89, 125, 401.

tainty the extent of this editorial prerogative. However, given what we know of Capgrave's interests, his English prose style, and his limitations as an original thinker, this remark seems to have been intended to reassure lay readers (perhaps a number of whom were women)—a readership that he was rarely used to having—that he would simplify the mysteries of Arrek's text. This process of simplification seems to be suggested in the following three lines near the end of the prologue,

> t[h]us endyth the prologue of this holy mayde,
> ȝe that rede it, pray for hem alle
> that to this werk eyther trauayled or payde
> (11.246–48)

We do not see the same degree of solicitousness for his readers acknowledged, for example, in his English verse *Life of St. Norbert*. In his *Tretis of the Orderes that be undyr the Reule of oure Fader Seynt Augustin* (1451), Capgrave makes explicit that the Norbert was composed for "the abbot of Derham that deyid last." Capgrave's intent to make his life of the saint "mor pleyn" reveals an attitude, or at the very least a narrative posture, in which the implied responsibility of the authorial voice is to report the biography as clearly as possible to his audience; it is a position which eschews interpretation. Such an authorial persona is used explicitly by Capgrave's acknowledged master in sacred biography, John of Tynemouth. It is a posture that Capgrave clearly approved. Tynemouth was fond of describing himself as an excerpter (*Apud Glastoniam de libris monasticis excerpsi*), an unbiased, indefatigable copier of texts. If he found two texts in disagreement, he simply copied both.[110] Tynemouth's remarks on his method are important because they also help to illuminate Capgrave's method: *Ego vero in prescriptis et dubiis, et in sequentibus non nullis, auctoritatem discutiendi et diffiniendi mihi non presumo, sed tamquam relator simplex, que in diuersis libris et locis sine laboribus et difficultate sedulus indagator reperire posui, ardua peritis ventilanda reliquens sine invidia, communico.*[111] The phrase *relator simplex*, "plain reporter," expresses in sum the attitude both Tynemouth and Capgrave brought to their work.

Although such fidelity might be laudable for copying a text, it does not follow that the idea of *relator simplex, a priori,* caused Capgrave to truncate his narrative skill in other contexts, such as in his use of

---

110. C. Horstmann, ed., *Nova Legenda Anglie* (Oxford, 1901), p. lii.

111. Ibid., p. lii. (Emphasis added.)

rhetoric or in the prologues to his translations. For in the very next lines, 3 and 4, he makes use of the figure of *captatio benevolentiae*. These two lines, besides being redolent with the sort of formulaic language we find in Middle English religious prose (e.g., "to write and to seyn") explicitly enjoin the reader's sympathy for his composition. In lines 5 and 6, we have an *invocatio* to his muses, Apollo and St. Paul. Such an *invocatio* indicates that, although in the vernacular, this text, written about one of the great heroines of the church, on occasion uses what the *ad Herennium* would refer to as the grand style, *unam gravem [elocutionem]*.[112] We will return to this point later, but for the moment I want to underscore the interesting choice of an invocation to Apollo in a *Life of St. Katherine*. Line 7, the final line in this stanza, contains a concise reference to the importance of the doctrine of sanctifying grace for its role in nurturing virtue in the human spirit. Capgrave understood this *vertu* as the sure sign of sanctity. Five centuries earlier, Agnellus likewise had justified the sanctity of his bishops by appealing to a similar idea of *virtus*, which also grew from the gift of grace.

Capgrave's *invocatio* deserves a closer look, for it has locked within it an insight into his thinking on sanctity and further illustrates his indebtedness to the tradition of sacred biography. Although the *invocatio* in the exordium of sacred biography is a common enough phenomenon, the one used by Capgrave contains some apparent surprises. Let us look first at the apparent incongruity of calling on Apollo in a work of sacred biography whose central character, the young Roman maiden Katherine, was tortured and beheaded for refusing to worship Apollo. Capgrave surely was not unaware that placing Apollo before St. Paul he seemed to confer additional status on the pagan deity at the expense of one of Christendom's greatest saints. The choice of Apollo appears singularly curious. What precisely does Capgrave intend?

The key to the meaning of the *invocatio* and Capgrave's placement of Apollo and Paul lies in the attributive phrase "Heuynly reyne." If we consider the *sensus literalis* of the phrase, we are reminded of the physical, the world of matter and creation. "Reyne" was common Middle English noun for rain.[113] The adjective "heuynly" is, then, an *amplificatio* broadening the associations we make between the rain and the heavens, the very "reyn" that God sends. And as assiduous an exegete as Capgrave knew that the God of the Old Testament was fre-

---

112. *Ad Herennium*, IV, 11, VII; see St. Augustine, *De Doctrina Christina*, IV, 18, XXXV.

113. *Middle English Dictionary*.

quently depicted raining his bounty from the heavens on his people. For example, in Genesis 27:28, Isaac blessed his son Jacob and beseeched God to give him the dew from heaven: *"Det tibi Deus de rore caeli."* And yet, parallels with such Old Testament examples, however they may underline the majesty and the power with which God freely gives his gifts to those who call on him, fail to adequately explain the significance of Apollo in this line.

The Middle English noun "reyn" also could mean a quality of light, a splendor, a brightness, or simply light.[114] This arena of associations seems immediately applicable to Apollo, whose most common epithet in antiquity, and one retained in medieval texts, was Phoebus, "gleaming one." Although Apollo's epithets in antiquity are many and not always distinctive, he has always had names which associate him with the sun. For the ancient Greek, Apollo actually shared in the brightness of the sun. He became, by a process of analogy, first the daylight, then clarity, and finally rationality itself. Returning to Middle English text the "heuynly reyne/that apollo bar a-bowte," it makes perfectly good sense to read this line as a reference to Apollo's gleaming, sunlike brilliance, the burning flash of his rationality in an otherwise black world. Of course, this still does not explain why Capgrave chose to keep Apollo in this line—assuming, of course, that he was in the nonextant text of Arreck—nor does it address the allusion to St. Paul.

The same "reyne" sent to Apollo is sent to Paul. If this "reyne" is light, Apollo's brilliance, his sharp wit in a world of suetlike judgments, then, following the line's syntax, this "reyne" must also point to a light associated with Paul. The most dramatic incident in Paul's life which concerns heavenly light is his conversion. It was on the road to Damascus, as Luke tells us in Acts 9:3, that Paul was blinded when "suddenly a light from heaven flashed all around him" (*et subito circumfulsit eum lux de caelo*). There is an interesting interpretation of this event which Luke places in the mouth of Paul himself. In Acts 26:13, Luke records the scene of the bound and chained Paul brought before King Agrippa to be examined for heresy. Paul recounts the incident on the road to Damascus of so many years ago, telling Agrippa that the light which blinded him was brighter even than the sun; indeed, this very light contained God: *die media in via, vidi, rex, de caelo supra splendorem solis circumfulsisse me lumen.* Paul goes on to tell Agrippa that a voice spoke out of the light and identified himself: *Dominus autem dixit: Ego sum Iesus quem tu persequeris.* This portrayal of Paul re-

114. Ibid.

flecting on the moment of his conversion underscores the importance of the event in particular for the early Christian church. It seems quite likely that Paul's conversion—an event which influenced other saints' lives, as in *Vita Sancti Eustachii*—lies behind Capgrave's expression "heuynly reyne." Moreover, we know from Bale's catalogue that Capgrave completed a commentary on Acts, testifying to his interest in this work and his inevitable reading of the considerable commentary on it.

Two questions remain unanswered, however. Why did Capgrave juxtapose the two figures of Apollo and Paul, and why was the figure of Apollo used in this life? First, I would propose that Capgrave is using the two figures appositively. The historically later figure of Paul is intended to extend and complete the associations begun and contained in the earlier figure of Apollo, the god of rationality. The light which blinded Paul was the light of Christian revelation; it was the blinding light of the paraclete which all the commentaries understood as fructifying the earlier light of wisdom unaided by revelation. As the New Testament emphasis on the commandment to love was meant to supersede the prescriptive legalism of the Old, then Paul, who from the perspective of the *sensus allegoricus* represents reason aided by revelation, must outshine Apollo, the representative of reason alone.

The figure of Apollo also serves to illustrate Capgrave's here unstated belief that in antiquity, prior to the birth of Christ, mysterious prophecies concerning the Incarnation circulated among righteous individuals. For example, in his guide to the city of Rome, *Ye Solace of Pilgrimes,* he explicitly argues in support of the common notion that Vergil had knowledge of the virgin birth of Christ:

> men may have mervelle that Virgille shuld have sweche knowinges of the mysteries of out Feith. And I answere therto that the Holy Host putte His ʒiftes not only in gode men of trew beleve, bot eke in other, as it is saide of Cayphas prephicied of Cristes deth./The Evangelist seith eke of him this: "These wordes sey he not of hymselff, bot because he was bisshop for that ʒere, therfore he prephicied."[115]

Notice the emphasis on prophecy, indeed, what one might call estatic prophecy; Capgrave claims the words Caiphas spoke were not his own but revealed. Apollo was widely held to have been the voice of prophecy, the most celebrated interpreter of symbols and the source of inspiration for the Delphic oracle. If we consider once again the grammatical apposition between Apollo and Paul in this line, it would seem that Capgrave intended that what Apollo was to the Greek, Paul was

---

115. *The Chronicle of England,* p. 358.

to the Christian. Paul is the Christian counterpart of the pagan Apollo: he is the high priest to the Gentiles; he is entirely dependent on the Christian God for his power, and his Epistles written in Greek (the first language of philosophy) are the first attempts at offering an interpretation of the hidden mysteries of the Christian religion. Paul and Apollo are thus both symbols of the hermeneutic struggle for explaining divine revelation.

The figure of Apollo is prominent in the rhetorical handbooks of the greatest rhetoricians, especially form the late seventh century, when he was frequently celebrated as the muse of music and poetry. He is cited as an apt figure for *invocatio* by such important rhetoricians as Rufinius of Antioch, Priscian, and Alberic of Monte Casino. In his *Dictaminum Radii* (formerly known as the *Flores Rhetorici*), Alberic, in a discussion of the importance of clarity in a theme, cites Apollo as a figure who enhances understanding and wisdom: "but if you deprive your theme of what is necessary to understanding it, how can you be of any more value to me than Apollo when he hides his face?"[116] By the fifteenth century, there existed a well-established tradition in verse of invoking Apollo's aid as a muse especially helpful to clarity and insight.

Capgrave and the Tradition of *Virtus*

The final line in our stanza—"It maketh vertu to growe in mannes soule"—moves the discussion of the importance of the "heuynly reyne" from the exalted level of Apollo and Paul to everyday mortals. The "It" in line 7 is, of course, the "heuynly reyne" of grace. This grace, which creates in men the predisposition to the virtuous life, Augustine referred to as *delectatio coelestis, inspiratio dilectionis,* and *cupiditas boni.* Such grace also is the means to effect individual redemption, and it may signify the most important characteristic of grace, the indwelling of the Holy Spirit in the human soul, what the Fathers called the *inhabitatio Spiritus Sancti.* It was a commonplace of medieval theology that grace transformed the human spirit. Further, the theology of grace is at the basis of any medieval theory of ethics. What is less discussed is the medieval idea that grace, which is the cause for *cupiditas boni* and the deeds subsequent to that desire, is crucial in medieval thinking on miracles and sanctity.

116. J. J. Murphy, ed., *Medieval Eloquence*, pp. 303–6.

Walter Daniel, in his *Epistola ad Mauricium,* argued that it was the
very deeds (*merita*) of the saint's life that produced the miracles: *ut
sciant Alredum merito miracula pepetrasse.* He argued from the Augustinian position that miracles are an expression of God's will—
repeating the widely held belief in the principle *voluntas Dei salvifica*—
and it is those men of good life who are able to do what God wills: *et
michi facile credibile uidetur homines uita bona preditos facere posse
quod Deus uoluerit.* Walter suggests that it makes perfect sense to believe that the virtuous deeds themselves are given freely by God to
those who live soberly, piously, and justly: *Quid autem rectius quam
ut intelligamus sobrie et pie et iuste uiuentibus a Deo dari uirtutis opera?* It would appear that a number of influential hagiographers, as well
as some theologians, saw grace, the desire for the good, the practice
of virtuous living, and the performance of miracles as intimately connected.

We have seen how Agnellus based his argument for the creditability
of the lives of the bishops in the *Liber Pontificalis Ecclesiae Ravennatis* on their virtue, assuring his readers that because the bishops were
castique et elemosinarii they could believe with certainty the narratives of their lives. In Jonas of Bobbio's *Vita Sancti Columbani,* the
very word *virtutes* is used to signify miraculous deeds. Capgrave's idea
of *vertu* owes much to this tradition; it is a *vertu* freely given by God,
which creates in individuals *cupiditas boni* and is most visible in the
saints. It is this *vertu* which transformed Saul from the Christian baiter
to St. Paul, and it is this self-same "heuynly reyne" which brought to
St. Katherine the *vertu* to secure the crown of martyrdom.

Let me give another illustration of Capgrave's belief in the power of
vertu to nurture sanctity. He wrote his *Life of St. Gilbert of Sempringham* (ca. 1451) at the behest of the prior of Sempringham, for the
sisters of that monastery, who knew no Latin "namelych for the soli-
tarye women of ȝour religion whech vnneth can vndyrstande Latyn,
that thei may at vacaunt tymes red in this book the grete vertues of her
maystyr."[117] He opens his prologue with the figure of *captatio benevolentiae:* "I ffrer I.C., amongis doctouris lest . . . haue take on hand
to translate out of Latyn rith as I fynde be-fore me, saue sum addicionis
wil I put thertoo whech men of that order haue told me, and eke othir
thingis that schul falle to my mynde in the writyng whece be pertinent
to the mater."[118] With the exception of a brief chronological portrait of

117. Munro, *John Capgrave's Lives,* p. 61.

118. Ibid., p. 62.

the saint's ancestry and childhood, the work is largely given over to a panegyric celebrating Gilbert as an English *thaumaturge*.

Capgrave solidly locates Gilbert's sanctity in his propensity to do good deeds. Loyal to his text, Capgrave brings out in his translation the figure of the blessed child. This was a well-established *topos* and, if not a universal characteristic of celebrating heroic figures, can be accounted for in sacred biography by its presence in the Gospels and in classical biography. A variant of the blessed child was used, for example, by Eddius Stephanus in his *Vita Sancti Wilfridi* and by Walter Daniel in his *Vita Sancti Aelredi*. Capgrave is not a slavish translator, for he changes the Latin text's remarks concerning Gilbert's slowness in school into a singular virtue. He relates that when the child Gilbert was first sent to school, he showed more interest in virtuous behavior than in learning his lessons: "was at that age set to skole . . . his *corage* at that tyme was more enclyned to lerne *good maneris* than sotil conclusiones, eke be-cause aftirward that he was ordeyned to be a techer of vertuous lyuyng, it was conuenient that he schuld first be a disciple in that *scole of honestie*."[119] A comparison with the Latin *vita* shows that he has chosen his words with care; his diction underlines his intention that his lay readers make no mistake that the young Gilbert is a child of miraculous power, a child already singled out for great things. For example, the Middle English noun "corage" was far more frequently used in an affective sense, to refer to emotions or metaphorically to the heart. The noun "maneris" is a word rich in nuances and could refer to deportment, decorum, character, behavior, and, in a collective sense, one's morals. Capgrave is using the word in this latter sense. This passage, which is ostensibly about the young Gilbert's time at school, is really designed to point out the singularity of the child's religious zeal. Substituting "heart" for "corage" and "true morality" for "good maneris," we can rewrite this as: "his *heart* at that time was more enclyned to lerne *true morality*." Shortly after this passage, Capgrave uses an *argumentum ad auctoritatem,* comparing Gilbert's youth to that of the saintly Athanasius. Such comparison was intended to provide a bridge between the legends (cited by Rufinus) which lauded the intelligence and piety of the child Athanasius with those of Gilbert.

The final phrase I wish to consider is "scole of honestie." Besides the associations of integrity and trust that "honestie" connotes, this word had wide application in Middle English. It could indicate such diverse characteristics as comeliness, splendor, moral purity, chastity,

---

119. Ibid., p. 63. (Emphasis added.)

virginity, justness, and virtue. Just as in his *Life of St. Katherine,* where Capgrave made virtue the sine qua non for the Saint's sanctity— and in so doing followed in the great tradition begun by Nepos, Plutarch, and the Evangelists and handed on to Athanasius, Sulpicius Severus, Agnellus of Ravenna, Eddius Stephanus, Walter Daniel, Reginald of Canterbury, and John Tynemouth—so, too, in his *Life of St. Gilbert,* the "scole of honestie" is more properly the "school of [Christian] virtue."

The theology of grace which united believers in a *communio sanctorum,* which in turn gave birth to the understanding of the corporate personality so perfectly encapsulated by Gregory of Tours, has its realization in the world in human behavior, that is, Walter Daniel's *uirtutis opera* and John Capgrave's "ministrations of the goostly giftis whech be vertue of our Lordes." It is this same understanding of virtue that Agnellus appealed to when he asked his readers to believe that the *vitae Episcoporum* which he acknowledged as contrived *composui* were nonetheless the true biographies of the saints, *verae vitae sanctorum.* And it is this same principle of verification based on virtue caused by grace that John Capgrave—writing nearly a millennium after Gregory of Tours—believed made historical documents of his sacred biographies.

5 / The Passion of Saints Perpetua and Felicitas and the *Imitatio Christi*

> Her comrades in martyrdom were also saddened; for they were afraid that they would have to leave behind so fine a companion to travel alone on the same road to hope.
>
> *Passio Sanctarum Perpetuae et Felicitatis*

The Ideology of Female Sanctity

Although the *vitae* of female saints of the later Middle Ages are indebted to the conventions of medieval sacred biography no less than those of their male counterparts, these lives possess sufficient distinctive features to warrant their separate consideration. Although the creation of a taxonomy of female sanctity is beyond the scope of this chapter, there are four types of experience taken together (they almost constitute an ideology of convention) within which female spirituality is exemplified in these lives. These types occur early in the tradition of Christian sacred biography and grow out of a necessary adaptation of the *vita apostolica* and the Gospel depictions of Christ; moreover, they appear to be gender-specific and diachronically constant.[1] They are: the redefinition of ideas of kinship; freedom from the Pauline notion of sexual "indebtedness"; the importance of prophetic visions; and the change from virgin, wife, or widow to *sponsa Christi*.[2]

1. Ernest L. Stahl, "Literary Genres: Some Idiosyncratic Concepts," pp. 80–91, and Johannes A. Huisman, "Generative Classifications in Medieval Literature," pp. 123–49, in *Theories of Literary Genre,* ed. J. P. Strelka, Yearbook of Comparative Criticism III (London, 1978). J. LeClercq, *Monks on Marriage: A Twelfth-Century View* (New York, 1982), p. 39: "Thus it is that certain texts [hagiographic], written at an earlier date, witness to a mentality which had survived and was still prevalent in the twelfth century."

2. Clarissa W. Atkinson, *Mystic and Pilgrim: The Book and World of Margery Kempe* (Ithaca, 1983), p. 159.

All of these categories exist in the Latin text of the *Passio Sanctarum Perpetuae et Felicitatis,* the primal document in the development of the conventions which were to shape female sacred biography for a millennium.[3] This *Passio* is early in the tradition (ca. 203). Its primary focus is the heroism of the two women, and although it is part autobiography and part encomiastic-biography, the author of the *Passio,* and other later influential commentators such as Augustine, seemed more concerned to establish its status as a paradigmatic model.[4] Aside from the complex issue of its autobiographical status (see below), Perpetua's diary was important for her contemporaries not because it described *sui generis* behavior but because in her words and deeds her "fellow travelers" could discern the presence of the shaping role of their God (*semper Spiritum Sanctum usque adhuc operari Testificantur,* XXI, 11). Its influence is already present in certain (apocryphal?) *passiones* of the early fourth century, such as the *Martyrdom of Marian and James* (ca. 304) and the *Martyrdom of Montanus and Lucius.*[5]

Before turning to a closer examination of the *Passio* and its influence on the genre, let me illustrate the first type noted above in a text of the early fifteenth century. Margery Kempe's autobiography reports a conversation which she had with her husband as they walked together on a Friday evening in midsummer. Her husband asked her: "'Margery,

3. The edition used for this study is that of C. I. M. I. van Beek, ed., *Passio Sanctarum Perpetuae et Felicitatis* (Nijmegen, 1936). I have also consulted his *Passio Sanctarum Perpetuae et Felicitatis, Latine et Graece,* in Florilegium Patristicum 43 (Bonn, 1938); and that of H. Musurillo, *The Acts of the Christian Martyrs* (Oxford, 1972). Hereafter, the text shall be cited simply as *Passio;* all citations are taken from van Beek. The bibliography on the *Passio* and *Acta* is considerable. For major items, see: *Analecta Bollandiana,* "Inventaire Hagiographique," (1983), p. 330; *Bibliotheca Hagiographica Latina,* Vols. K–Z, nos. 6633–36; *Bibliotheca Hagiographica Graeca* 2, no. 1489; H. LeClercq's essay in *Dictionnaire d'archéologie chrétienne et de liturgie* 14, pt. 1 (cols. 393–444); L. Robert, "Une vision de Perpétue martyre à Cartage en 203," *Comptes rendus des séances de l'académie des inscriptions et belles lettres* (1982): 228–67; M.-L. Franz, *Passio Perpetuae: Das Schicksal einer Frau zwischen zwei Gottesbildern* (Zurich, 1983); P. Dronke, *Women Writers of the Middle Ages* (Cambridge, 1984); E. A. Petroff, *Medieval Women's Visionary Literature* (Oxford, 1986).

4. The issue of author/editor is unresolved. Although Tertullian is an obvious choice, there may have been others who were learned and imbued with a similar eschatological zeal capable of writing such a text; see J. Quasten, *Patrologia* (Westminster, Md., 1950), Vol. 1, pp. 182–84.

5. Musurillo, *Acts of the Christian Martyrs,* pp. 194–213, 214–39.

yf her come a man wyth a swerd & wold smyte of myn hed les þan I schulde comown kendly [have intercourse] wyth ȝow as I haue do befor, seyth me trewth of ȝour consciens—for ȝe wyl not lye—wheyr wold ȝe suffyr myn hed to be smet of er ellys suffyr me to medele wyth ȝow a-ȝen as I dide sum-tyme?' 'Alas, ser,' sche seyd, 'why meue ȝe þis mater & haue we ben chast þis viii wekys?' 'For I wyl wete þe trewth of ȝowr hert.' And þan sche seyd wyth gret sorwe, 'For-soþe I had leuar se ȝow be slayn þan we schuld turne a-ȝen to owyr vnclennesse.' And he seyd a-ȝen, 'ȝe arn no good wyfe.'"[6]

The alienation of affection illustrated in the above dialogue was muted for a fifteenth-century audience; they would have likely understood that Margery and her husband were both correct in their dichotomous judgments. Moreover, they would have recognized that these judgments were themselves derived from two competing systems of authority in medieval religious thinking: *magisterium* versus what Gerhoh of Reichersberg called the *materia* of the sacred text.[7] The dispute is finally between competing authority systems. Margery's position pits an ancient church teaching on female chastity against her husband's reliance on Paul's injunction that explicit in the contract of marriage is a sexual debt which must be paid (*uxori vir debitum reddat/ similiter autem et uxor viro,* 1 Corinthians 7:1–16; Ephesians 5:21–33). Their domestic conflict is resolved not through the power of disputation but rather by her claim to a traditional prerogative of holy women—chastity—legitimized by her prophetic appeal to a higher authority (from the Montanists to Aquinas, prophecy was considered a divine gift which women had greater access to than men). She convinces her husband that if he attempts to sleep with her, God (who has revealed this to her) will kill him.[8] The threat works; she achieves her sexual independence and is freed from her sexual indebtedness. Although not taken from a saint's life, this vignette, coming from the early fifteenth century, captures in miniature the thesis which we can see in female saints' lives from Perpetua and Felicitas to the apocryphal life of St. Cecilia to Blessed Maria d'Oignies or St. Catherine of

6. S. B. Meech, ed., *The Book of Margery Kempe,* EETS O. S. 212 (London, 1940), p. 23.

7. G. R. Evans, *The Language and Logic of the Bible: The Earlier Middle Ages* (Cambridge, 1984), p. 31. The distinction is between subject matter and meaning (*sensus*).

8. Meech, *Book of Margery Kempe,* p. 23.

Siena: female spirituality is ensnared by an ethos of sexual indebtedness whose legitimacy is based on Scripture.[9] The *via media* for medieval female sanctity illustrated in the lives of saintly women is narrow and strictly prescribed;[10] its accomplishment requires a deliberate rejection of social and sexual mores rooted in the family, even if such bonds were sanctioned by a benificent authority.[11] The end of this *renuntio* is not nihilism but rather the visionary establishment of a transcendent utopia where loved ones, family, and authority figures all flourish under the rule of faith, not law. In the *Passio Sanctorum Montani et Lucii* (ca. 258/59?) the Christian woman Quartillosa describes a vision of her son's earthly suffering as past (he was martyred three days previously); she depicts him being refreshed by a heavenly youth who bears two drinking cups full of milk and who brings him news of his election.[12]

Although the vision of the future presented in these lives is apocalyptic and utopian, the authors' intention to create a paradigmatic tale seeks expression by characterizing the deeds of these female saints in language of the particular; threats, deeds of heroism, and, indeed, even visions and examples of extreme asceticism are rendered in language which continually evokes the home, kinship, the family. Perpetua's beautiful dream of her brother Dinocrates's change from spiritual sickness to well-being is accomplished through *effictio*.

As is the case for many saints, if Marjorie is to grow in spirituality, she must first confront the problem of sexual autonomy. The flight from sexuality, and its consequent denial of the legal and moral indebtedness of the female as the crucial link in familial continuity is a *topos* of female sanctity. Abstinence is most frequently depicted prior to marriage, as in the *vita* of St. Agnes or St. Christina, where the young women defy the familial wish that they marry, and thereby incur martyrdom. But it can occur even in the lives of women who have been lawfully married for some time, as in the idiosyncratic *Vita Sancti*

9. Ibid., p. 24.

10. P. Verdier, "Woman in the Marginalia of Gothic Manuscripts and Related Works," in *The Role of Medieval Women in the Middle Ages,* ed. R. T. Morewedge (Albany, 1975), p. 123.

11. Ibid., p. 123; R. Lane Fox, *Pagans and Christians* (New York, 1986), p. 409; Anne Yarborough, "Christianization in the Fourth Century: The Example of Roman Women," *Church History* 45 (June 1976): 149–65.

12. Musurillo, *Acts of the Christian Martyrs,* p. 220; see Psalm 115:13 and the *Passio,* pp. 110–12.

Theodora (Christina of Markyate, ca. 1096/98–1160). Theodora resorts
to disguises and deception to flee her Christian marriage and is aided
in her illegal flight from her husband by male and female religious.[13] In
either case, the goal of these women, whether virgins or wives, is a
closer union with Christ (I intend the word *union* to bear a conjugal
connotation) which depends on a successful outcome of the struggle
not only with their own sexuality but also with that of the men in their
lives. The war is with men, not with mankind—with pungent realities,
not abstract forms. The struggle is often depicted in a crudely misanthropic manner and gets perilously close (and here it is the opposite of
the romance) to presenting a rationale for misogyny. For example, in
the *Vita Beate Christinae Mirabilis* (1150–1224), we read that Christina
fled the city for the country because "she suffered from the smell of
men."[14] The presence of such sentiments in works which were the primary vehicle for the expression of ecclesiastical orthodoxy makes the
label of antifeminism, as applied to exemplary texts used in the
church's pedagogy, somewhat more problematic.

Imago Christi Transformed

The convention proposes that only after having achieved a modicum
of independence, having thrown off the yoke of male sexual dominance, having freed themselves from the ideal of Pauline indebtedness,
having resolved the actual struggle with a recognizable individual and
achieved self-control is the holy woman able to free herself from the
thrall of family, to exercise a propensity for her visionary inheritance,
and, finally and most crucially, to become the bride of Christ. The figure of Christ is a complex one in medieval female spirituality. He can
be both man and boy, mother and father, brother and lover, and he
may exhibit all these features in a single work.[15] The most prominent
depiction which we find in the lives of the female saints, however, is

13. C. H. Talbot, *The Life of Christina of Markyate: A Twelfth Century Recluse*
(Oxford, 1959), and his "Christina of Markyate: A Monastic Narrative of the Twelfth
Century," in *Essays and Studies* n.s. 15 (1962): 13–26.

14. *Vita S. Christinae Mirabilis Virginis, AS* July, t.5 (Paris, 1868), p. 651: "a presbytero ecclesiae sacramento constricta, est coacta descendere: horrebat enim, ut quidam autumant, subtilitas ejus spiritus, odorem corporum humanorum."

15. C. Bynum, *Jesus as Mother: Studies in the Spirituality of the High Middle
Ages* (Berkeley, 1982).

the polarity between male dominance and subordination: Christ the comely lover and Christ the helpless child. The lover, in turn, becomes the bridegroom par excellence—a tradition indebted to the allegorical interpretation of the Song of Songs—and the child becomes the innocent infant of the Gospels, to be protected, shielded, and suckled.

The earliest explicit example of Christ the bridegroom in the *vitae sanctarum* is that in the *Passio Perpetuae*. The author describes Perpetua's entry from her prison into the arena on the day of her death: she walked as the "wife of Christ, the beloved of God" (*ut matrona Christi, ut Dei delicata*, XVIII, 2). The association of Christ with infants and Christ the child, although not explicitly remarked in the *Passio*, was apparently made by early medieval audiences. For example, Quodvultdeus associates the birth of Felicitas's daughter with that of Christ, claiming "she gave birth for Christ."[16] From the late second century, epithalamic language and language extolling spiritual maternity become part of the convention when discussing the attributes of female saints (e.g., the death of Blandina).[17] Such conventional language maintained itself throughout the Middle Ages, as the treatises of Ambrose, Jerome, and Augustine amply reveal. Gregory of Nyssa uses the word *bridegroom* repeatedly in his description of St. Macrina's (327–79) devotion to Christ.[18] The visionary Abbess Hildegard of Bingen (1098–1179) had her nuns dress up as brides with rings, tiaras, and veils on special feast days.[19] In the *Revelations* of St. Gertrude of Germany (1241–98), Gertrude reports a vision in which she sees Christ as a handsome youth of sixteen years old, "beautiful and amiable (*amabilem et delicatum*), attracting my heart and my eyes."[20] In another of

16. *Sermo de Tempore Barbarico, PL* 40, cols. 703–4: "Una earum erat praegnans [Felicitas], alia lactans [Perpetua]. Felicitas parturiebatur . . . pro Christo." See also *Passio,* pp. 156–57.

17. Musurillo, *Acts of the Christian Martyrs,* pp. 78–79: ". . . rejoicing and glorying in her death as though she had been invited to a *bridal banquet* instead of being a victim of the beasts" (emphasis added).

18. Petroff, *Medieval Women's Visionary Literature,* p. 81.

19. *Sanctae Hildegardis Scivias, PL* 197, cols. 336–37. Hildegard's language is also one of interiority. Christ's gift of virtue to her is like a physical fire (col. 697): "Ob hoc tu, Domine, da mihi in virtute tua igneum donum, quod in me exstinguat hunc fomitem et hunc adorem perversitatis."

20. Gertrude d'Helfta, "Oeuvres spirituelles," ed. J. Hourlier and A. Schmitt, in *Sources chrétiennes: series des textes monastiques d'occident,* Vols. 127, 139, 143, 255, 331 (1967–86), Vol. 139, p. 220: ". . . astantem mihi juvenem amabilem et delicatum, quasi sedecim annorum, in tali forma qualem tunc juventus mea exoptasset exterioribus oculis meis placiturum."

her visions, on Christmas Eve, she desires to possess the infant in her soul (*intra se teneret anima mea*).[21] Gertrude's language, is a rhetoric of interiority—an affective language deeply imbued with physical images. She repeatedly uses words which denote possession, desire, penetration, unbearable sweetness. Although she is perhaps more directly indebted to the Song of Songs and Cistercian commentaries on that text, such language also has a long history in the lives of the female saints, such as Felicitas, Blandina, and Crispina, to note only a few.[22] Christina of Markyate sees Christ as the "fairness of the children of men."[23] St. Umilta of Faenza (1226–1310) pleads with Christ "to hold me in your arms."[24] The popular legendary life of St. Katharine of Alexandria, in Middle English, depicts a sequence of charged events leading up to Katharine's wedding with Christ, a wedding he insists on. First, she is disrobed by the Virgin Mary in preparation for her baptism; the baptizing priest is blindfolded so as not to jeopardize her modesty and his virtue; she is then brought to Christ for the wedding.[25]

These texts have recently attracted considerable scholarly attention, but an important point remains to be made: this final stage in the attainment of female transcendence—especially as it involves misanthropy (construed here in the broadest sense)—is deeply ironic, not in a purely figurative sense, but rather as an inevitable philosophical incongruity operating in early Christian ideas of history so that the achievement of liberation sanctioned by the conventions in the texts is

21. Ibid., p. 258.

22. Ibid., Vol. 127, p. 81, for such expressions of longing as "Eia Iesu, cordis mei dilectissime"; "Aperi mihi, et introduc me in suavitatis tuae plenitudinem. Ex corde enim et ex animo desidero te; oroque te, ut tu solus possideas me. Eia, ego tua et tu meus. . . . Affice me ad perfruendum te" (p. 82). It should be pointed out that Perpetua's language, like that of Hildegard, Gerturde, and other medieval female diarists and the great bulk of the *vitae sanctarum,* has this predisposition to concern itself with the inner self; their religiosity begins inside, affirming that realm as the sine qua non for religious truth. This is different from much of the spiritual writing of their male counterparts, who are preoccupied with creation and teleology and whose languge is heavily indebted to metaphors finding God outside, above, distant, and so on. Note Crispina's remarks to the proconsul Anullinus: "ipse mecum est adiuuans me et ancillam suam in omnibus confortans," in Musurillo, *Acts of the Christian Martyrs,* pp. 302–9.

23. Talbot, *Life of Christina of Markyate,* p. 187; Petroff, *Medieval Women's Visionary Literature,* p. 149; Psalm 44:3.

24. Petroff, *Medieval Women's Visionary Literature,* p. 250.

25. C. Horstmann, ed., *The Life of St. Katharine of Alexandria,* EETS O. S. 100 (London, 1893), pp. 237–45.

dialectical. This ultimate stage is the inevitable obverse to the orthodox ideas of family, male sexuality, and authority sanctioned by the *civitas hominis*. It is in this oppositional sense that I believe all of medieval female sacred biography is at once ironic and utopian.[26]

Although these three categories of experience may also have a basis in a morphology peculiar to the Western imagination—an extratextual argument which provides a quasi-anthropological rationale for their diachrony—the direct inspiration for such depictions of female spirituality in medieval saints' lives is textual. The *Passio Sanctarum Perpetuae et Felicitatis* stands at the very beginning of the tradition of female saints' lives; provides much of the convention which develops in the genre for the next millennium; exercises an inestimable influence on the development of the lives of female saints through the liturgy, popular preaching, and ecclesiastical art; and contains as powerful an exemplification of these three categories as we have in all of the medieval *vitae sanctarum*.

Passio Sanctarum Perpetuae et Felicitatis

The story of the martyrdom of Perpetua and Felicitias is told with restraint. We can easily imagine why it was held in such respect by Tertullian, Augustine, Quodvultdeus, and many others throughout the history of the church. The *Passio* tells that on either the second or seventh of March of the year 203, in the city of Carthage, twenty-two-year-old Vibia Perpetua, who had taken the "Christian name," was taken from her home, imprisoned, mauled by a wild heifer, and, finally, having endured torture and humiliation, had her throat cut while the mob looked on and jeered raucously.[27] Perpetua was not alone in this hideous spectacle; imprisoned and martyred with her were her maidservant Felicitas; Felicitas's husband, Revocatus; and two young male catechumens, Saturninus and Secundulus. Although this small group contained some who were Roman citizens, their defiant refusal to renounce Christianity and to offer sacrifice to the emperor and gods (an intransigence which Stewart rightly affirms as an inheritance from Ju-

26. K. Burke, *A Grammar of Motives* (Berkeley, 1969), pp. 511–17.

27. See Lane Fox, *Pagans and Christians,* p. 601, for the change in the audience's reaction.

daism)[28] was behavior contrary to Trajan's explicit remarks in his reply to Pliny (which were still being enforced). Moreover, their behavior was considered contemptuous of the religious and legal customs of the state—and the unavoidable sentence, if the magistrates could not get the Christians to sacrifice, was death. Such noncompliance was viewed, as Leitzmann avers, as political rebellion.[29] There was little else available to the authorities except to pass a sentence of death.

The story of the heroism of Perpetua and Felicitas has been celebrated and revered by the church for almost two millennia. The feast appears in the earliest Roman (354) and Syriac calendars (late fourth century) as well as in the Martyrology of Jerome. Perpetua appears in the Gelasian Sacramentary (fifth century), and likely appeared in the fragmentary Leonine Sacramentary.[30] The *Passio* was so popular in Africa during the late fourth and early fifth centuries that Augustine warned that their *passiones* were in some communities being placed on a par with Scriptures. The popularity of the cult is evident in liturgical texts and inscriptions and in church dedications and ornamentation.[31] Augustine's remarks point to an interesting feature of a text's achievement of what I have called canonicity and beg a brief digression. Sacred biography returns to the medieval audience the freedom to fictionalize in a genre which was seen as holy. Once the New Testament canon was fixed and the apocryphalizing literature based on the now inviolate sacred Scriptures was exhausted, the single outlet for continued recreation of the *vita apostolica* in succeeding ages was the biographies of Christian saints.

The language of Perpetua's diary in the *Passio* is unadorned and direct. Auerbach was the first to point out its richness as a representative of *sermo humilis*.[32] The lack of rhetorical conventions gives Perpetua's

28. Z. Stewart, "Greek Crowns and Christian Martyrs," in *Memorial Andre-Jean Festugière: antiquité païenne et chrétienne,* ed. E. Lucchesi and H. D. Saffrey (Geneva, 1984), p. 127.

29. H. L. Leitzmann, "The Christian Church in the West," *Cambridge Ancient History* 12 (Cambridge, 1971), p. 571.

30. The Leonine Sacramentary is missing the feasts for January through March, and hence the March 7 feast is not present.

31. E. Diehl, *Inscriptiones Latinae Christianae Veteres* I (Berlin, 1961), nos. 2040a–41; see also nos. 1959a, 1962, 3138.

32. E. Auerbach, *Literary Language and Its Public in Late Latin Antiquity and in the Middle Ages* (New York, 1965), p. 60.

voice greater realism and tends to confirm our reception of it as auto-biographical. We hear the singular voice of that isolated, at turns fright-ened and grieving, yet committed young woman—a voice whose avoid-ance of rhetorical polish, whose fractured syntax, simple lexicon, and dialogic naturalism underscore its authenticity, and hence draw the reader into the dark, hot dungeon, to follow this now courageous, now fearful, now joyous band of young people as they go to their deaths admidst the cacophony of the screaming crowds. Unlike other contem-porary *acta* in which women figure, such as the speech of Agathonice in the Latin recension of the *Martyrdom of Saints Carpus, Papylus, and Agathonice,* Perpetua keeps, as Dronke has written, "steadily to the essential—no observation seems gratuitous, no word excessive."[33]

The story stresses incidents that we find only infrequently in the idealized narratives more typical of sacred biography: scenes of inti-macy in prison between Perpetua and her infant son, her concern for her family, an economically portrayed tableau of the quick dispatch with which the authorities decided her case and scorned Perpetua's father, vivid images of the stifling reality of the Carthaginian prison, genuine expressions of fear not sanitized by religious dogma. All of the elements contribute to the text's special status in what Musurillo re-ferred to as the tradition of martyr literature.[34]

Perpetua's History

Perpetua was the daughter of a family of some standing in Carthage. She was married and had an infant son. We are told almost nothing of her husband. It would appear that Perpetua was a recent convert to apocalyptic African Christianity (*alterum aeque catechumenum*, II, 2) and as such fell under the recent constitutions of Septimus Severus (201–2, an emperor whose reign was otherwise tolerant of the Chris-tians), which, in order to stop Jewish and Christian propaganda, for-bade under pain of death new conversions to Judaism or Christianity.[35]

The figure of Perpetua's father is important in the argument of the

33. Musurillo, *Acts of the Christian Martyrs,* p. 34; Dronke, *Women Writers,* p. 17.

34. H. Musurillo, ed., *The Acts of the Pagan Martyrs* (Oxford, 1954), pp. 236–46.

35. S. N. Miller, "The Army and the Imperial House," *Cambridge Ancient History* 12 (Cambridge, 1971), p. 19.

narrative.[36] He speaks with his daughter at crucial moments throughout the story: at the outset early in the affair (III); during the trial which determines her guilt (V, VI); and, lastly, just before her death in the arena (IX). All three scenes provide the narrative with a logic to move closer to the denouement, her martyrdom; each rends the fabric of father-daughter relationship a bit more. This father and daughter were uncommonly intimate for provincial Roman citizens during this period. Perpetua's father tells her that he has favored her above all her brothers (*praeposui omnibus fratribus tuis*, V, 2), a clear sign of her special status in his eyes.

The depiction of Perpetua's father has an unavoidable political dimension as well. Christianity was found especially distasteful by the educated upper classes (where we must place Perpetua's father), as the Platonists Celsus and Porphyry make perfectly clear. Celsus condemned the cult's apparent abandonment of reason, he viewed Jesus as a fake making use of magical powers, and he believed that the movement had an inescapable political agenda and consequently was a threat to the stability of the state. Prophyry's challenge was more subtle: he praised Jesus as a hero, comparable to his revered Pythagoras, while condemning the Christians for perverting Jesus's genuine teaching.

Perpetua's representation of her father throws into relief her understanding of his two primary roles: first and most obviously as a distraught parent, but secondly as an embarrassed, angered, and threatened citizen who publicly followed the ancient traditions of the Roman family and state, that is, as *paterfamilias*. Because these roles are contradictory, the dialogue between Perpetua and her father often expresses otherwise unresolved dilemmas. In rejecting her father's public persona, she is forced into rejecting the loving parent figure. In the space of eight lines in chapter 3, Perpetua writes that her father came to persuade her to abandon Christianity because of his affection for her (*pro sua affectione perseveraret*, III, 1) but that immediately following the debacle of their conversation and his diabolic arguments (*cum argumentis diaboli*, III, 3), she was refreshed by his absence (*refrigeravi absentia illius*, III, 4). The conjunction of *diaboli* and *refrigeravi* (the latter an unmistakable Christian locution) points to her necessary, albeit rending, ostracism of her father and consequently that of her family.[37] Politics and parenting have become impossibly and tragically

36. Dronke, *Women Writers*, p. 4.

37. Auerbach, *Literary Language*, p. 62.

fused, and the image of the new father wrought from this lamentable collision is more threatening than nurturing to Perpetua. This complex characterization of her father becomes the dominant *topos* of the male parent in later female saints' lives.

At least one member of Perpetua's family, her brother, was a catechumen, and it appears that the rest of the family, with the exception of her father, if not Christian, respected her decision to persevere in her belief. Perpetua says that she spoke out of her anxiety about her child to her mother (*sollicita pro eo adloquebar matrem,* III, 8) and to her brother (*confortabam fratrem,* III, 8), who grieved for her (*tabescebam . . . videram mei beneficio,* III, 8). Her decision to embrace Christianity would cost the family its standing in the community, and it was to cost her life. Indeed, her father, appearing before the procurator Hilarianus, appealed to Perpetua to recant and not to destroy her family and her son's life (*Miserere . . .* [her father said] *aspice filium tuum, qui post te vivere non poterit,* V, 2–4). When she sends the deacon Pomponius to her father for her son, her father, acting in the best interests of his family and the state, refuses to return the child—the sole guarantor of a non-Christian future for his heirs—to her *Sed pater dare noluit,* VI, 8).[38]

If one can point to a dominant thesis in this complex narrative, it is the imperative for the Christian to witness in times of persecution. Spiritual autonomy as a precondition for salvation depends on this witness, and as natural corollaries of this act of public confessing come familial and political independence. Conversion to Christianity forces on the individual the choice between *fidei Christo* and *fidei mundo;* the *Passio* presents no acceptable *via media.* Such a radical (one might say suicidal) eschatology was being proselytized by Montanists at roughly this time. But what *consolatio* is awarded to those who seek the faith despite the threats of the state or family? Paulinus of Nola, writing to his friend and relative Melania the elder (a Roman Christian ascetic of some prominence), remarks: "We ought not to put loyalties or fatherland or distinctions or riches before God."[39]

In the *Passio,* not only does the promise of salvation console, but the *Spiritus Sanctus* will physically shield them—like the martyr Blandina, they will enjoy an "analgesic state" protected from even the most

38. Yarborough, "Christianization in the Fourth Century," p. 156.

39. Ibid., p. 164, quoting P. G. Walsh, *Letters* (Westminster, Md., 1966), Ep. 25, 2.

barbarous suffering.[40] Perpetua is unaware of her first trampling by the wild cow and initially refuses to believe it: "she refused to believe it until she recognized the cruel marks on her body and her dress" (*non prius credidit,* XX, 9). Although the *Passio* appears early in the development of the genre, it is well to note how conventionalized these antinomian ideologies have already become.[41] The invincibility of the saint—her immunity from the pain of physical violence as it crystallized into a conventional *topos* in later *vitae sanctarum*—in the Latin tradition has its ancestry here.

Whether the *Passio* is influenced by Montanism or edited by Tertullian or one of his followers is not an issue for our study. What is important is the legacy it bequeathed to the convention of later medieval saints' lives: women as models of unconventional heroism capable of autonomy; the idea of the chaste life as *primus inter pares;* the desire for union with Christ; the subordination of the blood family; the use of prophecy and apocalyptic visions; allegory; psychomachia; and the apparent indifference to persecution, pain, and suffering on the part of the saints. Although Lomanto attempts to restrict the breadth of the text's influence, its presence in the *canon missae* from the fourth century and its use in monastic *lectiones* provide an indisputable basis for a diffuse though not necessarily direct influence, an influence that may have served more to shape or to outline rather than to direct.[42]

40. Musurillo, *Acts of the Christian Martyrs,* pp. 66–73; see Frend, *Martyrdom and Persecution,* p. 264, citing Clement of Alexandria's belief in the martyr as an imitator of Christ.

41. J. Danielou, *The Origins of Latin Christianity* (London, 1977), p. 22.

42. Fox, *Pagans and Christians,* p. 752; *Early Sources of the Liturgy,* ed. Lucien Deiss, trans. B. Weatherhead (London, 1967), an immensely useful book, as it presents in summary fashion the liturgical observations of the earliest Christians. For example, Hippolytus of Rome describes a late-night practice called "Nocturnal Praise," in which the memories of "the men of old who bequeathed us this tradition" are prayed for. This may be a precursor of the remembrance of the saints in Matins. J. A. Jungmann, *The Early Liturgy: To the Time of Gregory the Great* (Notre Dame, 1959), pp. 181, 235; see also his monument, *Missarum Sollemnia: Eine Genetische Erklärung der Römischen Messe* (Wien, 1949), Vol. 2, pp. 207–19, 301–14. This is the standard work on the history and evolution of the Roman mass. Josef A. Jungmann, *Pastoral Liturgy* (London, 1962), p. 166. Jean Michel Hanssens, "Aux origines de la Prière Liturgique: Nature et Genèse de l'Office des Matines," *Analecta Gregoriana* 57 (1952): 87, in a discussion of the interval between the vigil and Matins, calls our attention to *Missae:* "en automne et en hiver, ils etaient séparés par un intervalle plus ou moins grand, rempli toutefois par des lectures entrecoupées de prières et de

The Latin text of the *Passio Sanctarum Perpetuae et Felicitatis* consists of a prologue and twenty-one chapters. Discussions of the language of Perpetua's diary remain controversial and, although of less importance to our discussion, they are worth mentioning briefly. Dodds and, most recently, Lane Fox argued for the original autograph to be Greek; Auerbach, Fridh, Musurillo, Petraglio, Dronke, and Hal-

---

chants, et nommées *missae*"; also p. 9: "Par le nom de matines, nous désignons l'heure de l'office canonique destinée à être célébrée à la fin de la nuit, en telle façon que sa conclusion coincide avec l'aube." See also B. de Gaiffier, "La Lecture des Actes des Martyrs dans la prière Liturgique en Occident, à propos du Passionnaire Hispanique," *Analecta Bollandiana* 82 (1954): 138–42, especially note 3 on p. 142, where Von Dobschutz comments on the practice in Rome at the time of the Council of Hippo (October 393): "Auch in Rom wurden die Martyrerakten an den bestimmten Tagen bei den dem betreffenden Heiligen gewidmeten Statten verlesen: aber eben nur hier, nicht auch in anderen Kirchen." See also Hadrian I's letter to Charlemagne, in which he discusses the readings of the passions: "Vitae enim patrum sine probabilibus auctoribus minime in ecclesia leguntur. Nam ab orthodoxis titulatae et suscipiuntur et leguntur. Magis enim passiones sanctorum martyrum sacri canones censuerunt, ut liceat eas etiam in ecclesia legi, cum anniversarii dies eorum celebrantur"; in J. Mansi, *Sacrorum Conciliorum Nova, Et Amplissima Collectio* 13 (Florence, 1767), col. 800, *Epistola Hadriani Papae ad Carolum Regem*. Although for a later period, see J. B. L. Tolhurst's exhaustive discussion of the *Cursus* in his edition of *The Monastic Breviary of Hyde Abbey, Winchester*, HBS, Vol. 6 (London, 1942), pp. 143–237; K. Young, *The Drama of the Medieval Church*, Vol. I, pp. 47–64. Although Young gives a quite thoroughgoing schematization of the entire *Cursus,* his model is based on twentieth-century practice. Young's commentary often does not clearly illustrate the development of the *horae* and thus is best supplemented with David Knowles's *The Monastic Order in England*, 2nd ed. (Cambridge, 1963); Eisenhofer and Lechner, *The Liturgy of the Roman Rite* (New York, 1961); I. H. Dalmais, *Introduction to the Liturgy* (Baltimore, 1961); Suitbert Baumer, *Histoire du Bréviaire,* trans. Reginald Biron, "Etat de l'office à la fin du XIIe ou au début du XIIIe siècle" (Paris, 1905), Vol. II, pp. 47–59. For a most illuminating discussion of the symbolic and typological implications of the liturgy, see Jean Danielou, *The Bible and the Liturgy* (London, 1960), p. 17: "the life of ancient Christianity was centered around worship. And worship was not considered to be a collection of rites meant to sanctify secular life. The sacraments were thought of as the essential events of Christian existence, and of existence itself, as being the prolongation of the great works of God in the Old Testament and the New." Although not specifically concerned with the presence of prayers to the saints in the mass, O. B. Hardison's essay, "The Mass as Sacred Drama," in *Christian Rite and Christian Drama in the Middle Ages* (Baltimore, 1965), pp. 35–79, illustrates the great importance of the ritual aspects of the liturgy. It is interesting to note, as Hardison points out on pp. 37–38, that Amalarius, in his *Liber Officialis,* although condemned by the Council of Quercy in 838, was very popular with the laity, who were said to have "read them [the alleogorizations of the Divine Office] assiduously."

porn support Latin.[43] There is circumstantial evidence supporting Latin. Early-third-century Carthage was overwhelmingly Roman in its upper classes—Perpetua may have been from this class; it is said that she was *honeste nata, liberaliter instituta,* and, even if she were able to speak some local Punic dialect and Greek, the daily speech of and within her class would have been Latin. The majority of the names in the *Passio,* including Perpetua's own, are Latin. And, if Juvenal's *Satire Six* is any barometer of actual female literacy, very few women, even those from the upper classes living in Rome in the opening years of the second century, could write Greek. Finally, the church in Carthage was founded from Rome, and Tertullian acknowledged that for the Carthaginian church Rome had apostolic authority. Therefore, we would expect a greater dominance of the language of the church of Rome.

The complex text of the *Passio Sanctarum Perpetuae et Felicitatis* breaks into two major sections, the biographical and the autobiographical. The biographical is that of the anonymous author (164 lines); the autobiographical is that attributed to Perpetua (166 lines); and to her fellow martyr Saturus (51 lines). The editor unambiguously states that both Perpetua and Saturus wrote their accounts in their own hand (*sicut conscriptum manu sua,* II, 3; *quam ipse conscripsit,* XI, 1). The prologue, the first three chapters, and chapters 14 through 21 are in the hand of the editor; chapters 3 through 10 are the diary of Perpetua; and 11 through 13 are by Saturus. The editor's contribution to the narrative is not inconsiderable, being only two lines shorter than that of Perpetua herself. Thus, his narrative not only gives to the autobiographical accounts a frame, but, because his text contains many of the hallmarks of sacred biography (i.e., it is allegorical and epideitic), it has the inevitable effect of placing for his contemporaries the recent autobiographical accounts (*nova documenta,* I, 2) in the larger tradition of exemplary biography (*Deus honoretur,* I, 2).

And yet, although one acknowledges the uniqueness of the images in the *Passio* and their lexical and syntactic similarities to natural dialogue, it is nonethess our recognition of these elements as they affect us which is the basis for believing the document to be autobiography.[44] The autobiographical claim is resolved in the perceptual bridge be-

43. Dronke, *Women Writers,* p. 283; and J. Halporn, *Passio Sanctarum Perpetuae et Felicitatis* (Bryn Mawr, Pa., 1984), p. 4.

44. Danielou, *The Bible and the Liturgy,* p. 60.

tween text and reception. There is no contemporary corroborating evidence outside the claim made in the text that it is autobiographical. Although we cannot establish its historical "authenticity" beyond a shadow of a doubt, we can affirm the power of the *Passio* to shape our reading of the text as autobiography or, perhaps more appropriately, as prison diary, and in so doing must perforce be satisfied to place it within a sphere of textual/historical indeterminacy.

Regardless of one's position on the authenticity of the autobiographical aspects of the text, those chapters attributed to Perpetua—chapters 3 through 13, written in a sometimes dislocated, sometimes rapturous, and sometimes jarringly realistic style—have served to distinguish it from the considerable number of *passiones* extant from the period of the persecutions. A number of effectively written *Acta* featuring the heroism of women date from roughly that period but they never created the same stir. For example, although *The Letter of the Churches of Lyons and Vienne* (for which Eusebius is our only source), written for distribution to the churches of Asia and Phrygia, described quite effectively the brutal martyrdom of Christians in Lyons in the summer of 177, it never approached the popularity of the *Passio Sanctarum Perpetuae et Felicitatis*.[45]

Perpetua's Dream

Slightly more than a third (62 lines) of Perpetua's complete diary (166 lines) is given over to her four dreams. Much scholarship has debated and illuminated the influences, classical, Christian, or universal folk, which her dreams appear to reflect and the relationships which exist between the dream and the world outside the dream.[46] In the discussion which follows, I would like to present an approach to understanding her dreams which is less an interpretation of the dreams but more of a methodology for interpreting them.

Before we pose the central question, let us begin by acknowledging the particular difficulties this text presents. First, the single greatest barrier to understanding Perpetua's dreams is paradoxically the very fact of their autobiographical status. This text is the only one which

45. Musurillo, *Acts of the Christian Martyrs*, pp. 62–85.

46. Dronke, *Women Writers*, pp. 1–17; E. R. Dodds, *Pagan and Christian in an Age of Anxiety* (Cambridge, 1965), pp. 47–53; M.-L. von Franz, *C. G. Jung, Aion* (Zurich, 1951), pp. 389–496, and *Passio Perpetuae: Das Schicksal*.

makes such a persuasive claim to autobiography by an educated Christian woman from late antiquity. As such, it presents all the attendant difficulties of historiography that uniqueness entails, not the least of which is the label *autobiography,* a word that evokes an expectation on the part of a modern reader which this text cannot meet and was never intended to meet. Her personal comments are meager and only indirectly indicate status, education, and reading habits. There are, however, a number of unambiguous citations of the Old and New Testaments in her dreams. The entirety of the *Vetus Latina* and, according to Danielou, Latin Judeo-Christian apocrypha such as *5 Esdras,* the *Ascension of Isaiah,* and the *Shepherd of Hermas* were available in late-second-century Carthage. By comparison, the classical echoes in the dreams are faint.[47]

Perpetua's personal reflections are set within the larger frame of the conventions of sacred biography and may themselves have been edited by the editor of the *Passio.* Thus, a strict separation between individual vision and paradigmatic expression seems impossible to assert conclusively. Further, as I shall argue, certain of Perpetua's remarks suggest that she may not have intended or believed that a clear distinction did exist between the individual and emblematic. An autobiographical memoir for Perpetua, I believe, was not a personal expression of an autonomous, individual spirit, which viewed the self as a congeries of intellectual and ethical impulses separable from all others. Rather, her reflections seem to suggest that the spirit is most nearly human when it is seen as a homunculus, reflective of more enduring paradigmatic realities. And in this regard, her diary is conceptually like St. Augustine's *Confessions.*

Instead of a traditional *Toposforschung* seeking to match an external text with Perpetua's image and thus to draw her intention from the match, let us begin by inquiring into what Perpetua understood her dreams to mean. Since we have her summary interpretation at the end of each of her dreams, my suggestion might seem otiose. On the contrary, although her conclusions at the end of each dream are crucial, they are nonetheless interpretations made after reflecting on what she has penned: her "dream records." They are interpretations which because of her imprisonment and threat of death we should expect to mollify her anxiety (*et expaui,* III, 23), and, finally, they are interpretations which, as with the fourth vision, I believe she reads as an allegory of her eventual triumph (X, 14). In other words, her summary

47. Dronke, *Women Writers,* pp. 9, 284; see van Beek, *Passio,* p. 20.

remarks to each vision, written after she completed the composition of her dreams, are interpretations of each dream record. To ask what her dreams signified to Perpetua is to seek the meaning which she believed the dream records bore in their telling as narratives independent and prior to her summary interpretation of them. Primary to my understanding of the nature of Perpetua's dreams is the consideration that her dreams are records which are already interpretations. The original dreams (of which we only have these records) were a way of giving some structure and coherence to these traumatizing (*multis diebus passa sum,* III, 5–9) experiences. The dreams as she has written them (*conscriptum manu sua,* II, 3) are literary memoirs, after-the-fact records and hence—despite what we think about their authenticity—are another attempt at coherence, at translating from the primal experience in light of her present situation. Crucial to this step is that now the structure is inevitably shaped by such matters as lexical choice, syntax, argument, *elocutio,* and the requirements of audience-intended discourse. These dream records are the public language-vested *fabulae* of her conscious reflection on her past visions. They are not the primary experience of the dream, nor are they the transparent data from which she has constructed her summaries. They are her memory of those closed, primary experiences given utterance in designedly symbolic language. As Donatus remarked about Aeneas's dream of the horribly wounded Hector, a reader could on the "basis of experience conclude that he [Hector] foretold calamity and death, even if he had not said a single word." The figures in Perpetua's dreams are a type of allegorized foretelling.[48]

Although I believe that Perpetua's dreams are probably genuine, the narrative she has written has nonetheless been shaped by her language which, in turn, has been chosen in response to the circumstances surrounding the dreams' recall. In light of this, her judgment at the end of each dream record is a verification that she believes her narrative description of the dream and her memory of the dream to be in harmony with each other. Moreover, although the dream record is the product of intentional conscious reflection, it would be naive to assume that the narrative which results can render a depiction that is complete and informational, accurate; language is only rarely, if ever, capable of doing that. What the dream records reports as "truthful" is the intention of the informant modulated by language, selection, context, and milieu.

48. P. Kragelund, *Dream and Prediction in the Aeneid* (Copenhagen, 1976), p. 14.

It is impossible to consider what Perpetua believed these dreams signified unless we see it from her vantage point. A brief summary of those factors which were most salient will therefore aid the discussion. She is in prison. She is a new convert to a religion, a catechumen receiving instruction but not yet baptized. The Roman authorities had recently forbidden new converts to this sect. She is a mother, wife, daughter, and member of a family with stature in the community. She has received some education beyond the modicum allotted to women. She will likely die for her beliefs. Her choices have deepened her alienation from her kin and have been the cause of much personal and public suffering. Although it is possible to exaggerate the nature of her religious zeal, her recent conversion and her willingness to abandon family and son are indicative of deeply committed personal choice.[49] Paul's conversion was a powerful example to catechumens like Perpetua for the imperative to make a complete break with their past (Acts 9:1–30). Such conversions invariably imply a massive process of intellectual and affective substitution: values, education, loyalties, beliefs are carefully screened and transformed so as to "fit" with the new *Weltanschauung*. Former positions which do not fit are jettisoned or so changed as to be unrecognizable. To suggest that something very like this change must have been going on in Perpetua is not to reduce her to the status of an intellectual pushover for Christianity or some other contagious contemporary ideology such as Montanism, but, on the contrary, it is to try imaginatively to reconstruct the process she was undergoing and to understand what she believed was happening to herself in the greatest crisis she was ever to face.

Given these complex factors, I read Perpetua's dream records as deliberately sought prophecies of her impending martyrdom. The paradigm on which these prophecies depend most is the Gospel accounts of Christ. The actions described in the *Passio* are deliberate, mimetic; they constitute an *imitatio Christi*. Perpetua's choice of words to describe her memory of the dreams must be deliberate, consonant with this intention. And although they claim to be autobiography, they are utterly different from our modern understanding of the dream's role in self-revelation. Because of this process of deliberate selection, we must not overestimate the degree to which we can impute motives to her unconscious and hence assign influences to the *figura* in the dream

49. Leitzmann, "The Christian Church," pp. 524, 535.

record.[50] There are some persuasive reasons which support this position: first, the entire complex milieu works on and in Perpetua's personality; second, the process from experience to dream, from dream to record of dream, is evolutionary—vestigial bits and pieces of past experience are borne unincorporated from one stage into the next— and this process involves at least four levels of translation, the last of which is the product of conscious selection and is written in prose; third, she prefaces her dreams with the remark of her fellow inmate that she seems especially blessed, perhaps in a state of grace (*Domina soror, iam in magna dignatione es,* IV, 1) and has a special status with the deity;[51] fourth, she acknowledges that she knew she could talk with the Lord (*sciebam fabulari cum Domino,* IV, 2); and, lastly, her dream records are *not* the products of an associative frame, free from a discernible teleology. Perpetua announces at the outset of the first vision that she has asked for the vision and that she will tell her comrade on the morrow whether she has learned if she will be freed or condemned (*Crastina die tibi renuntiabo,* IV, 2). Her second and third visions were similarly intentional and quite specific in focus. Only the fourth vision has no prefatory expressed intentionality, but then it is the only one in whose conclusion the interpretation is deliberately allegorical (X, 14).[52]

The dream records, whatever we make of the individual influences which may be present in them, are for the dreamer a whole cloth; they are her unique response to her deliberate intention to discern some larger truth in her dreams (this primary hermeneutic effort is not incompatible with her exemplary intention) to convey, however partially, something of that truth; and, lastly, they are dreams which she believed

50. Kragelund, *Dream and Prediction in the Aeneid,* p. 14. Perpetua's summary interpretations of each dream seem more in the biblical tradition than the classical, but we cannot rule out her knowledge of the latter. For Semitic dream interpretations, see A. L. Oppenheim, "The Interpretation of Dreams in the Ancient Near East," *Transactions of the American Philosophical Society* 46 (1956): 179–255; and M. Himmelfarb, *Tours of Hell: The Development and Transmission of an Apocalyptic Form in Jewish and Christian Literature* (University of Pennsylvania, Ph.D., 1981). For dreams in classical literature, see P. Kragelund and G. Williams, *Technique and Ideas in the Aeneid* (New Haven, 1983), pp. 106–8.

51. Van Beek, *Passio,* p. 16. *Dignatio* can have the force of grace in some early medieval Latin texts; see Halporn, *Passio,* p. 30.

52. Dronke, *Women Writers,* p. 7. Dronke's caveat that we resist turning the dreams into a consistent ideological whole, whether Christian, Gnostic, or Jungian, is salutary, but such an argument can, if taken too far, attenuate the dreams from their pointedly religious context, that of a woman being persecuted for religious conviction.

were sanctioned by God.[53] Indeed, we should be astonished to learn that someone intending to sacrifice herself for a religious principle would not seek to locate her event within some larger absolute frame. The absence of such paradigms would be *prima facie* evidence against the notion of autobiography. Her remarks concluding each dream are at once a thematic judgment and a commentary on the appropriateness which her intention realized in the written record pays to her total experience. In light of this, her narrative descriptions of her visions, the language employed, the figures depicted, her role projected in the visions must be viewed in a manner consonant with her present consciousness, a consciousness which, no matter how singular and unique, was nonetheless radically imbued with a commitment to a deeply eschatological, cultic, and apocalyptic religion, one in which women were especially revered for their prophetic ability.[54] It is this triumph of location of the individual within the ideal that the *Passio* bequeathed to the legion of *vitae sanctarum*.

Further, since Perpetua's recall is deliberate, designed to support both herself and her fellows in their travail, it is arguable that she has extended the interpretation not only to each dream but beyond to encompass the four dreams, and that the dream records have a teleology forced upon them by her language as it attempts to translate the meaning of her situation. Perpetua in her search for self-understanding seeks a rationale for her present situation in the historical past. The historical continuum in which she places herself is the tradition of the martyr. As she reveals her most personal reflections on her situation, she intuitively expresses the paradigm latent in her experience.[55] There is no contradiction here between the autobiographical and the emblematic voices.

53. Although it is not my intention to give a reading of the four dreams, it appears clear that they are deliberately connected, possess a symmetry of image, and mirror events outside their immediate contexts. Dreams 1 and 4 have images of dominant males; 2 and 4 contain images of immaturity; 1 and 3 are thematically opposed, death versus victory, as are 2 and 3 with the same opposition. Dreams 1 and 2 illustrate struggle leading to death; 3 and 4 illustrate struggle leading to a healing triumph.

54. F. C. Klawiter, "The Role of Martyrdom and Persecution in Developing the Priestly Authority of Women in Early Christianity: A Case Study of Montanism," in *Church History* 49 (1980): 251–61. Klawiter sees the *Passio* as "without a doubt authored by a member of the New Prophecy [Montanism]" and Perpetua's dreams as consonant with that tradition. See also P. Wilson-Kastner, *A Lost Tradition: Women Writers of the Early Church* (Washington, 1981), p. ix; and Yarborough, "Christianization in the Fourth Century."

55. Tertullian, *Ad Uxorem,* I, 4, cited in van Beek, *Passio,* p. 16.

If this manner of reading her narrative has merit, it is unlikely that Perpetua (unlike someone recalling a dream in a secure, nonhostile situation) would have been unaware of the sources of the elements in her narrative; she would have been sensitive to their nuances, she would have intuitively recognized the rightness of them, however partial and fractured the rendering, and she may have censored some; she was able to judge the appropriateness of the language she used (she knew the community was to have the text shortly—X, 15) to render the totality of her meaning. In those instances when the details of a particular image seem to contradict or do not fit a particular interpretive line, the first justification for any further interpretation in a work of putative autobiography must be to ask to what degree Perpetua would have found such explanations significant (a signification which cannot be divorced from her context). The problem of the intentional fallacy is minimized in this text by the larger historical paradigms within which Perpetua saw her experience, that is, by the text's placement of these visions in an arena not *sui generis*.

Having now presented some of the context, we can investigate how the autobiographical and the paradigmatic are brought together. In her record of her first dream, after having scaled the perilous ladder (Genesis 28:12; *Ascension of Isaiah*) and trod on the dragon's head (Genesis 3:15; *Testament of Levi*), she enters an enormous garden where she spies an old man with gray hair milking sheep. First, the vision of paradise as an immense garden (*vidi spatium inmensum horti,* IV, 8)—an expression used in Judeo-Christian apocalypses—arises from her need to disassociate herself from the cramped, hellish underground prison she was in (*in carcerem,* III, 5; *ad carcerem,* VI, 6).[56] The figure of the white-haired man milking sheep (*oves mulgentem,* IV, 8) who welcomes her and gives her fresh cheese (*de caseo quod mulgebat dedit,* IV, 9) is a complex image and the subject of considerable discussion. A number of conflicting interpretations have been given of this figure and of the event she described, ranging from the Christian Eucharist to an image symbolizing the embryo and rebirth commented on by Aristotle (see *The Generation of Animals,* I, 729a; II, 739b) to that of a Jungian universal folk motif.[57] All of these interpretations have as their starting point a heuristic which exists outside the subject who designed the narrative. They first seek an external motif to match the one given in the text; they employ traditional *Quellenkritik.* But we might reverse

56. Danielou, *The Origins of Latin Christianity,* pp. 60–62.

57. Dronke, *Women Writers,* pp. 9, 284.

this procedure and put the question somewhat more directly: what did Perpetua think this figure and action signified? Although such a question may seem somewhat naive, the context for her situation makes it appropriate. It makes perfectly good sense in light of Perpetua's threatening situation that she would have sought in her own language some way to shape her memory into a record which would have immediate value, symbolic or otherwise, for herself and for her fellow prisoners. Is it not likely that she would have sought primarily a *consolatio* in her dreams?

What we are trying to discern by testing her intention is not the *a priori* applicability of a particular figure, whether classical, Christian, or universal, but rather a rationale emerging from the persona of Perpetua which would lend credence to a particular interpretation, which might give us a means to weigh conflicting alternatives, to discern whether the figure and the food are more likely classical, Christian, or a universal motif. Hence the requirements for understanding the figure of the old shepherd should derive from what she has told us about the totality of her situation at this particular moment. He should be a *figura* of consolation both human and otherworldly. I emphasize his positive role because other male authority figures who were important to her, including her father, turned away from her. The shepherd must be otherworldly in order to confirm her present eschatological course. His quasi-divine status also serves as a guarantee for her earlier statement that in these visions she could speak with God (*fabulari cum Domino*, IV, 2), and, lastly, the figure should be apocalyptic, because this male figure will be the locus which allows the dream to serve as a shadowy prophecy of the future. We have, as it were, created an imaginative thesaurus with which we might now seek to validate external influences.

Perpetua promised one of her fellow martyrs immediately before having the dream that she would tell him whether the dream predicted their being set free or being sent to their death (*Crastina die tibi renuntiabo*, IV, 2). Her final words before she recorded her dream indicate her conviction that the dream is a gift, something she was worthy to receive (*Et postulavi, et ostensum est mihi hoc*, IV, 2). Having proposed this way of reading, we can now use the sum of these pertinent details to point toward a figure which would express a totality of meaning. Given the weight of her expressed intentions and the complexity of her milieu, it is most likely that this dream figure—rendered as ably as possible given the traumatizing circumstances she has experienced—would have been an acutely personalized image of the good shepherd and that the cheese given to her is sacramental, despite the absence of such an exact iconographic image at this time.

Given Perpetua's heightened emotional state, it would be an unnecessarily critical literalism to look to the dream record for *figurae* which followed precise external representations of them. Her language is intentional; she seeks to communicate in words images of intentionality, images which express, however refractory they may appear, her belief in their truth. Her images may appear to distort and may even appear to contradict what art history and extant liturgical texts tell us regarding the image of the good shepherd and the sacramental meal, but such distortion is more apparent than real; the critical quest is to discover what Perpetua believed these curious images signified. For instance, surely she is radically condensing time and forcibly conflating normally separable realities when she associates the milking of the sheep with the fresh cheese she is given to eat. But such temporal compression and union of unlike objects is typical of dreams. Here the contradiction of everyday experience in the dream record underscores the likelihood of the text's autobiographical authenticity as well as insisting on its exemplary message. There is no necessary contradiction between her autobiographical dream records and her intention to place those experiences within a larger paradigmatic frame.

Having established the basis for the inquiry, we can now weigh the evidence of particular external influences. The connection of significance between Perpetua's depiction of the old shepherd and his gift of food and religious symbols (which she would have known) would be more primary than, for example, the association of cheese with generalized ideas of birth which we see in Aristotle's discussion of conception in the *Generation of Animals*. Her depiction, while not a programmatic reading of a single influence, may well represent a conflated, perhaps attenuated union of different experiences so typical of oneiric accounts. The only caveat I want to raise against my reading is the use of the modifier *quasi* in the line *et de caseo quod mulgebat dedit mihi quasi buccellam. Quasi* typically serves to qualify expressions, to call attention to their unique particularity. If Dodds is correct and the joining of milking and cheese is the sort of thing one is liable to find in dreams, what must we conclude when we note that such an example of unconscious behavior as that found in dreams is followed by the use of *quasi,* a word which exists in order to qualify the experience being presented? Is *quasi* the result of a hypocorrective intention on the author's part, seeking to qualify and to give some literalness to an experience *de caseo quod mulgebat* so at odds with normative experience? I do not believe the question can be answered completely to anyone's satisfaction. We return to indeterminancy.

I would like to propose that this forcibly yoked account makes use of the *agape* meal, the morning Eucharist service, the Carthaginian practice reserved for those receiving first communion, and possibly a lingering memory of Perpetua's baptism which she said took place shortly before in prison seen through a matrix of liturgically meaningful events.[58] Let us now turn to these liturgies and some of their pertinent elements, especially their use of food, taken in liturgically appropriate order. Tertullian writes in *De Corona* that those who have just been baptized are given a mixed drink of milk and honey. The *agape* meal of fellowship (also described by Tertullian in the *Apology*) was an evening meal at which the initiates offered a prayer recited while standing (see Passio, IV, 8; and *sed agapem cenarent*, XVII, 1) before a meal, including milk and cheese, was eaten. The morning Eucharist, by this time a separate service, was described by Hippolytus in the *Church Order* (ca. 200); he emphasized the intimacy of the sacramental and sacrificial aspects of this liturgy: the liturgical practice of the consumption of the sacramental bread and wine was possible because it was a gift of the Spirit sent because of the suffering of Jesus. Also celebrated in Carthage at this time was the practice of giving to "candidates" (Perpetua's words at this point seem to be an echo, *et circumstantes candidati*, IV, 8) at their first communion, aside from the bread and wine, a cup full of milk and one of honey as a foretaste of the heavenly sweetness which awaited the blessed in heaven. Perpetua reports that she awoke with the taste of something still sweet in her mouth (*conmanducans adhuc dulce nescio quid*, IV, 10). Furthermore, Perpetua's use of *candidati* "clothed in white" was an almost traditional expression for martyrs (see Revelation 7:13–14; *Passio*, X, 2; and other historical *acta*). Another characteristic of the Eucharistic feast practiced during the late second century concerns the function of the celebrant who, according to Justin Martyr's *First Apology* (ca. 155), was to take the consecrated food to believers languishing in prison. Given the liturgical closeness of the Roman and Carthaginian churches and the spread of Latin translations of Justin Martyr's work, it is not unlikely that Perpetua and her fellow inmates would have known such a pertinent tradition. Hence, given the nature of the dream, her reception of the fresh

58. Leitzmann, "The Christian Church," pp. 524–36.

cheese with cupped hands seems most likely to be a sacramental gesture conflated with memories of other liturgical ceremonies in which food was administered and eaten.

At the very least Perpetua would have known, and perhaps been involved in, liturgies in which a variety of foods, some sweet, resembling those conflated in her dream (i.e., milk and cheese), were available and administered by a priest. But these correspondences allow a broader and deeper insight into her thinking and that of her community. Keeping in mind that Perpetua was a catechumen, someone who has not yet fully entered into the fellowship (i.e., not having received the *Eucharist*), we may conceive of this dream as an eschatological prophecy of her full reception into the community by virtue of her martyrdom. Such a reading is persuasive because it not only gives a coherent rationale for this dream but also helps place all the other dreams in an intelligible frame. Having achieved the foretold promise of her redemption, Perpetua can now exercise one of the traditional gifts associated with such extreme thinking on martyrdom: the power to forgive sins and to restore people to salvation. Such power was hitherto the sole prerogative of the bishop or priest, but as early as 177, Irenaeus in his *Letter to the Churches of Vienne and Lyons* allowed that martyr-confessors had such power through their continual prayers and their shedding of tears. Hence, Perpetua's next two dreams of her brother Dinocrates, who had died without receiving instruction in the faith, exemplify her ability to free him from his spiritual longing. She says she was confident that she could help him in his trouble (VII, 9), and that her help is in the form of daily prayer with tears and sighs (*Et feci pro illo orationem die et nocte gemens et lacrimans, ut mihi donaretur, VII, 10*). Her vision of his recovery of health is a symbolic restatement that her prayers were efficacious (*Tunc intellexi translatum eum esse de poena, VIII, 4*). Her last dream, the victorious fight with the Egyptian, is then the clearest ratification that she has achieved her desire. This dream is the final prophecy that the paradise, the eternal *refrigerium* sought by this apocalyptic community of Christians, is now hers. Further, her remark that on undressing she suddenly was a man (*et facta sum masculus, X, 7*) is, besides an attempt at appropriating male prowess in combat, a hitherto unrecognized echo of the thoughts of the Maccabean mother as she watched her last surviving son die (*et femineae cogitationi masculinum animum inserens, 2* Maccabees 7:21). This parallel is crucial because it extends the tradition of female martyrdom in 2 Maccabees for the first time into the *Passio* and suggests an awareness on the part of the author of an important paradigmatic model. Lastly, Perpetua's elevation and charismatic leadership appear to be acknowledged in Saturus's dream, in which the bishop Optatus and Aspasius the presbyter throw themselves at her feet and ask for her help in settling a dispute (XIII, 2).

If we believe in the authenticity of the tale and the teller, then we must try to understand the dream and the dream record from their point of view. In this case, that is the vantage point of someone about to face a brutal death because of conviction. Such a method of interpretation does the least violence to the historical character of Perpetua, because it views her intention (no matter how contradictory its expression may appear) as a primary factor in the reading of these complex dream records. Although such a reading emphasizes what I believe is her attempt to place her experiences within a paradigmatic frame—a contribution of immeasurable importance for the development of medieval *passiones*—such a reading does not denigrate the uniqueness of her personality.

If we attribute at least part of the success of the *Passio* to the eloquence of Perpetua's distinctive and heroically female voice—Auerbach compares her favorably to Antigone[59]—it is well to be reminded that the entirety of the text was filtered through a complex process of dictation, copying, and recopying, almost all of which was done by men. Given such a textual transmission, the author's intention, and what we can presume about the expectation of the community for whom the text was intended, we cannot underestimate their importance as factors which shaped the final outcome of the narrative (even in light of the redactor's comment *conscriptum manu sua*). Indeed, as I said at the start of this analysis, the text inhabits such a historical indeterminacy that all we can affirm with absolute certainty is how we respond to the claim of the autobiographical voice. The genuine woman who may have written this text or was the model for its composition is lost to us. The power of this claim on subsequent generations figured in the adoption of some of the *topoi* from her *Passio* in later examples of the genre.

Those chapters of the *Passio* explicitly written by the redactor also contributed to the text's importance in the history of sacred biography, and it is one of these which I wish to examine. But first, an obvious but sometimes overlooked point needs to be made: it is not the recog-

59. Auerbach, *Literary Language*, p. 63.

nition of the autobiographical voice alone which made this a seminal text for the development of the sacred biography of women in the medieval church. Indeed, it is virtually impossible to determine how major a role was played by the autobiographical voice for the broad spectrum of the medieval audience; it does not seem to have been a major role for Augustine, who considered the text's importance to reside in its exemplary status.[60] But Augustine was learned, and his position as bishop would have contributed to this broader exemplary outlook. Although there is no way to argue the following point conclusively, I assume that medieval audiences responded to claims of autobiography in much the same way as modern audiences do. In a related example, suppose it were learned that the diary of Anne Frank was not the product of a persecuted child hiding from the barbarism of the Nazis, but rather was written by a contemporary sympathetic Dutch national who knew the Frank family intimately and was thus able to present a very credible account of the matter. If such news was made public, the diary of Anne Frank would perhaps not fall into desuetude, but certainly readers' affection for it would be radically changed. Because we lack the necessary corroborating evidence to determine the authenticity of the autobiographical claim made by Perpetua, our focus should move to consider the effect the claim makes on us. Viewed from this perspective, we need to take seriously the issue of intention, because so many who read this text are moved to accept its authenticity.

The *Passio* tells the story of the heroism of two women. Felicitas (the editor explicitly takes full responsibility for her story) achieved as much fame as Perpetua during the Middle Ages. Medieval liturgical ritual and texts treat the two women as inseparably heroic. Furthermore, Felicitas is never mentioned in the diary attributed to Perpetua, only in the editor's frame. This fact is certainly an indication that a large segment of the medieval audience also found the more conventional part of the tale attractive, responding to the rhetorical conventions it employed. The *Passio* achieved its dominant position in the tradition because it represented in a singular manner the achievement of Christian sanctity by two women for whom the good things of this world were assured. They sacrificed all to gain entrance to an ethereal kingdom founded on faith.[61]

60. Van Beek, *Passio*, pp. 149–61.

61. Klawiter, "The Role of Martyrdom"; Wilson-Kastner, *A Lost Tradition;* and Yarborough, "Christianization in the Fourth Century."

The Ideal of Renunciation

Both in the frame narrative and in Perpetua's diary, considerable emphasis is placed on the idea that the commitment to Christianity requires a radical pruning of the old values and traditions. This demand to break with the past that the literature of martyrdom proselytizes is founded on a myth central to the experience of a persecuted church, that of the triumph of the righteous victim. Although this image has its primary roots in the figure of Christ in the Gospels—a sufficiently plastic image to allow for such different depictions as Christ the Eastern thaumaturge and the Anglo-Saxon "ȝeonȝ Haeleth"—it was also an image which underwent considerable change when it was used in the lives of the female saints. Here it takes the form of a radical asocial renunciation of virtually all the values of family life.[62]

Although these sacred biographies are built on what I have called a *mythos* of the triumphant victim, this *mythos* was not novel with the early Christian *Acta sanctorum* and *passiones* or with the Gospels, and indeed it is very likely a universal myth. However, for medieval sacred biography, its Judeo-Christian ancestry is the crucial influence.[63] A rather similar sentiment exists in much of the prophetic literature of the Old Testament, particularly in such late works as Maccabees. For the emerging Christian literature, however, the *locus classicus* for it is Christ's words in Matthew 10:34–36. His disciples believed his message sanctioned the most radical reappraisal of the habits of the human heart, demanding a new view of kinship, a destruction of traditional Semitic tribalism, and hence casting grave doubt on the importance of family for society. These words did not fall on barren ground in late second-century Carthage but instead took root and blossomed into a palpable and often bloody fruit.

The principle of Christian *renuntiatio* leading to martyrdom was a topic of serious concern for some of the most creative Christian leaders. For example, Origen looked back on the time of the Severian persecutions as a moment of crowning glory for the Alexandrian church. The fervor and zeal in the face of unspeakable danger that seized the imaginations of these beleaguered communities is evident in Origen's *Fourth Homily on Jeremiah,* in which he writes:

62. Klawiter, "The Role of Martyrdom," p. 254.

63. Stewart, "Greek Crowns and Christian Martyrs," p. 120.

This was when one really was a believer, when one used to go to martyrdom with courage in the church, when returning from the cemeteries whither we had accompanied the bodies of the martyrs, we came back to our meetings, and the whole church would be assembled there, unbreakable. Then the catechumens were catechized in the midst of the martyrdoms, and in turn these catechumens overcame tortures and confessed the living God without fear. It was then that we saw prodigies. Then too, the faithful were few in numbers but were really faithful, advancing along the straight and narrow path leading to life.[64]

Not only do we get a very similar sense of urgency with which the martyr responds to her call in the *Passio Sanctarum Perpetuae et Felicitas,* but the contest is often framed in such charged language as Origen's "narrow path leading to life." As remarked above, the lives of the saints were discussed and read in a variety of church settings, including somewhat later on in the *canon missae,* where their association with the idea of the sacrificial victim was unavoidable. It is in emotionally heightened contexts, such as the one reported by Origen, that one can appreciate the documentary importance of sacred biography and the role it played in providing both a linguistic and philosophical frame for the community's understanding of the experience and also for this experience's theological, moral, and political implications. The lives of the saints provided a small but growing community with an idiom free from the lexical hallowedness of Scripture, or what Augustine calls the *locutio divinae paginae.*[65] Such an idiom not only allowed public discourse to reinterpret its belief system in different contexts, but it also embodied a typology which reconfirmed anew each Christian community in its historic role.

The main targets of this Christian renunciation were those two guardians of Roman life, the family and the state. The terrible scenes of rending family ties between Perpetua and her father, who not only was the *paterfamilias* but also represented the old traditions, the Roman way, clearly illustrate this pattern of renunciation. Perpetua wrote movingly of the scene before Hilarianus, the Roman proconsul, who officiated at her trial and her father's public humiliation (VI, 5). Aside from the pathos of this scene and her genuine expression of distress as she views this man who gave her life and raised her, there is a compression in the narrative so that an ideological interpretation of the destruction of her family seems inescapable; a new family must be found for Perpetua. Her response to her father is complex and works on at least

64. Frend, *Martyrdom and Persecution,* p. 241.

65. Evans, *The Language and Logic of the Bible,* p. 5.

two levels: her feeling for him moves from intimate daughterly concern for his dejection and humiliation to ideological distance which now sees him as emblematic of an old order ("pathetic old age," *sic dolui pro senecta eius misera,* VI, 5; IX, 3). Her final report of the trial and the judgment rendered by Hilarianus is terse—"we were condemned to the beasts, and we returned to prison in high spirits" (*Tunc nos universos pronuntiat et damnat ad bestias; et hilares descendimus ad carcerem,* VI, 6)—and represents a complete reversal of a normative expectation; the sentence of death is here paradoxically the guarantee of an eternal spiritual life.

The Slaughter of the Innocents

Along with the disposition to insist on the *sensus literalis* of some of the more extreme pronouncements of the New Testament on self-sacrifice, the small Christian community to which Perpetua and Felicitas belonged had to contend with the historical fact of the persecutions. The idea of immolation and its agent had arrived at the appropriate star-crossed historical moment. Christianity was an officially outlawed sect, and those who called themselves Christians were called the *odium generis humani.* In this volatile climate, the radical Christian ideal, espoused by Cyprian, Tertullian, and Origen, which rapturously celebrated the virtue of martyrdom, became an ideologic *agent provocateur* in the Roman provinces of the late empire.[66] It is exceedingly difficult to comprehend without bias something of the mentality that brought Perpetua, an apparently educated woman of some social standing, to break so fundamentally with her cultivated past, with her family; it is also difficult to recreate any sort of appreciation for the circumstances which could cause her to write that her hovel of a prison was a palace (*et factus est mihi carcer subito praetorium,* III, 9) or how she could call her death a victory and not see this hyperbole as the product of brainwashing. The seeds for such an extreme position can be found in the New Testament and are succinctly stated by Paul in Ephesians 5:1–2. For Paul, Christianity is an imitation of God after the manner revealed by Jesus: "Be imitators of God as his dear children." He says much the same thing in a compressed manner in 1 Corinthians 11:1: "Imitate me as I imitate Christ." Perpetua's transformation of the given (prisons into castles) established this particular opposition as a convention for the lives of medieval female saints.

66. See Origen's *Dialogue with Heracleides,* in Frend, p. 291.

Clothed in the Armor of Love:
Sanctity and the *Imitatio Christi*

The passage of two thousand years has made it difficult for us to imagine the effect of Paul's remarks on recent converts to an aggressively eschatological and missionary church. The idea that there was contained in Scripture a model which mirrored the transcendent God's behavior and, moreover, that initiates to this new religion could incorporate this model in their lives was a prescription for the development of a new social order, which was a threat to the stability of the state. The communities depicted in the early *acta* and *passiones* accepted as a point of literal truth that an imitation of the example of Jesus in the New Testament was an imitation on earth, in their flesh and blood, of the God of Abraham and Moses. The literalness with which these texts were understood may be a historical accident, because the great bursting forth of theological and philosophical exegesis of Scripture was not to come until the middle of the third century.[67]

Such a theology was charismatic and profoundly eschatological, and the theological belief it gave rise to was the ultimate cause of considerable suffering. And yet it allowed women a reasonable latitude for self-expression and community leadership. They, no less than men, could imitate the *vita apostolica*. Although such enthusiastic religiosity and its concomitant recognition of female leadership seem to have diminished with the rise of episcopal authority in ecclesiastical (and in some secular areas) spheres from the third century, and with the increase of educated men entering Christianity seeking administrative positions from the middle of the fourth century, the lives of female saints preserved a memory of their earlier charismatic leadership role.[68]

The ministry of women in the church from the fourth century celebrated the life of celibacy as the apogee of their spiritual and administrative careers. From this period we have a great flowering of ascetical treatises praising female celibacy: Ambrose's *De Virginibus ad Marcellinam Sororem Suam*, Jerome's *Epistola ad Eustochium de Custodia Virginitatis* and *Ad Laetam de Institutione Filiae*, and later Caesarius of Arles, *Epistola Hortatoria ad Virginem Deo Dedicatam* (ca.

---

67. A. Pettersen, "To Flee or Not to Flee": An Assessment of Athansius's *De Fuga Sua*," *Studies in Church History* 21 (1984): 41.

68. Lane Fox, *Pagans and Christians*, pp. 498–504; Atkinson, *Mystic and Pilgrim*, p. 161; Klawiter, "The Role of Martyrdom."

513). Despite this official line, which made it impossible that the church should again see such powerful political figures as Perpetua or Felicitas and proposed a new ascetic agenda of female spirituality in actual fact, the genre of sacred biography had by the end of the fourth century so conventionalized its depiction of female heroines that women continued to be celebrated as heroic leaders, martyrs, and virgins in the liturgy and in countless biographies and cults (though almost universally spurious, these *acta* usually date some centuries later) which derive from this period, such as the lives of Sts. Agnes, Agatha, Cecilia and Margaret of Antioch. Charismatic female values and behavior which were no longer tolerable in practice were nonetheless continually being written and celebrated by the established church in the *vitae sanctarum.* Jerome, Augustine, and other fourth-century thinkers responded to this situation by presenting a new venue for Christian living which allowed these biographies to flourish while prescribing acceptable, albeit alternative, models for actual practice.[69]

This early third-century church believed the saint was a new Christ who combined the fire-breathing role of the Old Testament prophet with that of the New Testament shepherd who nurtured his flock. The theory of renunciation which we see in these texts was designed to simplify the depiction of the struggle between the good Christians and the evil pagans. The figure of the naked, bloodied martyr standing alone in the arena was meant to shock; it was a polemic to underline the barbarism at the core of the imperial civilization; it was a social alarum sounding the warning of the decadence of urban cultures. The contrast between the martyr and the state is stark and unforgiving. Moreover, this literature of ascesis condemned late Roman society wholesale, for these Christians believed *a priori* that any community which could not accept the truth of Christian revelation was in league with Satan and condemned to perdition.

The doctrine of the *imitatio Christi* and the literary types it gave birth to form the foundation for the development of sacred biography. Indeed, although it is not crucial to our discussion—it does illustrate the strength of these ideas across racial, ethnic, and temporal lines—it is well to recognize that the very ideal of asceticism and suffering for others that we see exemplified by Christ in the New Testament was directly influenced by an earlier Semitic tradition, most notably, as Manson argues, by the figures of the prophetic tradition: Elijah, John

69. Atkinson, *Mystic and Pilgrim,* p. 161; Yarborough, "Christianization in the Fourth Century," p. 160.

the Baptist, and the Therapeutae. Despite the arguments of those like Delehaye who would deny anything other than a Christian influence in the development of the cult of the martyrs and in their *acta,* Frend, Hummel, Downing, Grabar, and Manson have shown unequivocally the importance of the Semitic influence.[70]

In the later Jewish apocryphal books, especially the widely known *Martyrdom of Isaiah* and the *Lives of the Prophets,* pains are taken to establish beyond a doubt that the prophets died as martyrs for their faith. Furthermore, certain specific tales, such as the narratives of the Maccabean mother and her seven children and the death of Eleazar (2 Maccabees 7:1–42; 6:18–31) contributed to Christian sacred biographys' panegyrical style and characterization, and, along with the *acta martyrum,* may have bolstered the adoption of certain *topoi,* such as the debate. Both Sts. Augustine and Gregory Nazianzen testify that the church devoted services to the memory of these Maccabean heroes. In the later Middle Ages, their feasts were celebrated on the first of August, and basilicas were dedicated to them in Antioch, Rome, and Lyon.[71]

Martyrdom and Mimesis

The *imitatio Christi* was first employed as a literary convention, as we have seen above, in Luke's portrayal of Stephen's death in Acts. Luke, as pointed out earlier, patterned certain critical scenes and language attributed to Stephen on the passion and death of Christ. And, although Luke and the Christian sacred biographies which followed his example, borrowed from the Semitic tradition (and possibly were influenced indirectly by the lives of certain pagan philosophers, such as the *Life of Pythagoras*), they did introduce one fundamental and novel contribution to the understanding and exemplification of the *acta martyrum* that was not contained in these earlier traditions.[72] For Christians, the prospect of martyrdom was to be sought, to be received joy-

70. W. Manson, "Martyrs and Martyrdom," *Bulletin of the John Rylands Library* 39 (1957): 463–84.

71. St. Gregory of Nazianzus, *In Machabaeorum Laudem, PG* 35:911–34; St. Augustine, *Sermo CCC, PL* 38:1379. Augustine identifies a great basilica dedicated to the memory of the Maccabean martyrs. See also H. Delehaye, "Martyr et Confesseur," in *Analecta Bollandiana* 39 (1921): 30–64.

72. Dodds, *Pagan and Christian in an Age of Anxiety,* p. 31.

ously as a special grace from God, whereas martyrdom in either the Greek or Jewish context, if unavoidable, was accepted with a certain degree of stoiclike reserve. Christians believed martyrdom and persecution was a gift which made possible a virtually instantaneous union with God.[73]

The early apologists who wrote approvingly of Christian martyrdom did show respect for earlier pagan heroes and martyrs. Tertullian's *Apologeticum,* composed late in the year 197, mentions six pagan martyrs as worthy of Christian emulation. Clement of Alexandria, in his *Stromateis,* also cites with approval and appropriate exemplary figures some of the same pagan martyrs as did Tertullian.[74] But this early tolerance was not to last, and the more dominant attitude in the church was one which drew a sharp distinction between the behavior of the Christian martyrs and that of all others. St. John Chrysostom, in a sermon on the martyr St. Babylas, concisely states this point of view: Christian martyrs "are not like those Greek philosophers, who never expressed themselves with due moderation, but always more or less than was proper; and hence it is that they won a reputation not for fortitude but rather for futile suffering."[75] This negative view became the dominant Christian position throughout the Middle Ages, and we can see it, for example, in Bernard of Clairvaux, who is quite clear on the differences which separate the two traditions. Jewish martyrdom in Bernard's uncompromising view was a *descensus ad infernos,* whereas Christian martyrdom was a *transitus ad vitam.*[76]

Perhaps the most important early document, and one of enormous influence in illustrating this joyous reception of death and certain welcome by God, is Ignatius of Antioch's (ca. 35–107) *Epistle to the Romans* 4: "Suffer me to be eaten by the beasts, through whom I can attain God. I am God's wheat, and I am ground by the teeth of wild beasts that I may be found the pure bread of Christ."[77] Here the bar-

---

73. Klawiter, "The Role of Martyrdom," p. 253; Origen, *Exhortatio ad Martyrium, PG* 11:563–636; E. L. Hummel, *The Concept of Martyrdom according to Cyprian of Carthage* (Washington, 1946); H. Delehaye, *Sanctus: essai sur le culte des saints dans l'antiquité (Brussels, 1927).*

74. Musurillo, *Acts of the Pagan Martyrs,* pp. 243–44.

75. Ibid., p. 245.

76. Bernard, *Epistola XCVIII, De Machabaeis, sed ad quem scripta sit ignoratur, PL* 182:230–34.

77. K. Lake, *The Apostolic Fathers* (Cambridge, Mass., 1970), vol. 1, p. 230.

barous death inflicted by wild animals is the very conduit for his union
with God. In his *Epistle to the Ephesians,* Ignatius places the figure of
the martyr at the pinnacle of Christian heroism and explicitly urges his
disciples to imitate—in somewhat gnosticlike language—the suffering
and crucified Christ: "I am not yet perfect in Jesus Christ; for now I
do but begin to be a disciple . . . let us be imitators (μιμηταί) of the
Lord, and seek who may suffer the more wrong, be the more destitute,
the more despised."[78] Ignatius's teaching, especially his Christology,
was in part responsible for the exalted position of the figure of the
martyr in the early church.[79] Irenaeus of Lyons cites with warm approval the teaching and example of Ignatius (though without naming
him).[80]

If we consider the frequency of the persecutions—they comprised
129 years in the first two and a half centuries of the church's history—
and grant those instances when Christians belligerently refused any
opportunity to avoid punishment, it is nonetheless possible to see that
in this very volatile climate the martyr could be viewed as the embodiment of a miracle, of divine favor. His invincible faith in the face of
such cruel punishment decreed by the greatest imperial power to govern the world was an inspirational example to his fellows and an
equally powerful example to non-Christians of lunatic irrationality.
The single martyr, in the eyes of this nascent Christian community, had
triumphed over the state; the civil authorities were unable to deter him
from his commitment to imitate literally his crucified God. In keeping
with this growing religious rhetoric on the heroism of martyrdom, Tertullian taught that every new convert to the faith was a candidate for
martyrdom. He believed that martyrdom was the surest sign of the
effulgence of God's pleasure. Looking at the contest between the martyr and the civil authorities in light of remarks such as Tertullian's illustrates what I have called "the paradox of the triumphant victim."
Because the state's power to destroy was seen as its impotence and its
moral bankruptcy, the unmistakable sign that God's favor moved from
the grandeur of Rome to a humble stable in Bethlehem was the fact of
the persecutions.

In the earliest historical passions, those texts that can be accurately
assigned to the period before the mid-third century, the martyr is por-

---

78. Ibid., p. 184.

79. H. von Campenhausen, *Die Idee des Martyriums in der Alten Kirche* (Göttingen, 1964), pp. 59 ff.

80. Irenaeus, *Adversus Haereses, PG* 8:1200–1201.

trayed as uncompromisingly seeking to model literally his suffering and death on that of Christ. Special benefits were believed to accrue to those martyrs who were able to complete the *imitatio Christi.*

The Invincibility of Divine Rapture

There was yet another rationale for the *imitatio Christi* which is not so obvious and not nearly so well understood but which is quite important in the development of the cult of the saints. We can see in certain texts, such as the *Passio Perpetuae,* an understanding that if the candidates for martyrdom were of the proper spirit and were able to model his or her suffering and death on the paradigm of Christ, then just prior to death, he or she would experience a complete personal metamorphosis. This metamorphosis was not a self-actualized internal reorientation, the result of some blinding insight into the true nature of heroism. Rather, it seems to have been based on the belief that in the midst of the torment the martyr would be personally rescued by the Christian God.

The metamorphosis was expressed in figurative language (often using words from athletic contests), which suggested that this embattled community understood this moment of possession to be a lightninglike divine enveloping of the martyr's person. In sum, although this is an idea whose complete ethos is difficult to translate into our modern idiom, because it is so grounded in a profoundly radical religious eschatology, the promise of redemption is realized at once for those select few who choose to imitate literally Christ's sacrifice. God is present to them. Further, this transcendent presence changes the dynamics of the combat: the martyr is taken into the bosom of Abraham, and the successful outcome of the strife is guaranteed because now it is the Christian God who is ranged against the forces of religious intolerance. Perpetua announces that "she knew the victory was hers" (X, 14).

Before we actually examine an example in the *Passio Perpetuae,* I will briefly mention why this extreme understanding of *imitatio* is important to our examination of the continuity of sacred biography. This ecstatic religiosity formed the foundation of three major constitutents of sanctity: the saint as the perfect vehicle for such imitative expression of Christ's life; the saint as thaumaturge, miraculously bridging the human and the divine; and the saint as the epitome of the ethical excellence possible to human beings. The ritually correct observation of the *imitatio Christi* will cause the promised metamorphosis from ordinary believer to saint. The promise of this metamorphosis, which we find so clearly in the early *acta martyrum,* and as we shall see in the *Passio Perpetuae,* accounts for these three attributes becoming an integral part of the developing cult of sanctity. Indeed, as a result, these three early understandings of the dimensions of sanctity contributed enormously to the emerging characterization of saints within medieval religious culture.

The Importance of Ritual Suffering

Because the idea of metamorphosis is very clearly illustrated in the editor's development of the character of Felicitas, I would like to examine that narrative in some detail. Being only seven sentences long, chapter 15 is a marvel of economy. Nonetheless, in spite of its brevity, the narrative contains some of the most important points of the entire *Passio.* It is a chapter, presumably because it is not part of the autobiographical account of Perpetua, which has received less critical attention. Ironically, it is for this very reason—because it is conventional and not autobiographical—that it is important in tracking developments in the genre.

The chapter opens with a depiction of an apprehensive Felicitas awaiting her execution (*instante spectaculi die in magno erat luctu,* XV, 2). What sets Felicitas apart and deepens the verisimilitude of this chapter is her pregnancy. The realism that this fact forces on an otherwise intentionally exemplary narrative governs the arguments in this chapter: first, Felicitas was in her eighth month; second, it was against the custom of Roman law to execute someone who was pregnant; and third, Felicitas was fearful that because of her pregnancy her execution might be postponed. The chapter has a contradiction at its heart: the imminence of childbirth juxtaposed with that of death. Understood metaphorically, the birth of the child would contribute to the development of the *civitas hominis,* whereas the death of Felicitas contributes to the *civitas Dei.*

Note, however, that it is not the fear of losing her life or that of her unborn infant which distresses Felicitas. Rather, it is the context within which she will lose her life. Her deepest concern is that she might have to shed her holy, innocent blood afterward along with others who were common criminals (*et ne inter alios postea sceleratos sanctum et innocentem sanguinem funderet,* XV, 2). Her companions also share her anxiety: "Her comrades in martyrdom were also saddened; for they were afraid that they would have to leave behind so fine a companion to travel alone on the same road to hope" (*sed et conmartyres graviter contristabantur, ne tam bonam sociam quasi conmitem solam in via eiusdem spei relinquerent,* XV, 3). These lines underscore the dichotomy between earth and heaven; the utopian paradise implied was influential in later *passiones,* such as *Passio Sanctorum Mariani et Iaocobi* (ca. 300).[81]

But let us turn to what the text does not focus on, to the unconscious and unwritten text. Is it not significant that in a scene so full of pathos and the celebration of domesticity—a young woman expecting her first child—no concern is expressed for the life of this unborn child, for the imminence of motherhood? The absence of maternal concern—sharpened by deliberately juxtaposing Felicitas's response with the tender care Perpetua exhibited for her infant son's welfare—is a deliberate part of the thesis. There are at least two major reasons which help account for this apparent lack of interest in the innocent unborn life: first, "realism" is sacrificed to the exemplary so as to highlight the martyr's courage; second, the deliberate displacement of maternal concern focuses on what for this community was a more important *partus,* the separation of Felicitas from her fellows. Her pregnancy is a barrier to her self-sacrifice and hence, although a natural good, is, in a terrible irony, a barrier to her union with God. Here the normative expectations that the Western tradition has associated with birth—joyous expectancy, hope for the future, the renewal of the world—are turned upside down. Such unconcern is the most bleak statement of the *renuntio mundi.*

The focus on Felicitas's pregnancy, which gives pace and suspense to the story, adds another dimension as well: transience. The question never asked, but which is inescapable and comes to displace all others, is will she die in time (i.e., with her friends)? This question also has the effect of muting the barbarism of her impending martyrdom by focusing on (what may have been an infiltration from the romance) the race against time.[82] In the first fourteen lines of chapter 15, there are nine words out of the total of one hundred twenty whose exclusive concern is to mark time: "eighth month," "the day of," "postponed," "afterward," "two days before," "one," "immediately," "now," and "then." If we add to this preoccupation with temporality the anxiety of the pregnancy, it is hard to escape the point that what these martyrs

---

81. Musurillo, *Acts of the Christian Martyrs,* pp. 194–213.

82. Anderson, *Ancient Fiction,* p. 123.

are fleeing is not only the world but time itself in their search for an immutable present. To this end, it is well to note that this story concludes (as do most of the *acta martyrum*) with the words of the doxology celebrating eternity: "and boundless power forever" (*et immensa potestas in saecula saeculorum,* XXI, 11).

The figure of the martyr embodied in the character of Felicitas synthesizes complex and possibly antagonistic attributes: although she is depicted as very much a flesh-and-blood woman, Felicitas is also characterized as the "perfect" vessel and thus a member of the elect. Her character is a complex biographical amalgam of the humility associated with the Virgin Mary and ascetic Montanist ideals of feminine virtue. Such a complex ideology of self-abnegation embodied in its attendant victim, however, indebted as it is to its New Testament heritage, represents a considerable change from this heritage. Christ was crucified as a criminal between two criminals. His death was a vindication of the power of innocence in the midst of sin. The meaning of Felicitas's death, on the other hand, would be lessened, even polluted, if she were killed alongside criminals. Her very role as a witness to the faith seems compromised if she is kept from the group's sacrifice. From purely the perspective of the narrative, the pregnancy serves to underline the expected miracle of her delivery.

Felicitas's comrades' anxiety creates a dramatic context for the presentation of an apparently intractable problem. Will the fact of her pregnancy mean that Felicitas will die against her wishes and against those of her brethren, and, as a result, will her sacrificial death then be diminished? And if her death is diminished, is the victory given to Rome? Her pregnancy is used as a symbol to dramatize the tension between the desire for the continuity of human life on the one hand and the prospect of eternal life on the other. If this latter dialectic is being proposed, then the dilemma facing Felicitas is truly Solomonic. The young woman is caught, having to choose between living for her innocent unborn infant or for her God, a choice which for educated citizens of late antiquity would have been grotesque but a choice which, for these zealous third-century African Christians, was less fraught with moral compunction.

There is, however, a solution to the problem Felicitas faces. The way out of the dilemma lies in the answer to the following questions: is there some way that this band of faithful yet powerless imprisoned Christians can lawfully change the course of nature, that is, alter Felicitas's pregnancy, since she has at least another month left before parturition? The pregnancy must be the focus of their efforts and not the policy of the state because of the state's status as the necessary, albeit from their perspective malign, agent for their attainment of sacrificial sanctity. The state must remain invincible in its role as antagonist. The crude dualism of the argument is inescapable. Of course, the impossibility of this group's altering the laws of nature and, at the same time, denying the authorities the opportunity to make a propaganda victory out of Felicitas's not dying with her comrades forces the only possible solution to such a problem. That solution, deliberately couched in exemplary language, is the Christian weapon against the world: prayer.

There is no break in the narrative between the mention of the concern of the group for Felicitas's well-being—time is miraculously collapsed—their decision to pray for help, and the answer to their prayers. The text reads: "And so, two days before the contest, they poured forth a prayer to the Lord in one torrent of common grief. And immediately after their prayer the birth pains came upon her" (*statim post orationem dolores inuaserunt,* XV, 5). We expect the immediacy of the response, for without it the text's exemplary character would suffer. However, the compression of the narrative, the sudden miraculous nature of the birth, and the inherent didacticism of the event, although they all converge to cause a momentary disruption of the verisimilitude, do not detract from the writer's ability to continue to engage our sympathies. For example, the birth of the baby is not without difficulties, made more vivid through realistic language. The labor in this hovel of a prison is especially painful because of its prematurity: "She suffered a good deal in her labor because of the natural difficulty of an eight months' delivery" (*et cum pro naturali difficultate octaui mensis in partu laborans doleret,* XV, 5).

In the midst of the depiction of the childbirth, the narrative abruptly introduces a new and important character in the figure of a prison guard. Before examining the conversation between Felicitas and this guard, two points need to be made: first, the prison guard is a foil to exploit fully the argument of this group's estrangement from the state; moreover, as a male antagonist, he deepens the misanthropy latent in the depiction of the enemy. The guard is another type of the threatening male which we have seen in the figure of Perpetua's father, the proconsul Hilarianus, and the Egyptian gladiator. Although I have stressed how this figure extends the narrative's exemplary intention, I do not intend this argument to diminish the power of the text. Men held positions of public power in this society, and men made judgments about life and death; women were not so empowered. A text which did not work within these historically normative contexts could not appropriate sufficient credibility. A second reason for limiting the number of characters in this intimate scene concerns exigencies of narrative in a culture which was predominantly oral. It further enhances the utility of this text in a liturgical setting where such clearly depicted antinomies were required. Nowhere in the entirety of the *Passio* do we have an instance in which more than two people are in the foreground. This reduces the complexity of the plot, simplifies dialogue, underlines the essentially binary nature of the dialectic (good versus evil), and enhances the audience's ability to retain what the author believes thematically most important.[83]

The scene between Felicitas and the prison guard contains both the above conditions: it restricts the action to the archetypal contest between two individuals, the vulnerable woman and the armed guard. The narrative portrays the guard watching Felicitas in the throes of labor. Although it is not explicitly developed, the scene contains an inescapable air of voyeurism. On the one hand, we have the man's threatening presence and, on the other, Felicitas in the intimate *deshabillé* of childbirth. This voyeuristic element is not developed, but it exists to underline the degree of alienation separating these two individuals.

The scene opens with a coarse taunt: "Hence one of the assistants of the prison guards said to her: You suffer so much now—what will you do when you are tossed to the beasts? Little did you think of them when you refused to sacrifice [to the gods and emperor]" (XV, 5). It is difficult to think of another scene in the whole of Western medieval literature which so polarizes the potential for abuse latent in male and female role playing without destroying the realism of the action. The man's crude reminder of the imminence of Felicitas's death opposes the promise of life about to be born. The certainty with which he speaks of her death confronts the certainty of the new life she brings into the world. His derisive words, an emblem of a larger ideology, are rebuked by the birth of the innocent child. One cannot but marvel at the skill of this anonymous author as we acknowledge, deeply imbedded in this brief interchange, the author's indebtedness to the theology of the Lucan account of Christ's birth (1:23–56). At this point, the narrative has proceeded as far as it can in depicting the estrangement between the Christians and their fellow citizens. And yet it is at precisely

83. See Charles F. Altman, "Two Types of Opposition and the Structure of Latin Saints' Lives," *M&H* 6 (1976): 1–11. Altman differentiates structures which he calls "diametrical" and "gradational." I had come to an understanding of the binary nature of these texts prior to reading Altman.

this point, where the narrative has presented the conflict in the most savage of oppositions—where the antipathy between Felicitas and her prison attendant symbolizes the ruptured social fabric separating the Christian from the pagan, where even that nonideological inheritance of all people, human decency, is mocked—that we find what I believe to be the most influential pronouncement on the *topos* of the *imitatio Christi* and the idea of divine rapture and human metamorphosis in the entire corpus of sacred biography. Felicitas responds to the guard's taunts in the following manner:

> *Modo ego patior quod patior; illic autem alius erit in me qui patietur pro me, quia et ego pro illo passura sum.*

> What I suffer now, I suffer by myself; but then [the time of her martyrdom] another will be inside me who will suffer for me, because I shall be suffering for him (XV, 6).

These words are unsettlingly transparent. They bear such hallmarks of orthodoxy as the resigned acceptance of human suffering combined with the scripturally based belief that if suffering serves a religious ideal, it is elevated and transformed. However, the passage intends more than just an iteration of the orthodox position. Felicitas's words proclaim a peculiar ideology of suffering. They extend the arena of her personal pain to include within it the person of her Savior. Her retort to the guard "but then another will be inside me who will suffer for me, because I shall be suffering for him," was not intended to be understood either metaphorically or indeed sacramentally, but literally. The act of martyrdom is a type of conjuring; it precipitates an epiphany.

The language with which Felicitas testifies to her faith reflects the belief in a special covenant between the martyr and Christ: if the martyr remained faithful to her Lord, then he would not abandon her in her moment of need; indeed, Christ would stand between her and her tormentors as a shield, literally receiving blow for blow. Such sentiments can be seen in the writings of Tertullian, Cyprian, and Origen and other of the *acta martyrum* which date from this period. The martyr's pain was tempered by the certain knowledge that her Lord was taking on himself mutual suffering. At the core of such thinking, we can discern a radical eschatology which understood the promise of Felicitas's salvation to be based on an understanding of the sacramental covenant of martyrdom (certainly at home in Montanism), the real presence of Christ at such moments, and the apodictic nature of this covenant. The germ of this ideology is ancient and present in a fragment of a hymn Paul quotes in 2 Timothy (2:11): "If we have died with him, we shall also live with him." This verse, read literally by these apocalyptic-minded communities, affirms the blood covenant in the clearest and most unconditional way. And indeed, those who died with him were hallowed in a most reverent manner by the church. We learn in the *Martyrdom of St. Polycarp* that even the mutilated remains of that saintly man were regarded by the Christians as "dearer to us than precious stones and finer than gold."

Felicitas's statement is informed by some volatile ideologies concerning the mission of the Christian church and the death of the martyr, to wit, that a hypostatic union between a martyr and Christ at the time of persecution was a real possibility; that the church had a very radical eschatological view of its mission; that self-renunciation was the singular ideal within this fellowship of believers; that the dominance of the Christian fellowship throughout the late empire could only be realized through self-sacrifice, even if this required martyrdom; and, lastly, that the triumph of this total self-sacrifice was made manifest when Christ physically entered, in Felicitas's words came inside (*alius erit in me*, XV, 6), his martyr. These words, I believe, are (outside of the *Magnificat*) the most potent sanction for such language of interiority and provided a historical precedent for the tradition of such writing which emerges most notably from the late twelfth century with such masterpieces as the *Visions* of St. Elisabeth Schönau, the *Revelations* of St. Gertrude of Germany, and Mechtild of Magdeburg's *Book of Special Grace*.

Lampe has suggested that the depiction of such suffering in these early texts (he does not discuss the *Passio*) constitutes a "Christology of martyrdom."[84] There is certainly evidence for this position as early as the New Testament in the figure of Stephen in Acts. And indeed, there is striking corroboration roughly contemporary to Felicitas's claim that the initiate who remains faithful even to death can give birth to such divine cohabitation. In *The Letter of the Churches of Lyons and Vienne* (ca. 177), the death of another heroic female martyr, Blandina, is depicted quite unambiguously as an *imitatio Christi*:

> Blandina was hung on a post and exposed as bait for the wild animals that were let loose on her. *She seemed to hang there in the form of a cross*, and by her fervent prayer she aroused intense enthusiasm in those

---

84. G. W. H. Lampe, "The Reasonableness of Typology," *Essays in Typology*, ed. G. W. H. Lampe, and K. J. Woollcombe (Napierville, Ill., 1957), p. 34.

who were undergoing their ordeal, for *in their torment with their physical eyes they saw in the person of their sister him who was crucified for them,* that he might convince all who believe in him that all who suffer for Christ's glory will have eternal fellowship in the living God . . . and *tiny, weak, and insignificant as she was* she would give inspiration to others, *for she had put on Christ, that mighty and invincible athlete* (μέγαν καὶ ἀκαταγώνιστον ἀθλητὴν Χριστὸν ἐνδεδυμένη) . . . she hastened to rejoin them [those being killed], rejoicing and glorying in her death as though she had been invited to a bridal banquet instead of being a victim of the beasts.[85]

Deliverance

There remains one major concern in our consideration of the plight of Felicitas: the birth of her child. Following immediately her invocation of the power of God to succor her in her final torment, the text records: "And she gave birth to a girl; and one of the sisters brought her up as her own daughter" (*Ita enixa est puellam, quam sibi quaedam soror in filiam educavit,* XV, 7). This chapter fittingly closes with the denouement of the daughter's birth and her subsequent removal from the prison. Although the birth is an appropriate close to the chapter, signifying as it does the power of the prayer of the imprisoned Christians to defy the inexorable laws of nature, there is much about this last remark that tantalizes. For example, in a text which made so much of Perpetua's concern for her infant, there is not another word said about the birth of this child. Felicitas never gives vent to maternal feeling (how different from Perpetua's behavior); we never learn the little girl's name or anything about the mysterious woman *quaedam soror* who raised her. Further, the figure of the guard disappears completely from the narrative. The lack of any further details about these incidents forces the conclusion that the chapter has completed its task of freeing Felicitas from the thrall of pregnancy so she might join her fellow believers in the arena before the wild beasts. In doing so, it repulses our efforts to turn it into a realistic narrative of pain and suffering in an ancient prison; it returns it to the convention of the genre.

The final view of Felicitas is repugnant to any civilized sensibility, designedly so. She is depicted standing in the arena with her mistress Perpetua, her swollen breasts dripping the mother's milk she will no longer need (*alteram a partu recentem stillantibus mammis,* XX, 3).

85. Musurillo, *Acts of the Christian Martyrs,* p. 75. (Emphasis added.)

This image haunted the imaginations of medieval sacred biographers and their audiences. This last picture of Felicitas presents the reader or listener with a most complex icon: her person has become the place for the inexorable collision of the old world of Rome with the new world of Christianity; the subtext argues that, once unleashed, the sword which Christ said he brought into this world cannot be sheathed until fathers are rent from sons and mothers from daughters. Although Felicitas is only minutes away from sudden death, the promise of her triumph is clearly manifest in the powerful symbol of her maternity. Such a triumph is, however, won at enormous cost, a cost which placed religious principle above all other allegiances, to both the family and state, a cost which continued the breakdown of the fabric of late Roman society, a cost which enshrined in the emerging doctrine of the church the importance of self-renunciation and the virtue of a radical eschatology, a cost which gave to the later development of Christian sacred biography the necessity to depict sanctity as a dualistic struggle between the malign forces of this world and the benevolent forces of heaven.

The *Passio Sanctarum Perpetuae et Felicitatis* gave to medieval female sacred biography exquisite models for the portrayal of female heroism along with a complex philosophical matrix from which these biographies of saintly women were to be cast.

6 / Virgin Mothers

Do not fear, Mary. You have found favor with God. You shall
conceive and bear a son and give him the name Jesus. . . .
Mary said to the angel, "How can this be, since I do not
know man?" The angel answered her: "The Holy Spirit will
come upon you and the power of the Most High will over-
shadow you; hence the holy offspring to be born will be
called the son of God."

Luke 1:30–35

The young Mary, recently espoused, responds with a question indicative of her expectation that her marriage to Joseph would involve normal marital sexuality. If, for the moment, we read her question as an
actual response, literally that is, apart from Luke's interest in depicting
Christ as the messianic fulfillment of the Isaian prophecy (Isaiah 7:14),
and its dense "labryinth of Old Testament reminiscence," its historical
importance for the development of conventions concerning celibacy
becomes more apparent.[1] Mary's query provokes the fullness of the
angelic prophecy: female virginity is the ideal vessel for the reception
of the Spirit. But her question was perceived as fraught with nuance:
from the *Protoevangelium of James* (ca. 140?) to the English *Speculum
Sacerdotale* (ca. 1415), exegetes read her question as a troubled,
doubtful one: "sche was trowbiled in hure-self, and noȝt for the vision
of the angel but for his wordis."[2] Her virginity, they believed she knew,
would exact a great price: risk of losing her spouse, the denial of family
and children, and the burden, however blessed, of being the bearer of
the Christ, *Theotokos*.[3] While the exegetes dwelt on the manifold

---

1. M. Warner, *Alone of All Her Sex* (New York, 1976), p. 11; see Cadbury, *The
Making of Luke-Acts* p. 192, for a discussion of the quality of prose in the Gospel of
Luke.

2. M. R. James, ed., *The Apocryphal New Testament* (Oxford, 1924), p. 43. The
Protoevangelium (XI, 2, 1) says she "questioned" this revelation; E. H. Weatherly,
Speculum Sacerdotale, EETS O. S. 200 (London, 1936), p. 40.

3. The implications of this title were a primary cause of the Nestorian dispute, the

meanings of her remark, the conditions attendant on her virginity supplied the story line for the authors of the apocrypha and served as models for the sacred biographies of female virgins.[4]

Christian female sacred biography has its origins in Mary's questioning response to the angel. The Annunciation is heavenly, grandiose, prophetic, formulaic, redolent with mystery and authority, and, as Stuhlmueller suggested, it is possessed of a "strongly Hebraic tone . . . a cento of OT-LXX texts." Mary's response is lexically simple, charmingly naive, rhetorically unadorned, skeptical, and ultimately accepting. Annunciation and answer offer a dynamic exploration of the apparent antimonies which exist between woman and God; they outline the centrality of the female role in the literature of Christian sanctity (Mary as the human fulfillment of God's messianic purpose), and establish the frame for much of the convention in sacred biography. The spiritual fruit which grows from this dialogue is an unshakable conviction in revelation and woman's role in its reception; it is a conviction which will brave exile, anguish, and physical torment. The dialogue presents in miniature much of the later *topoi* of the *vitae sanctarum:* revelation and free choice, social ostracism attendant on sex roles, miraculous visions, power to contradict nature, and election of the socially inferior, the humble.

What Mary Wrought

If the family in ancient Israel was a great blessing, sterility was a great curse (Genesis 30:1; 1 Samuel 1:6–8), and virginity was a cause for mourning (Judges 11:37). The Annunciation brings us face to face with a religiosity which reverses this equation of shame. Mary's virginity, although socially undesirable, was seen as a sign of her election. But

---

Nestorians urging in its place *Anthropotokos* ("mother of man") or *Christotokos* ("mother of Christ").

4. R. E. Parker, ed., *The Middle English Stanzaic Versions of the "Life of Saint Anne,"* EETS O. S. 174 (London, 1928), pp. 15–21. Carroll underestimates considerably the influence of the *Protoevangelium of James,* of other apocrypha, and the lives of the virgin saints in propagating veneration to Mary; see his *The Cult of the Virgin Mary* (Princeton, 1986), pp. 4, 169. Quasten, commenting on the *Protoevangelium of James,* remarked: "the influence of this nativity Gospel cannot be overestimated. Liturgy, literature and art—all have been affected by it," *Patrology* I, pp. 118–22. For a useful bibliography, see G. Constable, ed., "Women in Religious Life," in *Medieval Monasticism: A Select Bibliography* (Toronto, 1976), pp. 56–61.

it was an election not without attendant pain: the Annunciation, besides bringing to Mary tidings of great joy, brought her opportunity for considerable sacrifice. As the anonymous author of the thirteenth-century poem on the Annunciation put it, "Of-dred wes þat mayde."[5] Mary's question gave rise to learned and popular commentary, the latter of which established as a literary convention for sacred biography an equation which depicted female virginity as embattled, and as socially beyond the pale.

Celibacy as a condition for union with God involved turning one's back on one's spouse, denying one's children, and living in the world as if one were dead to the world—in the words of the fifteenth-century translation of Aelred's *De Institutione Inclusarum,* "þu þat art deed to þe worlde."[6] The virgin lives partly in the world of the dead and hence becomes a medium for marvelous power and prophetic visions. The virgin becomes a visionary who lives a life of self-imposed exile; Paul in the apocryphal *Acts of Paul and Thecla* (ca. 160) remarks: "Blessed are they that have renounced the world . . . for unto them shall God speak."[7] The theology of virginity which developed from consideration of passages such as that from Luke extolled the female celibate's humility, her charismatic witness, and her martyrdom of the spirit. Priscilla, one of the founding priestesses of Montanism, known for her virginity, claimed that sexual purity allowed her to see visions and to hear saving (*salutares*) but secret (*occultas*) voices.[8] In his treaties *Exhortation on Chastity* (Montanist) and *For Wives* (Catholic), Tertullian saw the road to spiritual holiness, *sanctificatio,* involving three *gradus* ("steps"); the final one, entered after baptism, was celibacy in marriage.[9] Perpetua, it should be remembered, makes no mention of her actual husband and was martyred a few days after her baptism. She is described as she walks into the arena as having taken a new husband; she is now the wife of Christ (*ut matrona Christi,* XVIII, 2). It has not yet been suggested, but it seems eminently plausible, that Perpetua's

5. R. Morris, ed., *An Old English Miscellany,* EETS O. S. 49 (London, 1872), p. 100.

6. J. Ayto and A. Barratt, ed., *Aelred of Rievaulx's De Institutione Inclusarum,* EETS O. S. 287 (London, 1984), p. 36.

7. James, ed., *Apocryphal New Testament,* "Acts of Paul and Thecla," (II, 5, 3–4); Paul's preaching of virginity "corrupted our wives" (II, 15, 4).

8. Klawiter, "The Role of Martyrdom," p. 254.

9. Tertullian, "Exhortation to Chastity," I, 4; and "For Wives," VI, 2. Passages cited in Danielou, *The Origins of Latin Christianity* p. 84.

husband is not mentioned in the *Passio* because of the idea that follow-ing baptism the renunciation of the marriage debt was an achievement of the highest good.

Virginity, espousal, new marriage, visions, the gift of the spirit, and martyrdom are a complex of related beliefs which shape the conven-tions of female sanctity throughout the Middle Ages. The lives of the female saints of the later Middle Ages were equally indebted to this ideal of virginity as charismatic witness, as martyr, as women capable of superhuman feats, and as *sponsa Christi*. The twelfth-century life of the English saint Mildrith notes that when Mildrith was most severely tortured, the Holy Spirit remained unmoved in a small house (*domici-lium*) in her heart.[10] These characteristics of female sanctity and a lex-icon which uses a disproportionate number of words and metaphors drawn from or related to things physical, domestic, and interior, as we saw above, give it its singularity—the spirit of God takes his abode in a small house in Mildrith's heart; it is not resident in the abstraction of the *anima*. Paradox and contradictions are the raw materials from which the convention is developed. As Bokenham writes about the Vir-gin's birth in his *Vita S. Annae matris S. Mariae:* "Whos singuler pri-uylege was þis, þat she/Schulde mayde be & modyr eke of myssye;/ and hyr name þey dede clepe marye."[11] Before turning to consider such conventions in those lives written in the vernacular texts of the later Middle Ages, let us first examine briefly the major intellectual legacies which inform the tradition.

Sexual Encraticism as the Ideal *Imitatio*

In the period just preceding the advent of the Christian era, movements espousing adult celibacy and lives of rigorous asceticism were attract-ing increasing interest in Greco-Roman and Semitic society. Such sen-timent of self-denial is demonstrable in quite varied groups—the Stoics, the Cynics, the Indian "Gymnosophists," and that part of the Jewish community which revered the second and fourth books of Mac-cabees and apocrypha such as *1 Enoch,* which warned of the dangers of sexuality. The allure of celibacy lay in the belief that such encrati-cism was a sign of heroism and able to confer virtue on its practition-

10. D. W. Rollason, ed., *The Mildrith Legend: A Study in Early Medieval Hagiog-raphy in England* (Leicester, 1982), p. 124.

11. Bokenham, *Legendys of Hooly Wummen,* p. 55.

ers. An example of the lengths to which this ideal was pushed (caricatured) can be found in Lucian's dialogue *Philosophers for Sale,* in which the Cynic Diogenes proclaims that for a man to accept the Cynic's way of life "he must strip himself of all luxury, devote himself to sleep on the ground, drinking nothing but water, renounce marriage and children."[12]

Despite the many differences between pagan and Semitic ideals concerning celibacy, both communities allowed select members—usually individuals associated with more extreme religious groups or those who held official positions at cultic centers—to advocate publicly lives of chastity and asceticism, such as the virgin priestesses who served the Delphic Apollo and the members of the Essene community. Prior to the emergence of Christianity in both the Jewish and Greek-speaking communities, an ideological synthesis was being forged which joined ideas of celibacy, spiritual autonomy, hermeticism, charisma, and misanthropy with a nascent ideal of election. The implications of this new ideal were far-reaching and, I believe, of fundamental importance in shaping the conventions of the medieval *vitae sanctarum virginum.*

Although Christian celibacy undoubtedly borrowed from both Jewish and pagan ascetic traditions, virginity in the first-generation Christian community differed from these two models in both scope and theology: the early Christian church preached the virtue of celibacy to *all* its members (women no less than men) because of the deeply held eschatological belief in the imminence of the *parousia* expressed in the Apocalypse of John and 1 Peter 1:4, where the faithful are told of the "inheritance . . . kept for you in heaven." Given such a radical eschatology, there developed almost immediately wide differences of opinion concerning the celibate's responsibility in society. There were those who drew a clear line between the spirit and the body, who preached a rigid dualism, such as the encratic sentiments preached in the sermon *De Centesima, Sexagesima, Tricesima* (ca. 175), and others, such as Clement of Alexander, who argued in the *Stromateis* that although virginity was a high ideal, the body was nonetheless good; it was sin which made it a vehicle for evil. Clement inveighed against the crudely dualist division between body and spirit which came to dominate the mainstream of medieval thought from the mid-fourth century. On the whole, that which separated the Christians of whatever stripe from those around them was the ideal that the life of the virgin was no longer to be restricted to the few heroic zealots, the Pythagoras or Jeremiah

12. Musurillo, *Acts of the Pagan Martyrs,* pp. 269–70.

(Jeremiah 16:1), or those votaries necessary at cultic shrines, but rather celibacy was advocated for all members of the church.[13] Virginity was acknowledged by some of Christianity's greatest teachers, from Paul through Peter Damian, as a means for achieving salvation in a world about to end.

If the Stoic ideal of celibacy was an illustration of how self-control would allow one to live in greater harmony with the natural world, the Christian counterpart sought to widen the disjunction between the world and the spirit, to overcome love for the world through sexual abstinence and prayer, and to teach believers how to live in the world as if they were already living in heaven—sentiments preached by Tatian and the Montanists. The point of difference is precisely in their intellectual centers: for the pagan Stoic, it is the perfection of the will, whereas for the Christian of the second and third centuries, it is an abandonment of self so as to ensure a place in an imminently expected paradise, the eternal *refrigerium*.

Scriptural Authority

The guarantee of the rightness of Christianity's call for the many to enter the singular fold of the chaste is scriptural: the example of the virgin birth of Christ and Christ's own celibacy as interpreted by Paul. As with many of the essential props to medieval Christian belief, the virgin birth as a doctrine of unimpeachable divine truth was justified on scriptural grounds; not only was it repeated by the Evangelists and Paul, but it was believed to have been foretold in the Old Testament. The passage thought to be the most unequivocal prophecy of Mary's delivery of Christ was Isaiah 7:14: "Therefore the Lord himself will give you this sign: the virgin shall be with child, and bear a son, and shall name him Immanuel." Thus, the prophecy of Christ's birth to a virgin could be traced back to the God of Abraham.

Although every generation after the immediate post-Apostolic age to those exposed to the pungent satires of Erasmus considered the subject of virginity as worthy of intense discussion, it was largely the influence

13. J. McNamara, "A New Song: Celibate Women in the First Three Centuries," *Women and History* 6/7 (1983): 37. The Christian custom was at odds with Roman custom and law; the Augustan laws made marriage compulsory for all Roman citizens. For a view of the liberating potential that virginity may have had for classical women, see A. Yarborough, "Christianization in the Fourth Century: The Example of Roman Women," *Church History* 45 (1976): 160.

of the Pauline Epistles and their interpretation by the Fathers which established the importance of the life of the virgin for Western medieval Christianity. Such complex passages as Paul's remarks in 1 Thessalonians 4:1–8 and 1 Corinthians 7:1–16 ("A man is better off having no relations with a woman") were used to support a position which viewed celibacy as superior to marriage. The extreme eschatological context which governed Paul's thinking and which gave these passages their full dimension was either misunderstood or ignored by later commentators.[14]

If we add to these crucial New Testament *exempla* those contemporary encratic tendencies in Neoplatonism, and in Jewish gnosticism and mysticism, and locate all of this within the wider context of the rich blendings of autonomous hellenized ideologies, as Garnsey suggests, that we find in Roman provincial cities of the time of the Pauline Epistles, we not only have the catalyst that made the *vita virginitatis* so important to the early church and the Fathers, but emerging from this religious cauldron is a practicable ideal preached throughout the Middle Ages.[15] It is instructive to note that extreme encraticism as a literary convention used particularly in sacred biography emerges as a decisive *topos* from the second century. Virgins are recognized as a distinctive class as early as Ignatius's *Letter to the Smyrnaeans 13*.[16] If human sexuality as the occasion for sin is a primary theme in such Apocrypha as the *Apocalypse of Peter,* the *Gospel of Thomas,* the *Odes of Solomon,* the *Apocalypse of Paul,* and the proto-romance/ saint's life the *Acts of Paul and Thecla* (a celibate couple),[17] the saint's life is the thematic obverse of the apocryphal literature, illustrating how Christianity allows one to live a better life in this world by virtue of his or her celibacy.

There was virtual unanimity among both the Greek and Latin Fathers—beginning with Irenaeus and including Eusebius, Origen, Tertullian, Chrysostom, Jerome, and Augustine—that Isaiah's words were a prediction of the birth of Christ. Moreover, the fathers could point to other parallels in the Old Testament (reasoning *a posteriori*) in which

14. McNamara, "A New Song; see C. W. Atkinson, *Mystic and Pilgrim: The Book and the World of Margery Kempe,* p. 161.

15. P. Garnsey, "Religious Toleration in Classical Antiquity," *Studies in Church History* 21 (1984):24.

16. P. Wilson-Kastner, *A Lost Tradition: Women Writers of the Early Church* (Washington, 1981), p. ix.

17. McNamara, "A New Song," p. 5.

the Lord had rendered hitherto barren women fertile: Sarah, mother of
Isaac (Genesis 17:16–19); Samson's mother (Judges 13); and Hannah,
mother of Samuel (1 Samuel 1:9–20). Despite such commentary on the
truth of the virgin birth, this idea of virginal conception and *in partu*
birth was received with skepticism by some and with downright ridi-
cule by others. As early as 153, Justin Martyr in the *Apology,* writing
for a non-Christian audience (presumably a wholly Greek one), remarked that such a doctrine ought not to strain their credulity, since,
as they well knew, the pagan writers wrote of a number of sons of
Zeus. Justin's audience was obviously more than a bit skeptical of such
a position. Slightly later, Celsus mocked this belief of the virgin birth
as a mere Christian myth on a par with the Greek myths of Danae,
Melanippe, and Antiope. Despite the fact that the church, following
the councils of Ephesus (431) and Chalcedon (451), eventually established the virgin birth as a legitimate and binding dogma to be believed
by all, there is evidence that some degree of skepticism persisted for
some time. As late as the seventh century, Bede argued that those
members of the church who did not accept this article of faith as binding were traitors to the faith.[18]

Not only do the lives of the virgin saints represent a continuing effort
on the part of the church to inculcate the great virtue of celibacy as an
ideal for women, an ideal which was practiced by Mary, the paragon
of medieval feminity, but the ubiquity and continuity of these stories
throughout the Middle Ages serves to reinforce and elevate the importance of clerical celibacy. Moreover, because the two great models for
celibacy are Christ and Mary, the ideal has an unimpeachable pedigree.
These lives of the female virgins accomplish religious teaching and promote obedience to the church: women are given appropriate role
models, the clergy's singular life is located in the truth of Scripture and
the orthodoxy of the doctrine of the virgin birth, and the importance
of Mary is kept continually before the people. In Jerome's *Life of St.
Hilarion,* the sterile woman from Elutheropolis bursts in on Hilarion,
throws herself in the dust at his feet, and blurts out: "Forgive my bold-
ness, forgive my importunity. Why do you turn away your eyes? Why
do you shun my pleas? Do not look upon me as a woman, but as a
creature to be pitied [because of her inability to have a child], as one

---

18. *Apology* I, xxi; see R. L. Wilken, "Pagan Criticism of Christianity: Greek Religion and Christian Faith," in *Early Christian Literature and the Classical Intellectual Tradition,* ed. W. R. Shoedel and R. L. Wilken (Paris, 1979), pp. 117–34, Vol. 53
in *Théologie Historique*; Carroll, *The Cult of the Virgin Mary,* pp. 84–86.

of the sex that brought forth the Redeemer."[19] The woman's outburst points to the dichotomous Christian view of woman as cause of all sin and as *Theotokos*.

The Desire for Cultic Recognition

The fledgling Christian church sought a means to disassociate itself from the decadent moral life of the late empire, especially from such libertine sects as the gnostic Marcosians and Nicolites and the hellenized Jewish community. For example, that strain of what we might call evangelical puritanism which we see in Justine Martyr (150), Athenagoras (180), and Minucius Felix (200), in Tertullian's *Adversus Judaeos* and Commodian's *Carmen Apologeticum,* not only served as a genuine teaching for their respective communities but was intended principally to distinguish between themselves and the Jews, to show the error of the Jews in not recognizing Christ as the promised messiah. Although this process of individuation made use of the developing Christian ideal of celibacy, it was not limited to celibacy. The early church took every opportunity to proclaim its distinctiveness; celibacy was advocated along with an abandonment of the ritual of circumcision and the rules of *kashruth*. The Christians of the first century avoided the other major cultic trappings of "religion" during this period; they did not have shrines, temples, sacrifices, or cult statues, nor did they have festivals, pilgrimages, dances, or other public signs that would have acknowledged to their Jewish and pagan brethren that their members constituted a "religious" community. All of these efforts were part of an organized attempt to establish the Christian church's identity.

Early Christianity's search for a unique collective personality was antagonized by the Roman habit of considering Christians merely another example of heterodox Judaism. For example, the calumny of onolatry, the worship of an ass, first attributed by Tacitus to the Jews, was later used to defame Christians, by both non-Jews and Jews. Christ was sometimes depicted in graffiti as half human and half ass. Tertullian and Minucius Felix acknowledged this practice and bitterly

19. McNamara suggests that part of this evangelizing was designed to diminish the gender roles assigned to men and women in Jewish and Gentile society; see McNamara, "A New Song," p. 5. See also W. O. Walker, Jr., "The 'Theology of Woman's Place' and the 'Paulinist Tradition,' in *The Bible and Feminist Hermeneutics,* ed. M. A. Tolbert, in *Semeia* 28 (1983): 101–12.

denounced it. Their defense was as much motivated by a desire to distinguish themselves from heterodox Judaism as it was intended to defend the church from blasphemy. What is of interest here is that an important part of the program of individuation was directed at developing a corpus of texts which could illustrate the moral and practical superiority of Christianity as it transformed human life. The lives of the saints were to be that corpus. As with many other attempts at self-definition, the new sapling was grafted onto an older root.

Christian Neoplatonism

Two other traditions which contributed greatly to the developing Christian understanding of virginity and which shaped later medieval saints' lives were Platonism and Gnosticism. Late Platonism, although it achieved its apogee in thinkers like Numenius (fl. 175?) and in the Neoplatonic idealism of Plotinus (205–70) and Porphyry (233–303?), also influenced earlier fathers such as Justin Martyr. The syncreticism of late Platonism presented an attractive and ambitious philosophical system for some influential Christian thinkers. Origen, to cite one example, abandoned the professional teachers of philosophy to listen to the lectures of the Alexandrian dockworker and Neoplatonist Ammonius Saccas. In his *Stromateis,* Clement of Alexandria writes that Greek philosophy (he is referring to Neoplatonism) "prepares the way for the teaching that is royal in the highest sense of the word/λόγος, [the New Testament], by making men self controlled, by moulding character and making them ready to receive the truth."[20] Platonism for Clement is of value not so much for its metaphysical idealism as for the assistance it provides in the development of a Christian system of behavior.[21]

The depth of Platonic philosophy's hold on the creedal systems of late-second and third-century Christians, especially those nurtured by the Alexandrian church, can be seen in some Christian thinkers' attempts at giving Plato the status of the universal heroes of their ancestral faith. Some even argued in good typological fashion that Plato—to the same degree as Moses the founder of Judaism—was a prophetic foreshadowing of Christ. Both Clement in the *Stromateis* and Eusebius in the *Praeparatio Evangelia,* citing Numenius of Apamea, refer to

20. *Stromateis,* I, 80.

21. Frend, *Martyrdom and Persecution,* p. 259.

Plato as "the Attic Moses."[22] Christianity's intellectual debt to Neoplatonism from the late second through the fifth centuries, despite the occasional opposition of a Tertullian to Greek philosophical exegesis, is both widespread and deep. In fact, as Dodds and Cox have observed, the revival of late third century Neoplatonism shows a marked tendency to elevate the Christian emphasis on authority to the supreme place formerly accorded the Neoplatonic principle of reason. As Dodds succinctly put it, the theoretical Neoplatonism of Plotinus was transformed into "a religion with its own saints and miracle-workers."[23] The lives of the saints were to be the primary examples for what Clement of Alexandria referred to as the process of "moulding character and making them [the believers] ready to receive the truth."

Now, granting the breadth of this philosophical influence, let us ask the question germane for our discussion: did this Greek Neoplatonism influence the composition of sacred biographies of virgin saints, particularly those of women? The answer is a guarded yes—guarded because, although we have the example of Tertullian in his *Ad Nationes* (ca. 197?) and *Ad Martyras* (ca. 197?–203?) urging the faithful to imitate famous pagan women such as the queen of Egypt, the wife of Hasdrubal, Lucretia, Dido, and Cleopatra, there is little evidence of direct influence from a pagan text, such as *Acta Alexandrinorum,* on such Christian *vitae*. The influence of Neoplatonism on Christian sacred biography was not direct textual borrowing but was indirect in the formation of the Christian ideal of celibacy.

The early Christian concept of virginity, as it matured and changed, made its own the values its pagan predecessors had already attributed to a life of celibacy. The crucial appropriation from classical ideals of virginity—an appropriation which certainly influenced the Christian biographies of the *vita virginitatis*—was Neoplatonic idealism's radical split between the spirit, the intellect, and matter. Jerome incorporated into his teaching on virginity traditions indebted to the ascesis which grew from such Neoplatonic teaching. Such suspicion of the things of the world obviously suited a group with a strong eschatological ethos and provided an appropriate frame within which to cast the struggles exemplified in the *acta* and *passiones* of the Christian saints.

How did the asocial, antiurban attitude of fourth-century thinkers such as Jerome and Athanasius influence the composition of sacred

22. *Stromateis,* I, 150: 4, II, 93: 10; and Eusebius, *Praeparatio Evangelica,* XI, 10, 14, cited in Frend, *Martyrdom and Persecution,* pp. 258, 487.

23. E. R. Dodds, *Pagan and Christian in an Age of Anxiety,* p. 30.

biographies of women? To begin, the Christian ideal of celibacy in the thought of Jerome elevated celibacy to a position of far greater importance than it had enjoyed in either Judaism or Greco-Roman religion and gave it a systematic creedal foundation. The effect of this elevation was initially to offer a reordering of certain social norms. For example, because the vocation of Christian celibacy was a radical disavowal of one's sexuality, the role of the celibate within the young church minimized the importance of gender. In so doing, it allowed women, *in theory,* an opportunity to advance to positions of importance within the church; celibacy freed them from the demands of the roles of wife and mother (as Tertullian remarks in *Ad Uxorem*). Something like this attitude may be present at the level of subtext in Perpetua and Felicitas's acknowledged importance and their behavior's implicit disavowal of husbands. Jerome, though not an advocate of greater administrative responsibilities on the part of women in the church, does reveal his indebtedness, despite his misogyny, to this ideal of the transforming power in a woman's life. In his *Commentary on the Epistle to the Ephesians,* Jerome wrote that celibacy allowed a woman, for the very first time, to rise above her traditional status and become like a man: "As long as a woman is for birth and children, she is different from man as body is from soul. But when she wishes to serve Christ more than the world, then she will cease to be a woman and will be called man."[24] Extending Jerome's argument, men are souls, and women who are not celibate are bodies. The women who die to protect their chastity might be said to put on masculinity or, as Perpetua said, to have become men (*et facta sum masculus,* X,7).

Christian Gnosticism

The Gnostics also insisted on a radical dualism between matter and the spirit. However, they went further than the Neoplatonists and created a value-laden hierarchy. They argued that, if the spirit were a reflection of the intellect of the creator (the *nous*), it must have existed before matter and therefore be more primary (more worthy) than material creation. The Gnostics preached a classic antipathy between the spirit and the flesh, a coarse dualism which saw the spirit as elevated and matter as base. Further, believing physical creation to be a state of depravity, the Gnostics made the intellectual attainment of prophecy and wisdom

24. K. A. Wilson, ed., *Medieval Women Writers* (Athens, Ga., 1984), p. xxiii.

(*gnosis*) their primary goal, and as such they proselytized for a noetic hierarchy.

Celibacy, viewed from this perspective, is an eminently appropriate response to a flawed creation, because it eschews the continuity of creation. The achievement of true *gnosis* is greatly enhanced by the celibate state. Gnostic dualism was quite influential in the church and left its mark on such influential thinkers as Clement of Alexandria, Tertullian, and Origen, who in turn transmitted something of this spirit to the institutional church and thence to those who would be its saints. The vernacular sacred biographies from the high Middle Ages are imbued with this (by this time utterly assimilated) gnostic dualism, which pitted the saints, those enlightened leaders, against Satan and his evil legion. From the earliest times (in the *Passio of Perpetua* and the *Vita Antonii,* for example), the suffering endured by the martyrs and saints is a deliberate *bellum Satanicum.*

Theodicy

Dualism in the early church was reinforced from another quarter besides Neoplatonism and Gnosticism. The additional source for this dualism was less an established ideology than the product of a dialectic which attempted to reconcile the fact of an all-merciful creator with the obvious existence of uncaused or unjustified suffering in the world. How do we account for evil in God's sacred creation? The Christians, following Jewish tradition (cf. Wisdom 2:24; Job 4:18; Isaiah 14:12–15), believed that God created only two kinds of sentient beings—angels and men—and that these two, although created innocent, sinned, the angels through self-deception and man deceived by the fallen angels. This was a constant of orthodoxy throughout the Middle Ages and is succinctly stated in the language of the Fourth Lateran Council: *Firmiter credimus . . . Diabolus enim et alii daemones a Deo quidem natura creati sunt boni, sed ipsi per se facti sunt mali.* However, Satan was, no matter how powerful, forever subservient to God and the primal cause of human suffering and damnation.

The early church rejected the extreme dualism of the Manicheans, who believed in two equivalent principles, one of light and one of dark, one good and one evil, locked in eternal strife. However, this celestial battle between the forces of light and dark, between God and Satan, between demigods and malign forces, continued to rage in the lives of the saints. What orthodoxy did not tolerate in its official pronounce-

ments and teaching, it did not suppress in these exemplary tales. In his
life of St. Anthony, Athanasius, echoing Ephesians 6:12, refers thus to
the fight against Satan: "our wrestling is not against flesh and blood,
but against the Principalities and the Powers, against the world-rulers
of this darkness, against spiritual forces of wickedness on high."[25]

The Rational Basis for Virginity

If the theology of the virgin birth could silence most critics by investing
itself in the infallibility of Scripture, such an appeal to authority was
not possible for those who proposed chastity as the *summum bonum
naturale* in this life. Those who argued that complete chastity was preferable in the sight of God to married life justified their position by
claiming such a life was more in keeping with the dictates of reason.

Aside from the polemicists of the late fourth century, such as Ambrose, Jerome, Augustine, and John Chrysostom, the first genuine attempt to supply a reasoned rationale for celibacy emerges with the
School of Chartres and their attempt to harmonize theological belief
and nature.[26] However, it was Aquinas who provided an unimpeachable rational basis for celibacy. In his commentary on Aristotle's *Ethics,* Aquinas distinguished between man's animal nature, which is
obliged by natural instinct to mate, and his intellectual nature, which
is also obligated, although by the *ius gentium,* to make decisions. Aquinas's distinction is an important one, providing a reasoned account for
the superiority of celibacy. For example, if we compare a life of virginity with that of marriage, although both vocations are worthy and sanctioned by natural law, the chaste life is paradoxically somehow more
human requiring an additional exercise of this rational faculty, the *ius
gentium* open only to humanity, which is that higher faculty that gives
to mankind the disposition to know God, make moral judgments, and
live in community.[27] The life of virginity is therefore one in which we
participate more fully in the life of reason. It is reasonable to strive,
whatever the cost, for such a life. Thus, the lives of the female saints,

25. R. J. Deferrari, ed., *Early Christian Biographies* (Washington, 1952), p. 252.

26. A. Barstow, "Married Priests and the Reforming Papacy: The Eleventh Century Debates," *Texts and Studies in Religion* 12 (1982): 183–91.

27. D. E. Luscombe, "Natural Morality and Natural Law," in *The Cambridge History of Medieval Philosophy* (Cambridge, 1982), p. 710; B. Gottleib, "Feminism in
the Fifteenth Century," *Women of the Medieval World,* ed. J. Kirshner and S. F.
Wemple (Oxford, 1985), pp. 337–62; *Catholic Encyclopedia,* Vol. 4, p. 764.

even if their extreme behavior might appear hysterical, illustrate a desire to participate more fully in the complete dimension of what it means to be human. Aquinas's position represents an effort to augment with Aristotelianism the dualism so obviously a part of these sacred biographies.

It is misleading to speak about the dominance of an encratic ideal in the mentality of Middle Ages; from the fourth through the fourteenth centuries, proponents and opponents alike can be identified, from Jovinian and Jerome to Jean de Meun and Christine de Pisan. As a subject of intense public debate, its history is reasonably clear in works by Origen, Cyprian, Jerome, Augustine, Caesarius of Arles, Aldhelm, Stephen Langton, Bernard Silvestris, Hugh of St. Victor, Aquinas, the visionary work of Joachim of Fiore, and the related *querelle des femmes* of Lydgate and others from the fifteenth century. Although dualism would appear virtually a universally accepted article of faith, it is difficult to assess how influential the opinions of such thinkers were in all spheres; for example, what part did this encraticism play in the belief systems of the laity? From the later Middle Ages, that population is more accessible, and, judging from a considerable number of texts from the thirteenth century, such dualism, although perhaps the orthodox position, is often the butt of considerable humor, as in anonymous fabliaux like *Du prestre crucifie,* Marie de France's *Eliduc,* or Chaucer's *Canterbury Tales.* Contradictory sentiments abound, from the suspicious misogyny in the Latin *Lamentations of Matheolus* (ca. 1300) to Chaucer's Friar Lawrence's naive naturalism. Outside literature, we have the example of the peasant woman Grazida Lizier, born in the French village of Montaillou, who saw no harm in having been the mistress of the parish priest (nor did her mother, who arranged it) from the age of fourteen. Homans, Britton, and Razi have elucidated peasant marriage and indicated the frequency with which fornication, marital infidelity, and illegitimate birth were the subject of manorial court records in thirteenth- and fourteenth-century England.[28]

There is, however, one genre in which we can speak with certainty about the importance of an ideal of extreme asceticism, and that is the sacred biographies which lauded the heroism of the virgin saints. The life of the virgin saint, but chiefly that of the female virgin, was a powerful symbol for a certain element of the population throughout the

28. G. Homans, *The English Villagers of the Thirteenth Century* (Cambridge, Mass., 1941), pp. 109–207; E. Britton, *The Community of the Vill* (Toronto, 1977), pp. 34–37; Zvi Razi, *Life, Marriage and Death in a Medieval Parish* (Cambridge, 1980), pp. 130–53.

Middle Ages. Aside from the mass of apocryphal *vitae*, we can name just a few of the more important texts as Gregory of Nyssa's *Life of St. Macrina*, Rudolph's *Life of St. Leoba*, Thomas of Celano's *Life of St. Clare of Assisi*. In England from the thirteenth through the fifteenth centuries, there is a veritable avalanche of these biographies. A considerable number of important lives were written: the "Katherine Group," the numerous lives of the virgin saints in the *South English Legendary*, in de Voragine's *Legenda Aurea*, in the *Northern Homily Cycle*, in the *Gilte Legende*, and in Osbern Bokenham's *Legendys of Hooly Wummen*. Writers such as Chaucer and Capgrave composed lives of female saints, and some anonymous verse lives survive. Besides these collections and the unique work of the virtuosi, there remain *exempla* and epitomes of virgin saints extant in unedited sermon manuscripts of the period. The quantity of material which survives is clearly only a fraction of what must have existed, for we know from manuscript mutilation that the later reformers were not partial to such reminders of the *ancien regime*.

The Problem of Marriage

Within certain of the early Christian churches, especially those communities under the influence of one or more of the types of dualism mentioned above, the roles of the celibate and the married were in sharp opposition. The rift separating the two systems was based on theological and moral concerns. Marriage was a state to be avoided, because in intercourse the curse of original sin was passed on to the children of the union, forever corrupting them. Sexual pleasure not only endangered one's chances for salvation, but it placed at grave risk any fruit of such liaison. Athanasius's *Life of St. Anthony*, the first sacred biography of a non-martyr, underlines how revered certain of these encratic ideals had become by the late 350s. Anthony's first major temptation was a sexual one: "The contemptible Enemy [Satan] even dared to assume the appearance of a woman at night, imitating her every gesture solely to deceive Anthony."[29] If physical pleasure is already being held up as a paradigm of corruption, the less exalted way to live life, marriage itself becomes questionable because it interferes further with the totality of affection involved in loving Christ. In Cy-

29. Deferrari, *Early Christian Biographies*, pp. 139, 155.

newulf's life of *Juliana,* the heroine tells her father, Africanus, that she cannot marry Eleusius: "He must seek bridal love from another woman; he will not have any here."[30]

Marriage viewed from the perspective of Anthony or Juliana was a vehicle for the perpetuation of sin and should be avoided. Examples abound of virgin saints fleeing to avoid marriage. Malmesbury and Tynemouth record the legend of St. Frideswide, a Saxon princess from Wessex (680–735), fleeing into a forest and then to the city of Oxford to escape her suitor.[31] Margery Kempe, after having heard the celestial music played by the angels and saints in heaven, found "the debt of matrimony was so abominable to hear that she had rather, it seemed to her, eat or drink the slime or muck in the gutter than to consent to any fleshly communing [intercourse with her husband], save only for obedience."[32] Some argued that there were practical reasons not to marry. Family duties carried out responsibly could occupy a considerable portion of one's time, making it harder for the married to live with the imminence of Christ's coming as their sole concern (Tertullian, *Ad Uxorem*). Jerome, in his passion to discredit Jovinian, argued that the Apostle St. Peter, appointed to the primacy of the church by Christ, was inferior to St. John the evangelist. Jerome's argument was based on his belief that Peter's marital status made him less able to perform the Lord's service than the celibate John, a point of view shared by Aelred of Rievaulx.[33] In the great English Dominican Bromyard's chapter on *Matrimonium* in his *Summa Predicantium* (ca. 1345), less than a seventh of the discussion concerns the merit of marriage. Bromyard argued that if the Old Testament ideal of womanhood was fecundity, the New Testament ideal was virginity.[34] The tradition begun

30. Robert E. Bjork, *The Old English Verse Saints' Lives*, pp. 47–48.

31. C. Horstman, ed., *Nova Legenda Anglie*, pp. 459–60.

32. W. Provost, "The English Religious Enthusiast: Margery Kempe," in Wilson, *Medieval Women Writers*, p. 306.

33. Ayto and Barratt, *Aelred of Rievaulx's De Institutione*, p. 35.

34. G. R. Owst, *Literature and Pulpit in Medieval England* (Oxford, 1966), p. 378. Although one must bear in mind that from the thirteenth century, when extreme antipathy toward marriage is quite apparent, we also have clergy, such as Richard of Leicester and Richard of Weteheringsette, whose *Summa brevis* (ca. 1210?) contained sections on the goods to be found in matrimony; see L. E. Boyle, "A Study of the Works Attributed to William of Pagula" (D. Phil., Oxford, 1956), Vol. 2, pp. 20–22, and "Three English Pastoral Summae and a Magister Galienus," in *Studia Gratiana* 11 (1967): 133–44. See also F. Broomfield, ed., *Thomae de Chobham: Summa Confessorum* (Louvain, 1968), p. li. Broomfield points out that Chobham's great *summa*

in the mid-fourth century which extolled the primacy of virginity, although it obviously was changed to suit differing contexts—reinvigorated by the Gregorian reforms of the late eleventh century—came down to the high Middle Ages remarkably intact.[35]

The Virtue in the Chaste Life

These varied traditions governing virginity and asceticism coalesced by the mid-fourth century and gave birth in the Christian church to a theology which held sexual abstinence to be a sign of singular virtue. The conjugal life was at best a *necessaria culpa*. The more orthodox movements in the Apostolic and post-Apostolic church did attempt to combat severely ascetical practices, especially those demeaning marriage. In 1 Timothy 4:3, Paul's statements make abundantly clear that the fledgling Christian community at Ephesus was practicing such heterodox encraticism, going so far as to forbid its members to marry. The discussion of the virtues of marriage and virginity in 1 Corinthians (7:1–40) indicates that the church at Corinth was considering whether marriage was an acceptable practice. Paul's own ambivalence about the merits of marriage versus those of celibacy in 1 Corinthians 7 gave precious aid to the orthodox opponents of extreme sexual continence. It is necessary to add that the encraticism one suspects was being considered in Corinth and implicit in Paul's remarks need not illustrate a deeply felt anti-female point of view or that the status of women was purely a subordinate one.[36] Paul's reasoning is eschatological: if the world is to end soon, it is best not to prepare for a family. The Pauline letters indicate that women could serve various roles in the community,

---

did not rely on his knowledge of the Fourth Lateran Council's pronouncements on marriage. See T. N. Tentler, "The Summa for Confessors as an Instrument for Social Control," in *The Pursuit of Holiness in Late Medieval and Renaissance Religion,* ed. C. Trinkaus and H. Oberman (Leiden, 1974), p. 122. Although Tentler tends to see the *summae* as yet another indication of "clerical elites," this is nonetheless a valuable study. See also L. E. Boyle, "The Summa for Confessors as a Genre, and Its Religious Intent," also in Trinkaus and Oberman, for a response to Tentler.

35. M. W. Kaufman, "The Conception of Woman in the Middle Ages and the Renaissance," *Soundings: An Interdisciplinary Journal* 56 (1973): 143.

36. Walker, "The 'Theology of Woman's Place.'" Walker separates out the authentic Paul (1 Corinthians 7) from such passages which preach female subordination (1 Corinthians 11:3–16; 14:34–35; Colossians 3:18–19; Ephesians 5:22–23; 1 Timothy 2:8–15; Titus 2:4–5).

from the very important to the lowly. Meeks has suggested that the role of women in the first-century church was much greater and more equal to that of men than the role of women in contemporary Judaism, a conclusion given further substantiation by the model of the preaching of the virgin Thecla.[37] However, a substantial diminishment in the role of women in the church took place in the space of a century: while Justin Martyr was able to write of women's notable ministry as preachers, Cyprian viewed such ministry as a practice now past.[38]

The Ladder of Perfection

The debates concerning the relative merits of marriage and celibacy were to continue unabated throughout the Middle Ages. Bishop Eustathius of Sabasteia was condemned in 343 for preaching the complete rejection of marriage and urging Christians to shun those who were known to have had sexual intercourse. Although Bishop Eustathius was an extreme case, an interesting product of this dialectic between celibacy and marriage for the student of sacred biography was the development of a ranking of the value of various forms of Christian witness (e.g., martyr, virgin, widow, and married). Such hierarchies or ladders are redolent of the earlier gnostic systems. The values assigned to these vocations were fluid and continually being fine-tuned to suit the religious climate. Those vocations which consistently emerged at the top of the scale became the official vehicles for Christian heroism, that is, to those who would aspire to sanctity.

Martyrdom, as a ritualized reenactment of the *imitatio Christi* which led to death, was considered the apex of Christian heroism. Once the period of persecutions had passed, however, the forces supporting extreme encraticism were so strong that the virgin assumed the crown formerly held by the martyr. This change in position can be illustrated nicely through a comparison of the comments of St. Cyprian made in the mid-third century with those of St. Patrick from the mid-fifth century. Cyprian assigned a numerical value to the various ways in which a Christian could choose to live his life, giving the value of 100 to the martyr and that of 60 to the virgin. By the time we reach Patrick, such scales have become increasingly elaborate and hierarchical. With the demise of the physical persecutions, the role of martyr had fallen into

37. Meeks, *The First Urban Christians*, p. 81; *Acts of Paul*, II, 43, 4.

38. McNamara, "A New Song," p. 77.

desuetude. In Patrick's scheme, the virgin, along with monks, bishops, and doctors of the church (vocations restricted in almost every instance to celibates), received a ranking of 100; all other clergy and widows received a score of 60, with the faithful but unfortunately married laity in last place with a meager 30. Such tabulations may seem somewhat jejune, but they nonetheless illustrate the intensity of feeling which gave rise to them and underscore behavior which served as approved models in sacred biography.

Celibacy, the Vernacular, and the Laity

Although there was considerable variety within the ranks of the clergy concerning the actual practice of celibacy, as visitation and bishops' registers indicate, Jerome's ideas on celibacy as the highest ideal were preached in both Latin and vernacular sermons unceasingly throughout the Middle Ages. Lea has presented a plethora of evidence from the synods and councils which shows the church's interest in the ideal of such encraticism.[39] What is surprising in this mass of synodal material is not the hierarchy's reformist zeal in promoting celibacy for its ordained priests and professed nuns but also for the laity. Virginity was preached to married lay men and women in an often vulgar antimarital invective in vernacular sermons, treatises, lyrics, cathechisms, and saints' lives.

What was it about the married state that so upset the proponents of this anti-marital invective? The answer may appear too obvious, but it seems inescapably to be the fear of the pleasure derived from sexual intercourse bolstered by the notion that such behavior continued the curse of original sin in the world and hence must represent a violation of our highest faculties, reason and will. The argument was made that sexual intercourse, even within the bounds of a legally contracted Christian marriage for the purpose of procreation, was an impediment to spiritual growth and, as Aquinas had argued, to greater rationality.[40]

39. H. C. Lea, *History of Sacerdotal Celibacy in the Christian Church,* 2 vols. (London, 1907).

40. On the difficulty of a satisfactory definition of marriage, see J. A. Brundage, "Concubinage and Marriage in Medieval Canon Law," *Journal of Medieval History* 1 (April 1975): 7: marriage required the consent of the two partners and was ratified by sexual intercourse. See M. M. Sheehan, "The Formation and Stability of Marriage in Fourteenth-Century England: Evidence of an Ely Register," *MS* 33(1971): 239, ff.; his discussion of *Cum inhibitio,* Canon 51 of the Fourth Lateran Council, is most instructive.

When these encratic sentiments are rendered in the vernacular, the rhetoric becomes more strident, more vituperative. That singular vernacular document on virginity in thirteenth-century England, *Hali Meiðhad* (ca. 1225), makes precisely this point concerning sexual desire: "is al to muche lauerdom ant meistrie þrinne þis cunde [imerred tus] þe Davi∂ cleopet þi faderes hus. þet is, þe lust of lecherie þet rixle∂ þerwiþinne" (p. 5).[41] *Hali Meiðhad*, written as a guide for virgins, has, as one would expect, virtually nothing positive to say about marriage. Sharing in the theological spirit of Eustathius, Jerome, and Patrick, it subordinates marriage to celibacy. Given its purpose and audience, such a singular point of view is understandable. What is noteworthy, however, is the author's language when he does discuss the married life. Here he employs a rhetoric of bestiality, of detritus and putrefaction, to proscribe the married life: "þet bestelich gederunge, þet scheomelese sompnunge [copulation], þet ful of ful∂e, stinkinde ant untohe dede" (p. 4). Although written in English forty years before Aquinas worked out his rational basis for the superiority of the celibate life, *Hali Meiðhad*'s lexicon underscores the same point that the conjugal life is one of brute physicality, a life which eschews the higher faculty of reason. The treatise accepts implicitly the dualism in the gnostic position that every human vocation possesses a degree of intrinsic merit; it exhibits an influence from the Johannine Apocalypse and has the self-same penchant for enumeration which we have observed in Cyprian and Patrick (once again underscoring the continuity of these traditions), that such merit can be graded on a scale: "For wedlack haue∂ frut ∂rittifald in heouene; widewehad, sixti fald; meiðhad, wi∂ hundretfald, ouergea∂ ba∂e" (p. 11). Along this graded continuum, points are gained by those who seek the spiritual and avoid the physical; points are lost for those who marry: "hwase of hire meiðhad lihte∂ into wedlac, bi hu monie degrez ha falle∂ dunewardes" (p. 11). The spirituality which informs the theology of *Hali Meiðhad* is based on an intellectually naive interpretation of Christian-gnostic dualism.[42]

Marriage is placed on the lowest rung of the ladder of Christian vocation because the treatise views sexual intercourse as the most grave

---

41. Bella Millett, ed., *Hali Meiðhad*, EETS O. S. 284 (London, 1982). Page numbers are from this edition.

42. Such language was to become quite conventional in English treatises. See R. Morris and P. Gradon, eds., *Dan Michel's "Ayenbite of Inwyt,"* EETS O. S. 23 (London, 1975), p. 228; J. Bugge, *"Virginitas": An Essay in the History of an Ideal* (The Hague, 1975), pp. 15–90.

of sins. Sexual intercourse, even within the sacramental confines of a Christian marriage, is a pollution which not only disfigures the dignity of the human body but soils the spotless immortality of the soul and places a barrier between man and God: "Alle þe oþre sun[n]en ne beoð bute sunnen; ah þis is sunne, ant ec uncumel[i]cheð þe ant unwurðgeð þi bodi, suleð þi sawle ant makeð schuldi towart Godd ant fuleð þi flesch ec" (p. 17). Although the extreme nature of this teaching concerning intercourse in marriage was at odds with the official teaching of the church, the treatise's existence is testimony that deviance from the official *magisterium* was tolerated provided it moved in the general line of orthodoxy, in support of antimarital encraticism. The text proposes, perhaps with some self-conscious hyperbole, that it is better to be buried than married: "wel were ham weren ha on hare brudlakes dei [wedding day] iboren to biburien!" (p. 4).

Virginity over Martyrdom

The martyr, who had occupied the highest place within the heirarchy of Christian heroism, had slowly relinquished her laurel to the virgin (see ll. 319–30). The author of *Hali Meiðhad* appeals to his audience to be mindful of Sts. Katherine, Margaret, Agnes, Juliana, and Cecilia and eulogizes their memory more for their virginity than for their martyrdom (ll. 676–77). Such a transformation made eminently good sense when blood sacrifice was a thing of the distant past and his audience likely to have been celibate. If Anthony flounted Maximian's enforcement of Diocletian's edicts against Christians in the Great Persecution of 303–12, he was spared, Athanasius writes, because the "Lord was keeping him to help others that he might teach many the practice of asceticism."[43] Anthony's singular lack of success as an aspiring martyr points to the historical imperative which supported the ascetic ideal: virginity achieved its prominence in part because of the demise of martyrdom as a form of witness.

By the time we reach the mid-twelfth century, the proponents of virginity have virtually rewritten church history. Virginity is seen not merely as equal to martyrdom but as ancient in the church's history and as a tradition whose heroes are as noble as the early martyrs. Virginity, following the impetus it received from its great proponents in the late fourth century, and once again as a result of the Gregorian

---

43. Deferrari, *Early Christian Biographies,* p. 177. The date of Anthony's attempted martyrdom is debated, but it seems likely to have been between 303 and 304.

reforms of the late eleventh century, eclipsed the ideal of martyrdom as the most worthy *imitatio Christi*.[44] Its dominance as a literary *topos* is practically complete in the corpus of vernacular sacred biographies which begin in the late eleventh century and continue through the mid-fifteenth century. Lives such as the *Vie St. Alexis* and the translations of the lives of the virgins in the *Legenda Aurea* and treatises like *Hali Meiðhad* and the *Ayenbite of Inwyt,* which hold up an ideal of celibacy to the laity, not only reflect a milieu which, to use Southern's expression, had not "developed a plausible ethic for secular life," but they seem to argue against the establishment of such positive social identification on the part of the laity. I believe the conventions of piety and the anti-marital invective depicted in vernacular sacred biographies from the twelfth century seek as part of their dialectic to constrain the growth of the laity as an autonomous class with the capacity for some degree of self-determinism.

In the following passage from the *Life of Seinte Marharete,* a thirteenth-century English author considered the relative merits of these two types of witness.[45] Virginity is celebrated as the queen of all virtues:

> Cum quoth the culure with schilinde steuene, ant stih to the wunne & to the weole of heouene. Eadi were the meiden, tha thu chure meithhad, the of alle mihtes is cewn; for-thi thus schalt aa bruken in blisse buten ende crunene brihtest (44:23–27).

St. Marharete, in a reversal of the usual benediction *topos* in a virgin-martyr life, receives the promise of everlasting life, not because she dies for Christ, as did Perpetua and Felicitas and legions of other saintly women depicted in countless *libri sanctarum,* but because she has chosen to be a virgin. Even the devils in hell are moved by her purity and beseech her before her death: "Margarete, medien, leoðe nuðe lanhure & lowse ure bondes: we beoð wel icnawen þet nis na lauerd bute godd, þet þu on leuest" (52:7–9). Such new emphasis suggests a radical shift in spirituality from a piety which recognized the witness of martyrdom as the perfect *imitatio Christi* in a Perpetua or Felicitas to one which celebrates the purity of the virgin in Margaret.

How widespread was this sentiment celebrating virginity as the queen of the virtues and its corollary lamenting the ill effects, both

---

44. Lea, *History of Sacerdotal Celibacy,* Vol. 1, pp. 216–43.

45. R. W. Southern, *Medieval Humanism and Other Essays* (New York, 1970), p. 95. F. M. Mack, *Seinte Marherete* EETS O. S. 193 (London, 1958). All quotations are from this edition, page number followed by line.

physical and moral, deriving from sexual intercourse, in vernacular texts? We can find such expressions in the length and breadth of virtually all the western European vernaculars in both poetry and prose from the late eleventh century. In medieval England, texts of demonstrable popularity, such as the "Mirror of the Ages of Man," went so far as to propose that sexual intercourse caused depression and led inevitably to despair. This text supported a commonplace belief of the period that despair was the most craven of all the habitations of the human soul; the despairing soul was beyond the ministrations of God's salvific mercy. Thus, sexual intercourse was an indulgent type of suicide leading to damnation, as the *Speculum Sancti Edmundi* puts it, "whanhope of þe blysse of heuen."[46]

The opponents of human sexuality were not content with merely denigrating intercourse within marriage, and indeed marriage itself, but they also questioned the very basis for human affection. The primary argument was based on the observation that human love is self-serving and selfish and that the love celebrated, for example, by the Troubadors was not noble but base. The Vernon Manuscript treatise "Of Clene Maydenhood" proposes that what men celebrate as love is in fact not love but a chimera, a false illusion:

> Fikel. Fals and les
> Whon thou wenest. hit best to holde
> Hit wendeth a-wey. as wyndes bles.
> And bi-cometh wrest and colde
> For trewe loue. hit neuer nes.[47]

We should not be surprised to discover that the logic of these sentiments as they were slowly propounded in these vernacular lyrics should eventually propose that whatever that quality is which we label human love cannot exist in the same creature who feels a desire for human sexuality. Thus, not only is the act of sexual intercourse a barrier to higher spirituality, but even the thought of physical pleasure is inhospitable to genuine love. The lyrics in Lambeth Palace manuscript 853 (ca. 1400) make this point crystal clear: "wrong is an hiȝ seete there riȝt schulde be,/merci for mys deede is putt away;/letcherie hath made clennesse to flee, Loue may not abyde nyght ne day." If conjugal love which seeks expression in the fulfillment of human intimacy, delight in the pleasure of physical creation, and spouses who are more cherished

---

46. G. G. Perry, *Religious Pierces in Prose and Verse*, EETS O. S. 26 (London, 1867/1914), p. 25.

47. C. Horstmann, ed., *Minor Poems of the Vernon Manuscript*.

the more they contribute to such conjugal pleasure are portrayed as ignoble models, it is the opposite of these ideals which ought to be pursued. The encratic thesis is no more succinctly stated than in the words of St. Juliana—words which surely echo those of Felicitas to the prison guard—as she is being stripped by her father in preparation for a savage whipping. "So much," she said, "shall I be the dearer to him, as I suffer more pain for his love" ("Swa muche quoð ha ich iwurðe him þe leouere: So ich derure þing for his luue drehe").[48]

Dan Jon Gaytrige's sermon is a typical populist vehicle for the dissemination of the Lateran program in the late fourteenth century. It presents us with the very bold proposal that the desire for sexual intimacy of any sort is coupled with the illusory and inordinate desire for material wealth, a desire which all the faithful would acknowledge led inevitably to thralldom: "Temperance . . . controls physical lust and inhibits our desire for material goods" ("methe . . . kepes vs fra . . . luste of þe flesche, and ȝemes vs fra ȝernynges of werldly gudes)." Conversely, abstinence from sexual pleasure would stiffen the will's resolve to avoid the false desires of the world.[49]

Many Middle English texts from the thirteenth through the fifteenth centuries could be quoted to illustrate this polarity between human sexuality and true human spirituality. Broadly speaking, what one confronts in these saints' lives, poems, prose treatises, and sermons is an understanding of sexual desire as an indication of spiritual disharmony. The effect of this desire is to destroy the soul's innate longing for God. This view of virginity and its exemplification in medieval texts illustrates the influence, albeit muted, of the dualism of gnosticism, Patristic Neoplatonism's dialectic which placed a premium on the substantiality and primacy of the soul at the expense of matter. It remains to see the fullness of this encratic ethos depicted in a vernacular saint's life.

The Lateran Program and the English *Vitae Sanctarum*

In England, the period between the second decade of the thirteenth century and the middle of the fifteenth century witnesses the single greatest increase in the composition of sacred biography in the history

48. O. Cockayne and E. Brock, eds., þe *Liflade of St. Juliana*, EETS O. S. 51 (London, 1872), p. 16.

49. Perry, *Dan Gaytryge's Sermon*, p. 11; see also W. N. Francis, ed., *The Book of Vices and Virtues*, EETS O. S. 217 (London, 1942), pp. 43–46, 223.

of that vernacular.[50] Of special interest is the number of lives of heroic saintly women, those who achieved their sanctity either through virginity or martyrdom or both. Certainly, partial explanation for this marked increase in vernacular sacred biography is the reform program stimulated by Lateran IV, which urged—as that great reform bishop, Richard Poore of Salisbury (ca. 1217–21), stated—frequent preaching in the mother tongue, *frequenter domestico idiomate sane inculcent*.[51] But many of these sacred biographies, especially those which concern female virgin saints, do not show a strict indebtedness to the Lateran program. This pouring forth does, however, occur at roughly the same time as when the *chanson de geste* and the romance have reached the peak of their period of greatest productivity (1150–1225) and hence would be reflected in the circulation of these French texts or Anglo-Norman versions in England.[52]

Further, coincident with the decline of these two genres, that is, after 1225, in England the mendicants (the Dominicans arrived in Dover in the early summer of 1221 and the Franciscans in 1224)[53] began to reply

50. C. d'Evelyn, "Saints' Legends," in *A Manual of the Writings in Middle English* (Hamden, Conn., 1970).

51. W. Rich Jones and W. Dunn McCray, eds., *Charters and Documents of Salisbury* (London, 1891), p. 130. Poore is just one of a number of Thirteenth-Century reform bishops who specifically urged vernacular catechesis, such as Bartholomew of Exeter, John Pecham of Canterbury, Roger Weseham of Coventry, and Walter de Cantilupe of Worcester. See C. R. Cheney, *English Synodalia of the Thirteenth Century* (Oxford, 1968), pp. 51, 62–89, 150.

52. P. Zumthor, *Histoire littéraire de la France médiévale VIe–XIVe siècles* (Paris, 1954), pp. 206–54.

53. L. E. Boyle, "The Fourth Lateran Council and Manuals of Popular Theology," in T. J. Heffernan, ed., *The Popular Literature of Medieval England* (Knoxville, 1985), pp. 30–43. Although the mendicants gave great stimulus to the Lateran Council's emphasis on preaching, it is well to note that some secular and regular clergy were regularly preaching in the native tongue to the people generations before the council—Benedictines like Abbot Sampson of Bury St. Edmunds (ca. 1135–1212), Cistercians like Alain de Lille (ca. 1128–1202), Helinand de Froidmont (ca. 1170–1220), Caesarius of Heisterbach (ca. 1180–1240), the secular bishop of Paris Maurice de Suly (d. 1197), and the cardinal Jacques de Vitry (ca. 1180–1240). See T. Arnold, ed., *Memorials of St. Edmund's Abbey* (London, 1890,) Vol. 1, p. 245; G. Gonnet, *Enchiridion Fontium Valdensium* (Rome, 1958), p. 10; A. Piaget, "Sermonnaires et Traducteurs," in *Histoire de la langue et de la littérature française des origines à 1900* (Paris, 1890), Vol. 2, p. 233; T. F. Crane, ed., *The Exempla of Jacques de Vitry* (London, 1890), p. 146. Moreover, although the evidence is far harder to interpret, there are conciliar decrees from the Ninth Century which urge preaching in the "lingua romana" and which were repeated virtually verbatim through the Eleventh Cen-

to the undoubted success of the secular lyrics of the *trouvers* and their "songes of fowle rebawdry and of unclennes" with *exempla* and "songes of lawde and preysyng" concerning the Blessed Virgin and the saints.[54] The growth of biographies of female virgins was in part a response to the Lateran program, in part a response to the clergy's desire to compete with the *jongeleurs*—a group bitterly attacked by Aquinas, John of Mirfield, William of Nassington, and John Bromyard—and may also reflect a lay interest in the cult of the Virgin Mary.[55] Moreover, the lives of the virgin saints, not being constrained by the controlling authority of the New Testament, were able to go well beyond the propriety necessary for narratives of the Virgin.

The vernacular *libri festivales* from this period point to a recognition on the part of the clerical hierarchy of a need for a different vehicle for evangelization. Turning to such texts is an implicit recognition by the clergy of the growth of a vernacular religious culture and the prospect for a genuine lay piety. Furthermore, unlike the *chanson de geste* or the romance, these sacred biographies were not thought of as "imaginative" literature either by the clergy or apparently by the laity. Also unlike the romance and the *chanson de geste,* their claims as historical narratives were taken seriously. The distinction which separates the hold on the medieval belief systems of the respective genres lies in the identification of the romance and the *chanson de geste* as works of creative imagination, as *fabula,* and that of the saints' lives as *historia.* For example, in the 115 extant works labeled as Middle English romances, the characterization of females in those texts, although they provided entertainment, escapism, and inspiration, could not—unlike the sacred biographies of the women saints—claim a sacred historic past which required the audience's acknowledgment of such texts as

---

tury; see the Second Council of Rheims (813), Third Council of Tours, First Council of Mayence (847), and Third Council of Tours. For the actual canons from these councils, see J. Mansi, *Sacrorum Conciliorum Nova, et Amplimissa Collectio* (Florence, 1759–98) XIV, cols. 78, 85, 899. For the Dominicans, see A. Jessop, *The Coming of the Friars* (London, 1889), p. 32; and W. A. Hinnenbusch, *The Early English Friars' Preachers* (Rome, 1951), p. 282. For the Franciscans, see A. G. Little, ed., *Fratris Thomae Tractus de Adventu Fratrum Minorum in Angliam* (Manchester, 1931), p. 3. Their success was astonishing: by the middle of the thirteenth century, the Franciscans had established forty-nine houses and had twelve hundred friars preaching in England, with the Dominicans having fifty-one houses.

54. G. R. Owst, *Literature and Pulpit in Medieval England* (Oxford, 1966), p. 17.

55. Ibid., pp. 10–13.

part of the creedal system of orthodoxy.[56] The clergy who used such texts in their catechesis, presuming on their historicity and given the liturgical setting of many of these readings, presented these women as "models" of behavior for lay women. These biographies were, however extreme the behavior they recounted, a *speculum mundi,* an illustration of the potential for female Christian behavior.

The Problem of Voice

Before we turn to consider the audience for these *vitae,* a brief caveat about the "voice" which informs these narratives needs to be made. Since the "authors" were the clergy, and the audiences primarily the laity, we should expect the narrative to reflect a view consonant with the dominant ethos of the time. The obvious conclusion is that the voice which informs these narratives is not a female one. But is it a male one? Such a question might appear tendentious, muddled, if not downright obvious, but it nonetheless asks one to consider as problematic those judgments which see these texts as narrow products of a clerical elite. Such critiques seem too broad in light of the anti-authority, misanthropic content of these narratives, as well as the positive reception such texts received from women and men alike. Since we shall discuss this aspect at some length below, I would like to suggest that to the extent we can say anything about voice, the best characterization is one of androgyny.

The vernacular *vitae sanctarum* were popular with a variety of socioeconomic audiences.[57] Indeed, aside from their continuing use in the reading of an epitome at prime and during the third nocturn's *lectiones,* some early evidence indicates that preachers were using such texts regularly in their Sunday services, especially the mass which would have been attended by a mixed group. Morey pointed out that as early as the late twelfth century that it was an established article of canon law that every priest should have in his possession, among other books, homilies appropriate for Sundays and for feast days (saints' feasts).[58]

56. E. Reese, "Romance," in Heffernan, *The Popular Literature of Medieval England,* pp. 108–30.

57. On the problems associated with the use of the word *popular* when discussing medieval culture, see the introduction and the essays in Heffernan, *The Popular Literature of Medieval England.*

58. A. Morey, *Bartholomew of Exeter* (Cambridge, 1937), p. 192.

Du Meril has recorded the enthusiastic reception by the crowd of laity and the clergy (words such as *congregatio* and *turba* surely indicate women, men, and children) which greeted the narration on a Sunday of the life of that great ascetic St. Alexis recorded in the *Chronicon Laudaniensis,* dated 1173.[59] Although the evidence is limited, saints' lives appear to have been so popular that lay minstrels used them unexpurgated (i.e., did not turn them into romance) in their repertoires. Thomas de Chobham, in his *Penitential* (ca. 1230), reports that minstrels sang in the churchyards of the deeds of the lives of the saints.[60] Robert Mannyng, in *Handlyng Synne,* remarks on how popular saints' lives were with the people.[61] Moreover, these sacred biographies were not simply spiritual fodder for the benighted lower classes. Odericus Vitalis, in his *Historia Ecclesiastica,* tells of Gerald of Avranches, chaplain to early Hugh of Chester, and his efforts to draw the courtiers, the knightly class, to a more Christian life by describing the heroism of the saints.[62] Further evidence of their utility, and, one must conclude, their popularity, can be measured by their number of extant manuscripts. I shall simply cite the example of the *South English Legendary* (others could be offered), the most important of the thirteenth-century *libri festivales,* which survives in sixty-two manuscripts (a small percentage of the original number), outnumbered in extant Middle English texts only by the *Pricke of Conscience,* the *Canterbury Tales,* and *Piers Plowman,* three compositions written a century later.[63]

59. E. du Méril, *Études sur quelques points d'archéologie et d'histoire littéraire* (Paris, 1882), p. 296: "Is, quadam die dominica, cum declinasset ad turbem quam ante joculatorem viderat congregatem, ex verbis ipsius compunctiis fuit, et eum ad domum suam deducens, intense eum audire curavit. Fuit enim locus narrationis eus qualiter beatus Alexis in domo patris sui beato fine quievit."

60. C. Hareau, "Notices sur un penitential attribue à Jean de Salisbury," *Notices et extraits des manuscrits de la Bibliothèque Nationale* 24 (1876): 285: "Joculatores qui cantant gesta principum et vitas sanctorum."

61. F. J. Furnivall, ed., *Robert Mannyng: Handlyng Synne* (London, 1901–3), p. 3.

62. Ordericus Vitalis, *Historia Ecclesiastica, PL* 188, 451–52: "Luculenter enim enarrabat conflictus Demetrii et Georgii, Theodori et Sebastiani, Mauricii ducis et Thebaeae legionis, et Eustachii praecelsi magistri militum cum sociis suis, qui per martyrium coronari meruerunt in coelis."

63. M. Görlach, "The Textual Tradition of the South English Legendary," in *Leeds Texts and Monographs,* ns 6 (1974): viii–x. See also d'Evelyn, "Saints' Legends," p. 416.

The Polysemous Virgin

The dominant image of the model virginal life in English sacred biographies of the thirteenth century combines a number of seemingly contradictory motifs of the Virgin Mary: Mary as comely *sponsa Christi*, as spotless virgin, as loving gentle mother, as the regal queen of heaven, and as a synecdoche for the church.[64] Such a complex of overlapping images, themselves the process of a rich tradition—although observable separably from the beginning of the Catholic exegetical tradition in Tertullian, for example—began in earnest with twelfth-century commentaries on the Song of Songs, and with Bernadine and Victorine spirituality, and were developed somewhat more systematically in such works as Abelard's "Sermon of the Assumption" and in the commentaries of Rupert of Deutz and Honorius Augustodunensis, to name some of the more prominent. Even in the lyrics of the thirteenth century, many of these themes are prominently joined: "Moder of milce. and mayde hende," and such lyrics as:

Leuedi flour of alle þing.
rosa sine spina.
þu bere ihesu heuene king. gratia diuina.
Of alle þu berst þe pris.
Leuedi quene of parays.
electa.
Mayde milde. Moder.
es effecta.[65]

The affective spirit of Franciscan spirituality also introduced the image of the Virgin who felt her son's pain so grievously that she suffered physically:

Mayde and Moder þat astod,
marie ful of grace,
[O hu let þe teres al of blod]
uallen in þe place.[66]

The celebration of Mary's virginity, her espousal to Christ, her maternity, and her figure as the emblem of the church presents us with an enormously complicated icon. At the very least, this icon underlines a

64. P. Shine Gold, *The Lady and the Virgin* (Chicago, 1985), discusses the varying images of women, secular and religious.

65. R. Morris, ed., *An Old English Miscellany,* EETS O. S. 49 (London, 1872), pp. 88, 195.

66. Ibid., p. 198.

number of ambivalent traditions concerning the depiction of women, even if it does concern that most singular paradigm of womanhood, the Virgin Mary. The diversity of these *topoi* joined together in the single icon find additional expression in the lives of the female virgins. The saintly women whose lives we shall examine in this chapter are studies in paradox: they combine in a single icon images of the virgin, the mother, the rich and the poor, the humble and the regal, the frail and the strong, the captive and the free.

The depiction of the female saint, unlike those of the Virgin Mary, was not bound by the authority of the New Testament, and hence these varied and contradictory themes are exemplified with less circumspection: the erotic and the maternal feelings, the suffering and triumph of these holy women are treated in more detail and with greater hyperbole than that of the *mater Dei/Theotokos*. Like their virginal counterpart in the apocrypha, they supplied an outlet for imagination untrammeled by the authority of the sacred Scripture. Before turning to the important question of audience for these sacred biographies, there is one crucially important *topos* in the *vitae sanctarum* from the thirteenth century which is not found in the corpus of vernacular mariolatry, or in the *chanson de geste,* or in the romance: the image of the physically embattled woman who struggles against all lawful authority, whether political, familial, moral, or sexual. The narrative exemplification of such embattlement shows its most revealing side in the sexual abuse meted out to the virgin saints. Such abuse is ubiquitous and, as I hope to illustrate, a crucial, albeit paradoxical element (certainly much older than anything remotely like it in the romance) in the success of these sacred biographies with clergy and people alike.

Audience Reception

Any discussion of the audience for these texts must begin with a caveat: arguments concerning the audience are necessarily based on reasonable supposition; there is precious little firsthand evidence. The Middle English sacred biographies of the virgin saint are a complex of story types suggesting a varied audience which, while predominantly drawn from the lower echelons of society, was nonetheless socially and economically diverse. The *vitae sanctarum* contradict two persistent old saws: first, that "popular" non-courtly literature lacks sophistication and, second, that lower-class audiences were substantially alike. Clanchy has sensibly argued that vernacular texts were often composed by the "most sophisticated and not the most primitive authors,"

authors expert in Latin and dialectic, such as Jordan Fantosme of the Paris and Winchester schools and "Maister" Nicholas of Guilford, the author of *The Owl and the Nightingale,* and as I shall show, the anonymous authors of the lives of the saints.[67] To translate or compose in English in the thirteenth century, was a bold undertaking, indicative of one's confidence in one's abilities. Moreover, it was still so comparatively singular that we have to presume a reciprocal relationship between author and audience like that discussed in chapter 1. Although there is general agreement on the paucity of reliable firsthand evidence about parish "entertainments" in the thirteenth and fourteenth centuries, the lives of the saints, though *prima facie* catechetical works, provided considerable literary diversion for their audiences.[68]

Social Strata

Although we might expect greatly extended affinial and consanguinal ties in agrarian communities in rural England, the depth of feeling for extended kinship relations beyond that of the nuclear family can, as MacFarlane and Cressy have argued, be exaggerated.[69] Ideas of community homogeneity based on models of close extended kinship relations, related vocations, shared levels of learning, comparative amounts of wealth, and similar legal and social status may be more apparent than real, a product of modern nostalgia for a simple past. J. S. Furnley has rightly pointed out the enormous variety one finds in medieval English civil government: "in the Middle Ages . . . there was no uniformity; the system of government in a town depended on its individual history."[70] If towns, where we should expect to find some degree of standardization, because of the exigencies of social order when larger populations are concerned, were not possessed of uni-

67. M. T. Clanchy, *From Memory to Written Record,* p. 170.

68. A. F. Johnston, "Parish Entertainments in Berkshire," in *Pathways to Medieval Peasants,* ed. J. A. Raftis, (Toronto, 1981), pp. 335–37.

69. A. MacFarlane, *The Origins of English Individualism* (Cambridge, 1978), introduction, and more recently his essay "The Myth of the Peasantry: Family and Economy in a Northern Parish," in *Land, Kinship and Life-Cycle,* ed. R. M. Smith (Cambridge, 1984), pp. 333–49; David Cressy, "Kinship and Kin Interaction in Early Modern England," *Past and Present* 113 (November 1986): 65–69. For a brief and balanced summary of the differences between those who hold out for nuclear families and those who support extended, see E. Britton, "The Peasant Family in Fourteenth Century England," *Peasant Studies* 5 (1976): 2–7.

70. J. S. Furnley, *City Government in Winchester* (Oxford, 1923), p. 1.

formity, should one expect such uniformity in the composition of smaller agrarian communities, the habitation of much of the audience who listened to saints' lives, simply *because* of their size? Razi has shown in his study of the manor of Halesowen in Worcestershire that although such a manor contained a few hamlets and outlying farms, or nucleated villages, its populations, although peasantry, were nonetheless varied with respect to social status and wealth. Manorial tasks spanned a variety of occupations which possessed varying degrees of status, from the skilled artisan to the unskilled field hand; for certain duties, such as those of the reeve, literacy was undoubtedly of great assistance. Indeed, even the sons of the poorest villeins, if they were bright and had a chance to enter the church, might rise to very high office, as did Robert Grosseteste, bishop of Lincoln, the son of a villein.[71] Land tenure situations ranged from those who were bondmen to free tenants. Although economic well-being for most came principally from their land and its fertility, some peasants regularly received wages for work. Hilton has shown the degree of economic inequality that existed amongst the peasants.[72] Tenancy arrangements existed in which wealthy tenants were able to employ less prosperous tenants; and some "kulaks" such as Adam Jop and Adam Pistor of Redgrave Manor in Suffolk, who acquired considerable land during the 1260s through 1289, did so without incurring the wrath of the manorial lord.[73] Marriage status differences existed between peasants consecrated by the church and those who lived conjugally by mutual consent. By the fourteenth century, wealth rather than legal status determined social standing, and, as Robertson has suggested, such a situation could give rise to the otherwise anomalous condition in which "a bondman might have a higher status in the manorial community than many of his free neighbors."[74] Indeed, as Britton has argued, villages had hierarchies of families from the "best" to the "worst," all of whom were nonetheless peasants.[75] The manor of Writtle in Essex, for example, seems to have divided its tenantry on a "hierarchical" basis determined by the type

71. Homans, *The English Villagers*, p. 135.

72. R. Hilton, "Reasons for Inequality among Medieval Peasants," *Journal of Peasant Studies* 5 (1978): 271–84.

73. R. M. Smith, "Families and Their Land in an Area of Partible Inheritance: Redgrave, Suffolk 1260–1320," in Smith, *Land, Kinship and Life-Cycle*, pp. 165–71, 194.

74. D. W. Robertson, "Who Were the People?" in Heffernan, *The Popular Literature of Medieval England*, p. 5.

75. Britton, "The Peasant Family," p. 19.

of tenure held and the size of the land holdings.[76] In sum, although one must be careful not to use this variety to portray these communities as proto-mercantilist villages, the English peasantry which made up the majority of the audience for the lives of the saints constituted a complex spectrum of economic, social, and moral attitudes set in a matrix of an important but, in England, informal system of extended kinship ties.[77]

Given such variety of status-bearing social roles, to understand the lives of the saints as hoary *exempla,* pushing a monolithic type of orthodoxy which one might find in the conciliar decretals, both misrepresents the quality of these texts and assumes that the audience for whom it was intended was a homogeneous, malleable mass. The recent work of historians on the family undercuts that stereotype. Moreover, insisting on the saints' lives' exemplary status without qualification raises particularly troublesome questions. For example, what exemplary merit would a married audience find in a narrative whose central figure is a young woman who celebrated the virtue of celibacy over that of marriage, who arrogantly rejected her father, and who sought to destroy even the nurturing aspect of the mother? Would those single men and women in the audience have seen an Agnes, an Alexis, or a Katherine as models for their future, and, if so, why? Would an audience of agricultural workers and artisans take seriously a narrative which praises aristocratic female heroism and makes not a single reference to the dignity of labor, indeed by its very absence appears to dismiss the worth of labor? What would women, married or single or widowed, make of tales which subjected women who defended principle to an encyclopedia of violent sexual abuse, ending in death? A too obvious answer might be that, indeed, there is little in these tales which seeks to reinforce the dignity of the work done by these audiences, precisely because the narratives are the products of a clergy which sought, along with their responsibility for *cura animarum, to control* the moral, social, and political mores of their flocks. Although such an argument does provide a rationale for the success of this catechetical program, it operates on the presumption that the audience is a "simple peasantry," a homogeneous gathering of hard-working illiterates under the thumb of the local clergy. Moreover, such an argument has not seriously examined the evidence of the texts themselves.

76. K. C. Newton, *The Manor of Writtle: The Development of a Royal Manor in Essex, c. 1086–c. 1500* (Chichester, 1970), pp. 42–52; see Robertson "Who Were the People?" p. 8, for hierarchy.

77. Cressy, "Kinship and Kin Interaction," p. 68.

The saint's tale takes many of the apparent norms of medieval society—class stability, the role of women, the fear of sexuality, and authority, whether parental, clerical, or political—and turns them upside down. To view these vernacular texts chiefly as exempla intended to aid in a worldwide program of catechesis following the lead of the Fourth Lateran Council is far too limiting. The positive reception which greeted these vernacular narratives of the saints suggests some degree of sophistication on the part of its audience, an audience whose attitudes are not easily categorized despite the hegemony of orthodoxy, an audience in which men and women were aware of gender problems, and audience familiar with sexually explicit and deviant behavior, an audience who enjoyed stories which exploited class conflict, and an audience who believed that authority figures, whether clerical or political, often had feet of clay.

Such audiences, although intensely local, primarily peasant, agrarian, and illiterate, nonetheless appear to have had a fondness for the saint's life, when one considers the welter of cathechetical texts produced. The flood of exemplary narratives from this period—nearly three hundred authors of *artes praedicandi* have been identified, and many of these *artes* acknowledge the value of the saint's life in catechesis—as indicated above, was unparalleled. Voragine's *Legenda Aurea*, the hagiographic epitomes in Vincent of Beauvais's *Speculum Historiale*, the epitomized legends collected by Etienne of Bourbon, by Odo of Cheriton, Johannes Junior's *Scala Coeli*, the *Gesta Romanorum*, the *South English Legendary*, the *Northern Homily Cycle, Gilte Legende*, and hundreds of *distinctiones* suggest the existence of a veritable industry attempting to meet audience demand and further testify to an interest in narratives which entertain as well as instruct. But now we must turn to the actual texts themselves and to see whether we can learn the secret of their success.

Narrative Structures: The Archetypes

All successful narratives are built from creative structural models. Structures can be both universal and local, embodying the primary ideals of a particular era. This bipolarity is certainly true for the medieval saint's life. The English lives of the saints are structurally unambiguous and, I submit, consist of three distinct archetypes of behavior: renunciation, testing, and consummation. These archetypes are not arbitrarily imposed on the material but rather are the primal constituents of the Christian experience of conversion. Because this conversion story informs all sacred biography, these archetypes grow naturally out of the exigencies of that narrative type. The fundamental thesis of the conversion story is a universal one: the rejection of one belief system in order to accept a new one which selectively controls the choices made as the narrative unfolds. Although such a thesis is universal and hence appropriate for virtually any religious conversion, from Christianity to Zoroastrianism, it is particularized through the adoption of motifs with cultic significance—specific professions of faith, images of sacramentalism such as baptism and reception of the Eucharist, the *imitatio Christi*, and so on. These motifs are, in turn, generated by the logic of the archetypes they are developed in. For example, in the renunciation, one frequently sees initial professions of faith followed by a baptism, whereas in the testing and the consummation, the imitation of Christ's suffering is necessarily dominant. Such archetypes and their attendant motifs are genre-specific and inform these narratives from inception to end, from the *Passio* of Perpetua and Felicitas to Capgrave's life of St. Norbert. All conversion stories begin with the call for the renunciation of former allegiances, move to the testing of the faith in early stages of spiritual growth, and lastly signify the maturity of conversion with some signal emblematic sign, such as the *imitatio Christi* leading to martyrdom.

I discuss these archetypes and their motifs in more detail below, but I want now to comment briefly on the reasons for the lack of structural ambiguity in the saint's tale. The reason for this narrative clarity is twofold, based on exigencies of the audience and the binary nature of the plot. The audiences were primarily illiterate, and the context for most of these texts (at least from the first quarter of the thirteenth century through the first quarter of the fifteenth century) was an oral one. They were read to an assembly, and the demands of orality required texts that were lexically familiar, mnemonically engaging, possessed of clear theses, and comparatively brief. A survey of two important collections from the late thirteenth century finds all these qualities: both collections follow verse patterns indigenous to their respective dialect areas, eschew lexical difficulty, are easily remembered, and are short. The metrical *vitae* in the *South English Legendary* are of an average length of 292.9 lines; those in the *Northern Homily Cycle* average 300 lines.[78] Details, dialogue, and dominant figures, as Orlick has shown, were also severely restricted. Further, the dualist nature of the thesis,

---

78. These two collections are unequivocally intended for oral delivery and therefore seem to be indicative of an optimal length in such circumstances.

good versus evil, works effectively in an oral setting, advancing unambiguously the particular theological and moral ethic being promoted. In short, the oral and binary characteristics of these lives underline the dialectical exigencies of the conversion story. The binary nature of the narrative action is dictated by the conversion story. The Christian saint, in order to turn to Christ, must turn from the world; her conversion is away from something before it is toward something. Such conversion, such turning away, is for medieval Christian ideals of sanctity inescapably dialectical and conflictual. In particular, the attainment of Christian sanctity for medieval women required a struggle between women and men, between the chaste and the lewd, between Christ and Satan, between the righteous and the damned. Before Christian women could turn to Christ, they first had to turn away from those totemic figures in whom the society had invested power and charisma—father, lover/husband, state/emperor—those men to whom, as Franklin has noted, they were indebted for nurturing, for providing sexual pleasure, and for securing protection.[79] To conclude our analysis here, however, would treat these texts in an ahistorical manner and offer a reductionist caricature of a feminist critique. The conflict between the saint and her male antagonist, no matter how realistically portrayed, no matter how inescapably dualist and sexually abusive it appears to our sensibility, was nonetheless a complex allegory for the medieval mentality. It was an allegory which included (but was not limited to) understanding the narrative as an exemplification of Satan's temptation of Eve, the heroism of the Virgin Mary, the ability of woman to resist what medieval exegetes believed to be her special nemesis: her sexual appetite, and her capacity for independent judgment. These *vitae sanctarum* are elaborate tales whose meanings are far more complex than one which praised misanthropy or feminine heroics, as the following discussion of the three archetypes will show.

Renunciation

The anonymous life of St. Margarete (ca. 1220) acknowledges at the beginning that the maiden ("þis meiden þet we munieð wes Margarete ihaten; & hire flesliche feder Theodosie hehte, of þet heðene folc patriarche & prince"). Likewise, the *South English Legendary* text of the

---

79. P. Franklin, "Peasant Widows' 'Liberation' and Remarriage before the Black Death," *EHR* 39 (1986): 195.

life of St. Katherine (ca. 1280–90) opens with the following genealogy: "Seinte Katerine of noble kunne: cam, bi olde dawe;/Hire fader was king, hire Moder Quyene: boþe of þe olde law." Lastly, Osbern Bokenham writes that St. Agnes (ca. 1445) was of the "nobyllest blood eek of þat cuntre/Lyneally succeedyng she dede descende."

The depiction of the maiden as well bred, sometimes aristocratic, comely, forceful, intelligent, and eminently desirable is a *topos* specific to the archetype of renunciation, and it informs virtually all these vernacular lives. There is no single source—if source is required for such universally appealing qualities—from which these particular characteristics entered the genre. The influence of the Virgin Mary is, if present, indirect; both the Matthean (1:18–25) and Lucan (1:23–45) accounts of Mary only mention her virginity and suggest her youth. However, apocryphal legends of Mary which did celebrate her beauty, wisdom, and chastity must have existed; both the *Protoevangelium of James* and, to a greater degree, the *Psuedo-Matthew Gospel* (ca. eighth century) dwell on Mary's beauty, wisdom, and chastity. Another likely influence, themselves perhaps reflecting the influence of no longer extant early apocrypha of the Virgin Mary, are the depictions of female martyrs recorded in their Latin *acta*. Virtually all the qualities mentioned above appear in the depictions of such early female saints as Agathonice, Agnes, Perpetua, Catherine of Alexandria, and Cecilia.

A genteel background dramatizes the degree of commitment in the young woman's conversion; she literally gives up all to follow Christ. And in this respect, her behavior is exemplary. Indeed, if her life is to be an *imitatio Christi,* renunciation of her material possessions is a first public precondition for this undertaking. However, the dispersal of her goods, her desire for voluntary poverty, given the lay context for this tale, must have raised for the audience the issue of virtue as a birthright versus virtue as a result of merit. Such subject matter was bound to have complex resonances in a hierarchical society. St. Agnes, in rejecting her suitor's offer of "gold and seluer . . . broches and eke ringus," affirms the creation of the world from nothing, thereby acknowledging the primacy of poverty: "God made this world from nothing and gave us all we need/Al þene world he made of nouȝt: and ȝaf us ovre fode" (*SEL,* l. 29). Mary of Egypt, who lived as a prostitute for seventeen years, abandoned everything and went into the desert: "she took but two and a half loaves of bread with her/þe tweie loues and þe halue lof: þat heo with hire nam" (*SEL,* l. 104). Thus, the initial act of renunciation is a complex of ideas which invariably raises such issues as the origins and attainment of virtue.

Furthermore, the maid's renunciation, as mentioned above, is not effected without struggle. It can only be accomplished by a series of struggles with male antagonists. The situation described immediately before St. Katherine's debate with the fifty pagan philosophers makes use of a language of physical combat: "Shot forth some word," "strife," "foes," "contest," "sickle forth," "to fight," "under shield," and to "throw down/*adweschen*" her disputants (ll. 688–836). Thematically, the renunciation is followed immediately by the vanquishing of her male superiors. This, too, follows a sequence dictated by the maturation of her faith, and her triumph serves to move the narrative from domestic melodrama, to sexual empowerment, and to the foundation of a new political order. Typically, her first dispute is with her father; the next, being with someone who is also a suitor, is fraught with sexual overtones; and the last, when she is fully matured in her belief, is political, being with the representative of the state. In all three of these contests, the saints' lives exemplify the maid's intelligence (she defeats all comers in offering a rationale for hew newfound religion), her irresistible beauty (all of her interlocutors, including the parent, are physically attracted to her), and her insistence on principle (she is killed for her belief). The choice of chastity as the main prop of the religious conviction is social and moral rebellion.

Thus, the archetype of renunciation presents the modern reader with a complex icon of female heroism which embodies in its complex nucleus ideals of female integrity, autonomy, and intellectual skills which are not easily recognized in our traditional view of the models presented to medieval audiences. Let us consider one of the thematic points invariably raised by the lives.

Property and Virtue

Although many of the virgin saints are depicted as members of the upper classes, paradoxically an important function of this aristocratic heritage in Middle English sacred biography (and I would extend this to the Latin texts)[80] is to underscore that virtue is not class-dependent or inherited at birth, but the prerogative of every individual, serf or knight, free villein or bondmen, married woman, single, widow, or

---

80. Agathonice: "when the crowd saw how beautiful she was" (*pulchritudinem eius*, VI, 5). Perpetua: "a newly married woman, well educated and of good family" (*honesta nata, liberaliter instituta, matronaliter nupta*, II, 1). Katherine: "there lived a certain young maid of eighteen, attractive in appearance" (*erat quedam puella annorum duo de viginti. speciosa valde*).

mother superior. But in addition, these biographies raise, albeit indirectly, the inescapable issue of the value of such ancient familial heritage, wealth, and the varied trappings of social prominence. Although St. Katherine of Alexandria was orphaned by her wealthy parents at an early age, "she kept only a small part of her parents fortune giving all the rest to the needy and the naked (of hire ealdrene/& spende al þe oþer/in neodfule & in nakede, (ll. 101–3). Property, as an extension of a societal material good, inhabited a problematic area in orthodox medieval Christian spirituality. To consider this thesis in the context of a lay audience raises some difficult problems: for the entire class of the peasantry, land guaranteed not only status but survival. The argument that property is a potential evil cannot avoid opening, even if only implicitly, the question of the importance of wealth and class in a Christian state.

Along with the populist Franciscan insistence on the value of voluntary property, which called into question the inherent rightness of social status, this issue was finding a voice in another more learned context. Luscombe pointed out that throughout the scholastic period, debates which espoused such principles as "people sovereignty" and the "ascending" theory of government challenged "ruler-sovereignty" and "hierocratic theory" in both civil and ecclesiastical spheres. Thirteenth-century scholastic thinkers were keenly interested in Aristotle's thesis in the *Politics* (I, 1, 8, 12) that man is by nature a political animal but one whose status as a citizen is distinct from his status as subject (*subditus*).[81] They adduced this in support of the view that moral and civic virtue is not dependent on economic, civil, or legal status (virtually all of which were conditional on the size of one's landholdings), because the responsibilities of the citizen and the subject are divergent. Peasants as well as priests and rulers could achieve virtue; indeed, peasants because of their poverty, may have easier access to Christian truth.

The crucial point is that we can find such issues raised in vernacular texts expressly designed for catechizing the lower classes. For example, St. Katherine is described as keeping watch over her servants and maintaining them in her household "not because she believed in her heart it was good to have many under her, and be called lady, a title many speak well of, but because she feared sin and shame; if she released those whom her ancestors had raised, evil would befall them" (ll. 85–97). The phrase "þe feole telleþ wel to" is heavy with irony and

---

81. D. E. Luscombe, "The State of Nature and the Origin of the State," *Cambridge History of Later Medieval Philosophy*, pp. 757–68.

surely raised the question for these audiences of what is the value of lordship, class, property, and their relationship to Christian virtue. The answer given in the line immediately following is breathtakingly direct, to wit, they are impediments to virtue: "For herself she [Katherine] cared nothing for the world (For hire seolf ne kepte ha/nawt of þe worlde"). The judgment that virtue is not a birthright, although on one level a commonplace of the Christian ethic and discussed in scholastic *quaestiones* and by the mendicants, takes on additional weight by virtue of its present context, a vernacular tale of a female virgin intended for reading to a subordinate class. Although one must be cautious in attributing sentiments to congregations who left no records, it would naive to imagine that these audiences heard such tales which treated such topical problems, albeit shrouded by the veil of the historical past, and did not see the present application of such sentiments. For indeed, if they did not make such judgments, the tales cease to have any exemplary value at all.

I am not proposing that these vernacular saints' lives systematically argued the philosophical merits of this populist view of the potential for all men to attain virtue. This would be to caricature the lives of the saints. But it is nonetheless the case that these texts present behavior which dramatically illustrates such issues. For example, the young maiden's rejection of her wealthy family frees her to embrace Christianity. The Christians often appear in these tales as the lower classes. Although not lauded for their poverty, they are presented as the chosen, the anointed people of God. Their poverty is not an emblem of their shame but a sign of their worth. Hence the normative relation between the different classes in the *vitae sanctarum* is set awry: the rich are rejected and the poor exalted. Although it was not the intention of these sacred biographies, or that of those who read them, to preach class antagonism, or to proclaim the natural goodness of the common man (*une espece de bon sauvage*) at the expense of his wealthier neighbor, it is difficult to deny their abiding interest in furthering an ethic that was populist, more sympathetic to the lower classes than to the upper. Read in this light, such sacred tales become the poor man's equivalent of the chivalric tales of the *chanson de geste* and the romance enjoyed by a more privileged class. They confront issues pertinent to his group, promote fantasies she can identify with, and raise expectations they can dream about. If this is true, literary historians must view these tales as at least potentially promoting something more than a rigidly understood category of imitation more or less based on the precepts of orthodoxy.

The obvious question is whether the institutional church would have sanctioned such a message, even if this commentary was more subtext than explicit narrative. I believe the church did countenance such narrative depictions for two reasons: first, because they made possible an even more comprehensive encratic statement and, second, because the accounts were generalized and part of a centuries-old tradition. For example, the maiden's rejection of her family was a *de facto* rejection of their wealth, their position in the society, the state itself; indeed, it was also a rejection of the values which these represented. In short, her behavior was a repudiation of the corrupting influence of the world and, as such, represented a timely redaction, in English, of the *contemptus mundi* theme, the basis of Innocent III's ecclesial reform, a program nurtured by the reformist spirit of the English episcopacy from Bishop Poore through Archbishop Courtenay. The single fortress of truth which remained for those who, like Katherine, sought virtue in a postlapsarian world was the ecclesial embrace of Mother Church, an embrace open to all but more generously proffered to the poor. Once these accounts were rendered from Latin into the vernacular, they were no longer the exclusive provenance of the church but joint properties with the people and, as such, open to valid interpretations from both groups. The vernacular provided more latitude for initiative, even if such initiative could be the ground for class conflict. For example, manorial court records from the thirteenth century show that when medieval English peasants discussed land inheritance, they did not use the simple Latin formulae of the lawyers but invariably found English equivalents, thereby attempting to assert their claims outside the systems employed by the lawyers.[82]

The Test

Let us begin our discussion of the most complex of the three archetypes with three quotations from texts more than two centuries apart. The anonymous life of St. Margaret (ca. 1225) remarks that her tormentors "stripped her naked and hung her up high by virtue of sharp hooks, and burned her flesh with flaming tapers." In the *South English Legendary* (ca. 1275–90) life of St. Agnes, the duke says to Agnes, "'If you do not leave off your folly, before nightfall you shall suffer great

82. Homans, *The English Villagers*, p. 121.

pain'; he ordered them then to fasten sharp hooks to her breasts, and ordered her torturers to cut off her breasts." In Osbern Bokenham's life of St. Lucy (ca. 1445), Judge Pascass orders the young Lucy, for her intransigence, to be imprisoned in a house of prostitution. Whereas in the first archetype—the renunciation—the action was restricted to dialectic, to oral debate on the efficacy of competing theocracies, in the second archetype we find the action dictated by the saint's sexual choice. The second archetype—the test—moves the concern from argument to action. Broken, naked bodies are the concern of these narratives. Here, in the guise of suitor, magistrate, governor, or emperor, the saint's male antagonist combines his interest in forcing her to recant her Christianity with his desire to possess her sexually. The action turns on both her ability to defend her religious principle and her chastity at once. The subject is enmeshed in an erotic matrix. It is precisely because she is comely, because she remains *virgo intacta,* that she is attractive and will be forced to suffer and die. Sexual dominance is the game and intercourse the forbidden prize.

Whereas the archetype of renunciation provided an occasion for the display of intellectual debate and raised questions of public social importance, the test examines the strength of individual conviction under duress. The tortures undergone by the saints generate images and questions that are private, figments of the imagination, and inescapably erotic. The issue is no longer a debate concerning public virtue but individual value—Margaret's, Agnes's, or Lucy's virtue. Before we examine this erotic element in more detail, let us turn to the final archetype, the denouement of this tale of chastity besieged—the consummation.

Consummation

This final archetype presents the moment of the virgin's death and her prophesied union with her savior, Christ. It ends with an invocation of the now sainted virgin's memory and a request for her to succor all who call on her. The consummation is the shortest sequence of actions in these lives. Its brevity serves both a thematic and a structural purpose. A rapid denouement serves as a catalyst to focus all the elements of the narrative together in one moment of grand drama, the blood sacrifice of the young woman and her consequent achievement of salvation. After considerable suffering and torment, Osbern Bokenham presented the death of St. Agnes succinctly:

Comaundyd a swerd both bryht & clere
Into hyr throte depe for to be sent,
And þus þis holy mayde, þis innocent,
Cruelly martyrd for crystys sake.
To hym as hys spouse he dede take.

All the lives of the female virgin saints of the early church (e.g.,
Agatha, Agnes, Cecilia, Christina, Juliana, Feyth, Margaret, etc.)
which were rendered into Middle English possess these archetypes and
their constituent motifs. Can we provide a coherent explanation that
will account for the predominantly lay audience's apparent interest in
such action, focused on a main character barely out of girlhood? The
image of the prepubescent girl undertaking independent actions normally reserved for mature males cannot have been held in high regard
in the thousands of villages throughout medieval England. If there was
any member of the household who was dispensable, whose contribution to the success of the household was problematic, it was the unmarried daughter. The pertinent historical records, manorial court records, provide virtually no evidence of young females acting
independently. Females of this age were completely under their fathers' tutelage until marriage, as the following characterization in the
customs of Cirencester, Gloucestershire (ca. 1209), makes perfectly
clear: "while they are under the rod and power of their father."[83]

Virtually all the documentary sources from the thirteenth and fourteenth centuries agree that first marriages for peasant women were generally between the ages of eighteen and twenty-two and that the daughters of wealthier peasants, those endowed with richer dowries, married
younger.[84] Thus, the prospect for land inheritance and dowry determined the appropriate marriageable age; girls younger than fourteen
were viewed, especially among the poorer families, as potential future
liabilities on the family. Surely this ethos of young females as property
played a role in the depiction of the young virgin saint as rebellious, as
one who rejects family and patrimony, as the locus of sexual abuse.
This point can be pushed too far, but if the pubescent child is "property," it would be emotionally less problematic for a male parent to
project sublimated sexual fantasies onto the image of the naked, beaten
maid. The sinful violation of the daughter is vitiated by her status as
property, as object, and her uncommon rebellion.[85]

83. Ibid., p. 210.

84. Razi, *Life, Marriage and Death*, p. 65.

85. E. Searle, "Seigneurial Control of Women's Marriage: The Antecedents and
Function of Merchet in England," *Past and Present* 82 (1979): 3–43.

Turning again to the saints' lives, we note that none of those sacred biographies which were repeatedly translated and copied in Middle English presents us with an older heroine. The heroines are on the verge of mature female sexuality. These lives hold up for praise an image of femininity, the child-woman, whose legal status was little more than chattel in these households. Surely the sexual ambiguity of the central character, neither child nor woman, is an important aspect in the narrative's popularity, especially since her heroism is such an anomaly within the normal range of expectations for communities which were agrarian, containing the married and their children and single men and women, all of whom were involved to some extent in subsistence demesne farming.[86]

To see these lives as mimetic *exempla* designed by the church for implementation of the program of moral uplift planned by the Fourth Lateran Council, though this aspect was undoubtedly present, is surely to isolate a small part of their message. The encratic moral implicit in the abusive sections of the vernacular lives of the virgin martyrs contributes to a complex vision: conflict, eroticism, a new social order, and salvation are bound tightly in a spirituality which seeks transcendence through deliberate abandonment of the material. Ironically, the success of this synthesis depended on a minute exploration of the very thing it found so reprehensible: the physicality of human sexuality.

The Virgin and the Erotic

Since the aim of sacred biography is a celebration of the process through which Christian sanctity is achieved, the *vitae sanctarum*'s depiction in scene after scene of a beautiful young woman—often an adolescent on the verge of puberty—embattled, partly clad, suffering a variety of punishments at the hands of her male captors, although within the convention, is nonetheless so dense with the gospel of sexual encraticism that it is at first glance difficult to see what a medieval audience would have understood as being celebrated.

The discussion which follows concentrates on those scenes which depict a holy woman's sexuality under attack, for two reasons: first, although part of the convention, the explicit and extended preoccupation with sexual matters is an anomaly in medieval literature, and, second, this very preoccupation, this *idée fixe*, is likely to assist us in understanding the *mentalité* for such texts.

86. J. L. Bolton, *The Medieval English Economy* (London, 1980), pp. 97, 104.

It goes beyond the limits of the evidence to assert that a segment of the audience took conscious pleasure in these scenes—which within the frame of church law would be considered sexually deviant and hence sinful. The fact, however, that such scenes explore at length topics otherwise forbidden and unavailable to the laity (even in the love poetry of the *amour courtois* and *minnemystik* or the *fabliaux*) suggests that the *vitae sanctarum* provided a forum, controlled by the clergy and the liturgy, for the officially sanctioned presentation of erotic behavior in order to promote an ideal of a new social order.

The "gospel of asceticism" proselytized in the *vitae sanctarum* has both individual and communitarian dimensions. An ethic based on encraticism is functionally different when viewed from the solitary and the collective stance. To preach asceticism to an individual through an appeal to the model lives of the saints represents an attempt at reforming individual judgment and behavior; it seeks to change private morality through an exclusively *ad hominem* appeal. Viewed collectively, however, the appeal for social reform implied by the themes in sacred biography seeks to promote a utopian social system founded not on blood kinship but on Christian ideals of fraternity. This hope to create an eschatological brethren of the spirit, a sexless *civitas Dei,* has an unavoidable political dimension, albeit one sanitized by literary convention and association with non-threatening female adolescents. The positive disregard for familial symbols of authority, blood kinship, and human sexuality in the *vitae sanctarum* underscores this thesis, as I will illustrate below.

Although one must be careful about the use of modern labels to describe medieval categories of experience, there is an inescapable element of "sadism" in the Middle English lives of the holy virgins. This label does no more than convey the texts' preoccupation with the depiction of physical abuse and the debasement of female sexuality. Sadism as a category in the *vitae sanctarum* has received little analysis, and yet it contributes significantly to the success of this genre and was part of Latin medieval sacred biography's inheritance from Greek romance. In the popular *Vita Sancti Eustachii,* one of the prominently narrated events is the attempted rape of Eustace's wife by a sea captain, an incident which derives from romance. But if the erotic is a plausible element in the romance, its presence seems less so in the lives of the medieval Christian saints. Nevertheless, the erotic element in these lives was neither bowdlerized nor understated, but on the contrary was highlighted. The reason eroticism is so prominent must concern any analysis of these texts.

The Conventionality of Sexual Abuse

Let us begin with the convention, since such depictions are the product of an ancient inheritance and can be found in the earliest *acta*. The conventionality of these depictions is a historical sign to modern readers that these depictions are not to be treated simply as a *speculum mundi* for a given period.[87] It is not only their remoteness in time which causes their otherness, but the human experiences they describe and the response of past audiences to these texts. The convention of sacred biography presents paradigms, not depictions of individuals. Furthermore, the correspondence between the paradigm and the individual is difficult to measure given the paucity of the historical documents. With this caveat before us, we can turn to the texts.

The sexual abuse in these lives occurs mainly in the archetype of the test. Suffering is presented as a prerequisite for the prize of salvation: a wealthy young maiden, a Perpetua, Agnes, Agatha, Cecilia, or Christina, who has renounced her privilege, must traverse a gauntlet of physical suffering—a cultic *rite de passage*—before achieving her goal of *sponsa Dei*. Once the maid has become the bride, the next transformation is into *mater Dei*. The transformation from virgin to bride to mother is thematically complex and theologically essential, and it informs all these texts. These three transformations present us with three distinctive textual images of medieval womanhood: the allure of the sexually attractive but unapproachable nymph/goddess, her emergence into full sexual maturity as the *sponsa,* and the icon of the fecund, reproductive mother. The three images represent the breadth of medieval female experience, from child to mother, from adolescent desire to sexual possession, from tutelage to tutor.

The Prize of Enormous Cost

Two traditional themes effect these transformations and are inextricably entwined: salvation and suffering. Such punishment and suffering

---

87. Although social science can make major contributions to our understanding of the past, there is always the danger that in one's application one loses respect for the otherness of the medieval experience. For example, two recent studies have allowed their preoccupation with theory to obscure the manifold complexity of the historical experience and have misrepresented medieval female ideas of sanctity and the holy by turning them into a modern pathology. See D. Bell, *Holy Anorexia* (Chicago, 1985), and M. P. Carroll, *The Cult of the Virgin Mary* (Princeton, 1986).

are explicitly directed at female sexuality. The attainment of the chaste
bridal veil is accomplished only if the maid continually places her virginity at risk. Her sanctity is not achieved by virtue of her virginity,
but at the risk of it; it is only a beleaguered virginity that is able to gain
the crown. The irony of the heroine's situation is that to gain sanctity
through the maintenance of prized chastity, she must continually flaunt
her virginity as a prize for her antagonists in her struggle toward saintly
perfection. St. Juliana tells her tormentors that the more they abuse
her, the greater will be her reward ("for eauer se ȝe nu her mearreeþ
me mare: se mi crune schal beon brihttre ba & fehere"). Looked at
from a theological perspective, the maiden's actions illustrate a pop-
ularized Augustinianism; that is, they reflect in dramatized narrative a
theology of grace which proposed that merit was only attainable in
virtue which was tested. Moreover, since grace alone was unable to
provide salvation, the exercise of the will against the vicissitudes of
nature was necessary to withstand the depravity resultant from original
sin.

The attainment of sanctity depended on testing the maid's vow of
celibacy, so the audience's attention was continually directed away
from the fact of her continence toward those scenes which put her virginity in jeopardy. Juliana's father in a savage voice ordered her
stripped stark naked (*strupen hire steortnaket*) before her male captors.
Because it emphasized the young woman embattled, the narrative
highlights the allure of her sexuality and as a result throws into contrast
her vow of chastity. The audience knows from the outset that the saint
is *virgo intacta,* and thus the drama of the narrative depends on those
scenes which place her vow in jeopardy. The judge Pascass in Bokenham's "Lyf of seynt Lucye" orders her to be sent to a bordello: "For
to þe bordelhous þou led shat be." The narrative must illustrate the
extent of the testing she can endure before she is forced to give up her
prized chastity or her life.

Sexual Abuse and the Symbol of Femininity

There are innumerable Middle English lives of virgin saints in which
the litany of abuse which the maid undergoes is encyclopedic and
chiefly directed at her sexuality. I want to discuss two examples of such
behavior, the disrobing of the maiden and the physical abuse of her
breasts. Both are part of the convention, and, as such, they are central
to "eroticizing" the narrative.

Before the heroine is tortured, she is forcibly disrobed by her antagonists. It might be objected that disrobing is logically prior to scourging, but these scenes are invariably described in language with erotic overtones. Scenes of disrobing occur in most of the biographies of female virgins and serve to introduce the archetype of the test and the onset of the physical tortures. The earliest example I have found of disrobing associated with the beauty of the saint's nakedness is in the Latin recension of the martyrdom of Agathonice (ca. 175?): "And when she was led to the spot, she removed her clothing and surrendered [*tradidit*] to the servants. But when the crowd saw how beautiful [*pulchritudinem*] she was, they grieved in mourning for her."[88] Two important elements are linked even at this early stage in the genre: subordination (*tradidit*) and physical attraction (*pulchritudinem*).

The typological paradigm for such scenes is Christ before his crucifixion, but the stripping of the female's garments has clear erotic overtones lacking in Christ's disrobing. Indeed, none of the Gospels actually mentions the disrobing of Christ; they simply comment that his garments were divided among his tormentors. The earliest mention of the stripping of Christ's garments that I am aware of is in the *Acta Pilati*.[89] The absence of this motif in the Gospels and its occurrence in the apocrypha is a complicated matter, but the one thing it unambiguously underlines is the increased interest in the centuries following the formation of the canon—a period coincident with the beginning of the genre of sacred biography—in embroidering the official account with details more appropriate to romance than to Scripture.

The disrobing allows the text to draw attention to the beauty of the maiden's nakedness. It is a ubiquitous motif and can be observed in the *vitae* of Juliana, Margaret, Agnes, Katherine, and others. The next element to be factored in to the equation of subordination and comeliness is physical abuse. In the life of St. Katherine, for example, she was stripped naked and her fair body (*hire freoliche bodi*) beaten so that her lovely body might be lathered in blood (*swa me dude sone, þat hire leofliche lich/ liþerde al o blode*). I am unable to account for the appearance of this element on purely historical grounds.

The naked body can be the object of sexual arousal as well as physical abuse, and various attempts at shielding the maid are employed. Of course, such attempts actually focus the audience's attention on the desired but forbidden object. Osbern Bokenham described a miracle

---

88. Musurillo, *Acts of Christian Martyrs*, p. 35. This scene is missing in the Greek recension.

89. *Acta Pilati*, James, p. 102.

wherein St. Agnes's hair grew long and luxuriant so as to hide her naked body on her imprisonment in the bordello: "And alle hir nakydnesse fully dede hyde." The tortures of St. Christina begin with her disrobing. In a scene similar to the disrobing of St. Juliana, Christina's clothing is removed by her father: "He [her father] let hure naked strupe anon & tormentors inowe with harde scorgen legge hure on. and al hure bodi todrowe." The attention of the congregation would surely have been arrested by this image of the suddenly naked Christina, the most beautiful of all virgins ("sche had grete bodyly beute"). Although her nudity ought to suggest her vulnerable maidenly innocence, and hence parallels the figure of Christ stripped in preparation for his death on the cross, in this instance her nakedness does not present an icon of maidenly innocence, of human vulnerability, but rather serves to arouse the passions, to whet the bloody appetite of her aggressors who "with harde scorgen legge hure on."

The denouement of the Gospel story is not the disrobing of Christ or the Crucifixion, but the Resurrection; the disrobing of Jesus before his death is a lesser element in a much greater plan. In Christina's case, however, her heroism is rooted in her desire to control her sexuality, for she claims the role of virgin. Thus, the disrobing presents at least the opportunity to challenge the strength of her vow, the prop around which she seeks to achieve sanctity. When she is disrobed before her antagonists, her father chief among them, the naked maiden is a complex image: her comeliness and her refusal to give herself are locked in a kind of contradictory embrace. From the point of view of the antagonist, such beauty should submit to the dictates of nature and should be used for sexual gratification. For Christina, however, such extraordinary beauty makes her decision to abandon willfully the sexual ways of the world all the more imperative; indeed, such beauty makes the struggle more worthwhile, promising to be all the more difficult to maintain such a vow.

Christina's refusal to share herself is a defiant challenge to traditional male dominance; her refusal to enter into marriage is a striking rejection of the New Testament's teaching that men and women were bound to pay the marriage *debitum,* that is, a legitimate request for intercourse.[90] Although the image of the nude Christina seems to project an

90. The image of the parent forcing the daughter is a complex one and presents two historical moments. During the historical period which this sacred biography claims as its origin (period of the early church persecutions), the practices of the church concerning marriage more or less accepted local and family customs and followed the dominant practice of the region. Thus, Christina's father was well within his historical

aura of passive innocence, her nakedness presents nonetheless a re-statement in the subtext of the age-old struggle for sexual dominance between men and women, as Chaucer's Wife of Bath so aptly put it: "Wommen desiren to have sovereynetee/As well over hir housbond as hir love." The saint's nakedness is thus a challenge, a girdle draped across the field of battle.

Because Christina's *virginitas intacta* is the point around which the rest of the themes play, the narrative seeks to hold the interest of the listener through action which continually threatens to violate Christina's chastity. Thus, it is not the denouement of her death, her final achievement of sanctity, which the audience expected, but rather the many smaller narrative frames which illustrate episodically her battle to remain a virgin. The congregation was presented with a sacred tale which used a depiction of a plethora of physical abuse in a sexually deviant but undeniably erotic manner to illustrate this young woman's triumph over Satan, herself, and, finally, men.

Sexuality, Suffering, Shame and Salvation

The lives of the female virgins rely so exclusively on the importance of sexual innuendo and struggle for the achievement of sanctity that they, more than any other type of sacred biography, represent a hybridization of the saint's life and the romance. This concern is present throughout the tradition from the romantic tryst hinted at in the *Acts of Paul and Thecla* through Bokenham's *Legendys of Hooly Wummen*. The dominant image of the female invariably turned sacred biography into something akin to a sexual melodrama, replete with anguish and

---

local rights to force his daughter to marry whomever he chose. However, by the middle of the twelfth century, with the publication of Gratian's *Decretum* and Lombard's *Libri IV Sententiarum*, a major change had entered the church's understanding of marriage, and that was the idea that the marital bond was created by consent. Note Gratian's rubric to a canon from the decretal of Urban II (1088–99): "A father's oath cannot compel a girl to marry one to whom she has never assented." Such commentary led to the publication of the marriage banns in England early in the thirteenth century and to their support by the Fourth Lateran Council. Thus, a late-thirteenth-century audience viewing Christina's father's actions would have found them, according to canon and civil law, indefensible, albeit possibly still practiced. (Thomas Chobham's need in his *Summa Confessorum* to defend a villein's right to free consent suggests that it was honored more in theory than in practice.) See M. M. Sheehan, "Choice of Marriage Partner in the Middle Ages: Development and Mode of Application of a Theory of Marriage," *Studies in Medieval and Renaissance History* 1 (1978): 3–33.

physical cruelty depicted in an unabashedly erotic manner. The eroticism grows out of the torment the maid is forced to endure and hence
is inseparable from the debasement of her sexuality. Female sexuality
is never treated as a positive attribute; rather, it is reified, and presented as a liability, a potentiality for sin or a disabling illness. Such a
message could do little more than countenance the abandonment, the
renunciation of this "occasion of sin."

The vernacular texts of sainted female virgins are profoundly gnostic
in their implication that human sexuality is a stigma hindering one from
a fuller participation in that perfection which is an experience of the
divine. If the label *gnostic* appears to carry too much weight for these
vernacular texts to support, it is well to note that such sentiments were
common in the didactic treatises of the time, as in the following remark
from the popular *Speculum Sancti Edmundi:*

> To the knaweyng of thi selfe thou may come on this manere. Thynke
> besely and ofte what thou erte, what thou was, and what thou sall be.
> ffyrst als vn-to thi body. thou erte nowe vylere thane any mukke. thou
> was getyne of sa vile matire and sa gret fylthe that it es schame for to
> nevunne and abhomynacyone for to thynke.

These sentiments suggest quite unambiguously the crude polarity between spirit and flesh that is the later medieval inheritance of the gnostic tradition, a polarity equally apparent in the *vitae sanctarum.*

But let us probe a bit deeper. If the body is the locus of such
"muck," why did it take center stage in these sacred biographies? At
the very foundation of such strident dualism, whether it has its roots
in Christian gnosticism or in the evangelical asceticism of the mendicants, is the emotional conflict between pleasure derived from the body
and the fear of the consequences of that pleasure, whether that fear
has a theological or moral basis. If the congregation did receive some
degree of titillation from the depiction of the sufferings of Christina or
one of the other lives of the female virgins then this pleasure could only
have been derived from a narrative which maltreated the desired but
forbidden object, the naked maiden. Such an outlet for sexual fantasy
could only obtain a public hearing by denigrating the young woman's
sexuality and in so doing could instill a religiosity of shame concerning
human sexuality in the congregation.

Severed Breasts and Chaste Mothers

Lest it seem that I linger on this issue of sexuality in the lives of the
female virgin saints, I want to reiterate the degree to which female

sexuality is jeopardized in these lives and to point out that much of the actual narrative in the archetype of the test is concerned with depicting such physical molestation. In the overwhelming majority of scenes of physical abuse in the lives of virgin saints, the focus of torture is the symbol of woman's maternity and sexuality, the breasts. The maiden's breasts are not only mutilated, but, in a number of instances, completely severed from her body. The earliest English life of St. Agnes in the *South English Legendary* is a case in point:

> "Nelþou [nou]ȝt," seide þe duyk: "þine folie ȝuyt bi-leue,
> In strong pine þov schalt beo-i-done: to-day are it beo eue."
> hokes and witthene he let nime: and faste to hire breoste binde,
> And let is tormentores with þe withþene: hire breostene of wynde.

Physical mutilation is a leitmotif of dozens of the lives of the virgin saints, and indeed mutilation of the maiden's breasts is depicted in the lives of those most popular vernacular saints, Agatha, Christina, Dorothy, and Katherine, and in such early *acta* as the depiction of Blandina in the martyrs of Lyon. These Christian heroines are depicted stoically enduring this cruelty to their person; their breasts are flailed, cut, pierced, battered, burned, beset by serpents, and in some instances severed entirely.

Why do we find such a preoccupation with the mutilation of the breasts of young women, who, just emerging from puberty, have taken a vow of perpetual virginity? Leaving aside for the moment the erotic element and the appeal in the subtext to the desires of sublimated male sexual aggression, a partial explanation of this phenomenon lies in one of the important themes of the lives of the female virgins, the *topos* of transformation: the movement from virgin to bride to mother. Surely this transformation produces one of literature's most complex icons: the virgin becomes the bride of the God, and finally the mother of the God, while retaining her virginity. Her breasts as the symbol of her maternity are mutilated and finally severed, to underscore the miraculous metamorphosis of the virgin into a nurturing mother, virtually a deity in her own right. The physical mutilation is also the sign of her election, as the stigmata are the authenticating sign of Christ's crucifixion (John 20:24–29).

The Miraculous Power of Transformed Flesh

Let us examine an example, again from the popular life of St. Christina, of this ideal of transformation and its consequences. Osbern Bokenham narrates a scene in which poisonous snakes are tossed on Christina's head and shoulders in the hope that their venomous bites will kill her:

> And wyth that woord, to doon hir wrake,
> Vp-on hir heed the serpentys to
> He dyd do cast and eythyr snake,
> Wenyng that thei hir harm shuld do.
>
> (ll. 2947–50)

The scene opens with an opposition, juxtaposing the unblemished warmth of the maiden and the cold flesh of the serpents.[91] This portrayal of Christina is dense with intentional (and, for a medieval audience, recognizable) typologies. The image is a complex composite of three women: Eve, the Blessed Virgin, and the woman in Revelation (12:1–17). All three scriptural analogues share some common characteristics: tempted by serpents, suffered anguish, and gave birth to important male children who in turn were perceived as a type of sacrificial victim; and at least two of the three, Mary and the woman in Revelation, were virgins before and immediately after the birth of their children. Eve and the woman in Revelation are preyed on by serpents, whereas the Virgin was the fulfillment of the prophecy (Genesis 3:15), the bearer of the fruit which would crush Satan, and the paradigm for medieval female virginity. Part of the complex religious teaching intended by this image of Christina and the serpents was the transforming power of Christian revelation to overcome evil, the primacy of the new revelation as it nullified the Old Testament curse of eternal enmity between female and serpent uttered by God in Genesis 3:15: "I will place enmity between you and the woman, between your seed and hers." The lesson being urged on the congregation underlines the possibility of the impossible, the reconciliation of the irreconcilable, the transparent truth of paradox, the prospect of attaining a faith able to move mountains, and the recognition of the miraculous latent in creation awaiting actualization through Christian belief.

In Christina's person, particularly that symbol of her nurturing ma-

91. Some may find in this scene a wealth of subliminal phallic associations, but such conclusions would be utterly unrecognizable in a medieval context, are imposed on the text, do not emerge from the intentionality of the text, and do not provide us—no matter how illuminating—with the necessary tools for further examination. Further, such psychological interpretations run the great risk of not respecting the otherness of these long-dead men and women. Finally, such an examination is likely to reveal more about our reading habits than about the *mentalité* of the thirteenth century, an important task, but not that of the present author.

ternity, her breasts, contraries were reconciled. The depiction of the saint allowed for the representation of the most obdurate of oppositions. Christina—like that exemplar of medieval maternity, the Virgin Mary, and unlike the exemplar of postlapsarian womanhood, Eve—transforms the serpents from demonic succubi into "smal infaunts." The cold, venomous serpents become like warm, adoring infants. Bokenham here seems to be following the similar depiction in the *Legenda Aurea* quite closely:

> But als soon as þe serpentys comyn hir to,
> Thei claspyd hir helys ant þe dust dyde lykke
> þer-fro, & heng up-on hir pappys also
> Lyk small infaunts wych kun no wykke.
>   (ll. 2951–54)

The serpents were transformed, made like children, from their suckling of her virginal breasts. The *South English Legendary* version makes this transformation of the serpents so complete that it has given them human characteristics. To show their gratitude for her fondling, they embrace the saintly maiden and kiss her: "Hi custe hure."

This metamorphosis of the deadly serpents through the presence of the saint appears to share sympathetically in the transformation of the saint; that is, the serpents are transformed by the self-same faith which is changing her. But several questions beg hearing: why has the narrative introduced the idea of maternity in so central a position in the life of a virgin saint? Does this mixing of types of female models, the maiden and the mother, not detract from the central theme celebrated in the narrative, the triumph of asceticism (in this case chastity) in an avaricious world, a world wherein greed is another face of *luxuria?* Does such contamination not detract from the positive face the clergy is trying to put on encraticism even for those who are married? An answer to this question begins with the conventions of the genre and the theological point being made. The application of the principle of binary opposition is conventional in the narratives of female sanctity, and indeed is as old as the *Passio* of Perpetua and Felicitas. In this instance, the convention works by juxtaposing apparent opposites, virgin and mother, and the clash of opposites proposes that there is a profound identity which, although not apparent, does unite them. To wit, both Christian virgins and mothers beget children, albeit the one spiritual and the other biological. Further, the theological message is that the transformation of human nature was achieved through the incarnation which was effected by a virgin. Such "play" between the paradoxical relatedness in the opposition of virgin and mother, in the ability of barren women to conceive, was a deep and abiding aspect of medieval Christianity's spiritual legacy and exemplified in both the Old and New Testaments in the figures of such "saintly" women as Sarah, Samson's mother, Ruth, Hannah, Elizabeth, and Mary.

Mother and Mediatrix

Medieval saints, aside from any local cultic characteristics that surrounded their worship, were understood by the hierarchical church as crucial mediators in the plan of Christian soteriology. The faith of the saints, demonstrated in the teeth of adversity, was the sure sign of God's presence and favor, a favor that could render the miraculous commonplace. Moreover, this earthly promise of God's redemptive favor, exhibited in such manifold ways in the saints, was extended to all the faithful who prayed to the saints. The saints were an exemplification of that salvation and the achievement of Christian heroism, open to all, the great and the small, the rich and the poor, women and men. Read in this light, the complex image of woman, available to the congregation in the story of Christina, may have offered to medieval women a model of female celibacy as deeply fulfilling as that of marriage and maternity. For those in the convent or contemplating a monastic vocation, it legitimized a type of spiritual betrothal and maternity. For the unmarried woman in the village, whether a widow or not yet of marriageable age, it may have provided a model conferring some degree of status on females who remained single. Although direct address is not common in these texts, the life of Seinte Marherete admonishes widows, married women, and maidens to listen carefully to Margaret's story:

> Hernecð, alle þe earen & herunge habbeð: widewen wið þa iweddede, & te meidnes nomeliche, lusten swiðe ȝeorliche hu ha schulen luuien þe liuiende lauerd & libben i meiðhad, þet him his mihte leouest. (4:7–11).

From a socioeconomic point of view, it is worth noting the interest in encratic female behavior, exemplified in the lives of the saints, coincides with an inexorable decline in the amount of arable land available, along side a considerable increase in population throughout the thirteenth century, at least through the beginning of the great famine of 1315.[92] This situation presented a real diminution in the prospects for

92. Razi, *Life, Marriage and Death*, p. 81. See also A. R. H. Baker, "Some Fields and Farms in Medieval Kent," *Archaeologia Cantiana* 80 (1965): 156–57. Baker pro-

the formation of viable new peasant families throughout the thirteenth century and for a considerable part of the fourteenth.[93] This is borne out in records that indicate an increase in the average marriageable age for young men and women and the frequency with which recently widowed women were sought in marriage.[94] An ideology that provided a sanction for celibacy in times of economic depression and famine (1315–18) would no doubt have found a ready, sympathetic, and commonsensical response in parents who faced the prospect of being unable to provide dowries for their daughters and land for their sons.

Lastly, because Christina is transformed into a nursing mother at the end of the tale, married women with children would have seen their importance in the scheme of Christian soteriology publicly acknowledged.

Although Christina gave up her chance to bring children into the world, in the final hours before her death she is depicted as giving birth to a spiritual truth so potent that it can transform the minions of Satan. Moreover, like the Virgin Mary, she conceives and bears this fruit without the taint of intercourse, without perpetuating the curse of original sin. Thus, the figure of Christina, although virginal and, as such, indebted to a long tradition of Christian ambivalence toward sexuality, does not disparage the role of most medieval women, that of wife and mother. And indeed, her image projects a powerfully complex yet consolidating thesis for medieval women, and one which affirms the value of the opposing traditions of celibacy and the conjugal life.

Bearing in mind the importance of coupling these apparently opposite roles of mother and virgin, we are better able to interpret the final scene of humiliation immediately before Christina's martyrdom. The *South English Legendary* account reads:

He let hure swete tendre bresten. kerue of bothe to
Awei the seli tendre limes. lite hadde hi misdo
Wiȝt milk com out of the wonden. & neuere a drope blod
Ou Iesus that the holy maide. clene was and god
This maide stod and bihuld. with wel glad mode
The milk stremes that orne adoun. as for defaute of blode.

(ll. 321–26)

---

93. Britton, "The Peasant Family," p. 143.

94. Razi, *Life, Marriage and Death*, p. 63.

The miracle of the flow of milk from the wounds inflicted on a virgin's breasts is not a common motif and is unexpected in this particular context. Once again, however, it has its roots in the exigencies of the narrative's structure, that is, in the principle of binary opposition and in the theology that provides the catechetical basis for the narrative. The system of binary oppositions creates an expectation of dislocation of experience, as the most likely expression of what we might call an excess of meaning. We have been prepared for this final miraculous event by the earlier episode of Christina's suckling and pacifying the poisonous serpents. Christina, the pagan child-woman and the Christian virgin, at this point in the narrative has been utterly transformed into the *sponsa Christi/mater Dei*. With her potential for maternity now demonstrated beyond a shadow of a doubt, she is the mediatrix between her earthly children, who call on her, and her divine husband/child. She is both triumphant virgin and spiritual mother, uniting these opposing themes in a vacillating, indeterminate middle ground. The miracle of the maternal milk is the emblem that signals the union of these themes.

The Rejection of the Family

Earlier in this chapter, I discussed the image of parental rejection. This is another complex image difficult to account for within the horizon of "exemplary literature" without extending our appreciation for the nuances of reception such an image was likely to receive. Again, I would like to introduce this motif by using the life of Christina. Christina's great beauty is the cause of her misfortune; in order to protect her from the rapacity of men, it is necessary for her father to shut her off from society by locking her and her equally fair handmaidens in a forbidding tower. Her sexual attractiveness gives to the narrative its initial and perhaps its primary motivation for action. The archetypal perilous tower—a symbol for her maidenly chastity—is a foil which her antagonist will attempt to overwhelm as the tale unfolds:

> Vrbane, consyderynge the frech coloure
> Off Crystyn hys doughtyre, and the grete beute,
> Dyde maken ane hye and a ful solenne toure,
> In wych wyth tuelue maydyns put was she.
>   (Bokenham, ll. 2131–34)

In addition to the contest between the maiden and her antagonist, the narrative is indebted to the romance for a series of contrapuntal antipathies on which are based some of the important themes of the *vita*. The first and most basic of these is her struggle against her father and mother.

Christina's struggle with her parents, especially her father, is crucial to the encratic thesis of the text. The young maiden spurns the companionship of both her mother and her father. In rejecting her father, however, she scorns a wider venue than that of the family alone; with him, she rejects the religion and the society of the state, since Urban, her father, is an official representative of that world: "an hei Iustice/ Under the luther emperor. Dioclisian." These sacred tales tend to maximize dramatic situations through stark polarities. Christina could not denounce what her father represented and still remain a faithful daughter. The break with the father represents an attempt to inculcate in the audience a distrust for the things of this world. The rejection of the male parent reminds the listener that the very fabric of Christian society is temporal, passing, illusory, and something to be transcended:

> And no dout thys blessyd cristyne
>   Disposyd was all on a-nother wyse
>   Than hyr fadyr wende or cowde devyne,
>   For hoolly hyr hert to goddys seruyse
>   Applyed was, wher-fore sacryfyse
>   To ydols done she ne wolde
>   As hyr fadyr bedyn had, but hertly dede despyse
>   All hys goddis forgyd off syluyr & golde.
>   (11. 2147–54)

This eschatological thesis complemented the reformist theology promulgated by councils and synods throughout England during the thirteenth and fourteenth centuries.

Before we turn to scenes of rejection of Christina's mother, I would like to acknowledge the *topos* of conflict between father and daughter in another very important text. The *Vita Sanctae Margarete* was one of the most widespread of the female virgin sacred biographies. Translations of a number of different Latin variants appear in virtually every European vernacular. In England, St. Margaret's cult was no less popular, with a number of translations and more than two hundred churches dedicated to her, including fifty-eight in rural Norfolk alone.[95] Her feast was celebrated on July 20, and, though a virgin, she was

---

95. For a bibliography see *BHL*, nos. 5303–13; *AS*, July vol. V; A. Mabellini, *Leggenda di Santa Margherita* (1925); and H. Delehaye, *Legendes hagiographiques*, pp. 187–92.

revered as the patron saint of childbirth.[96] Although the account of
Margaret in Bokenham's collection contains much of interest, I want
to restrict my discussion to the motif of enmity between father and
daughter. We begin, as with all these lives, with the conventional genealogy. Margaret is of high birth, being the daughter of Theodosius,
the patriarch of Antioch, a high priest of paganism. She is extremely
intelligent and is unmatched throughout the land for her great beauty.
She is the delight of her parents. However, as is the custom in the city,
she is sent, as a child of "statys hy," to be raised by a nurse. The nurse
is secretly a Christian and converts the young Margaret. On hearing of
the death of her mother, Margaret decides never to return to her father:

> But whan hyr moder was from hens past,
>   Wych deyid whil she was tendyr of age,
>   Margarete hyr affeccyoun set so fast
>   Vp-on hyr noryhs bothe wyhs & sage,
>   That she forsook al hyr hey lynage,
>   And purposyd hyr fully ther to soiourne,
>   For to hyr fadyr she nold hom returne.
>   (Bokenham, ll. 386–91)

Her conversion to Christianity not only gives her the resolve never to
see her father again, but it also produces in her a positive revulsion for
him and everything he stands for:

> And for she ded wurshepe crist & loue,
>   And wold not ageyn turne to paynymry,
>   Hyr fadyr hyr hatyd & dede reproue
>   And yaf no force what vylany
>   She had had; but the souereyn lord on hy
>   Thergeyn hyr fyllyd wyth so gret vertu
>   That in fewe yerys she perfyht greu.
>   (ll. 393–99)

Within the space of less than fifty lines, there is depicted the father's
joy at the birth of his daughter ("Hyr fadyr ful glad was of hyr byrthe")
and the daughter's utter rejection of him ("Hyr fadyr hyr hatyd & dede
reproue"). But would a contemporary audience (especially those male
parents who had daughters of marriageable age) have found this rapid
reversal of analogous figures of authority somewhat puzzling, if not
provocative? What would a predominantly lay audience find of interest

96. This curious association may result from the depiction of Margaret being swal-
lowed by the dragon and the miraculous opening of his stomach to free her because
of the irritation given his stomach by the cross she held in her hand.

in a saint's life which demeaned the role of the family and positively stressed the apparent good of childhood rebellion? To read these saints' tales as catalogues of the bizarre and the supernatural (elements which they seem to contain in abundance for modern readers) or as didactic treatises methodically inculcating the conciliar canons, glosses over a critical part of the social message these lives spread, intentionally or not, and the realities of the socioeconomics of everyday life.

If we consider the ideal of female heroism that the lives of the virgin saints proffer—an ideal according to which women reject not only family, friends, society, and law but, most violently, males—we must ask how this ideal was received and, indeed, why it was listened to at all by lay audiences. This question should be raised in the face of our certain knowledge that there is no satisfactory historical record with which to construct our answer other than the texts themselves.

Christina's rejection of her mother underlines, almost as a counterpoint to that of her father, how utterly radical was her dissolution of the family ties. Her mother is not explicitly identified with a context outside the family and, further, is never depicted as a physical threat to her daughter. Thus, Christina's rejection of her mother has a gratuitousness about it; it does not appear essential to her immediate theological aims and does not serve to move the action of the narrative. However, it is precisely in its apparent lack of thematic importance that its meaning lies: her rejection of the love of her mother shows the lengths to which the Christian must be willing to go in order to follow the message of the Gospels. Christina responds to her mother's plea to return to the religion of her family in the following manner:

> "But þou þan trauaylist," quod she, "in veyn,
> To clepe me doughtyr, & lesyst þi labour;
> For þis I wyl þou know in wurdys pleyn
> My name I haue of cryst my creatour.
> He is my fadir, he is my modir also."
> (ll. 2423–27)

If Christina's father is also a symbol of officialdom, her mother is the hearth, the nurturing spirit of aristocratic pagan femininity. Christina's mother was a member in good standing in the community, whose job it was to ensure the continuity of society through the household. Christina's rejection of her parents represents a radical denial of all the merit of pagan society in both its public and familial domains. This denial underscores the Christian polemic by showing Christina as now utterly alone in a barbarous world. Christina, although still a mere child and not yet a Christian, is well on her way to sainthood; she has seen the evil of this world and has had the strength to reject it.

But two nagging questions remain: why depict such militant behavior on the part of women in a traditional society which not only denies but also punishes women for such behavior? Might not such texts subsequently be used as models with which to legitimize antisocial or anticlerical behavior? There is little evidence with which one might construct an answer to this query, but I have discovered one highly suggestive fact. It is little known that Peter Waldo, the founder of the Waldensians, traced his interest in studying and preaching the Gospels in the vernacular to having heard a *jongleur* recite the life of St. Alexis. Furthermore, Etienne Bourbon records that the legends of the saints were held in special esteem in the Waldensian communities generally. (Interestingly, they called these stories *sentences,* judgments.) These communities granted considerably greater religious freedom to women than did the established church.[97] Thus, although the *Vie St. Alexis* lauds male encraticism, it nonetheless seems quite significant that the founder of a heretical movement with strong populist sympathies and a more tolerant attitude toward female autonomy traces his spiritual growth to a sacred biography.

Images of Female Militancy

The figure that dominates these virgin saints' lives is that of the youthful, beautiful maiden. However, this is not the maiden of romance, attractive and wily but finally submissive to the entreaties of the hero. The heroine of sacred biography is a far more complex compound of negative and positive behavior than her counterpart in romance. She upsets everyone's expectations of her. She rejects her parents, her brothers and sisters, her friends, her lover, the society, and its laws in single-minded pursuit of her goal, to embrace Christian fraternalism, to love Christ. Her deepest antagonism, however, is reserved for men, whether they be members of her family or strangers. In text after text, the saintly maiden is shown deceiving, rebuking, outwitting, displaying more courage, and finally triumphing over men. Despite this virtual

97. J. L. Willyams, *A Short History of the Waldensian Church* (London, 1845), pp. 36–37; A. Lecoy de la Marche, *Anecdotes historiques* (Paris, 1877), p. 290 ff. Peter's interest in preaching flew in the face of established clerical practice. Alain de Lille wrote passionately against lay preaching; see his *De fide Catholica contra Haereticos sui Temporis,* in G. Gonnet, ed., *Enchiridion Fontium Waldensium* (Rome, 1958), p. 106.

abhorrence of males, these lives were held up to the faithful as models for living the virtuous life. Bokenham writes that he translated the life of St. Katherine:

> to excite
> Mennys affeccyoun to have delyte
> Thys blyssyd virgyne to loue and serue
> From alle myscheuys him to preserue.

When we consider the misanthropic behavior of Katherine described in Bokenham's text, we cannot but wonder how males would have responded to this invitation.

Although, as Britton points out, there has been a tendency to exaggerate the drudgery and subordination with which peasant women actually lived as opposed to the manner in which the law provided for them, female assertiveness, when it threatened a prevailing social norm, custom, or statute, was quickly checked.[98] Dozens of examples could be adduced, but that of Agnes de Felixthorpe will illustrate my point. Agnes, a nun of St. Michael's convent in Stamford, abandoned her convent on nine different occasions. She was each time forcibly returned very much against her will. Further, for her pains, she was excommunicated by Bishop Dalderby in 1309 for apostasy, throttled by restricting chains, and placed in solitary confinement until she agreed to wear her habit. When records mention women from the lower strata of society, it is usually incidental to a case involving another more important individual. We see this quite frequently in parish visitation registers which sometimes record investigations into the sexual fidelity of individual clergy, indicating the woman involved simply as *uxor*. In the manorial court records, the fines charged to women for sexual infidelity (the "lerwyte") and for bearing a child out of wedlock (the "childwyte") are among the most common levied for wrongdoing. With some small exception, the clerks usually recorded in the rolls that the woman (seldom identified by name) had fornicated (*deflorata est*) and the amount of the fine she or her family was forced to pay.[99]

Suffice it to say that, although one might adduce some instances of female self-expression which were directed against the social mores of late medieval England, the overwhelming evidence points to a female

---

98. E. Britton, *The Community of the Vill*, pp. 20–21.

99. Razi, *Life, Marriage and Death*, pp. 64–65. Razi reports that the pre-Plague instances of illegitimacy were astoundingly high. From the Halesown court rolls between 1270 and 1348, he estimates that "for each 1.9 women who married, 1 woman gave birth to a child out of wedlock."

populace not given to such actions. The inspiring courage of Perpetua
and Felicitas, the military heroism of Boudiecca, the determined zeal
for religious converts of St. Leoba, Hrostvita's acknowledged skill as
a dramatist, the fierce independence of Eleanor of Aquitaine, the intellectual gifts of Eloise, or Agnes de Felixthorpe's determined efforts
at asserting her right not to be a religious are memorable because they
are singular when we place them in the context of the history of a
millennium of medieval women. If this is so, it is important to know
what sort of experience or passion the images of militant virgin saints
were designed to arouse in the majority of the laity constrained by innumerable familial and vocational burdens who heard such stories as
part of their regular liturgical obligations.

Assumptions of Autonomy

Can we assume that these tales of women who rebelled against repres-
sive parents and society in their search for religious independence reflect a deeply felt, albeit perhaps not conscious, desire for self-expression in the imagination of medieval women, a desire as important for
the female audiences listening to Gregory of Tours preaching in the late
sixth century in the cathedral of St. Martin on the life of St. Monegund
as it was to those listening to a Franciscan preaching the life of St.
Clare of Assisi in a rural English mendicant church of the late fourteenth century? For the moment, let us assume that this hypothesis
has some plausibility (reasoning *a posteriori* from the evidence of the
texts).

The assumption of the existence of such displaced desire has, if
nothing else, a superficial correctness about it. The autonomy of the
great spectrum of medieval woman—the freedom to choose among
modes of behavior—was dictated by the daily round of her labor,
whether physical as in the case of the peasant, physio-spiritual for the
nun, or as a cohort or partner to a male who held a position of authority. In light of this proscription of behavior, texts that portray women
exercising this decision-making capacity may have provided a safe opportunity for female audiences to celebrate independence by identifying with the heroic rebelliousness of the female saint. It is a commonplace of virtually all schools of psychology that if an individual is
denied something essential for emotional growth, something as crucial
as self-expression, he or she will likely continue to seek it, if not publicly, then privately and passively, perhaps entirely in the realm of the
imagination. The saints' lives which recount great feats of self-expres-

sion on the part of female virgins may have provided a stimulus for such imaginative identification.

There are, however, two difficulties with respect to this conjecture. First, it is far from clear whether the women of late medieval England (it need not be said how varied a group this was, differing in wealth, status, vocation, and privilege within particular socioeconomic classes) felt themselves to be members of an oppressed group. And, second is it likely, if we grant this first point concerning the corporate mentality of the women of this society, that the clergy would offer them such provocative role models or that spouses, brothers, and fathers would have welcomed them? Why would the church direct its clergy to present such potentially provocative *vitae* to their congregations? Certainly, the role model which the female saint presents to medieval women defies all the strictures which society and church had constructed. Until these questions can be answered, our conjecture must remain simply that.

Embracing the Deity

The rejection of the parents is an ironic parallel to the saint's acceptance of Christ; she accepts the Christian God completely, without hesitation. The figure of Christ becomes father and mother, lover and protector, state and family to her. Christina announces to her mother that Christ "is my fadir, he is modir also/Wych me hath clepyd to heuenly cheualrye." The person of Christ is the new locus for the natural good which she believed, when a pagan ("wych men peynyms call"), existed in the parents and ideals she has rejected. The following scene between Christina and her mother, set in her prison cell, illustrates this transference of the maiden's belief from parent to Christ:

> The moder for hure doȝter loue. made deol inou
>   He[o] porueide hure time wel. & to the prison drou
>   Doȝter he[o] sede swete herte. wepinge wel sore
>   For the loue that louest me. bilef thi false lore
>   For euerich strok that me ȝifth. thoru myn herte geth
>   Certes bote thou the withdrawe. ichot it worth my deth
>   Dame quath this holy maide. thi doȝter nam ich noȝt
>   For ich bere my fader name. that deore me hath iboȝt
>   After Crist that is my fader. Cristine is my name
>   Ich forsake the to moder. vare wel leoue dame.
>
> (*SEL*, ll. 133–42).

This poignant moment between mother and daughter was designed to impress on its listeners the singularity of Christina's love for Christ and, by extension, his church. The moral for this late-thirteenth-century Gloucestershire congregation[100] was as simple as it was impracticable for them: if you wish to live as a true Christian, follow the example of this heroic child. It is a commonplace of Middle English sacred biography to speak in absolutes, especially when prescribing behavior to be evaluated by the laity. However, in this instance, the practical impossibility of this moral for a lay audience suggests a wider intention on the part of the author. For surely the church in its catechetical literature is not encouraging familial strife. What then can we construe from this passage and from the life of Christina? I believe that part of the intention of this text is twofold: to uphold the importance of the celibate life and to establish an arena in which lay celibacy, even celibacy within marriage, might be seen as an appropriate model for lay conduct.

Christ as Lover

Following the scene in the prison with her mother, the young Christina undergoes a fundamental change of heart: she falls in love with Christ. The first indication of this in the prison scene with her mother is her choice of a new name, a feminized form of the name of her Savior. Her name change is the first step toward her goal of becoming the Savior's spouse. Her single desire is to subordinate her very person to her Lord, to become the beloved bride of Christ. Although this narrative lacks the power and verisimilitude of the scenes between Perpetua and her father, its moral is no less dramatic: a child rejects her parents in order to celebrate a hoped-for union with God.

The New Submissiveness

If her goal was to marry Christ, what steps did this child-woman take to realize her ambition? The primary obligation enjoined on wives by St. Paul in his Epistle to the Ephesians was that "Wives should be submissive to their husbands," a religious conviction which found analagous expression in the law.[101] With few exceptions, the ideal of the

100. A preponderance of the manuscripts have been localized by language to that region. Görlach has proposed that the "Z" version may have been written as far north as Worcester and brought into Gloucestershire through the "A" version later.

101. Britton, *The Community of the Vill*, p. 20.

Pauline verse was the practice, both legally and in matters of familial authority, throughout the Christian Middle Ages. However, submissiveness in the sacred biographies of medieval female saints has an unusual dimension. On the surface, the behavior of these female saints constitutes a rejection of the Pauline position. Moreover, the issue of sanctity in these female sacred biographies turns the Pauline notion of submission into a radical test of the woman's loyalty. The women in these *vitae* are anything but submissive, anything but dominated by the traditional male figures in their lives. They are submissive, however, to the exigencies of their belief, no matter the penalty. The ideal of feminine subordination is transformed into an ethic which demands, as primary, allegiance to one's religious conviction, even if that conviction turns the world upside down.

The slow, excruciatingly drawn-out depiction of doomed bravery in these females must have galvanized audience attention. The tests of loyalty to which these heroines are subjected are a battery of unspeakable tortures. The transformation from pagan nymph to Christian *sponsa* which began with Christina's testimony of faith in the dark prison cell now awaits the searing light of public ratification. In the following scene, Christina has been left to drown in the sea because of her refusal to renounce Christ:

> Oure Louerde hure nom bi the hond. & haf hure al aboue
> Christina he sede muche thou hast. itholed for my loue
> Beo stable and hard for thi sege. in heuen is ido
> & ichelle ar ich fram the wende. marki the therto
> He baptized with is owe honde. this maide in the se
> And softe with is angles suthe. to heuene aȝe
> Cristene he[o] miȝte hote wel. so ich vnderstonde
> Wanne Criste hure baptizede there. [with] is owene honde
> Cristene he[o] was tho ariȝt. & Cristes owe spouse.
>
> (*SEL*, ll. 197–205)

The passage, though lacking rhetorical polish, has a simple charm. There is a genuine pathos in the image of the young girl, abandoned, left to drown in the sea by her father—the protecting *paterfamilias*—being rescued by the tender ministrations of Christ. The listener's attention is directed to Christ's extended hand three times in these nine lines. The hand of the Lord first rescues her from drowning—a counterpoint to the rejecting hand of the father—to become the means for her baptism. The open hand is a conventional symbol for comfort, compassion, and trust. The virtues formerly supplied by her parents are now being proffered to this abandoned and abandoning child by the welcoming hand of Christ (the church?). This public avowal of Christina's merit by her savior is subtly crafted. This scene embodies a clash of opposing symbolic traditions. The Christian water of baptism restores a spirit dead from the ravages of original sin. Conversely, the image of the "maid in the se" shows the limitless power of nature. This sea destroys life as easily as the water of Christian baptism restores it.

If the water of the Christian liturgy of baptism brings new life, then this threatening water, this primeval maelstrom, bespeaks chaotic force, *natura naturans,* a universe without God. The turbulent sea represents the opposition of two traditions: the classical and the Christian. Christ's hand (typologically reminiscent of Moses's pacification of the Red Sea) extended to save and to baptize quiets the raging sea. The pagan maiden Christina is born anew, born a Christian from this ancient deluge. She is the new Aphrodite. The legacy of her past has been subdued and dies in the limitless sea. In its final appearance, the image of Christ's "owne honde" moves us beyond Christina's need for succor and baptism to her need for affection. The open hand represents the caress of the lover; Christina becomes through this divine touch his "owe spouse." Her girlhood past, her biological youth, has now been washed away. Christ is now protective father, nurturing mother, and adoring lover to the newly baptized maid.

I would like to suggest that the social and civil upheaval depicted in the tales of the female saints, the rejections of family and state, the coarsely depicted sexual abuse and bodily mutilation suffered by these godly women pointed the way to an approved version of a type of asceticism the church felt was available to women, whether clerical, married, or single, in order to establish a new order of Christian sisterhood. Moreover, in every narrative of female sanctity of which I am aware, the issue of personal allegiance, respect, or love of the family are always presented in a binary equation in which God is the primary element. Whatever is given up or rejected is done to allow the sacred heroine to move into a deeper relationship with the Christian God. Thus, the rebellious behavior, even the rejection of the deepest ties, is subsumed into a larger pattern of obedience to the divine will.

The liturgical setting of many of these saints' lives—their being read in lieu of the sermon preached following the Gospel at a Sunday mass, for example—reinforced the positive quality of what appears to be unwomanly behavior. The liturgical context surely sent a quiet but unmistakable message that such behavior was sometimes necessary. We may consider further the impact on the congregation of a priest reading

in the holy precincts of the church from a life of a saint who has rejected all male influences in her life from father to emperor, who has
spurned marriage, childbirth, and the religion of the state; the priestly
presence must have acted as a visible sign that the organized church
recognized that women might have such desires for autonomy and that
these feelings, even if socially unacceptable, need not cause them to
fear losing their place in the Christian community. Looked at in this
light, these sacred tales play a far more complex role than mere exemplary models for behavior. The liturgical context supplied by the
church makes it easier to see how these lives might also allow women
and men to indulge in a type of ritualized emancipation from their rigidly appointed roles, free from the personal stigma of sin and guilt.

Select Bibliography

This select bibliography is intended to be a listing of the most important texts used.

Primary Sources

Acta Sanctorum. J. Carnandet, ed. 64 vols. Paris, 1863–87.

Alanus de Insulis. *De Fide Catholica contra Haereticos Sui Temporis. Enchiridion Fontium Waldensium.* G. Gonnet, ed. Rome, 1958.

———. *Liber in Distinctionibus Dictionum Theologicalium. PL.* Vol. 210.

———. *Summa De Arte Praedicatoria. PL.* Vol. 210.

Ambrose, St. *De Interpellatione Job et David. PL.* Vol. 14.

———. *De Mysteriis. PL.* Vol. 16.

———. *De Poenitentia. PL.* Vol. 16.

———. *De Virginibus. PL.* Vol. 16.

Anonymous, ed. *The Legends and Commemorative Celebrations of St. Kentigern: His Friends and Disciples Translated from the Aberdeen Breviary and the Arbuthnot Missal.* Edinburgh, 1872.

Aquinas, Thomas, St. *Contra Gentiles,* Lib. III, cii.

Arnold, Thomas, ed. *Memorials of Saint Edmund's Abbey.* Vol. 1. London, 1890.

———. *Selected English Works of John Wyclif.* 3 vols. Oxford, 1869–71.

Athanasius. *Vita Sancti Antonii. PG.* Vol. 26.

———. *Vita Sancti Antonii.* Sister Mary Emily Keenan, trans. *The Fathers of the Church.* New York, 1952.

Augustine, St. *Contra Faustum Manichaeum.* Lib. XX, XXI, cols. 370–402. *PL.* Vol. 42.

———. *De Doctrina Christiana. CCSL,* Vol. 32, part IV, I. J. Martin, ed. Turnhout, 1962.

———. *De Humilitate et Timore Domini. Sancti Aurelii Augustini.* Congregatione S. Mauri, ed., Vol. 5, part 2. Paris, 1838.

———. *De Mendacio. PL.* Vol. 40.

———. *De Opere Monachorum. PL.* Vol. 40.

———. *St. Augustine's Confessions.* William Watts, trans. Vol. 1. London, 1912.

———. *Sermo CXVII. PL.* Vol. 38.

———. *Sermo CCVII. PL.* Vol. 39.

———. *Sermo CCC: In Solemnitate Martyrum Machabaeorum. PL.* Vol. 38.

———. *Sermo CCCXV. PL.* Vol. 39.

Barlow, F. *The Life of King Edward the Confessor.* London, 1962.

Barnes, John (printer). *Two Short Treatises, against the Order of the Begging Friars, Compiled by That Famous Doctour of the Church, and Preacher of Gods Word John Wickliffe.* Oxford, 1608.

Bazire, J. *The Metrical Life of St. Robert of Knaresborough together with Other Middle English Poems.* EETS O.S. 228. Oxford, 1958.

Beauvais, Vincent of. *Speculum Historiale.* 3 vols. Augsburg, 1474.

Bede. *De Psalmorum Libro Exegesis. PL.* Vol. 93.

———. *Ecclesiastical History of the English People.* B. Colgrave and R. A. B. Mynors, eds. Oxford, 1969.

———. *Historia Ecclesiastica Gentis Anglorum. PL.* Vol. 95.

———. *Kalendarium Anglicanum. PL.* Vol. 94.

———. *Vita Metrica Sancti Cuthberti. PL.* Vol. 94.

Bennett, J. A. W., ed. *Piers Plowman.* Oxford, 1972.

Bernard of Clairvaux. *Epistola XCVIII: De Machabaesis, sed ad quem scripta sit ignoratur. PL.* Vol. 182.

Bibliotheca Hagiographica Graeca; Seu Elenchus Vitarum Sanctorum, 3rd ed. Brussels, 1954.

Bibliotheca Hagiographica Latina Antiquae et Mediae Aetatis. Vol. 1. Brussels, 1898–1901.

Bibliotheca Hagiographica Latini Supplementi. Socii Bollandiani, ed., Brussels, 1911.

Birgitta, St. *The Revelations of St. Birgitta.* Oxford, 1929.

Blunt, J. H., ed. *The Myroure of Oure Lady.* EETS E.S. 19. London, 1873.

Boswell, J. *The Life of Samuel Johnson.* London, 1791.

Breviarum Ad Usum Insignis Ecclesie Eboracensis. Surtees Society no. 71. London, 1871.

———. Surtees Society no. 75. London, 1882.

Brown, B. D. *The Southern Passion.* EETS O.S. 169. London, 1927.

Budge, E. A. W., trans. *Coptic Martyrdoms in the Dialect of Upper Egypt.* London, 1914.

Burgundius, Vincentius. *Bibliotheca Mundi Seu Speculi Maioris.* Tomus Quartus. Duaci, 1624.

Caesarius of Arles. *Ammonito ut Silentium in Ecclesia Praebeatur.* Sermo LXXVIII. *CCSL* 103. G. Morin, ed. Turnhout, 1953.

Cassian, John. *De Coenobiorum Institutis. PL.* Vol. 49.

Cassiodorus. *De Institutione Divinarum Litterarum. PL.* Vol. 70.

Chambers, J. D., ed. and trans. *The Psalter, or Seven Ordinary Hours of Prayer: According to the Use of the Illustrious and Excellent Church of Sarum.* London, 1852.

Chambers, R. W., and W. W. Seton. *A Fifteenth-Century Courtesy Book and Two Franciscan Rules*. EETS O.S. 148. London, 1914.

Charland, Th.-M., ed. *Artes praedicandi: contribution à l'histoire de la rhétorique au moyen âge*. Ottawa, 1936.

Chepman, Walter, ed. *Sancti Servani Episcopus et Confessor. Breviarium Aberdonense*. London, 1845.

Christina of Markyate. *The Life of Christina of Markyate: A Twelfth Century Recluse*. C. H. Talbot, ed. and trans., Oxford, 1959.

Chrodegang. *Regula Canonicorum. PL.* Vol. 89.

Colgrave, B., ed. and trans. "The Earliest Life of St. Gregory the Great, written by a Whitby Monk." *Celt and Saxon: Studies in the Early British Border*. N. K. Chadwick, ed. Cambridge, 1963.

———. *Felix's Life of St. Guthlac*. Cambridge, 1956.

———. *The Life of Bishop Wilfrid*. Cambridge, 1927.

———. *Two Lives of St. Cuthbert: A Life by an Anonymous Monk of Lindisfarne and Bede's Prose Life*. Cambridge, 1940.

Collins, A. Jefferies. *The Bridgettine Breviary of Syon Abbey*. Worcester, 1969.

Crane, T. F., ed. *The Exempla of Jacques de Vitry*. London, 1890.

Crawford, S. J., ed. *Byrhtferth's Manual*. EETS O.S. 177. London, 1929.

Cyprian, St. *Ad Fortunatum. CCSL 3*. R. Weber, ed. Turnhout, 1972.

———. *De Lapsis. PL.* Vol. 4.

Dalton, J. N., ed. *Ordinale Exon*. 3 vols. London, 1909–40.

Damascus, John of. *De Imaginibus Oratio III. PG.* Vol. 94.

d'Ardenne, S. T. R. O., ed. *An Edition of the Liflade ant te Passiun of Seinte Iuliene*. EETS O.S. 248. London, 1961.

Day, M., and R. Steele, eds. *Mum and the Sothsegger*. EETS O.S. 199. London, 1936.

Deferrari, R. J., ed. *Early Christian Biographies*. Washington, 1952.

D'Evelyn, C., and A. J. Mill. *The South English Legendary*. EETS 235–36. London, 1956.

Eadmer. *Vita Sancti Anselmi. PL.* Vol. 158.

Einenkel, E. *The Life of Saint Katherine*. EETS O.S. 80. London, 1884.

Ellis, F. S. [William Caxton] *The Golden Legend or Lives of the Saints*. 7 vols. London, 1900.

Erbe, T., ed. *Mirk's Festial*. EETS E.S. 96. London, 1905.

Eustace, St. *De Sanctis Eustachio, Uxore Ejus et Filiis. AS.* September VI. Antwerp, 1757.

Evagrius. *Vita Beati Antonii Interprete Evagrio Presbytero Antiocheno. PL.* Vol. 73.

Fell, C. E., ed. "Dunstanus saga." *Éditiones Arnamagnaeanae*. LXXXVI. 1963.

Feltoe, C. L., ed. *Sacramentarium Leonianum*. Cambridge, 1896.

Fontaine, J., ed. "Sulpicie Severe 'Vie de Saint Martin,'" *Sources chrétiennes*, no. 133, 3 vols. Paris, 1967.

Freemantle, A., *A Treasury of Early Christianity*. New York, 1953.

Frere, W. H., and L. E. G. Brown, eds. *The Hereford Breviary.* 3 vols. London, 1904–15.

Furnivall, F. J., ed. *Robert of Brunne's Handlyng Synne.* EETS O.S. 119. London, 1901.

Giles, J. A., ed. *Venerabilis Bedae Opera Quae Supersunt Omnia.* 12 vols. in 6. London, 1843.

Graesse, Th., ed. *Legenda Aurea.* Leipzig, 1840.

Gregory the Great. *Dialogorum Libri Quartus. PL.* Vol. 77.

———. *Epistola XXX. PL.* Vol. 77.

———. *Vita S. Benedicti. PL.* Vol. 66.

Gregory Nazianzen, St. *In Machabaeorum Laudem. PG.* Vol. 35.

Gregory of Nyssa, St. *Ascetical Works.* Washington, 1967.

Gregory of Tours. *Historia Francorum. PL.* Vol. 71.

———. *Liber de Gloria Confessorum. PL.* Vol. 71.

———. *Liber Vitae Patrum. MGH: Scriptores Rerum Merovingicarum.* B. Krusch, ed. Hanover, 1969.

Griffiths, R. G., ed. *Registrum Thome de Cantilupo. Canterbury and York Society.* Vol. 2. London, 1907.

Habig, M. A. *St. Francis of Assisi, Writings and Early Biographies, English Omnibus of the Sources for the Life of St. Francis.* Chicago, 1972.

Hampson, R. T. *Medii Aevi Kalendarium.* Vol. 2. London, 1841.

Herbert, J. A. *Catalogue of Romances in the Department of Manuscripts in the British Museum.* Vol. 3. London, 1910.

Herolt, John. *Promptuarium Exemplorum.* Rothmagi, 1511.

Herzfeld, George. *An Old English Martyrology.* EETS O.S. 116. London, 1900.

Heyworth, P. L., ed. *Jack Upland, Friar Daw's Reply and Upland's Rejoinder.* Oxford, 1968.

Hilduin of St. Denis. *Areopagitica. PL.* Vol. 106.

Hingeston-Randolph, F. C., ed. *The Register of John de Grandisson.* 3 vols. London, 1894–99.

Holder-Egger, O. *Agnellus Liber Pontificalis Ecclesiae Ravennatis. MGH: Scriptores Rerum Langobardicarum.* Hanover, 1878.

———, ed. *Cronica Fratris Salimbene de Adam. MGH: Scriptores.* Vol. 32. Leipzig, 1913.

Holweck, F. G. *Calendarium Liturgicum Festorum Dei et Dei Matris Mariae.* Philadelphia, 1925.

Honorius of Autun. *Speculum Ecclesiae. PL.* Vol. 172.

Horstmann, C. *Altenglische Legenden, Neue Folge mit und Anmerkungen.* Heilbronn, 1881.

———., ed. *Barbour's des Schottischen Nationaldichters Legendsammlung.* Heilbronn, 1881–82.

———., ed. *Capgrave's The Life of Saint Katherine.* EETS O.S. 100. London, 1883.

———. *The Early South English Legendary.* EETS O.S. 87. London, 1887.

————., ed. "Die Evangelien Geschichten des Ms. Vernon." *Archiv für das Studium der Neuren Sprachen und Literaturen* 57 (1877): 241–316.

————. *Nova Legenda Anglie.* Vol. 1. Oxford, 1901.

Hurst, D., ed. *Bedae Venerabilis Opera: In Lucae Evangelivm Exposito.* CCSL. 120. Turnhout, 1960.

Innocent III. *Regestorum sive Epistolarum Liber Primus. PL.* Vol. 214.

Irenaeus. *Adversus Haereses. PG.* Vol. 8.

Isidore. *Etymologiarum Libri XX. PL.* Vol. 82.

James, M. R. *A Descriptive Catalogue of the Manuscripts in the Library of Corpus Christi College, Cambridge.* Vol. 1. Cambridge, 1912.

————. *A Descriptive Catalogue of Manuscripts in the Library of King's College, Cambridge.* Cambridge, 1895.

————. *The Lost Apocrypha of the Old Testament.* London, 1920.

Jerome, St. *Epistola ad Laetam. PL.* Vol. 22.

————. *Liber contra Vigilantium. PL.* Vol. 23.

————. *Liber Ecclesiastici. PL.* Vol. 30.

Julian of Norwich. *A Book of Showings to the Anchoress Julian of Norwich.* E. Colledge, ed. Toronto, 1978.

Junior, Johannes. *Scala Coeli.* Louvain, 1485.

Justin Martyr. "The First Apology" and "The Second Apology." *Fathers of the Church.* T. B. Falls, ed. Washington, 1965.

Karrer, O. *St. Francis of Assisi: The Legends and the Lauds.* London, 1947.

Kempe, Margery. *The Book of Margery Kempe.* S. B. Meech, ed., Oxford, 1940.

Lactantius. *Ad Donatum Confessorem de Mortibus Persecutorum. PL.* Vol. 7.

Lake, Kirsopp. *The Apostolic Fathers.* 2 vols. Cambridge, Mass., 1970.

Legg, J. Wickham, ed. *Missale ad Usum Ecclesie Westmonasteriensis.* Vol. 2. London, 1893.

————. *The Sarum Missale: Edited from Three Early Manuscripts.* Oxford, 1916.

Lind, L. R. "The Vita Sancti Malchi of Reginald of Canterbury." *Illinois University Studies in Language and Literature* 27 (1942): 1–245.

Little, A. G. *Fratris Thomae Tractatus de Adventu Fratrum Minorum in Angliam.* Manchester, 1931.

Logeman, H., ed. *The Rule of St. Benet.* EETS O.S. 90. London, 1888.

Loserth, J., ed. *Johannes Wyclif Sermones.* London, 1890.

Luard, H. R., ed. *Roberti Grosseteste Epistolae.* London, 1861.

Macarius. *Verba Seniorum. PL.* Vol. 73.

McCann, J., ed. *The Rule of St. Benedict: In Latin and English.* London, 1952.

Mack, F. M. *Seinte Marherete the Meiden ant Martyr.* EETS O.S. 193. London, 1928.

Macray, William Dunn. *Chronicon Abbatiae de Evesham, ad Annum 1418.* Rolls Series no. 29. London, 1863.

Madden, Sir Frederick. *The Ancient English Romance of Havelok the Dane.* London, 1828.

Mansi. J. *Sacrorum Conciliorum Nova, et Amplissima Collectio.* Florence, 1759–98.

Marche, A. Lecoy de la, ed. *Anecdotes Historiques Légendes et Apologues d'Étienne de Bourbon.* Paris, 1877.

Maskell, William. *Monumenta Ritualia Ecclesiae Anglicanae,* 2nd ed. 3 vols. Oxford, 1882.

Matthew, F. D., ed. *The English Works of Wyclif.* EETS O.S. 74. London, 1880.

Miracles de Nostre Dame Collected by Jean Mielot. G. F. Warner, ed. London, 1885.

Munro, J. J. *John Capgrave's Lives of St. Augustine and St. Gilbert of Sempringham.* EETS O.S. 140. London, 1910.

Musurillo, Herbert. *The Acts of the Christian Martyrs.* Oxford, 1972.

———. *The Acts of the Pagan Martyrs.* Oxford, 1968.

Napier, A. S., ed. *The Old English Version of the Enlarged Rule of Chrodegang together with the Latin Original.* London, 1916.

Natalibus, Petrus de. *Catalogus Sanctorum.* N.p., 1521.

Oesterley, H., ed. *Gesta Romanorum.* Berlin, 1871.

Orientius. *Commonitorium. PL.* Vol. 61.

Origen. *Exhortatio ad Martyrium. PG.* Vol. II.

———. *Homiliae in Canticum Canticorum. PG.* Vol. 13.

———. *Prayer, Exhortation to Martyrdom.* J. O'Meara, trans. London, 1954.

Parker, R. E. *The Middle English Stanzaic Version of the Life of St. Anne.* EETS O.S. 174. London, 1928.

Peacock, E., ed. *Myrc's Instructions for Parish Priests.* EETS O.S. 31. London, 1868.

Perry, G. G., ed. *English Prose Treatises of Richard Rolle of Hampole.* EETS O.S. 20. London, 1866.

Petre, H., ed. "Etheria Journal de Voyage." *Sources chrétiennes,* no. 21. Paris, 1948.

Pope, John C. *Homilies of Aelfric.* EETS O.S. 259, 260. London, 1967–68.

Power, P., ed. and trans. "Lives of Saints Declan and Mochuda." *Irish Texts Society 16.* London, 1914.

Powicke, M. *The Life of Ailred of Rievaulx.* Oxford, 1950.

Proctor, F., and E. S. Dewick, eds. *The Martiloge in Englysshe: after the Use of the Church of Salisbury and as It Is Redde in Syon with Addicyons.* London, 1893.

Proctor, F., and C. Wordsworth, eds. *Breviarum ad Usum Insignis Ecclesiae Sarum.* Vol. 1. Cambridge, 1882.

Prudentius. *Liber Peristephanon. PL.* Vol. 60.

Robertson, J. C. *Materials for the History of Thomas Becket.* 7 vols. London, 1877.

Ruinart, Theoderici. *Acta Primorum Martyrum Sincera et Selecta.* Paris, 1689.

Salmon, Pierre. *Le Lectionnaire de Luxeuil. Collectanea Biblica Latina.* Rome, 1944.

Sapegno, N. "Dante Alighieri: La Divina Commedia." *La Letteratura Ital-iana: Storia e Testi.* Rome, 1957.

Sarisburiensis. *Portiforum seu Breviarium Insignis Sarisburiensis Ecclesie Usum: Pars Hyemalis.* Paris, ca. 1518.

Savage, H. L. *St. Erkenwald, A Middle English Poem.* New Haven, 1926.

Schoedel, William R. "Polycarp, Martyrdom of Polycarp, Fragments of Papius." *The Apostolic Fathers.* Robert M. Grant, ed. London, 1967.

Sedulius. *Carmen Paschale. PL.* Vol. 19.

Selmer, Carl. *Navigatio Sancti Brendani Abbatis.* Notre Dame, 1959.

Serjeantson, M. S. *Osbern Bokenham, Legendes of Hooly Wummen.* EETS O.S. 206. London, 1938.

Severus, Sulpicius. *Dialogi III. PL. Vol. 20.*

Shepherd, Geoffrey. *Ancrene Wisse: Parts Six and Seven.* London, 1959.

Skeat, W. E., ed. *Aelfric's Lives of the Saints.* London, 1881-1900.

———. *Havelok.* EETS E.S. 4. London, 1868.

———. *Pierce the Ploughmans Crede.* EETS O.S. 30. London, 1867.

Small, J. *English Metrical Homilies.* Edinburgh, 1862.

Smetana, C. *The Life of St. Norbert by John Capgrave, OEAA (1393-1464).* Toronto, 1977.

Smith, L. T., and P. Meyer, eds. *Les contes moralisés de Nicole Bozon.* Paris, 1889.

Southern, R. W., ed. *The Life of St. Anselm, Archbishop of Canterbury by Eadmer.* London, 1962.

Southwell, Robert. *An Epistle of Comfort, to the Reverend Priestes, and to the Honorable, Worshipful, and Other Laye Sort Restrayned in Durance for the Catholicke Fayth.* Paris, n.d.

Stephen, St. *Vita Sancti Stephani jun. PG.* Vol. 100.

Strecker, K. *Rhythmi Aevi Merovingiei et Carolini. MGH: Poetae Latini.* Vol. 4. 1923.

Stubbs, William. *Epistola Adelardi ad Elfegum Archiepiscopum de Vita Sancti Dunstani. Memorials of Saint Dunstan: Archbishop of Cantebury.* Rolls Series no. 63. London, 1874.

———. *Willelmi Malmsbiriensis Monachi: De Gestis Regum Anglorum.* Rolls Series no. 90. London, 1889.

Sweet, H., ed. *King Alfred's West-Saxon Version of Gregory's Pastoral Care.* EETS O.S. 45. London, 1871.

Swoboda, E., ed. *Odo of Cluny. Occupatio.* Leipzig, 1900.

Symons, Dom Thomas, ed. and trans. *Regularis Concordia.* London, 1953.

Tertullian. *De Corona Militis. PL.* Vol. 2.

———. *De Exhortatione Castitatis. CSEL.* Vol. 2. Turnhout, 1954.

———. *De Fuga in Persecutione. PL.* Vol. 2.

———. *Liber de Oratione. PL.* Vol. 1.

Theodore of Studium. *Antirrheticus. PG.* Vol. 99.

Thompson, H. J., ed. *Peristephanon Liber.* Vol. 2. Cambridge, Mass., 1961.

Thompson, Stith, ed. *Motif Index of Folk Literature.* 6 vols. Bloomington, 1955–58.

Thorpe, Benjamin, ed. *The Homilies of the Anglo-Saxon Church: The First Part Containing the Sermones Catholici.* Vol. 1. London, 1844.

Tolhurst, J. B. L. *The Monastic Breviary of Hyde Abbey, Winchester.* HBS, no. 6. London, 1942.

———. *The Ordinale and Customary of the Abbey of Saint Mary.* Vol. 3. London, 1963.

———. *The Ordinale and Customary of the Benedictine Nuns of Barking Abbey.* London, 1927.

Usardus. *Martyrologium. PL.* Vol. 124.

Van Beek, C. I. M. J., ed. *Passio Sanctarum Perpetuae et Felicitatis.* Nijmegen, 1937.

Van der Westhuizen, J. E. *John Lydgate, The Life of Saint Alban and Saint Amphihal.* Leiden, 1974.

Walther, Hans. *De Excidio. Corpus Initia Carminum Ac Versuum Medii Aevi Posterioris Latinorum.* Göttingen, 1959.

Webb, C. C. I., ed. *Ioannis Saresberiensis Episcopi Carnotensis Policratici.* Oxford, 1909.

Weber, R., ed. *Bibla Sacra Iuxta Vulgatam Versionem.* 2 vols. Stuttgart, 1969.

Wilkins, D. *Concilia Magnae Britanniae et Hiberniae.* London, 1737.

Wilkinson, John. *Egeria's Travels.* London, 1971.

Wilson, H. A., ed. *The Gelasian Sacramentary, Liber Sacramentorum Romanae Ecclesiae.* Oxford, 1894.

Woodward, G. R., and H. Mattingly, trans. *St. John Damascene: Barlaam and Ioasaph.* Cambridge, Mass., 1967.

Wooley, R. M., ed. *The Gilbertine Rite.* Vol. 1. London, 1921.

———. *The Officium and Miracula of Richard Rolle of Hampole.* London, 1919.

Wormald, F., ed. *English Benedictine Kalendars after A.D. 1100.* London, 1939.

———. *English Kalendars before A.D. 1100.* London, 1934.

Wright, T. *A Selection of Latin Stories.* London, 1842.

Wright, W. A. *The Metrical Chronicle of Robert of Gloucester.* London, 1887.

Secondary Sources

Aaron, David. *Studies in Biography.* Cambridge, Mass. 1978.

Aigrain, René. *L'Hagiographie: ses sources, ses méthodes, son histoire.* Paris, 1953.

———. "La liturgie dominicaine." *Liturgia: encyclopédie populaire des connaissances liturgiques.* Paris, 1930.

Allard, Paul. *Dix leçons sur le martyre*. Paris, 1907.

Allen, Hope Emily. *Writings Ascribed to Richard Rolle Hermit of Hampole.* New York, 1927.

Aston, S. C. "The Saint in Medieval Literature." *MLR* 65 (1970): 25–42.

Atkins, J. W. H. *English Literary Criticism: The Medieval Phase*. London, 1952.

Auerbach, Erich. *Literary Language and Its Public in Late Latin Antiquity and in the Middle Ages.* R. Manheim, trans. New York, 1965.

———. *Mimesis: The Representation of Reality in Western Literature.* W. Trask, trans. New York, 1957.

Baker, D., ed. *Medieval Women, Dedicated and Presented to Professor Rosalind M. T. Hill.* Oxford, 1978.

———. *"Vir Dei:* Secular Sanctity in the Early Tenth Century." In *Popular Belief and Practice*. Cambridge, 1972, pp. 41–53.

Baldwin, W. *Alexander III and the Twelfth Century*. Westminster, Md., 1966.

Baudot, J. L. *Dictionnaire d'hagiographie mis à jour à l'aide de travaux les plus récents*. Paris, 1925.

Baumer, S. *Geschichte des Breviers: Versuch einer quellenmassigen Darstellung der Entwicklung des Altkirchlichen und des Römischen Officiums bis auf Unsere Tage*. Freiburg, 1895.

Baus, K. *From the Apostolic Community to Constantine*. London, 1965.

Benko, S. *The Meaning of Sanctorum Communio*. Napierville, Ill., 1964.

Bennett, R. F. *The Early Dominicans*. Cambridge, 1937.

Benton, J., ed. "Fraud, Fiction and Borrowing in the Correspondence of Abelard and Heloise." In *Pierre Abélard-Pierre le Vénérable: les courants philosophiques, littéraires et artistiques en occident au milieu du XIIe siècle*. Paris, 1975.

Bjork, R. E. *The Old English Verse Saints' Lives*. Toronto, 1985.

Bolton, B., ed. *Women in Medieval Society*. Philadelphia, 1976.

Bonnet, M. *Le Latin de Grégoire de Tours*. Paris, 1890.

Bonniwell, William R. *A History of the Dominican Liturgy*. New York, 1945.

Bouyer, Louis. *The Meaning of the Monastic Life*. London, 1955.

———. "The Spirituality of the New Testament and the Fathers." M. P. Ryan, trans. *A History of Christian Spirituality*. L. Bouyer, J. Leclercq, and F. Vandenbroucke, eds. New York, 1963.

Boyd, B. "A New Approach to the 'South English Legendary.'" *PQ* 47 (1968): 494–98.

Brandt, W. J. *The Shape of Medieval History*. New Haven, 1966.

Braswell, Laurel. "Sir Isumbras and the Legend of St. Eustace." *Medieval Studies* 27 (1965): 128–51.

Breisach, E., ed. *Classical Rhetoric and Medieval Historiography*. Kalamazoo, 1985.

Brewer, D. "Towards a Chaucerian Poetic." *Proceedings of the British Academy* 60 (1974): 1–35.

Brown, B. "Robert of Gloucester's *Chronicle* and the Life of St. Kenelm." *MLN* 41 (1926): 13–23.

Brown, Carleton, and Russel Hope Robbins, eds. *The Index of Middle English Verse*. New York, 1943.

Brown, Peter. *Augustine of Hippo: A Biography*. Berkeley, 1967.

———. *The Cult of the Saints: Its Rise and Function in Latin Christianity*. Chicago, 1980.

———. *The Making of Late Antiquity*. Cambridge, 1978.

———. *Relics and Social Status in the Age of Gregory of Tours*. Reading, Eng. 1977.

———. "The Rise and Function of the Holy Man in Late Antiquity." *JRS* 61 (1971): 81–101.

———. "The Saint as Exemplar in Late Antiquity." *Representations* 1 (1983): 1–25.

Brown, R. E., and J. A. Fitzmeyer, eds. *The Jerome Biblical Commentary*. Englewood Cliffs, 1968.

Bugnini, A. "Passionario." *Enciclopedia Cattolica*. Vol. 9, cols. 915–17. Citta del Vaticano, 1952.

Burke, K. *A Grammar of Motives*. New York, 1945.

Burckhardt, J. *Die Zeit Constantin's des Grossen*. Basel, 1853.

Burrow, A. J. *The Ages of Man: A Study in Medieval Writing and Thought*. Oxford, 1986.

Bynum, C. *Jesus as Mother: Studies in the Spirituality of the High Middle Ages*. Berkeley, 1982.

Cabrol, F. "Liturgie: attitudes et gestes liturgiques." *Dictionnaire de théologie catholique*. Vol. 9. Paris, 1926.

Cadbury, H. J. *The Making of Luke-Acts*. London, 1958.

Caplan, H. "Rhetorical Invention in Some Medieval Tractates on Preaching." *Speculum* 2 (1927): 284–95.

Carle, B. "Structural Patterns in the Legends of the Holy Women of Christianity." In *Aspects of Female Existence*. Copenhagen, 1980.

Chapman, John. *St. Benedict and the Sixth Century*. London, 1929.

Chaytor, H. J. *From Script to Print*. Cambridge, 1945.

Cheney, C. R. *English Synodalia of the Thirteenth Century*. Oxford, 1968.

———. "Rules for the Observance of Feast-Days in Medieval England." *Bulletin of the Institute of Historical Research* 34 (1961): 117–47.

Clanchy, M. T. *From Memory to Written Record*. London, 1979.

Clemoes, P. "The Chronology of Aelfric's Work." *The Anglo-Saxons: Studies Presented to Bruce Dickins*. London, 1959.

Coleman, J. *Medieval Readers and Writers*. New York, 1981.

Cox, P. *Biography in Late Antiquity*. Berkeley, 1983.

Cross, F. L., ed. *The Oxford Dictionary of the Christian Church*. London, 1957.

Cunningham, L. *The Meaning of Saints*. New York, 1980.

Curtius, Ernest Robert. *European Literature and the Latin Middle Ages.* W. Trask, trans. New York, 1953.

Dalmais, I. H. *Introduction to the Liturgy.* Roger Capel, trans. London, 1961.

D'Ancona, A. *Poemetti Popolari Italiani.* Rome, 1881.

Danielou, Jean. *The Bible and the Liturgy.* London, 1960.

Davis, R. H. C., and J. M. Wallace-Hadrill, eds. *The Writing of History in the Middle Ages.* Oxford, 1981.

Davy, M. M. "Les sermons universitaires Parisiens de 1230–1231." *Études de Philosophie Médiévale* 15 (1931): 149–414.

Deanesly, M. *The Lollard Bible.* Cambridge, 1920.

———. *The Lollard Bible and Other Medieval Biblical Versions.* Cambridge, 1966.

———. *The Pre-Conquest Church in England.* London, 1961.

———. "Vernacular Books in the Fourteenth and Fifteenth Centuries." *MLR* 15 (1920): 349–58.

De Bruyne, Edgar. *Études d'esthétique médiévale.* Brugge, 1946.

De Gaiffier, B. "La lecture des actes des martyrs dans la prière liturgique en occident: A propos du passionaire hispanique." *Analecta Bollandiana* 62 (1954): 138–42.

———. "De l'usage et de la lecture du martyrologe: témoignages antérieures au XIe siècle." *Analecta Bollandiana* 74 (1961): 40–59.

———. *Recueil d'hagiographie.* Brussels, 1977.

Deiss, Lucien, ed. *Early Sources of the Liturgy.* B. Weatherhead, trans. London, 1967.

Delaruelle, E. *La piété populaire au moyen âge.* Turin, 1975.

Delehaye, Hippolyte. "La légende de Saint Eustache." *Bulletins de la classe des lettres.* Brussels, 1919.

———. *The Legends of the Saints.* Notre Dame, 1961.

———. "Les passions des martyrs et les genres littéraires." *Subsidia Hagiographica.* Brussels, 1921.

———. *Sanctus; essai sur le culte des saints dans l'antiquité.* Brussels, 1927.

D'Evelyn, C. "Collections of Saints' Legends." *A Manual of the Writings in Middle English, 1050–1500.* J. Burke Severs, ed. Hamden, Conn., 1970.

Dodds, E. R. *Pagan and Christian in an Age of Anxiety.* London, 1965.

Dörrie, H. "Die Griechischen Romane und das Christentum." *Phil* 93 (1938): 273–76.

Douie, D. L. "Archbishop Pecham's Sermons and Collations." *Studies in Medieval History Presented to E. M. Powicke.* Oxford, 1948.

Drake, H. A. *In Praise of Constantine: A Historical Study and New Translation of Eusebius' Tricennial Orations.* Berkeley, 1976.

Dreves, G. M. "Historiae Rhythmicae Liturgische Reimofficien des Mittelalters." *Analecta Hymnica Medii Aevi.* Vol. 5. Leipzig, 1889.

Dronke, P. *Women Writers of the Middle Ages.* Cambridge, 1984.

Dubois, M. M. *Aelfric: sermonnaire, docteur et grammairien*. Paris, 1942.

Duby, G. *William Marshall. The Flower of Chivalry*. New York, 1985.

Dugmore, C. W. *The Influence of the Synagogue upon the Divine Office*. Oxford, 1943.

Dummler, E. "Rhythmen aus der Carolingischen Zeit." *Zeitschrift für Deutsches—Altertum* 23 (1879): 273–80.

Ebert, A. "Zu den Carolingischen Rhythmen." *Zeitschrift für Deutsches Altertum* 24 (1880): 148–50.

Edel, L. *Literary Biography*. New York, 1973.

Eisenhofer, Ludwig, and Joseph Lechner. *The History of the Roman Rite*. A. J. Peeler and E. F. Peeler, trans. H. E. Winstone, ed. London, 1961.

Faber, F. W. *An Essay on Beatification, Canonization and the Processes of the Congregation of Rites*. London, 1848.

Ferrante, J. *Woman as Image in Medieval Literature*. New York, 1975.

Ferster, J. *Chaucer on Interpretation*. Cambridge, 1985.

Fierville, M. Charles. "Notice et extraits des manuscrits de la bibliotheque de Saint-Omer." *Notices et Extraits des Manuscrits de la Bibliothèque Nationale* 31 (1884): 49–88.

Finucane, R. C. *Miracles and Pilgrims: Popular Beliefs in Medieval England*. London, 1977.

Fletcher, J. R. *The Story of the Bridgettines of Syon Abbey*. London, 1933.

Foley, J. M. ed. *Oral-Formulaic Theory and Research: An Introduction and Annotated Bibliography*. New York, 1985.

Fontaine, J. "Alle fonti dell'agiografia europea." *Rivista di Storia e Letteratura Religiosa* 2 (1966): 187–206.

Foucault, M., *The Order of Things*. New York, 1970.

Freemantle, A., ed. *A Treasury of Early Christianity*. New York, 1953.

Frend, W. H. C. *Martyrdom and Persecution in the Early Church*. Oxford, 1965.

Freud, S. *Leonardo da Vinci and a Memory of His Childhood*. London, 1910.

Fristedt, S. W. "The Dating of the Earliest Manuscript of the Wycliffite Bible." *Studier i Modern Sprakvetenskap* 28 (1956): 61–86.

Gadamer, H.-G. *Truth and Method*. New York, 1981.

Gay, P. *Style in History*. New York, 1976.

———. *The Enlightenment, an Interpretation: The Rise of Modern Paganism*. New York, 1966.

Geertz, C. *The Interpretation of Culture*. New York, 1973.

———. *Local Knowledge: Further Essays in Interpretive Anthropology*. New York, 1983.

Gerould, G. H. "The Hermit and the Saint." *PMLA* 20 (1905): 529–45.

———. "Review of J. Mosher's Exemplum in England." *ES* 47 (1913): 81–84.

———. *Saints' Legends*. Boston, 1916.

Gianakaris, C. G. *Plutarch*. New York, 1979.

Gibbon, Edward. *The Decline and Fall of the Roman Empire*. New York, 1952.

Goodich, M. "A Profile of Thirteenth-Century Sainthood." *Comparative Studies in Society and History* 18 (1976): 429–37.

Görlach, Manfred. "The Textual Tradition of the South English Legendary." *Leeds Texts and Monographs* 6 (1974): 1–317.

Gransden, Antonia. "Anglo Saxon Sacred Biography." *Historical Writing in England*. London, 1974.

———. *Historical Writing in England c. 550 to c. 1307, and Historical Writing in England c. 1307 to the Early Sixteenth Century*. Ithaca, 1974–82.

Grant, R. M. *The Earliest Lives of Jesus*. London, 1961.

———. *Eusebius as Church Historian*. Oxford, 1980.

Gurevich, A. Ja. *Categories of Medieval Culture*. London, 1985.

———. *Contadini e santi*. Turin, 1986.

*Hagiographie cultures et sociétés IV–XIIe siècles.*Actes du colloque organisé à Nanterre et à Paris 2–5 Mai 1979. Études Augustiniennes, 1981.

Hanning, Robert W. *The Vision of History in Early Britain*. New York, 1966.

Hardison, O. B. "The Mass as Sacred Drama." *Christian Rite and Christian Drama in the Middle Ages*. Baltimore, 1965.

Hareau, C. "Notice sur un penitentiel attribue à Jean de Salisbury." *Notices et extraits des manuscrits de la Bibliothèque Nationale* 24 (1876): 269–87.

Hargreaves, H. "Wyclif's Prose." *Essays and Studies* 19 (1966): 1–17.

Hart, A. Tindal. *The Country Priest in English History*. London, 1959.

Hart, Cyril. "Byrhtferth and His Manual." *MAE* 41 (1972): 95–109.

Hay, D. *Annalists and Historians: Western Historiography from the Eighth to the Eighteenth Centuries*. London, 1977.

Heffernan, T. "An Analysis of the Narrative Motifs in the Legend of Saint Eustace." *MEH* 6 (1975): 63–89.

———. "The Authorship of the 'Northern Homily Cycle': The Liturgical Affiliation of the Sunday Gospel Pericopes as a Test." *Traditio* 41 (1985): 289–309.

———. "The Rediscovery of the Bute Manuscript of the *Northern Homily Cycle*." *Scriptorium: revue internationale des études relatives aux manuscripts* 36 (1982): 118–29.

———. "Sermon Literature." In *Middle English Prose*. A. S. G. Edwards, ed. New Brunswick, N. J., 1984.

Hengel, M. *Judaism and Hellenism: Studies in Their Encounter in Palestine during the Early Hellenistic Period*. 2 vols. Philadelphia, 1974.

Herrnstein-Smith, B. *On the Margins of Discourse: The Relation of Literature to Language*. Chicago, 1978.

Hinnebusch, W. A. *The Early English Friars' Preachers*. Rome, 1951.

Hogdson, M. G. S. *The Venture of Islam*. 2 vols. Chicago, 1974.

Hoster, Dieter. *Die Form der Frühesten Lateinischen Heiligenviten von der Vita Cypriani bis zur Vita Ambrosii und ihr Heiligenideal*. Diss. Cologne, 1963.

Hudson, Anne. "A Lollard Compilation and the Dissemination of Wycliffite Thought." *JTS* 23 (1972): 65–81.

——. "A Lollard Sermon-Cycle and Its Implications." *MAE* 40 (1971): 142–56.

Hummel, Edelhard L. *The Concept of Martyrdom according to St. Cyprian of Carthage.* Washington, 1946.

Hurt, James. *Aelfric.* New York, 1972.

Inventaire Hagiographique des Tomes 1 à 100 (1882–1982). In *Analecta Bollandiana* 100 (1983).

Jackson, K. H. *International Popular Tale and Early Welsh Tradition.* Cardiff, 1961.

James, E. *Gregory of Tours: Life of the Fathers.* Liverpool, 1985.

——. *Aesthetic Experience and Literary Hermeneutics.* Minneapolis, 1982.

Jauss, H. R. *Toward an Aesthetic of Reception.* Minneapolis, 1982.

Jeffrey, D. L. *The Early English Lyric and Franciscan Spirituality.* Lincoln, Neb., 1975.

Jessop, A. *The Coming of the Friars.* London, 1889.

Jones, Charles W. *Saints' Lives and Chronicles in Early England.* Ithaca, 1947.

Jones, E. "The Authenticity of Some English Works ascribed to Wycliffe." *Anglia* 30 (1907): 261–68.

Jungmann, Josef Andreas. *The Early Liturgy: To the Time of Gregory the Great.* London, 1960.

——. *Pastoral Liturgy.* London, 1962.

——. *Missarum Sollemnia: Eine Genetische Erklärung der Römischen Messe.* Vol. 2. Freiburg, 1952.

Kaminsky, J. *Language and Ontology.* Carbondale, 1969.

Kasmann, Hans. "Das Kirchenjahr." *Studien zum Kirchlichen Wortschatz des Mittelenglischen 1100–1350.* Tübingen, 1961.

Ker, N. R. *Medieval Libraries of Great Britain.* London, 1964.

Keyes, C. "Charisma: From Social Life to Sacred Biography." *Journal of the American Academy of Religious Studies* 48 (1982): 1–22.

Kieckhefer, R. *Unquiet Souls: Fourteenth Century Saints and Their Religious Milieu.* Chicago, 1984.

King, M. *The Desert Mothers: A Bibliography.* Saskatoon, 1984.

Kirsh, J. P. *The Doctrine of the Communion of the Saints in the Ancient Church.* St. Louis, 1910.

Kissinger, W. S. *The Lives of Jesus.* New York, 1985.

Kittel, Gerhard, ed. *Theological Dictionary of the New Testament.* G. W. Bromiley, trans. and ed. 9 vols. Grand Rapids, 1964.

Klawiter, F. C. "The Role of Martyrdom and Persecution in Developing the Priestly Authority of Women in Early Christianity: A Case Study of Montanism." *Church History* 49 (1980): 251–61.

Knowles, David. *Great Historical Enterprises: Problems in Monastic History.* London, 1963.

————. *The Monastic Order in England*, 2nd ed. Cambridge, 1963.

Knust, H. *Dos obras didácticas y dos leyendas sacadas de mss. de la Bibl. del Escorial*. Madrid, 1878.

Kranz, Gisbert. *Europas Christliche Literatur von 500–1500*. Munich, 1968.

Kris, E. *Psychoanalytic Explorations in Art*. New York, 1964.

Kurtz, B. P. "From St. Anthony to St. Guthlac: A Study in Biography." *University of California Publication in Modern Philology* 12 (1926): 103–46.

La Capra, D., and S. L. Kaplan, eds. *Modern European Intellectual History: Reappraisals and New Perspectives*. Ithaca, 1982.

————. *History and Criticism*. Ithaca, 1985.

Laistner, M. L. W. *Thought and Letters in Western Europe A.D. 500 to 900*. London, 1931.

Lampe, G. W. H. "To Gregory the Great." *Cambridge History of the Bible*. 2 vols. Cambridge, 1969.

Latham, R. E. *Revised Medieval Latin Word-List: From British and Irish Sources*. London, 1963.

LeClercq, Henry. *Dictionnaire d'archéologie chrétienne et de liturgie*. Paris, 1932.

LeClercq, Jean. *The Love of Learning and Desire for God in the Middle Ages*. C. Misrahi, trans. New York, 1961.

Lee, S. *Life of William Shakespeare*. London, 1898.

Legge, M. E. *Anglo-Norman*. Oxford, 1963.

————. *Anglo-Norman in the Cloisters*. Edinburgh, 1950.

Le Goff, J. *The Birth of Purgatory*. Chicago, 1984.

————. *Time, Work, and Culture in the Middle Ages*. Chicago, 1980.

Leo, F. *Die Griechisch-Römische Biographie nach ihrer Literarischen Form*. Leipzig, 1901.

Linge, D. E. "Dilthey and Gadamer: Two Theories of Historiography." *Journal of the American Academy of Religion* 41 (1973).

————. *Philosophical Hermeneutics*. Berkeley, 1977.

Little, A. G. *The Gray Friars in Oxford*. Oxford, 1892.

Little, A. G., and F. Pelster. *Oxford Theology and Theologians*. Oxford, 1934.

Lord, A. B. *The Singer of Tales*. London, 1960.

Lyon, B. *The Origins of the Middle Ages*. New York, 1972.

McDonald, William J., et al., ed. *New Catholic Encyclopedia*. New York, 1967.

McFarlane, K. B. *Wycliffe and English Nonconformity*. London, 1952.

McKisack, M. *Medieval History in the Tudor Age*. Oxford, 1971.

McNamara, J., and S. Wemple. "Sanctity and Power: The Dual Pursuit of Medieval Women." In *Becoming Visible: Women in European History*. R. Bridenthal and C. Koonz, eds. Boston, 1977.

Manson, W. "Martyrs and Martyrdom." *Bulletin of the John Rylands Library* 39 (1957): 463–84.

Marche, A. Lecoy de la. *La Chaire française au moyen âge.* Paris, 1868.

Mehl, Dieter. *The Middle English Romances of the Thirteenth and Fourteenth Centuries.* London, 1968.

Méray, A. *La Vie au temps des libres prêcheurs.* Vol. 1. Paris, 1878.

Meyer, P. "Une Ancienne version française des fables d'Eude de Cherrington." *Romania* 14 (1885): 381–97.

———. "La Vie de St. Grégoire le Grand." *Romania* 12 (1883): 145–208.

Meyer, Robert T. "Lectio divina in Palladius." In *Kyriakon: Festschrift Johannes Quasten.* P. Granfield and J. A. Jungmann, eds. Münster Westfalen, 1970.

Misch, G. *A History of Autobiography in Antiquity.* 2 vols. London, 1950.

———. *Das Mittelalter.* 3 vols. Frankfurt, 1959–70.

Molinari, Paul. *Saints: Their Place in the Church.* New York, 1956.

Momigliano, A. *The Conflict between Paganism and Christianity in the Fourth Century.* Oxford, 1963.

Moorman, J. R. H. *Church Life in England in the Thirteenth Century.* Cambridge, 1945.

———. *The Grey Friars in Cambridge 1225–1538.* Cambridge, 1952.

———. *A History of the Church in England.* London, 1953.

———. *A History of the Franciscan Order.* Oxford, 1968.

Morey, Dom A. *Bartholomew of Exeter.* Cambridge, 1937.

Morris, C. *The Discovery of the Individual, 1050–1200.* London, 1972.

Mosher, J. A. *The Exemplum in the Early Religious and Didactic Literature of England.* New York, 1911.

Murdoch, V., and G. S. Couse. *Essays on the Reconstruction of Medieval History.* Montreal, 1974.

Murphy, J. J., ed. *Medieval Eloquence, Studies in the Theory and Practice of Medieval Rhetoric.* Berkeley, 1978.

———. *Medieval Rhetoric: A Select Bibliography.* Toronto, 1971.

———. *Rhetoric in the Middle Ages: A History of Rhetorical Theory from Saint Augustine to the Renaissance.* Berkeley, 1981.

———. *Three Medieval Rhetorical Arts.* London, 1971.

Murray, R. "The Features of the Earliest Christian Asceticism." In *Christian Spirituality: Essays in Honour of Gordon Rupp.* P. Brooks, ed. London, 1971.

Nadel, I. B. *Biography: Fiction, Fact and Form.* London, 1984.

Nielen, J. M. *The Earliest Christian Liturgy.* P. Cummins, trans. St. Louis, 1941.

Oesterley, W. O. E. *The Jewish Background of the Christian Liturgy.* Gloucester, Mass., 1965.

Olney, J., ed. *Autobiography: Essays Theoretical and Critical.* Princeton, 1980.

Owst, G. R. *Literature and Pulpit in Medieval England.* Cambridge, 1933.

————. *Preaching in Medieval England*. Cambridge, 1926.

Pächt, Otto. *The Rise of Pictorial Narrative in Twelfth-Century England*. Oxford, 1962.

Page, William, ed. *The Victoria History of the Counties of England: Gloucestershire*. London, 1907.

Paris, Gaston. *La Littérature française au moyen âge*. Paris, 1913.

Parsch, Pius. *The Breviary Explained*. W. Nayden and C. Hoegerl, trans. London, 1952.

Pelikan, J. *The Christian Tradition: A History of the Development of Doctrine*. Vol. 3: "The Growth of Medieval Theology 600–1300." Chicago, 1978.

————. *Jesus through the Centuries*. New Haven, 1985.

Perry, B. E. *The Ancient Romances*. Berkeley, 1967.

Petroff, E. A. "Discovering Biography··in Hagiography: Lives of Women Saints." *Lady-Unique-Inclination-of-the-Night* 2 (1977): 34–45.

————. *Medieval Women's Visionary Literature*. Oxford, 1986.

Pfaff, R. W. "Principal Modern Editions of Medieval English Liturgical Texts." *New Liturgical Feasts in Later Medieval England*. Oxford, 1970.

Pfander, H. G. *The Popular Sermon of the Medieval Friar in England*. New York, 1937.

Piaget, Arthur. "Sermonnaires et traducteurs." *Histoire de la langue et de la littérature française des origines à 1900*. Petit de Juleville, ed. Paris, 1896.

Popper, K. *The Poverty of Historicism*. New York, 1957.

Power, Eileen. *Medieval English Nunneries, c. 1275–1535*. Cambridge, 1922.

Powicke, M., and E. B. Fryde, eds. *Handbook of British Chronology*. London, 1961.

Preminger, A., O. B. Hardison, and K. Kerrane, eds. *Classical and Medieval Literary Criticism*. New York, 1974.

Press, G. A. *The Development of the Idea of History in Antiquity*. Montreal, 1982.

Rabinow, P., and W. M. Sullivan. *Interpretive Social Science: A Reader*. Berkeley, 1979.

Reynolds, F. E., and D. Capps, eds. *The Biographical Process: Studies in the History and Psychology of Religion*. The Hague, 1976.

Rickman, H., ed. *W. Dilthey: Pattern and Meaning in History*. New York, 1961.

Robertson, D. W. *A Preface to Chaucer*. Princeton, 1962.

Rosenthal, C. L. *The Vitae Patrum in Old and Middle English Literature*. Philadelphia, 1936.

Schatkin, Margaret. "The Maccabean Martyrs." *Vigiliae Christianae* 28 (June 1974): 97–113.

Silverman, H. J., and D. Ihde, eds. *Hermeneutics and Deconstruction*. New York, 1985.

Smith, W., and S. Cheetham, eds. *Dictionary of Christian Antiquities*. London, 1875.

Spearing, A. C. *Criticism and Medieval Poetry*. London, 1972.

Spengemann, W. C. *The Forms of Autobiography: Episodes in the History of a Literary Genre.* New York, 1980.

Stancliffe, C. *St. Martin and His Hagiographer.* Oxford, 1983.

Stebler, V. "Die 'Horae Cometentes' des Benediktinischen Stundengebetes." *Studia Anselmiana* 42 (1957): 15–24.

Steidl, B., ed. *Antonius Magnus Ermetica 356–1956: Studia ad Antiquam monachismum Spectantia.* Rome, 1956.

Stevenson, F. S. *Robert Grosseteste, Bishop of Lincoln.* London, 1899.

Talbert, E. W. "The Date of the Composition of the English Wyclifite Collection of Sermons." *Speculum* 12 (1937): 464–74.

Ten Brink, B. *History of English Literature.* H. M. Kennedy, trans. New York, 1889.

Turner, V. *Dramas, Fields, and Metaphors.* Ithaca, 1974.

Van Dam, R. *Leadership and Community in Late Antique Gaul.* Berkeley, 1985.

Van Dijk, S. J. P. "The Bible in Liturgical Use." *Cambridge History of the Bible.* Cambridge, 1969.

Van Engen, J. "The Christian Middle Ages as a Historiographical Problem." *American Historical Review* 91 (1986): 519–52.

Van Austin Harvey, W. *The Historian and the Believer.* New York, 1966.

Vauchez, A. *La sainteté en occident aux derniers siècles du moyen âge: d'après les procès de canonisation et les documents hagiographiques.* Rome, 1981.

Vinaver, E. *The Rise of Romance.* Oxford, 1971.

Von Camphausen, H. *Die Idee des Martyriums in der Alten Kirche.* Göttingen, 1964.

Weinstein, D., and R. M. Bell. *Saints and Society.* Chicago, 1982.

Weintraub, K. J. "Autobiography and Historical Consciousness." *Critical Inquiry* 1 (1975): 821–48.

Wells, J. E. *A Manual of the Writings in Middle English.* New Haven, 1916.

Wells, M. E. "'The South English Legendary' in Its Relation to the 'Legenda Aurea.'" *PMLA* 51 (1936): 337–60.

Welter, J. T. *L'Exemplum dans la littérature religieuse et didactique du moyen âge.* Paris, 1927.

White, H. *Metahistory: The Historical Imagination in Nineteenth-Century Europe.* Baltimore, 1973.

———. *Tropics of Discourse: Essays in Cultural Criticism.* Baltimore, 1979.

White, Helen. *Tudor Books of Saints and Martyrs.* Madison, 1963.

Williams, M. A. "The Life of Antony and the Domestication of Charismatic Wisdom." *Journal of the American Academy of Religion Studies* 48 (1982): 23–45.

Willyams, J. L. *A Short History of the Waldensian Church.* London, 1845.

Wilson, S., ed. *Saints and Their Cults: Studies in Religious Sociology, Folklore and History.* Cambridge, 1983.

Winn, H. E. *Wyclif: Select English Writings.* Oxford, 1929.

Wolpers, Theodor. *Die Englische Heiligenlegende des Mittelalters*. Tübingen, 1964.

Woolf, Rosemary. "Saints' Lives." In *Continuations and Beginnings in Old English Literature*. E. G. Stanley, ed. London, 1966.

Young, Karl. *The Drama of the Medieval Church*. Oxford, 1933.

Zumthor, P. "Autobiography in the Middle Ages." *Genre* 6 (1973): 29–48.

———. *Speaking of the Middle Ages*. Lincoln, 1985.

Index